# Duties of the Heart
## by Rabeinu Bahya ibn Paquda

*with commentaries*

*translated by Yosef Sebag*

### VOLUME 2

### OTHER WORKS BY YOSEF SEBAG

Ethics of the Fathers     - www.dafyomireview.com/489

Path of the Just     - www.dafyomireview.com/447

Gates of Holiness     - www.dafyomireview.com/442

Vilna Gaon on Yonah     - www.dafyomireview.com/259

Torah Numerology     - www.dafyomireview.com/543

Marks of Divine Wisdom - www.dafyomireview.com/427

Torah Authenticity     - www.dafyomireview.com/430

yosefsebag@gmail.com

בס"ד

Chovos ha'Levavos, the monumental work of Rabeinu Bachye ben Yosef Ibn Pakuda, a judge in Islamic Spain (circa 1040), is one of the earliest works on Jewish philosophy and beliefs. It remains one of the fundamental works of Musar and Hashkafah. Even the great Rambam (Maimonides) bases a large part of his treatises in these fields on the revered words of the Chovos ha'Levavos. (It has been suggested that Rav Shlomo Ibn Gevirol took ideas from the Chovos ha'Levavos as well.)

Originally written in Arabic, this classic was translated into Hebrew not longer after its original publication, and more recently to many other languages. Among works of Jewish philosophy, its prominence in even the most traditional houses of learning makes it unique. The Chovos ha'Levavos' methodical and systematic analyses or every aspect of the human character makes reading it an experience in growth through introspection.

We owe a debt of gratitude to Rabbi Yosef Sebag for his exceptionally readable English translation of this important work. By adding translations of classic commentaries on the text, he has made the depth of the work available to all. Rabbi Sebag's investment of time and effort is evident in every part of the work, but especially in the Sha'ar ha'Yichud, the somewhat "controversial" section dealing with philosophical proofs of G-d.

I have known Rabbi Sebag for many years, and I have witnessed firsthand his overwhelming dedication to Torah-study and to raising a family on Torah-true ideals. His careful adherence to the instructions of our Torah giants, coupled with his strong will to teach others the timeless lessons of the Torah, has made him a true "Ben Aliyah."

May his investment bear the dividends of allowing him to help many of our brethren improve their faith and strength of character!

With Torah blessings,

Rabbi Mordecai Kornfeld

Israel office: P.O.B. 43087, Jerusalem 91430, Israel • US office: 140-32 69 Ave., Flushing, NY 11367
Tel. - Israel: (02) 651-5004 • Fax - Israel: (02) 591-6024 • email: daf@dafyomi.co.il
http://www.dafyomi.co.il • http://dafyomi.shemayisrael.co.il/
U.S. tax ID: 11-3354586     580-28-908-0 עמ'ר מס' ע"ר

# *** SHAAR YICHUD HAMAASE - Gate of Devotion to G-d Alone ***

* Introduction

* Chapter 1 - What is devotion of actions to G-d.

* Chapter 2 - What leads to it.

* Chapter 3 - On which actions is devotion incumbent

* Chapter 4 - Which things damage devotion.

* Chapter 5 - Ways to distance from them until one can successfully devote all actions to G-d.

* Chapter 6 - To guard, protect and rule over one's thoughts.

# *** INTRODUCTION ***

(*Tov Halevanon*: After having demonstrated in the previous gate the ways of trust in G-d, and that trusting in any creation is foolish and useless, for it yields no benefit as derived through reason and through scripture - thus it is certainly proper to devote all our actions to G-d. This is the subject of this gate.)

Since the topic of our preceding discussion was placing one's trust in G-d, I deemed proper to follow with a clarification of the ways in which it is incumbent to devote all actions of religious service to G-d alone. For this leads to purification of thought and heart from mixtures of other intents which diminish the quality of the actions, and saves one from all sorts of embellishment and flattery to try to win the approval of other people, as Elihu said "I will show partiality to no one, nor will I flatter any man" (Iyov 32:21).

(*Pas Lechem*: when a man desires to embellish himself, namely, to appear good to his colleagues in his service to G-d, then, even though his motive is good, nevertheless, over time, through this he will come to the trait of flattery. Namely, that his motive in the service of G-d will be out of hypocrisy. The author calls hypocrisy with the term "flattery", because anything which is not "tocho kebaro" (inner being matching exterior appearance) is called in hebrew "flattery").

It is now proper to clarify six matters on the subject of devotion of actions to G-d:
1. What is devotion of actions to G-d?
2. What leads to it?
3. On which actions is devotion a duty?
4. Which things damage devotion?
5. Ways to distance from them until one can successfully devote all actions to G-d
6. To guard, protect and rule over one's thoughts

## *** CHAPTER 4 ***

Three things damage one's devoting his act of service to G-d alone:

| (*Marpe Lenefesh*: Through these three things will come loss and spoiling of his deeds, that undoubtedly, they will not be l'Shem Shamayim (for G-d alone). He will now explain them, one by one.)

(1) Ignorance of G-d and His good.

| (*Pas Lechem*: He does not understand His loftiness, blessed be He, nor His good traits..)

(2) Ignorance of G-d's mitzvot and His torah.

(3) Thoughts and suggestions the yetzer presents a man to endear to him this world and distance him from the path that leads to [his good in] the next world.

Explanation of the above three:
Ignorance of G-d causes lacking in the service because one who does not know his master will not serve him devotedly. Rather, he will only serve someone who he is familiar with and which he expects benefit or harm from.

Hence, if one who does not know G-d does an act of service, his intent will be to people that he is afraid of or that he hopes to get some benefit from. Therefore, he is serving people not He who created them, because he is ignorant of G-d's matter.

Similarly we can say for the idol worshipper, that ignorance of G-d is what brings him to this (he hopes to get benefit or protection from the idol). However, the idol worshipper is to be preferred over the flatterer (hypocrite) in the following four ways:

(1) In our times, there are no prophets which can perform miracles to clarify to the idol worshipper his faulty outlook. But the flatterer in G-d's torah (who performs the service of G-d to impress people, as above), there are grounds for a claim against him. For he undertook the commandments to serve G-d alone and undertook the prohibitions not to serve someone else (than G-d).

(2) The idolater worships something which does not rebel against G-d (sun, moon, stars). But the flatterer in G-d's torah worships a human being who rebels against G-d as well as one who does not rebel against Him.

(3) The idolater worships one thing alone, whereas for the flatterer, there is no limit to those he worships.

(4) The idolater's status is visible for all to see, and people guard themselves from him due to public knowledge of his denial of G-d's existence. But the flatterer's denial is not visible, and people trust in him. Therefore, he is more likely to damage them (influence them with his false beliefs)than the idol worshipper.

It comes out that the flatterer is the greatest disease in the world. He is called in our writings, the flatterer, the haughty, the enticer.

> (*Tov Halevanon*: It is an evil sickness of which there is none greater. They will cast behind them all of G-d's orders and commandments of the duties of the heart which are concealed, and will choose, in exchange for them, visible religious service, which they fabricated from their hearts in order to show off their praise to the public. While for the commandments which do not bring them any benefit or honor - they will abandon them completely. And many of the masses take them as a proof and an example, and will hasten to do like them. Woe to their souls for they caused themselves evil.
>
> *"the haughty"* - He becomes arrogant in seeking honor and a good name from people, and he is not embarassed to make himself appear better than everyone and to justify himself before those bigger and better than himself.
>
> *"the enticer"* - he entices people to believe in him and to follow him, like Yeravam ben Nevat, who sinned and caused others to sin.)

One who does not understand the commandments of G-d and His torah is not capable of devoting his acts wholly to G-d. For as he does not know the ways of service prescribed and their roots in the torah, much less will he understand how to perform them properly, namely, with wholehearted devotion to G-d. Because he is not sure whether he is in truth under duty to perform them. Nor does he know what is detrimental to wholehearted devotion in his service of G-d, even if he is knowledgeable of G-d and of His goodness, as our Sages said "an ignorant man cannot be pious" (Avot 2:5).

(*Marpe Lenefesh*: since he is unsure if he is obligated in such and such a mitzva or not. And even if he does the service, it will be only by rote practice, and for ulterior motives, not l'Shem Shamayim (for G-d), like our sages said: (Avot 2:5) "A boor cannot fear sin nor can an ignorant man be pious"

*Tov Halevanon*: "all the more so, he does not understand how to complete them properly" - to complete the duties of the heart wholeheartedly, without doubts.)

## TEMPTATION OF THE YETZER HARA
(which is the third of the three things that damage [one's devoting his act of service] mentioned earlier - *ML*)

The temptations of the yetzer (evil inclination) divide into two categories:

(1) Thoughts which cast doubt on truths and confuse his emuna (faith), so that he cannot do any religious act properly to G-d.
(2) He comes in the way of arguments and proofs that his zeal and exertion in the service of G-d is neither a duty nor meritorious, and advises him to instead work for this world and its inhabitants.

# *** CHAPTER 5 ***

## INTRODUCTION TO THE YETZER HARA

I saw fit to clarify for you in this subject some examples (of the ways of the yetzer and his strategies - *TL*) which will teach [even] on things I do not mention in order that people will watch out for them, and so that their hearts will be complete with G-d. As the wise man said: *"Let the wise man hear and increase understanding"* (Mishlei 1:5).

> (*Tov Halevanon*: *"which will teach [even] on things I do not mention"* - because there are many more snares, traps, and strategies of the yetzer on people which are too numerous to specify.
>
> *Marpe Lenefesh*: These are examples and illustrations to learn to apply to other enticements of the yetzer because there is no end to his enticements. Therefore, who can possibly mention all of them?
>
> *Pas Lechem*: *"that people will watch out for them"* - from these examples, people will learn and acquire for themselves the trait of "zehirut"/watchfulness.)

O Man! You should know that the great archenemy you have in this world is your own yetzer (evil inclination). He is interwoven in the forces of your soul and intertwined in the order of your spirit. He associates with you in the guidance of your physical and spiritual senses. He rules over the secrets of your soul and of what is hidden in your breast. He is your advisor in all of your movements whether visible or invisible that you wish to do. He lies in wait, watching your steps to lead you astray. You are asleep to him but he is awake to you. You look away from him but he does not look away from you.

He masks himself as your friend, and pretends to show love. He enters in your inner circle of close friends and advisors. From his gestures and signs it appears he is running to do your will but in fact he is shooting deadly arrows at you to kill and uproot you from the land of the living (Olam Haba - *PL*), as the verse speaks of one like this "like a madman who throws firebrands, arrows, and death; so is a man who deceives his friend and says, 'Am I not joking?'" (Mishlei 26:18).

> (*Tov Halevanon*: *"You are asleep to him"* - i.e. you are like one sleeping who does not think about his deeds and plans against you.

*"deadly arrows"* - arrows which are smeared at their tips with various deadly poisons and venoms, so that when they are shot in the flesh of a man, the wound can never heal and the man will die due to this wound.
*Pas Lechem*: *"watching your steps to lead you astray"* - this is the correct text version. Literally in each and every one of your steps, he lies in ambush to entice you after his will, namely that this particular step be with intent for something opposed to the will of G-d.

*Marpe Lenefesh*: *"He is interwoven in the forces of your soul"* - the yetzer is mixed in all of the forces in a human being's soul. Likewise, he is mixed and merged in the spirit of a man, and in his physical senses, namely - sight, hearing, smell, and touch. He is mixed in and associates with all of them, to steer them according to his will.

Examine closely the book Shaarei Kedusha to see what is the evil inclination. See there in detail. Fortunate is the eye which saw all its words. You will understand from there. (Translator: see there also for the difference between the soul (nefesh) and the spirit (ruach) in a human being)

*"has control of the secrets of your soul..."* - That which you think in your heart and in your thoughts, which is something concealed and hidden from all creatures - he rules over all of them, and can steer them according to his evil way.

*"He is your advisor in all of your movements whether visible or invisible that you wish to do"* - you think that your physical movements and invisible movements (thoughts, decisions, etc.) are according to your will. But you don't put to heart that in all of your movements, he counsels you according to his will. If you don't stand up against him to reflect on whether or not your ways are just - immediately you will fall into his net and be ensnared like a bird in a trap.

*"to kill and uproot you from the land of the living"* - from Olam Haba (the afterlife), since, behold, we see that he entices people from small things and builds up to big things, until he tells you "go and serve idols" (i.e. rebel against G-d). How many have gone off to evil ways, r"l, and it is all due to the enticements of the yetzer hara. Therefore scripture tells us to guard "very much" from him, as written (in the Shema - Devarim 11:16): "guard yourself lest your heart be enticed, and you stray and will serve other gods, and worship them" i.e. when you stray from the way of the torah, even for small things, eventually you "will serve other gods, etc." (ibid), and in the end: "then the L-ord's wrath be kindled against you", etc. (ibid) until finally, "you'll be swiftly destroyed from the good land" (ibid), like our Sages told us in books, and likewise we saw with our own eyes. Here is a

quote from the "Magid" (angel) to the Beis Yosef (Rabbi Yosef Karo, sefer magid Parsha Vaera):

Yom Revii (Wednesday) at the time of mincha, while I was studying mishnayot: (The Heavenly messenger said in the Name of the Shechina:) Chazak v'Ematz (be strong and courageous) in my torah, and unify your heart to not separate your thoughts from my torah, my yirah, cleave to my nitzchi, my nekiyus, my sod, my oz, etc, my tiferet, my torah, my teshua, my teshuva, because that which you seek from the Holy One bb'H, that He guide you in the ways of His teshuva, these are the ways I am teaching you, i.e. these are the ways of His teshuva.

Strengthen yourself so that you do not part your thought for even a second from my torah and my yira. Annul from your heart all the hirhurim (urges, thoughts) which come to you from the yetzer hara, the serpent, the Samal (Satan). They put these in your heart to make you lost, to confuse/disorient you, to destroy you. And you - stand up against them. Annul them from your heart, let not their words enter your ears. Thereby, you will cause them to be lost and confused/disoriented, and you will destroy them. Their desire is in you but you will rule over them (a reference to Gen.4:7 "If you do well, you will be uplifted. And if you do not do well, sin crouches at the door, and to you shall be its desire. Yet you can rule over it")

That which you see that sometimes I speak to you but the words do not "happen", you know what the Sages said: "shema yigrom hachet" ("sin may cause" [the forfeiture of future good]). Furthermore, even if it does not cause, nevertheless, the hirhurim (thoughts) which enter your heart cause that my words do not happen and they also cause my words to stagger and I do not reveal to you all the words.

Therefore, be watchful and guard yourself from these hirhurim, and especially at the time of prayer, annul all these thoughts and unify your heart to my prayer and my service. It is necessary for you to not mesiach daat (become distracted) at all, because the moment you become distracted, your yetzer hara will make you lost, confuse/disorient you, topple you, destroy you, and cast you into the bor tachtis (depths of the pit).

Therefore, you must be constantly alert to his strategies. Do not be forgetful of him for even one second. Be always watchful of him, because zehirus (watchfulness) brings to cleanliness. And thereby, you will make him lost and will destroy him, confuse/disorient him, submit him under you. You must exert yourself exceedingly to not neglect your watchfulness of him for even one second. And especially during the time of Shema and prayer, to burn all hirhurim and machshevot betelot (useless thoughts) with the straw of keriat shema. And thus, you will become elevated and exalted. See and reflect that all the thoughts that a man ponders on his affairs, they do not increase, decrease, or annul in the least from what was decreed for him.

Therefore, annul the hirhurim (thoughts/worries) from your heart.

(later on Parsha Bo) Friday night 4th of Shevat: "G-d is with you, etc. only cleave in me and in my yira and in my mishnayot. Do not part your thoughts for even one second because, I, I am the mishna (i.e. the Shechina) which is speaking through your mouth. I am the mother which is chastising her child. Strengthen and cleave to me, because I and all of my legions are all around you.

And you are among us like a king with his army. If the eye had permission to see, you would see out as far as your eye could behold in every direction everything full of troops (angels) which were created from the breath of your mouth, when you toil in mishna. They are encamped all around you, and they surround my troops. And you are in their midst like a king in his army. And all of them proclaim and say 'give honor to the holy form of the King, because he is our teacher, etc.' Therefore, be careful for yourself in all your ways to be constantly clinging to me, and do not part your thoughts for even an instant from Me, and I will elevate you to exceedingly lofty levels...

Translator: The Vilna Gaon, who spent his life in almost total isolation toiling day and night in torah study, once asked a torah scholar to give him harsh words of rebuke. The scholar trembled "who am I to give words of rebuke to the Gaon of Vilna!?". "Please, I decree on you to do this", insisted the Gaon. The scholar openened his mouth and said "Hoy, Eliyahu, Eliyahu, you serve the Creator of the universe in a bounded circle, in the secrets of your chambers, and in your own 4 cubits of space. Go out, please, to the land of the living, to the world of action, and there stand up to the daily tests. There serve the Al-mighty from the stumbling and the traps of the yetzer hara lurking on every side. The Vilna Gaon burst into tears and said: "To do marvels, to walk on a tightrope stretched out over a raging sea - I am afraid." (from letters of the Chafetz Chaim pg.247)
I once heard from Rabbi Nissan Kaplan: "if you don't feel the war every day, then it means he got you already."

Among the strongest of his weapons which he will fire at you and wage war with you in your innermost being - is to try to cast doubt on things you deem to be true (through faith - *PL*), and to confuse what is clear to you (through reason - *PL*), and to confuse your mind with false thoughts and erroneous arguments, and to draw you away from what is for your benefit, and to cause you to doubt what is clear to you in your faith and religion.

(*Marpe Lenefesh*: *"to draw you away from what is for your benefit"* - i.e. by putting bad thoughts in your heart constantly, so that through this you will be distracted from looking and thinking about what is for your benefit, namely, your torah and your faith.

*Pas Lechem*: "*your faith and religion*" - "faith" corresponds to the duties of the heart, while "religion" corresponds to the duties of the limbs, which contain [physical] acts.)

If you will guard yourself from him, and have ready the weapons of your intellect to wage war with him, and deflect his arrows away from you, you will be saved and will escape from him with G-d's help. But if you leave your matters to him, and you are drawn after his will, he will not let up on you until he destroys you from both worlds, and uproots you from both lands, as written of one member of his legions: "For many are the dead that she has felled, and numerous are all her victims; Her house is the way to hell, going down to the chambers of death" (Mishlei 7:26-27).

(*Marpe Lenefesh*: The proverb is referring to a promiscuous woman, and the lust for her and the seduction towards her is one branch of the strategies of enticement of the yetzer hara. The [hidden] meaning of a "promiscuous woman" is to apikorsus (heresy) and idolatry as the Talmud says (Avodah Zara 17a). The verse gives a double expression of death corresponding to death in this world and in the next.)

Therefore, let no other war distract you from his war, no battlefield from his battlefield, no sword of a distant enemy from the sword of the enemy which is at close quarters and inseparable from you. Let not the effort to repel the enemy who will not approach you without permission (of G-d) prevent you from repelling the enemy who approaches you without [needing] permission, since he exists within you.

(*Tov Halevanon*: Do not distract your mind by fighting any war besides the war of the yetzer.

*Pas Lechem*: Do not say that you are not free to fight with him due to being busy fighting with others, namely, human beings which harass you. Because his war is more necessary... Furthermore, if a man comes to damage you, certainly, he is not capable of damaging you unless he was given permission through the decree of the Creator. Unlike the yetzer which does not need permission because he was created for this...)

It is said of a pious man who met some men returning from a war against enemies, and they brought spoils after a raging battle. He said to them: "you returned from the small war with spoils, now prepare for the big war!" They asked: "which big war?" He answered: "the war of the yetzer and his legions".

(*Marpe Lenefesh*: Rav Moshe Alshich wrote in parsha "Ki Tetze" similar to these words, see there. He concluded saying: "for two great and important reasons war with human beings is small compared to the war of the yetzer. The first: war with humans is not in a man's hands, but rather it belongs to G-d since "Ha-shem Ish Milchama" (G-d is the Master of war) (Shmos 15:3) and without Him "no man shall lift up his hand" (Bereishis 41:44). But the war of the yetzer belongs to man, not to G-d, since "Everything is in the hands of G-d, except for fear of G-d" (Berachot 33b). Free choice is unrestrained, to whatever way one desires, he may pursue.

The second: One who wages war with his yetzer is like a young lad who approaches a city he does not recognize. Inside it is a seasoned warrior, trained in warfare from his youth, knowledgeable in all the roads and alleys of the city, since he dwelled there all of his life.

There are over 600 troops there who are all like slaves of that seasoned warrior and follow his orders, powerful warriors which do his will. The city is barricaded shut, with the seasoned warrior and his troops inside it. And behold, this young lad comes and bold-heartedly decides to wage war with the seasoned warrior and topple him and conquer the entire city, capture all of its inhabitants, and enslave them all to himself, and change their hearts to accept him as their master.

In truth, if a man does thus with his yetzer hara, this is the ultimate degree of mightiness, because this is like the lad who wages war with the seasoned warrior as above. And this is what our sages said (Pirkei Avot 4:2): "Who is mighty? He who conquers his yetzer, as it is written (Proverbs 16:32) "One who is slow to anger is better than the mighty, and one who rules over his spirit is more than one who captures a city", [a city] as above. (Translator: There the Alshich explains that the yetzer tov (good inclination) is like a young lad since it comes on a man only at Bar Mitzvah, while the yetzer hara (evil inclination) comes at birth. Therefore the yetzer hara is already seasoned and has established rulership over the 600+ troops which are the body's 248 limbs and 365 sinews when the good inclination comes. see there.))

Translator: If you ask, "what is this great war? I don't feel any major war?" To this the classic book "Path of the Just" writes in the introduction: "The Holy One Blessed be He has put man in a place where the factors which draw him further from the Blessed One are many. These are the earthy desires which, if he is pulled after them, cause him to be drawn further from and to depart from the true good. It is seen, then, that man is veritably placed in the midst of a raging battle"
And likewise, the Tanya explains with powerful words:

"the term 'Avodah' (service [of G-d], literally 'work') only applies on something that a man does with tremendous exertion against his nature (yegia atzuma neged teva nafsho), only that he nullifies his nature and will to the will of G-d, for example to strain himself in torah study or in prayer until his soul is totally exhausted, etc." - *Tanya Igeres HaKodesh 12*
And also in the *Tanya L.A. Ch.30*:
"It is indeed a great and fierce struggle to break one's passion, which burns like a fiery flame, through fear of G-d; it is actually a huge trial. Therefore, each person according to his place and rank in the service of G-d must weigh and examine his position as to whether he is serving G-d in a manner commensurate with the dimensions of such a fierce battle and test - in the realm of "do good," as, for example, in the service of prayer with kavanah (devotion), pouring out his soul before G-d with all his strength, to the point of exhaustion of the soul. All the while waging war against his body and animal soul within it which impede his devotion. It is a strenuous war to beat and grind them like dust each day before the morning and evening prayers. Also during prayer, he needs to exert himself with the exertion of the spirit and of the flesh, as will be explained later at length.

Any one who has not reached this standard of waging such strenuous war against his body, has not yet measured up to the quality and dimension of the war waged by one's evil nature which burns like a fiery flame, that it be humbled and broken by fear of G-d...
So, too, in the matter of one's occupation in the study of the Torah, to learn much more than his natural or trained desire and will, by virtue of an enormous war with his body. For one who learns only a little more than his nature - this is but a small war, which has neither parallel nor any comparison with the true war of one's evil inclination which burns like fire; he is called utterly wicked (rasha gamur) if he does not conquer his inclination so that it be subdued and crushed before G-d." End quote.

Translator - it seems the point is that adhering to the torah requires enormous effort against one's nature. For example, the biblical commandments love your fellow as yourself, don't hate, do not covet, do not hurt others with words, to walk in His ways (which includes cultivating compassion, humility, wisdom etc.) - all these things require enormous work against one's nature.

It is a wonder, my brother, that for any enemy that one has, if one defeats him once or twice, he will back down from you and not consider waging war again, thinking your strength is greater than his, and he abandons thoughts of defeating you and overpowering you.

But the yetzer, is not satisfied with one battle or even a hundred battles, whether he has defeated you or you have defeated him. Because if he defeats you, he will slay you, and if you defeat him, he will lie in wait all of your days to defeat you, as our Sages said "do not believe in yourself until the day of your death" (Avot 2:4). He does not consider the smallest of the smallest of your matters as too insignificant a means of defeating you, in order that he will gain a step to defeat you on a higher matter.

> (*Marpe Lenefesh*: As the sages said (Avot 3:2) "one sin induces another sin", and (Shabbat 105b) "whoever breaks an object in anger is as if he worshipped idols... since today he tells you to do this and tomorrow that until he tells you to go worship idols".)

Therefore, it is proper for you to be on your guard against him. Do not fulfill the slightest of his requests. Rather, let it be big in your eyes the smallest of the smallest victory over him, or the least increase of your power over him, so that you will gain a step for defeating him on higher ground. For his lust [to destroy] you will soon return, but he will not be capable of standing up to you when you stand firm against him as written: "he will desire in you, but you will rule over him" (Gen.4:7).

> (*Tov Halevanon*: Even though it appears at the beginning of your war against him that he is a mighty and powerful warrior, when you stand up to him with a strong hand and an outstretched arm, immediately, he will turn around and run away from you, and like our sages said (Shab.104a): "one who comes to purify himself is helped from above")

Therefore do not panic at his word despite his mighty armies, and do not fear him on account of his many helpers, because his primary intent is to make the false appear true, and his goal is to establish lies (as truth). How near is his downfall, how swift is his destruction, if you will realize his weakness! And as the wise man describes him: "there was a small city with few inhabitants, and a great king came and surrounded it, he built high towers (to conquer it), but a poor wise man from the city defeated him with his wisdom but no one remembered that poor man" (Koheles 9:14).

The analogy is as follows: a man is the "small city", because man is called a "miniature world", the man's limbs and organs, and the traits of the [lower] soul are the "few inhabitants". Because they are small relative to the greatness of his heart's continuous desires for the lusts of this world, and lack of ability to attain them (that the whole world and everything in it be his - ML). The yetzer is the "great king", due to his possession of many tactics, soldiers, and legions. Then he "surrounds it", because he encompasses all matters of a man, whether public or private. Then he "built high towers", which refers to the many bad urges, bad thoughts, and disgraceful incidents which he strives to slay a man with, as we will explain later in this gate, with G-d's help.

(*Tov Halevanon*: *"bad thoughts"* - they damage him, as our sages said: "thoughts of sin are worse than sin" (Yoma 21a). And even though a man is not punished for his thoughts, nevertheless, they damage his soul, and they are like snares on his footsteps to bring him to actual sins.

*Pas Lechem*: *"the many bad urges, bad thoughts, and disgraceful incidents"* - "bad urges", refers to thoughts of sin. "bad thoughts" to stray from the good.
"disgraceful incidents" - he is given permission to set up incidents on a man to steer him away from the service [of G-d].)

And the "poor wise man" refers to the intellect, "poor", since its men and helpers are few as the verse continues "no man remembered this poor man...and the wisdom of the poor man was despised".

Despite [the man's] weakness, the text tells further of the yetzer's eager lust to wage war with a man, and how its power to injure him was easily removed because a little truth defeats much falsehood, just as a little light dispels much darkness.

From this analogy, there is to stir a person to wage war against the taavot (base desires), and to stand up to the yetzer with diligent exertion. Because we have seen that the yetzer is too weak to stand up against the Understanding, and how quickly he falls before it, as written "the evil ones bow before the good" (Mishlei 14:19).

(*Marpe Lenefesh*: See [Torat Moshe] by Rabbi Moshe Alshich on parsha Ki Tetze who explains the account of Ki Tetze to be referring to the war of a man with his yetzer, and how he can overcome it. See there amazing words.

Rabbi Mendel Weinbach zt'l said: "The Imerei Tal brings the Zohar of how important it is to learn torah b'simcha (with joy). the yetzer tov and yetzer hara are not static forces. They're capable of growing in power. It all depends whether you do a mitzva b'simcha and thus increase the power of the yetzer tov or ch"v find diversions of the yetzer hara and do that b'simcha and give him power" (from ohr.edu/2154).

## THE ENTICEMENTS OF THE YETZER

## *1 - NO LIFE AFTER DEATH*

The first matter the yetzer will try to cast doubt in your mind, and will try to convince you is that the soul cannot exist without a body, and that the soul perishes along with the body, and has no existence after the death of the body. He uses imaginative arguments, which don't hold if a man contemplates them, and the purpose of this is to induce you to pursue the temporary pleasures, and fleeting desires, and so that you adopt the outlook of the group of men which the verse describes "let us feast and drink because tomorrow we will die" (Yeshaya 22:13). If you take counsel with your understanding on this, you will distance from this outlook with clear proofs which the early ones already brought (see Kuzari maamar 5 siman 12 and our commentary there - *TL*) and which are mentioned in the words of the prophets.

(*Pas Lechem*: "the soul cannot exist without a body" - i.e. that the soul came to existence simultaneously with the coming into existence (formation) of the body, and that it cannot exist without the body. Not like our sages said on the verses in Bereishis 7:4 and 8:7 and the verse "Let the earth bring forth living creatures" (1:24) and the verse in Divrei Hayamim 4:23, and in many Midrashim that the souls preceded the world.

*Tov Halevanon*: "the purpose of this is to induce you to pursue the temporary pleasures" - i.e. in this, the physical nature of man tends quickly towards adopting [this view] because it is an excuse to pursue bodily pleasures...)

## 2 - NO G-D

When the yetzer abandons hope of casting doubts in your mind on this, he will attempt to cast doubt on the [existence of the] blessed Creator. He will tell you that the world is neither new nor created. It was never different from what it is now nor will it ever be any different, and there is no existence which is more fitting to be (called - *PL*) a creator than a created (being), and no one is under duty to serve anything since everything is ancient and has existed eternally.

(*Tov Halevanon*: it is impossible to create something from nothing, rather everything exists because the universe existed eternally in one form or another. Thus one will refrain from serving G-d...

*Marpe Lenefesh*: that the universe never ceased existing, that it is eternal, and likewise will never cease to exist. Therefore, nobody created the world and one is not under duty to serve anything.

*Translator*: *"there is no existence..creator than created"* - for only a true Unity can be Eternally existing, namely, that which is absolutely One, no parts, properties, limits, borders, definitions, etc. etc. as explained at length in Gate 1.

If he comes to you with this claim, return to your understanding and it will show you the fallacy of this claim from the discussion of the first gate of this book, and prove to you that this world has a Creator who created it from nothing.

(*Marpe Lenefesh*: Really you can deduce through reason that the universe has a Creator, as explained in the first gate, since even a small pebble cannot possibly create itself, all the more so for this entire vast universe. Translator: It is not relevant to ask "what brought G-d into existence?", because He is the framework of existence, or more precisely, He is the Existence itself as explained in the first gate.)

## 3 - FALSE GODS

When he gives up trying to make you doubt these matters, he will try to confuse you with matters of associating G-d, such as the beliefs of the dual gods, or the three god belief of the Christians, or the naturalists, or the beliefs of the foolish worshippers of the stars, according to their various views. When it will be clear to you that the Creator is one and eternal, according to the introductions of the beginning of this book, all of these doubts will leave you.

(*Pas Lechem*: *"naturalists"*: (literally "men of descendants") Who believe that the creator fathered another divinity. You already know who these people are. Alternatively, the intent is to the scientists (who believe that everything has a materialistic, naturalistic explanation - *MH*).

*Tov Halevanon*: *"naturalists"*: these are the sorcerers and necromancers. *"worshippers of the stars"* - who make offerings to the heavenly forces (angels, etc.), such as in Yirmiya 7:18. This group is better than the previous cases (the atheists), as explained in the Kuzari that the atheist philosophers are worse than the worshippers of the stars. And likewise this is the way of the yetzer to bring down a person from level to level. So too the entire matter mentioned on this [here is in this order].)

## 4 - YOUR RELIGIOUS SERVICE IS POINTLESS

When he gives up trying to mislead you in these matters, he will try to entice you regarding the duty to serve the Creator, saying "the service from the servant to the master is only when the master needs it. Since the Creator does not need His creations, and does not lack anything, therefore your service to G-d has no reason and no purpose. But when you examine with your understanding, in the previous Gate of Reflection, regarding the beneficence of G-d towards us, and in the "Gate of the Obligation to assume the service of G-d" due to this (see Gate 3 ch.2 and ch.4 - *TL*), then this doubt will disappear, and you will obligate yourself in the service of G-d.

(*Pas Lechem*: *"does not need His creations, and does not lack anything"* - He does not need nor lack anything that would need to be completed through our service. He doubled the expression "does not need" and "does not lack" because it is impossible from both perspectives. If from the perspective that all of us are His creations, and since He created us from absolute non-existence, if so, we and everything we have, and everything that results from our power is all given to us from His hand and from His power it came to be... Therefore how is it possible to claim that He needs us? For this the author wrote "He does not need His *creations*". Secondly, besides that we are His creations, needs of any kind does not apply to Him because He lacks nothing. Corresponding to these two he wrote: "therefore your service to G-d has no reason and no purpose".)

## 5 - TORAH'S AUTHENTICITY

When he gives up trying to entice you in these ways, he will try to cast doubt on the matter of prophecy and the prophets, the torah and the principles of its authenticity and necessity.

(*Pas Lechem*: *"on the matter of prophecy"* - whether or not there is such a thing as prophecy.
*"and the prophets"* - even if there is prophecy, it is doubtful whether or not there are human beings, who are all of coarse physical bodies, that are suitable for the prophecy to rest on them.
*"the torah and the principles of its authenticity and necessity"* - the true principles which it depends on (see the 13 principles compiled by the Rambam).
*"and necessity"* - if it is necessary from a logical perspective that the torah be given from G-d [to man], because the giving of the torah is something which is logically necessary.

*Translator:* - many aspects of the natural world on our planet appear to have been designed with vast wisdom and ability. Since man is the star here, and this Intelligence is hiding from us, it follows logically that some sort of communication should exist for Him to explain to us what this enigma is all about. This leads us to the first and foremost book on prophecy, the source and basis of most religious belief on our planet...

But if you stand up against him with your intellect, and fight him using the argument from the third gate of this book, all of these doubts will disappear from your heart. The fact of prophecy, the necessity of the torah and the sending of a prophet, and the ways in which the torah stirs [a person's heart to serve his Creator - PL] will be established as truths.

(*Pas Lechem*: "*sending of a prophet*" - it was necessary to send a [human] prophet, that through him the torah would be given to human beings. Likewise, the sending of the other prophets, each in his era, to strengthen it and safeguard it.)


## 6 - ORAL LAW IS NOT ESSENTIAL

When he gives up on this matter, he will try to cast doubt on the Tradition (the oral torah - PL). He will tell you that what reason obligates and what the written torah obligates are both true, but what the Sages said is not essential and its acceptance is not obligatory.

(*Tov Halevanon*: "*what reason obligates*" - i.e. what reason obligates regarding the Unity of G-d, reflecting on His good, and serving Him. Likewise for other commandments which reason obligates and abstinence from (excessive) physical pleasures, in addition to what the torah writes - it is all truth.)

But if you examine with your understanding, you will see that the rational laws as well as the scriptural laws are both greatly in need of the tradition. Because not one of them can be fulfilled completely without the tradition.

For rational laws: without the boundaries and explanations of the oral torah regarding amount, kind, time, place, and other circumstances, it is impossible to derive the laws from logic alone. Similarly for scriptural laws, without an explanation from the oral torah on how to read it properly, the meaning of the words, its explanation and that of its derivatives, it will not be completely understandable from the verses alone. Therefore our Sages taught "with 13 attributes the torah is expounded.." (Beraita of Rabbi Yishmael) and "the tradition is a boundary to the torah" (Avot 3:13).

(*Tov Halevanon*: "*with 13 attributes the torah is expounded*" - these are all traditions, except for the "kal v'chomer" (major to minor logical inference) which a man can deduce on his own since reason obligates it. But the "hekesh", the "binyan av", and the other attributes, according to Rashi (in

Sukkah 31a) a man is not allowed to deduce on his own but rather must have received it from the tradition...

*Pas Lechem*: *"explanations of the oral torah regarding amount, kind, time, place, and other circumstances"* - As an example, "marital relations" is among the rational matters since reason mandates that it is necessary for the survival of the human race. Likewise, promiscuity and excessiveness is evil and very damaging. However, it is not in man's power to determine the correct "quality", i.e. which woman is permitted and which is not. However we found in the tradition the boundaries, whether in "amount", namely the "onah" which the sages set for each [type of] person, and this also includes the "time", and likewise the "kind" which are the "sheniyot l'arayot" (secondary forbidden [incestual] relations not specified in the torah). The "place" here means in a modest place and to refrain from it b'achsanya or in a holy place or a place near holy books or tefilin.)

Furthermore, the torah itself, refers us to the tradition for its details as written "If a matter eludes you in judgment,...then you shall rise and go up to the place the L-rd, your G-d, has chosen; And you shall come to the Kohanim, to the judge who will be in those days, and you shall inquire, and they will tell you the words of judgment." (Devarim 17:8-9), and "And the man who acts intentionally, not obeying the priest who stands there to minister the L-rd, your G-d, or to the judge that man shall die" (Devarim 17:12).

(*Marpe Lenefesh*: The torah itself tells us that whenever we have any doubt in a torah matter, we should go to ask the Kohanim in the temple, because they are the pillars of the tradition. The explanation of the torah never left them from Moshe until then, since they are free to toil in the torah due to being supported from the priestly gifts.

*Pas Lechem*: Behold, the torah punishes by death to one who rebels against the tradition. Therefore, it must be that it is primary and not a "higher measure of piety" [i.e. non-essential].

*Tov Halevanon*: The torah was stricter with matters of the oral law than matters of the written torah. Since one does not incur the death penalty except on specific, known capital offences. But the Zaken Mamre ("rebellious elder" - a scholar who disobeys a decision of the supreme beit din in Jerusalem, which the above verse is referring to), incurs the death penalty for even one detail of a torah mitzva ruled by the supreme Beit Din. And according to the Rambam, even for a part of a mitzva d'rabanan (Rabbinical law) he also incurs the death penalty.)

When you understand all of this, the doubts will leave, and it will be clear to you that [in addition to] the knowledge derived from reason and the scriptures, the oral tradition [is also indispensable].

## 7 - NO REWARD AND PUNISHMENT IN THIS WORLD

When he gives up trying to entice you in these ways, he will try from the aspect of reward and punishment. He will claim that the course of events in the world does not follow the lines of justice because if there were justice in this world, the wicked would not prosper, and the righteous would not suffer, as one whom we mentioned in gate 4 (end of ch.3) of this book said.

> (*Pas Lechem*: To believe in astrological fate or that the world was abandoned to chance. People are confused about these things as explained in the Moray Nevuchim and the book "Haemunot".)

But when the understanding will show to you the justice [of divine wisdom] in both of these ways as we introduced in the Gate of Trust, these doubts will vanish, and your heart will be at peace from this confusion.

## 8 - NO REWARD AND PUNISHMENT IN THE AFTERLIFE

When the yetzer abandons the hope of overcoming us in these topics, he will try to cast doubt on us regarding the reward and punishment in the afterlife. He will try to confuse and distort this on us, due to the little mention of it in the torah and the little apparentness in it.

> (*Pas Lechem*: There is little explanation of it in the torah, and the torah did not mention it much. And even this small amount is not clearly apparent, and is not revealed openly nor explicitly explained for all to see. This is what the author meant by "little apparentness in it".
>
> *Tov Halevanon*: Even the places which mention the afterlife do not explicitly explain it and what it is, but rather only hint to it briefly, such as the matters of Karet (cutting off) as our sages expounded (Sanhedrin 4b) [on the verse in Bamidbar 15:31: "Because he has despised the word of the L-ord, and has broken His commandment, that soul shall utterly be cut off; his iniquity shall be upon him"] (the double expression "cut off" in hebrew refers to "cut off" in this world and "cut off" in the next world. And likewise as on the verse (Devarim 5:15): "[Honor your father and your mother, as the L-ord your G-d has commanded you;] that your days may be prolonged", they expounded in Kidushin 39b that it is referring to the day which is totally prolonged (i.e. the eternity of the afterlife)

But if we examine what there is in the books of the other prophets (besides

Moshe Rabeinu) on this matter [which is mentioned explicitly], for example "[And the dust returns to the earth as it was,] and the spirit returns to G-d, Who gave it" (Koheles 12:7), and "I will give you a place among these who stand here" (Zecharia 3:7), and "How great is Your goodness that You have laid away for those who fear You" (Tehilim 31:20), and "no eye has seen O G-d besides you, who prepares for those who wait for Him" (Yeshaya 64:3), "your righteousness shall go before you; the glory of the L-rd shall gather you in" (Yeshaya 58:8) (i.e. the gathering in of his soul in Olam Haba with the light of the glory of G-d - *TL*). When we study these and many more other similar verses in addition to what our Sages taught us in this, and with what our reason tells us, our souls will be at peace, and will be assured of the inevitability of reward and punishment in the afterlife.

## 9 - PREOCCUPY IN SECULAR INTERESTS

When the yetzer abandons hope of trying to make us doubt in all the previous matters mentioned, he will try to make us lazy in the service of G-d, and will try to preoccupy us in our secular interests - eating, drinking, dressing, riding, and to derive enjoyment from other physical pleasures.

> (*Pas Lechem*: "(1) to preoccupy us in our secular interests - eating, drinking...etc, and to (2) derive enjoyment" - he specified two evils. One, through being stuck in these things and wasting his time in them, he will be preoccupied and without any time for the service [of G-d]. On this, he wrote "to preoccupy us, etc". The second, deriving enjoyment from physical pleasures - they themselves destroy a man's heart, and inflate his mind to kick (be ungrateful) like a wild cow. On this, he wrote: "to derive enjoyment".)

And when we listen to him regarding eating, which we cannot exist without, he will make superfluous things that are secondary to food appear so embellished, and rejoicing and pleasure so charming that we will envy kings and their ministers, strive to live like them, adopt their practices, and go in their statutes, in pursuit of physical enjoyments.

> (*Pas Lechem*: "And when we listen to him regarding eating" - i.e. to have intent for enjoyment in the necessary eating, from this he will embellish to us the superfluous things.
> "strive to live like them" - in their great [desire of] heart.
> "adopt their practices" - to rule over the masses.
> "go in their statutes" - the pursuit of physical enjoyment is constant and habitual, a statute that cannot be broken. Like the necessities are for the masses.

*Marpe Lenefesh*: *"he will make superfluous things that are secondary to food appear so embellished"* - i.e. the yetzer embellishes to a man to run after the superfluous and the enjoyments which are the causes of all iniquities and all sins, as this is written at the end of the first gate and in the gate of abstinence, "that it is the El Zar (strange god) in the body of a man. see there.)

When the yetzer observes our desire and willingness in this, he will say:

(*Pas Lechem*: when the yetzer sees that we desire and want in this. He said "desire" which means "yearning" for them, before we attain them, and "willingness", i.e. delighting in them after attaining them.)

"Girdle your loins, bare your arms, O enticed man, exert with all your strength, O seduced man, to serve this world, and to serve its people, and you may attain some of your desire in it. Do not toil in matters of the next world. Rather, only in things which will help you in this world, to find favor among the people and the leaders, from kings to the rest of the people."

(*Pas Lechem*: *"Girdle your loins, bare your arms"* - i.e. tighten your belt and roll up your sleeves so that the clothing does not encumber you in swift movements. It is a phrase of encouragement to move to action.
*"O enticed man"* - now that I have found that you are like a friend and brother to me, being that you are enticed from my words, if so, why are you acting sluggishly and not [eagerly] pursuing my matters.)

"Don't exert your mind in any field of wisdom except those which will bring you honor from the public and favor in the eyes of the great men of your generation, the leaders, rulers, or anyone who occupies a high position. This includes the knowledge of languages, the essentials of prose, fundamentals of grammar, music, charming riddles, amazing parables and unusual sayings. Try to frequently meet with charismatic people, and be knowledgeable of cultures to be able to converse with all types of people and won't sit silent and be considered a fool and a simpleton. Leave the other wisdoms because their work demand is high but their practical benefit is low."

(*Pas Lechem*: *"to converse with all types of people..."* - that you become knowledgeable of all worldly matters. And then, when you are among a group of people who converse in their matters, you will also be able to converse with them and will not be forced to be silent and regarded as a fool, etc.

*Tov Halevanon*: *"considered a fool and a simpleton"* - in that you don't
know of the things happening in the world.)

But if from the beginning we did not open a door to the desires and satisfy
their wants (i.e. we do not leave any path or entrance to the yetzer - *TL*),
nor accustom ourselves to indulge in superfluous things and chase after
them, but instead we reply to the yetzer that we have no need for the
superfluous things and that we already have enough mental anxiety in
working to obtain what we need. If G-d sends us extra income without our
having to trouble our heart or straining our mind for it, we will spend them
in the right and proper manner as duty dictates. And if this does not
happen, we will be satisfied with the basic necessities, and won't require
more than this, then the [power of the] yetzer will be broken and smitten.

But if we listen to the yetzer in these things (to pursue the [physical]
enjoyments - *ML*), we will descend step by step until he has brought us to
hopeless destruction in this world and in the next.

All these example illustrations were on the first kind of enticements, which
the yetzer uses to cast doubt on a man who is weak in wisdom and in the
knowledge of G-d and of His torah.

## SECOND KIND OF TEMPTATION OF THE YETZER

(*Tov Halevanon*: these are the two kinds of enticement brought at the end
of chapter 4 of this gate. Until now was the first kind. From now on the
second kind.)

## 10 - TOPPLING THE WISE PERSON

But if a man is wise in understanding of G-d and His torah, the yetzer will
strive to damage and confuse his wisdom and actions by objections and
arguments from whichever side he can - from reason, scripture, and
tradition. He will bring spurious proofs whose premises are not true and
whose conclusions do not necessarily follow.

(*Tov Halevanon*: It is known that through two ways a [logical] proof is
established. One, through true premises. Two, through conclusions that
necessarily follow. i.e. if there is a foundation of premises which are
undoubtedly true, then when the premises are combined with each other,
the conclusions that are drawn from them must undoubtedly follow... a

spurious and faulty proof is due to either one of the premises is not true or that the conclusion does not follow these premises on proper consideration. This is what the author wrote that for the proofs of the yetzer, neither the premises are true nor do the conclusions follow.

*Pas Lechem*: For example, if we start with the premise that Reuven is taller than Shimon and Shimon is taller than Levi. Then the conclusion that necessarily follows is that Reuven is taller than Levi. However, it is possible that the premises are not true, that Reuven is not taller than Shimon or that Shimon is not taller than Levi, and the conclusions are automatically null and void. The second example, if we establish that Reuven loves Shimon and Shimon loves Levi, and we want to draw the conclusion that Reuven loves Levi. Even though the premises are true, the conclusion does not necessarily follow.

*Pas Lechem*: "rash/hasty proofs" - which suddenly grab the heart of a man, and are impressed on his mind before he can calmly deliberate it. Like a man in a panic, who is frenzied and rushed.)

If your intellect is sharp and your wisdom is strong in analyzing and defending and debating a position, you will see the various fallacies in the proofs of your yetzer, and the truth will become clear to you. The correct view will be apparent to you, your knowledge will be freed from doubts and your actions, from confusion.

(*Pas Lechem*: that you are wise and know the ways of proofs, which ways they are headed, then automatically you will know how to guard yourself from their fallacies when you contemplate them and see that they do not tread on the path of truth.)

But if your knowledge and ability in this is deficient (in the ways of proofs - *PL*), his enticements on you will be (increasingly - PL) stronger. He will overcome you more frequently. His ruling over you and surrounding you in your outer and inner life will become more imperative because he comes to you with wisdom, and leads you using proofs which your mind relies on. If your understanding has become seduced by him, he will let up from you, and it will help him work against you, because you rely on your mind when you have doubts, and trust its reasoning when some matter is not understood by you.

(*Tov Halevanon*: "his enticements on you will be (increasingly) stronger" - at first he comes with an argument of "maybe". Afterwards, he strengthens on you to establish his view as truth.
"more imperative" - you will accept his view with great imperative.

*"because you rely on your mind when you have doubts"* - you will rely on him. You think that this is not the acts of the yetzer since he has infiltrated in you with wisdom.

*Pas Lechem*: *"his enticements on you will be increasingly stronger"* - this is referring to the simple enticements mentioned earlier (for enjoyments). And on his overpowering a man by arguments and proofs, he wrote: *"and will overcome you more frequently"*. After he has habituated your mind with the arguments and proofs, they will be more prepared and readily available to invoke on you one after the other.
*"His ruling over you"* - he will rule over you to entice you to do disgraceful acts, and surround you with the hardship of the lusts of the world.
*"in your outer and inner life"* - i.e. in your actions and in your thoughts.
*"he will let up from you"* - he will let up on you and leave you a bit, since he no longer needs to strain himself on you because your intellect has become evil and stands in his place to entice you and help him.

*Marpe Lenefesh*: When your mind is seduced to believe his advice, then your intellect will depart from you, i.e. the intellect/conscience was given to a man to guide him to the just path, and the yetzer will divert it from you to help him do all the things G-d considers abominations with support of reason. Therefore our sages said (Pesachim 49b): "[Greater is the hatred wherewith the amme haaretz (ignorant Jews) hate the torah scholar than the hatred wherewith the gentiles hate Jews...It was taught:] He who has studied and then abandoned (the Torah, hates the torah scholar) more than all of them.")

And when the yetzer has overcome you, and rules you with the aid and support of your understanding, now, by deceiving you (away from the good - *PL*) and representing in your eyes falsehood (false imaginations to attract you to evil - *PL*) in the form of something demonstrated [as true], he will transfer you from this level, which was near to truth, and where falsehood was still concealed, and descend you to a lower level, where there is less truth and more falsehood.

(*Tov Halevanon*: *"which was near to truth, and where falsehood was still concealed"* - the falseness was not visible there, only the truth was visible and the falsehood was concealed inside it.
*"and descend you to a lower level"* - where the falsehood is more visible, and from level to level until you will be confident in yourself and will believe in that which is complete falsehood.)

And thus, he will not cease to lower you from one level to the next, until he will bring you to the level where the truth is completely concealed, and there is complete falsehood. And he will uproot you from this world, and topple you from the levels of reward in the next world. And your wisdom will become an evil for you (in this world - *TL*), and your intellect, the cause of your destruction (in the next world - *TL*), as written *"Hoy! They are wise in their eyes, and think they are understanding"* (Yeshaya 5:21), and *"they have rejected the word of the L-ord; and what wisdom is in them?"* (Yirmiyahu 8:9), and *"For the ways of the L-ord are just, and the righteous do walk in them; but transgressors do stumble therein"* (Hoshea 14:10).

(*Pas Lechem*: *"Hoy! They are wise in their eyes"* - the wise man said: He who thinks himself wise is a fool. Because one who is truly wise does not think of himself as a wise man.
*"they have rejected the word of the L-ord; and what wisdom is in them?"* - from this verse one can recognize and test himself. If he senses that his wisdom has led him to evil, certainly it is not true wisdom.
*"For the ways of the L-ord are just...etc"* - Perhaps a man will think that he will not be punished for this since his wisdom has deceived him and he is unintentional in this. On this he answered that it is not so, because no one will err except he who seeks to err and desires in it so as to be liberated through it (i.e. to go after the vanities of this world), because "the righteous will certainly walk in the ways of G-d while the sinners themselves will stumble in them" (Hoshea 14:10).

On this the Talmud says (Bava Basra 14b): *"Moshe wrote and he who wants to err will err"* - specifically *"he who wants to err"*, i.e. no one will err except he who wants to err and seeks excuses for doing so.

*Manoach Halevavos*: The ways of G-d and His torah are just. But they correspond to those who learn them. The righteous who learn them will go in them, like their way and justness. But the sinners will stumble more in learning the wisdom of the torah. For their wisdom will be a cause for their harming themselves. (Translator: The Vilna Gaon brings the analogy that torah is compared to water. Just like water causes good plants and bad plants (weeds) to grow, so too the Torah causes whatever is in a person's heart to grow, whether it is good or bad.)

*Marpe Lenefesh*: *"and topple you from the levels of reward in the next world"* - i.e. even if you are a torah scholar and toil in mitzvot - you will not have any reward in the next world when you heed to the yetzer that all your actions be not l'Shem Shamayim (for G-d), as will be explained. You will be like Doeg and Achitofel or the like, and the apikorsim in every generation who have no portion in the next world despite that they were big Chachamim (sages),... through the torah they became wise men to commit evil.)

It has been said that when wisdom is used in the proper way (to attain through it the favor of G-d - *PL*), it is a cure for all illnesses (of the soul - *PL*), but if one sways from its proper path, then it becomes an all-encompassing disease without cure and without medication.

(*Pas Lechem*: through this swaying away, a man is prepared to do all sin and iniquity whether inwardly or outwardly.)

On this, the torah is compared to fire as written *"Is not My word like fire?"* (Yirmiyahu 23:29), because it enlightens the eyes, as written *"the commandments of the L-ord are pure, enlightening the eyes"* (Tehilim19:9) and *"Your word is like a candle to my feet, and a light to my path"* (Tehilim 119:105). But anyone who turns away from its proper path, it burns up with its fire, as written *"by fire G-d will exact judgment"* (Isaiah 66:16), and *"on the wicked He will rain fiery coals"* (Tehilim 11:6), and *"Should I say; I will not mention Him, and I will no longer speak in His Name, but this was in my heart like a burning fire"* (Yirmiyahu 20:9).

(*Tov Halevanon*: One benefits from fire if he is far away and it enlightens the eyes. But if one gets close and clashes with it, it burns. So too for wisdom, it is beneficial in being like a candle to the feet of the torah and the religion. Then the light is sweet and good to the eyes of the intellect. But it burns those who enter it to damage and extinguish the flames. On this it says *"do not stray after your hearts"* (Bamidbar 15:39) and in the end they will inherit Gehinom (where he is punished by the fire of the torah itself - *PL*).
*"but this was in my heart like a burning fire"* - Lest you think that one who is very close to the torah also gets burned even if he is good. On this he brought this verse to teach that, on the contrary, closeness from torah and yira (fear) is the level of the prophets. The torah only burns those who stray from its paths.)

Therefore, be careful that your steps not stray from the path of the forefathers and the path of the early ones towards a new path you have devised, and be careful to not rely on your intellect nor to take counsel only with yourself. Do not reason on your own. Do not distrust your forefathers in the tradition they bequeathed to you as to what is good for you. Do not reject their advice in what they taught you because none of the plans you can think of were not previously known and (all of - *PL*) their good and evil consequences were already weighed.

(*Pas Lechem*: *"nor to take counsel only with yourself"* - nor with other

people of the same level as you who are also enticed by their yetzer lest they lead you astray. (i.e. get a wise Rav) Take counsel on how to wage war with the yetzer and to avoid his traps. This is for turning from evil.
*"Do not reason on your own"* on how to sustain the yoke of G-d's service . This is for doing good. (as in the verse in Tehilim *"turn from evil and do good"*).
*"Do not distrust your forefathers..."* - that you inherited falsehood. *"Do not reject their advice in what they taught you"* - in what they taught us as to how to wage war with the yetzer. These are the fences they enacted to distance from his traps.)

According to your reasoning, you may be impressed by the advantages which your plan brings at the beginning, but the long term negative consequences which the plan will bring are hidden to you. In your short sightedness, you will see its initial benefits but not its error and eventual damage. And the wise man said *"do not remove an ancient boundary stone set up by your forefathers"* (Mishlei 22:28), and *"listen my son to your father's instructions"* (ibid 1:8), and it is said of one who condemns the ways of his forefathers (who sees himself more righteous than his forefathers - *TL*) *"a generation clean in its own eyes, and yet are not cleansed of their excrement"* (ibid 30:12), and *"there is a generation that curses its fathers"* (ibid 30:11) (i.e. his forefathers are primitive in his eyes and he abandons their torah - *TL*), and *"the eye that mocks a father, [that scorns obedience to a mother will be pecked by the ravens of the valley, will be eaten by the vultures]"* (ibid 30:17).

(*Pas Lechem*: You think that this thing is just, and it is possible that it truly is good in the beginning, but its end will be evil and bitter. Hence with your little yishuv daat (clear-headedness), you grasp its beginning but not its end.

*Tov Halevanon*: *"a generation clean in its own eyes, and yet is not cleansed of their excrement"* - he sees himself more pure and clean than the early generations and seeks actions to become more righteous than them. But in truth, he is not even clean of the filth and waste of nursing babies. i.e. he transgresses sins that are known even to the [talmud torah] school children.)

However, if you see fit to take on yourself additional duties, what you can, beyond what is required, then, provided you are fulfilling those that are obligatory and that your motive is love of piety, and after your understanding has [examined it and] agreed, and that it is far from lusts - then the resolution is good.

(*Pas Lechem*: *"far from lusts"* - Since sometimes the stringency is a ploy of the yetzer in order to satisfy through this another desire such as the lust for honor and [to receive] praise for this, or the like. Therefore he said that one must examine himself in this if it is remote from his lusts.)

You will receive reward for this and are not deviating from the way of the forefathers. Because they already said *"make a fence for the torah"* (Avot 1:1), and *"why was Jerusalem destroyed? Because they pursued the letter of the law, and did not go above and beyond the letter of the law"* (Bava Metzia 30b), and "says Rav Huna - he who only occupied himself is as if he had no G-d, for it is said: 'Now for long seasons Israel was without the true God' - What is meant by 'without the true G-d'? - It means that he who only occupies himself with the study of the Torah, it is as if he has no G-d" (Avodah Zara 17b).

And one of the pious would say *"he who does no more than his duty is not doing his duty"*. But these "extra" acts are not accepted until one first fulfills the obligatory duties.

(*Pas Lechem*: It appears to us that the author's intent in this is that whoever performs his deeds only within the bounds of the torah is not fulfilling his duties. Rather one must be stringent and add to the obligation... And the verse which says 'without the true G-d', the intent is that he does not put to heart to fence himself [with stringencies] in order to not come to stumble in the mitzva itself. This is the intent of the "additional" [things].

If so, he is not mindful that G-d is described with the attribute "the G-d of truth". The intent of the word "truth" is eternity and permanence. Therefore the sages said: "the seal of the Holy One is truth" (Shabbat 55a), and just like He is permanent, so too His words are permanent. Likewise the blessing on the shema "He is permanent (kayam),etc. and His words are kayam (permanent/everlasting)". Understand this.

*"he who does no more than his duty is not doing his duty"* - i.e. the extra is not secondary. Rather it is primary for one who needs it, just like the duty itself. This is what the sages said (Yevamos 109b): "Whosoever says that he has only [an interest in the study of the] Torah, does not even have torah [study]"... Nevertheless, one should not precede the extra to the duty itself because *"these extra acts are not accepted until one first fulfills the obligatory duties"*.)

Our Sages already permitted us, and even [sometimes] obligated us to add on to the commandments, as they said (regarding friday evening) *"one must add from profane to holy"* (Yoma 81:2). Other examples are additions to fasts, prayer, charity, and refraining from the unnecessary permitted foods. They also warned us against taking an oath in G-d's Name, even for the truth, and from talking excessively even if the words are free of falsehood, and from discussing the affairs of other people, even if the words are not derogatory. Likewise, to refrain from lavishly praising someone even if it fitting, and to not speak bad or be disgusted by those who are falling short in fulfillment of their duties even if they deserve it, and many more things like this.

(*Manoach Halevavos*: *"To refrain from lavishly praising someone even if it fitting"* - Our sages taught (Arachin 16a): "He that blesses his friend with a loud voice, rising early in the morning, it shall be counted as a curse to him?", since from the praise, there will come derogatory remarks. Because there is no man who does not have enemies who hate him and are jealous of him, and when they hear the praise, they will speak bad of him...

*Marpe Lenefesh*: The Ramban wrote (on Devarim 6:18) that all the good conducts, even though they are not [explicitly] mentioned in the torah, the torah nevertheless exhorts us on them, as written there: *"And you shall do that which is right and good"* - that everything which is good in the eyes of G-d and man, you are under duty to do it all, see there. Likewise he wrote on the verse (Vayikra 19:2): *"You shall be holy"*, that this is a commandment on a man to be holy and pure in all of his conducts and traits. That he should be entirely holy. He then went to explain the good conducts, see there. He ended off: "even though these enactments are Rabbinical, the main intent of the verse is to exhort us in this, to be clean, pure, and separated from the masses of men who dirty themselves with superfluous and ugly things".)

It is proper for us to now bring some examples of the second type of enticements of the yetzer which one can learn to apply to other matters and to guard oneself from them with G-d's help when he understands them. Because necessarily, every good thing has corresponding bad things which can spoil it. Therefore, one who understands the things that damage good deeds will be capable of guarding himself from them. But one who knows only the good deeds, and does not know the things which can damage them will end up with nothing due to the abundance of damaging things which will beset him.

(*Marpe Lenefesh*: i.e. there is no good thing which does not have a corresponding damaging thing which can ruin and spoil that good thing. And the more good something is, the more quickly it can become spoiled. Similar to silk clothing which can be ruined with a bit of oil or a

| stain...unlike coarse cloth..)

One of the pious would instruct his disciples: "learn the bad things first to avoid them, and afterwards learn the good things and do them, as written *'Plow for yourself a furrow and do not sow upon thorns'*" (Yirmiyahu 4:3).

Rabbi Yochanan ben Zakai would say regarding the falsification of weights and measures (Bava Basra 89b) "woe to me if I say, woe to me if I don't say; if I say - perhaps the swindlers will learn from my words, if I don't say - perhaps the swindlers will say that the Sages are ignorant of our tricks.", the question was raised: "did he speak of them or not?", and concludes "he did speak of them", relying on the verse *"for the ways of the L-rd are right, and the righteous shall walk in them, while the wicked shall stumble on them"* (Hoshea 14:10).

(*Marpe Lenefesh*: From here is a proof that one need not refrain making known and publicizing the various types of incitements of the yetzer on a man. And we need not worry lest people may learn from these things to deceive others.)

## EXAMPLES OF THE SECOND KIND OF TEMPTATION OF THE YETZER

### 11 - STRIVE TO FIND FAVOR WITH HUMAN BEINGS
We have already mentioned in this gate regarding the ways in which the yetzer tries to cast doubts in a man's mind. If he is not successful in raising such doubts, he will attempt the method of arguments and proofs in order to revoke the truths of his faith. When you stand up to his superficiality and the weakness of his proofs and he is not capable of standing up to you, nor of annulling what you know to be clear and true of the matters previously mentioned in this gate, he will return to flatter you and mislead you in regard to yourself.

He will say to you: "How I rejoice for you on your good faith and devoted heart to G-d. You have already reached a degree of piety which others in your generation have not been able to reach (i.e. you are among the just and pious - *ML*), and you have already thanked G-d sufficiently for His goodness and kindness to you. Now it is proper for you to also work to pay your debts of gratitude to your fellow men. Because you already know that they are means to your benefit and harm, and it is clear also that when they like you, you will be honorable in their eyes. But if they are angry with you, you will incur losses. Therefore, endeavor in things that will please them and that will find favor in their eyes, as our Sages said: "One who is pleasing to his fellow men, is pleasing to G-d. [But one who is not pleasing to his fellow men, is not pleasing to G-d]" (Avos 3:10).

(*Pas Lechem*: The matters of your benefit must come through human beings since a man is social by nature. You are also liable to be damaged by them if you are not loved and considered important in their eyes.
*"endeavor in things that will please them"* - (1) that your deeds will please them, namely, some favor and benefit that you do to them. (2) And on self-embellishment before them without benefiting them he continued: *"and that will find favor in their eyes".*)

Answer the yetzer:
"What will I benefit from finding favor with someone who is weak like me, who does not have the ability to help me or harm me (see gate of trust), and the verse says: 'Withdraw yourselves from man whose [life] breath is in his nostrils, for by what should he be esteemed?' (Yeshaya 2:22). And even if it were my duty, how could I possibly find favor with all my contemporaries when I don't even have the ability to find favor with the members of my own household?!"

"And the proofs which you brought from the words of our Sages does not imply that one needs to try to find favor in the eyes of everyone. Rather this is like the case of the wise man that left in his will a command to his son:
'My son, to find favor with the public is not in your ability. Instead try to find favor with the Creator and He will grant you favor with the public, as written "When G-d finds favor in a person's ways, He will cause even his enemies to make peace with him" (and all the more so everyone else - *TL*) (Mishlei 16:7).

And likewise, when you see a man whom everyone, young or old, praises him and finds favor in his deeds, it is a proof that G-d has implanted love of him in their hearts, and established a good name for him on their tongues. The Creator does not do this for those He hates. And this is a clear and powerful proof that the Creator is pleased with him. But that a pious person should exert himself and strive so that others will praise him due to his service of G-d - this is not the way of the pious.

(*Pas Lechem*: Just like if one's enemies make peace with him, it is a sign that G-d is pleased with him, so too if the public loves him, without any exertion on his part, it is a sign for this. Hence, the intent of the sages teaching ("One who is pleasing to his fellow men, is pleasing to G-d") is only as a sign. And the sign is only valid if there is no exertion on his part. *"And this is a clear and powerful proof that the Creator is pleased with him"* - because love of good simply because it is good, not because of any enjoyment or benefit received - this is something found only in virtuous men. However, in this case, all the public praises and loves him. Then, certainly this is not a natural love and must be from [divine] providence.)

Therefore, be careful of this or similar things among the enticements of the yetzer toward you. Because he will try to lead you in this until he topples you in the trap of (the trait of - PL) flattery.

(*Marpe Lenefesh*: this is the complete flatterer, who worships human beings. He is like the idol worshipper, as written earlier in chapter 4.

Translator: Nevertheless, Rabbi Avigdor Miller zt'l would say that you should make every effort to try to make people like you because this makes you into a better person. It is not a contradiction to here. The intent of the author is that your motive should be to serve G-d when doing this, not to try to obtain some benefit from people, as the author brought in the Gate of Trust ch.4 category 3: "The person, whose motive in fulfilling their wishes is one of the [reprehensible] motives we mentioned above, will not obtain what he wants from them in this world. He will tire himself for nothing, and will lose his reward in the afterlife. But if his sole motive is to serve G-d, the Al-mighty will help them to make a return to him in this world, and G-d will place his praise in their mouths and they will hold him in high esteem, and he will reach the great reward in Olam Haba.." see there)

And on his praising you, answer him: "what is this that you are congratulating me on? Is it because I know my duties to G-d? Just the opposite - because I know my duties to G-d, there is grounds for a claim against me, namely, that I am not acting in accordance with my knowledge.

And even if I were doing enough according to my knowledge of my duties to G-d, would this be enough of an expression of gratitude to the blessed Creator for even the smallest benefits He bestows on me? And what is the measure of my days relative to the measure of the days of the universe? Even if it were equal to the age of the universe, it would not be enough time for me to recount all the favors G-d has bestowed upon me. How much less then is it possible for me to repay my debts of gratitude to G-d for them? (since even to recount all of them, all the days of the universe does not suffice. All the more so, to repay for them with service - *TL*) And scripture has already said: *"All flesh is like grass, and all its kindness is like the flower of the field"* (Yeshaya 40:6), and our Sages said *"If I am not for myself, who is for me? And if I am only for myself, what am I? And if not now, when?"* (Avos 1:14).

(*Marpe Lenefesh*: *"All flesh is like grass"* - Like a flower of the plants of the field which wilts and dries up swiftly, so too are human beings.
*"all its kindness is like the flower of the field"* - the kindness that a human being does is like a flower which blossoms and swiftly withers and falls from the fruit and does not endure. So too the deeds of human beings do not endure. And if so, how can a man be haughty?

*Pas Lechem*: All kindness that a man does to his Creator is insubstantial, like the flower of the field which is charming to the eye but has nothing substantial in itself.

*Tov Halevanon*: *"If I am not for myself, who is for me?"* - These words are directed to the understanding. (Not to the yetzer.) If I don't watch over myself using my understanding to stand up against the arguments and lusts of the yetzer, who will help me? For the free will is granted to me and there is no outside help.
*"And if I am only for myself, what am I?"* - even if I were free from the yetzer in my mind (as the Talmudic saying for emancipation (Gitin 85b): *"you are for yourself"*), and I could serve G-d according to my knowledge, *"what am I"*, would this be enough of an expression of gratitude to the blessed Creator, etc., as he wrote above.
*"And if not now, when?"* - This is corresponding to what he wrote: *"what is the measure of my days, etc."*, i.e. since all the days of a man and even all the days of the universe do not suffice for the due service, if so, if one wastes one second from the service of G-d, when can he ever repay this?)

## 12 - TO LOVE BEING PRAISED AND ACQUIRING A GOOD NAME

(*Pas Lechem*: In the previous case, he spoke of the yetzer's enticements to a man, that from today on, he will do his deeds with intent to receive benefit from human beings, and that it is sufficient what he did until now to have intent for the service of G-d. Now, he comes to entice him that he can continue to have intent for the service of G-d, only that he should reveal his deeds and not conceal them (so that human beings will also observe him - TL). Thus he will gain from this praise of people and it will not damage his service of G-d in the least.

*Manoach Halevavos*: In the previous case, he spoke of the need to pay back his debts to human beings. That since he has payed back his debts to G-d sufficiently, according to the yetzer, he should endeavor to pay his debts to human beings, and to do deeds for their benefit alone which are not related to the service of G-d. Thus, they will love him and honor him. Here, the yetzer abandoned this. He tries instead to induce him to do the service of G-d in such a way that human beings see him so that he attains honor and a good name.)

When the yetzer gives up trying to entice you in this way, he will try to entice from the angle of love of praise and of acquiring a good name in this world. He will say to you:

"I rejoice at your service of G-d with good trust, in that you have placed all your matters to Him, and have freed your heart from [the thought] that any created being can possibly benefit you without G-d. Now you are truly trusting in G-d wholeheartedly. It is not proper for you to conceal from people the high degree of piety you have attained. Rather it is proper now that you have ruled over your inclination and overcome your base desires to show your piety to others, and to reveal your heart to them. In this way you will be honored by them in this world, and will have good name and a good remembrance among them, as the verse says: "I will give them in My house and in My walls a memorial and a name, better than sons and daughters" (Yeshaya 56:5). It also says: "I will make for you a great name, like the name of the great ones of the land" (II Shmuel 7:9). Additionally, so that they will learn from your deeds, and you will receive reward for them. Hence, don't hide your deeds from them except those things that cannot be shown to people. Therefore, you will receive honor and a good name in this world and good reward in the next".

(*Pas Lechem*: *"you have ruled over your inclination"* - forced yourself to steer from the traps of evil.
*"and overcome your base desires"* - to sanctify yourself also with the permitted things, namely, the trait of chasidut (extra piety). And since it requires great strengthening to distance from the permitted, he wrote *"overcome"*.)

Answer him: "what will I benefit from praises of people, and from a good name among them, when I know that I am lacking in my obligations to the Creator? What benefit can I have from their honor and esteem, when they are incapable of helping me or shielding me from harm? In this regard, aren't they like plants and animals (who cannot benefit or harm me without G-d's decree as explained in gate 4 - *ML*). And maybe if I have these intents in my deeds, I will not find favor in their eyes. Rather, they will see me as a flatterer and I will become an object of disgust and contempt, and the result will be that I will lose my good deeds in that I did not have intent to G-d and will also fail in what I had hoped to attain from people in this world.

> (*Pas Lechem*: *"I will lose my good deeds in that I did not having intent to
> G-d"* - I will lose my deeds regarding the reward of the next world.
> Because any intent, whether a little or a lot, which strays a little bit to
> something other than G-d is necessarily a form of hypocrisy and ruins the
> reward, even though his primary act was for the service of G-d.)

It is said of one of the kings of Israel who was asked: "how did you like the
(torah) reading of the Chazan? His voice was pleasing and he was an
expert in the chanting of the cantillation notes." The king answered them:
"How could I like his reading. He was reading it only so that it would be
pleasing to me, and to find favor in my eyes. But if he had intent for
pleasing the Creator alone - then it would have been pleasing to me".

We can likewise say about all those leading the congregation in prayers,
and the chazanim who compose new piyutim (liturgical prayers), whose
intent is to find favor in the eyes of men and not of G-d - that their prayers
are not acceptable to the Creator.

Answer him further: "Maybe, if I receive honor in this world for my deeds,
nothing of my reward will be left in the next world, because I received it
already in this world".

It is said of one of the pious who entered a market to buy something. He
came to one of the shops to buy it and the shopkeeper's neighbor told the
shopkeeper: "give in to him, and do his will since he is a pious scholar".
The pious man answered him: "Thank you but I don't need special
treatment. I came to buy with my money, not with my torah knowledge".
He refused to buy from that shop, and instead went to another shop where
he was not recognized (since it is forbidden to benefit from the torah - *TL*).

(Answer the yetzer also:) "And that which you brought from the verse: 'I
will make for you a great name..', this is just like the other things people
aspire to in this world, such as wealth, honor, which the Creator bestows
on His servants when His wisdom deems this proper, as written *"And I
have also given you that which you have not asked for, both riches and
honor"* (Melachim 3:13), and also *"long life is in its right, to its left, wealth
and honor"* (Mishlei 3:16). But the pious do not intend for any of these
things in their service, rather their sole intent is for the Creator who
bestows good to who He wishes, among his servants or others, believers or
non-believers, as His wisdom dictates, as written *"wealth and honor is
Yours"* (Divrei HaYamim 29:12).

(Answer further:) "And what is this world? (since the benefit from honor is only in this world - *TL*) Even if my name becomes known to the whole world, what is the measure of my days? Even if my name does go out to part of the world, certainly my memory will reach an even smaller part, and even then it will fade away after a short time and be forgotten as if it had never existed. And scripture says: 'The sons of men are but vanity, and men of distinction are a falsehood; were they to be put on a scale, together they would equal vanity' (Tehilim 62:10), and 'his breath leaves, he returns to his dust' (Tehilim 146:4), and 'there is no memory of the early ones' (Koheles 1:11)."

"Therefore, for me to trouble myself for this world, and put my thoughts in it, is clear pettiness and a disgraceful mistake on my part. It is told of one of the pious that asked his friend: 'have you achieved equality?, he answered 'on what?', he replied 'is it equal in your eyes whether you are honored or insulted?'. He answered: 'No'. He said: 'if so, you have not yet arrived. Keep trying, maybe you will reach this level, because it is the highest of the levels of the pious, and the most desirable of qualities.'"

(*Translator*: Here is an excerpt from the book Shaarei Kedusha by Rabbi Chaim Vital (Part 4 Gate 3) on the trait of "equality" :
...After a man has merited to the clinging (of his thoughts to G-d), he will merit to the secret of 'equality', and if he merits the secret of 'equality', he will merit to the secret of 'meditation', and after he has merited to the secret of 'meditation', he will merit Ruach HaKodesh, and from this to prophecy, which means, he will prophecy and say over future events.

And on the matter of "equality", Rabbi Avner said to me: A wise man, among the misbodedim (meditators) came to me seeking that I accept him among the meditators. The master said to him: "blessed are you my son to G-d, your intentions are good. However let me know if you reached the level of 'equality' or not." He answered: "Rebbi explain your words." He said "For two men, if one of them honors you and the second insults you, are they equal in your eyes?"

He answered: "no my master. Because I feel pleasure and contentment from the one who honors me, and pain from the one who insults me, but I don't bear any grudge against him."

He answered "My son, go in peace, because as long as you haven't reached 'equality' until your soul does not feel the honor from someone who honors you, nor the embarrassment from someone who shames you, you're not

prepared to have your thoughts tied with the supernal when you come and
meditate. Go and humble more your heart in truth until you have reached
'equality', then you'll be able to meditate."

The matter of equality, comes through the clinging of one's thoughts to
G-d, blessed be He. Because the clinging to G-d causes that man not look
at others' honoring him, nor at their shaming him. He will also not be
worried about forces of evil.

You can see when G-d was with [King Shaul], and Shaul's thoughts were
clinging to Him, he removed the sorcerers from the land, and similarly, he
did not care when the evil men insulted him when he was coronated as king
over Israel (Shmuel I 11). But when G-d left him, he transformed into a
different person. He went after the sorcerers (Shmuel I 28:7), and also he
became furious with anger on the righteous Kohanim which did not sin
against him and he spilt their blood for nothing...And if so, a man must first
do a great humbling in order to merit the hisdabkus (clinging to G-d) and
this comes through fulfilling the mitzvos with all his strength. And also to
cling absolutely to the trait of humility, that his eyes should be below and
his heart above.)

## 13 - ENDLESS WORRIES AND DISTRACTIONS OF THIS WORLD
When the yetzer gives up trying to entice you in these ways, he will try to
ruin your [religious] deeds by distracting your mind with this world and its
people and with your extensive desires so that you forget your final end.

(*Marpe Lenefesh*: He will cause your mind to always worry and think on
this world, and from where will come your livelihood and desires, so that
you forget your end. Not only that, but even at the time you want to pray or
learn torah, he will put in your heart every which way he can [to distract
you] as will be explained.)

When he sees that you wish to turn your attention to matters of the next
world, such as during prayer, whether obligatory or voluntary, or when you
study the torah or some other wisdom related to emuna (faith) or mussar
(ethics), he will confuse you and distract your thoughts with secular
matters, such as thoughts of merchandise, buying and selling, profit and
loss. He will say to you: "you should be happy that now you have some
free time, an opportunity which will not return due to your many business
dealings. Now, think about your business partner, and make an accounting
of what he owes you and what you owe him, and how much you have
collected of your debts, and how much is due to you. Consider which
financial means of gaining livelihood are suitable to you and which are not.

Reflect on which matters brought you satisfaction and which made you regret, and if you have a court case against someone, review in your mind all of your claims and all of his claims against you, and all the ways you can outsmart him when the case is brought to court."

So too, if you have money [to invest], or sheep and cattle, or land for sowing, or you have a job to do for the nobleman or a commoner, or you need to make an accounting with either, or if you owe debts which you are unable to repay, or you have friends which you must watch over and think about, he will bring one of these to your mind when you turn to devote some time to matters of service of G-d. This is to distract you and ruin your deeds. Because when you do them, you are ready in body but distracted in mind and spirit.

> (*Pas Lechem*: The reason the yetzer is successful in his plan and is able to distract you is because while doing these things, namely, prayer or torah study, you were ready in body; i.e. you prepared only the limbs of your body but did not prepare for this your heart and mind. If you had mustered them for this completely, there would not have been any opening for the yetzer to enter in your heart/mind.
>
> *Marpe Lenefesh*: Why was he able to put in your mind all these things? Because you recite your prayers without kavana (intent) of your heart. But if you would pray with all of your kavana, to understand every word that comes out of your mouth - none of this would happen to you.)

If he does not distract you with one of the things mentioned previously, he will remind you of riddles, or other subjects which require much thought. If a man is among those who play dice or chess, or the like, he will bring him to picture as if the game is arranged before him and he needs to think about which moves to make, and which strategies to use to win the game.

## 14 - DISTRACTING WITH GOOD DEEDS

If a man will escape from all that we mentioned previously, and belongs to the men of wisdom and understanding (becomes a talmid chacham), the yetzer will bring to his attention a difficult matter of wisdom, and he will distract him with questions and answers, with difficulties and solutions, and he will show him which matters he missed and which he should have investigated more. He will also show him how much he still has to learn in this wisdom so that he makes a personal accounting and resolves to learn it. This way, the yetzer will distract him in all his acts of service of G-d, and will cause him much more damage than gain.

(*Marpe Lenefesh*: Even though he will think, during the time of prayer, on doing mitzvot and good deeds or to answer (Talmudic) difficulties, which are good things, nevertheless, the loss, namely that he ruined his prayer with outside thoughts is a greater sin in his hand and outweighs all of what he gained, and our sages said (Shabbat 10a): "Torah and Tefilah each have their own time"...as in the Shulchan Aruch: "prayer is in place of the temple korbanos, therefore one must be careful that it is like a korban with kavana, to not mix it with other thoughts just like improper thoughts can invalidate a korban", see there)

(Due to all of these distractions) it is possible that he will do the service of G-d but be outside of it, and that his thoughts are always distracted in some other secular interest. It may even be that he will seek forgiveness from G-d with his tongue, all the while eagerly rushing in his mind and spirit to rebel against Him (i.e. greatly desiring something prohibited - *PL*).

On this one of the pious said: "this kind of seeking forgiveness requires seeking forgiveness". And he pleas to G-d with his limbs, but turns from Him in his heart and thoughts, similar to the verse: "These people come near to Me with their mouth and honor Me with their lips, but their hearts are far from Me. Their worship of Me is nothing but acts of rote" (Yeshaya 29:13), and "But then they would flatter Him with their mouths, lying to Him with their tongues; Their heart was not sincere with Him" (Tehilim 78:36).

(*Pas Lechem*: "(1) seek forgiveness....(2) And he pleas to G-d" - it appears from the movement of his limbs that he is truly pleading but his heart and thoughts turn from Him. In both ways, his external contradicts his internal. From the first way, where he was seeking forgiveness for the past while [internally] preparing himself to sin in the future. From the second way, where he pleas and seeks some matter, but one who pleas must cleave his thoughts to the One he is pleading to and to find favor with Him... and promises to be faithful.. but here his heart is not with G-d.)

If you will wake up then and make an accounting with your soul and say to yourself: "How could I conduct myself towards the Creator in a way that would be improper for me to conduct myself with His creations when I need something from them, or likewise, for them to act towards me when they need something from me?

Because, if I went to borrow something from someone, and I asked him for the thing with my lips but my heart was against him, if he noticed this, he would be disgusted and repulsed by me. All the more so, that he would not grant me my request. And certainly, even more so, if he knew that I were planning in my thoughts not only things which would not find favor with him but rather even things which would make him angry with me. Surely, his hatred for me would be greater and his refusal more appropriate. And certainly, I would act in this same way towards someone who asked me to borrow something and if I knew his thoughts, just like the Creator knows what is in my heart.

Therefore, how then while [standing] before my Creator could I not feel ashamed? How can I expect to please Him with my conduct when I would not want a weak, created being like myself to conduct himself thus towards me, and which a fellow weak, created, and dependent creature like myself would likewise not be pleased to find in me, as it is written "Were they ashamed when they had committed abomination? nay, they were not at all ashamed, neither could they blush:[therefore shall they fall among them that fall: in the time of their punishment they shall be cast down, says the L-ord]" (Yirmiyahu 8:12)."

Then the yetzer will be smitten.

(*Marpe Lenefesh*: In the Orchos Chaim of the Rosh siman 47: "have intent in your prayer. For prayer is the service of the heart. If your son spoke to you not from his heart, would it not anger you? What will you do, putrid drop, before the King of the Universe, the Holy One, blessed be He. Are you not like a slave charged with an important job, for his own benefit, who then corrupts it? How then can you stand before the King of kings, the Holy One, blessed be He... if you cannot do this for the entire prayer, at least do not lack this for the first blessing of the Amida and for the Shema because one who did not have intent in these did not fulfill his obligation." In the Shl"A (Mesechet Tamid p.ner mitzva): "Let one reflect in his mind, if he were to speak before a flesh and blood king and between his words, he would speak other nonrelated things, certainly, he would be liable for his head to the king. And behold, for the King of kings, the Holy One, blessed be He, thoughts are just like words, "for the L-ord searches all hearts, and understands all the plans of the thoughts" (Divrei Hayamim 28:9). Therefore, what is the difference if one interrupts with other thoughts or other words during the prayer?"

Translator: Rabbi Beniyahu Shmueli, a famous Rosh Yeshiva and Kabalist in Jerusalem, wrote on Parsha Vaetchanan: How should our prayers appear? Rabbi Avraham Cohen of Tunis wrote in his book "Millel L'Avraham" about a holy rabbi who heard about a circus which came to the city, and that in the circus show there is an amazing acrobat who walks on a tightrope stretched out between two mountains and over a river. The Rabbi said: "I am going to watch". The pious people wondered "what does the Rabbi want with the circus?" Afterwards, the Rabbi answered: "I watched the face of the acrobat, and I saw how he focuses all of his thoughts in this walking. Because he knows that the danger of falling is imminent every second and were he to turn his thoughts to something else, immediately, he would fall to the depths and be no more. At that time, I learned mussar that when a Jew prays, he is under duty to focus all of his thoughts with total kavana for the prayer. If not, he will fall.")


## 15 - CONCEAL YOUR RELIGIOUS DEEDS COMPLETELY

When the yetzer gives up trying to entice you in this way, he will try to entice you from the angle of distancing from flattery, and he will say to you: "you cannot possibly serve G-d with a perfect heart until you distance yourself completely from flattery whether it is a little or a lot. And to distance yourself from flattery towards other people requires completely hiding all of your deeds from them, and showing them the opposite of what is in your heart.

(*Pas Lechem*: Since if you merely conceal them, perhaps they will ponder you and realize that you conceal your deeds. Then they will investigate and examine to know them. Therefore, you must be smart and show others the opposite of what is in your heart. Thus, they will think you are one of the simple people and will not ponder you at all. Then, you will be successful in concealing your deeds and will not become known.)

Therefore, when you pray, be brief, and let there be no appearance of desire or striving in them. When you learn wisdom, do so in seclusion so that none but the Creator knows. Let no good trait in you become apparent. Show others laziness and heaviness in the service of G-d so that your name will not go out and you will lose your reward. Do not instruct others to do good nor rebuke them against evil. Do not show your wisdom nor teach others, and let there be no sign of fear of Heaven on you, and no sign of being a servant of G-d so that others will not honor you on account of this. In order that your zeal in hiding your deeds to people is complete, mix with and befriend all the different classes of people. Adopt their customs and walk in their ways regarding laughter and laxness in words of truth.

(*Tov Halevanon*: i.e. let everything be equal in your eyes, and do not differentiate on them, lest they consider you pious, and give you a reputation for being an ascetic and a pious man, whereby you will lose your reward.)

Do not guard so much from lies and oaths. Join them in their feasts and drinking parties, in their riddles, in their excessive indulgences and abundant laughter. Speak of people, and speak of their faults. To summarize, avoid all things that will bring you a reputation for asceticism."

(*Marpe Lenefesh*: i.e. to abandon flattery completely. The intent is to not do any good things before people. Hence, he abandons the service of G-d because of the praises of people, so that they do not praise him for it. He is fleeing from a small fire, namely, the trait of flattery, and into a big fire, namely, he will abandon all good deeds one by one.)

If you listen to him in this, slowly without noticing, you will wind up losing even your faith. But if you answer him: "you have already helped my enemies by waging war with me, by your cunning planning to destroy my strength and promote my downfall. How could I flee from a small fire towards a big fire? I have tried to flee from love of recognition and honor in order to not embellish myself towards people, and you are instructing me to embellish myself to them by leaving the service of G-d!"

(i.e. two evils, to embellish myself to them in leaving the service of G-d - TL, with the excessive things, laughter, and the other things mentioned - PL)

*Pas Lechem*: *"slowly without noticing, you will wind up losing even your faith"* - This is the way he snares people with his traps. After confusing you in the good, he will topple you into the light bad, and from the light bad to the heavy bad, and from the deeds to the faith, until he eventually brings you to kefira (denial of G-d). And since he comes slowly in stages, and especially since the initial enticement appeared good in your eyes, therefore you did not even notice your downfall.
*"you have already helped my enemies..."* - since in this enticement, the yetzer disguises and enclothes himself as if he is a loving friend, as if he is the good inclination, and that he is coming to help a man against the evil inclination. Therefore, a man should tell him: I recognize that you have not come to help me, but rather to help my enemy, the yetzer hara. You, like him, are waging war against me.)

"Rather, the religious deeds which it is proper for me to conceal are those which can be done (wholly - PL) from beginning to end without knowledge of people. But to pray with the congregation, to instruct others to do good, to rebuke others from evil, the study of wisdom, doing acts of kindliness, or the like - it is not right to neglect and abandon them due to concern for flattery (i.e. out of concern that I will appear to be a servant of G-d so that people will praise me - *TL*). It is my duty to do them with intent to G-d. If people praise me or honor me for this, my reward will not be diminished in the least because while doing them, this was not my goal."

It was already said: when you do a good deed that others know about, and you want to know if your motives (are proper), test yourself in two ways. (1) Examine what reward you hoped to receive, and from whom you intended to receive it. If from G-d, this is good. If from anyone else, it is not good.

> (*Pas Lechem*: Even though the sages said: *"do not do a mitzva in order to receive a reward"* (Avos 1:3). However, [here] his intent is for reward which is acceptable to G-d, namely, that *"a mitzva leads to another mitzva...[and the reward of a mitzva is a mitzva]"* (Avos 4:2), or likewise the motive *"[One thing I ask of the Lord]...to behold the pleasantness of the L-ord"* (Tehilim 27:4) through this deed. Understand this.)

(2) To consider, if you were alone (and no one were observing you besides G-d - *TL*), would you still do this deed in the way you did it? If the answer is yes, your deed is wholly devoted to G-d. Continue doing more like these. But if it would be less than this, stop doing it until (you sense - *PL*) your heart has become more purely devoted to G-d. Then the yetzer will be smitten. (when you tell him that you do not need to be concerned for flattery of people after testing yourself with these two things - *TL*)

> (*Marpe Lenefesh*: If you were alone by yourself, would you have also done this? If yes, then you can do more deeds like this one even in front of people and it will not damage you. If no, that your heart is not yet whole so much, it is better to refrain from it, and not to do a fraudulent thing with bad motives.)

## 16 - WORSHIP YOURSELF

If the yetzer will not find a way to entice you in these ways, he will try to outsmart you with a subtler approach, namely, through the ways of reward and punishment in this world and the next. He will say to you: "behold, you are among the pious of the Creator, and His treasured ones. A person like you is surely worthy of reward in this world and in the next. You must exert yourself according to your abilities (in the service of G-d - *TL*), maybe you will earn the reward through your good deeds and your zealous pursuing of the service of G-d with a good heart and with great joy. Set the reward before your eyes, and work your hardest to reach it, because this is the greatest success and joy, as king David said: "A light is sown for the righteous, and for the upright of heart, joy" (Tehilim 97:11).

If you listen to him and you rely on his words, he will topple you by making you worship hidden association (G-d and something else - *TL*), namely, self-worship, in that you exert yourself in things that will bring you selfish pleasure and joy, and that will repel from you worries and despairs. If it were not for your hopes for these, you would deny the constant favors G-d bestows on you and not obligate yourself to serve Him on account of them. And furthermore, you don't see that it is befitting to serve G-d (even without these benefits) due to His greatness, infinite power, and the manifestations of His wisdom. On this the Sages said: "do not be like servants who serve their master in order to receive reward, but like servants who serve their master without [the condition of] receiving reward" (Avos 1:3).

(*Marpe Lenefesh*: Your worship is for yourself, so that you obtain this world and the next. And if not, you would not serve G-d with a complete heart.

"*in that you exert yourself in things that will bring you selfish pleasure and joy*" - you only do those things that bring you joy.

*Pas Lechem*: "*self-worship*" - You serve yourself since all of your aspirations are to benefit yourself. Behold you are both the worshipped and the worshipper. This is evident from "*that you exert yourself in things that will bring you selfish pleasure and joy*", "*pleasure*" in the hope for reward, and "*joy*" in being saved from punishment, and "*that will repel from you worries and despairs*", "*worries and despairs*" also corresponding to these two things.

"*If it were not for your hopes for these*" - you revealed your attitude that were it not for the hopes of reward, you would not be zealous and would not see yourself under duty in this. Hence, you are a denier of the beneficence of G-d. In addition to this, you revealed your understanding that you don't know the greatness of G-d, and that it is fitting to serve Him, due to His power, etc.

"*due to His greatness, infinite power, and the manifestations of His wisdom*" - the author included in this the three attributes (in the Amidah prayer) "*Hagadol, Hagibor, Ve'Hanora*" - on "*Hagadol*" (the Great), he wrote "*due to his greatness*". On "*Hagibor*" (the Mighty), he wrote "*infinite power*". On "*Hanora*" (the Awesome), he wrote "*the manifestations of His wisdom*", that when a man contemplates His wisdom (exhibited in nature), he is very amazed, and is in awe of Him, as it is written by Shlomo (Melachim 3:28) "and they held the king in awe, for they saw that the

| wisdom of G-d was in him".)


## 17 - G-D's DECREE VS. FREE WILL

When the yetzer gives up trying to entice you in the ways mentioned, he will hurl you in a sea of doubts regarding necessity and righteousness (predestination and free will).

> (*Tov Halevanon*: Whether all of a man's matters must necessarily follow only the decree of G-d or whether they depend on the righteousness and the deeds of human beings, as discussed at length in the gate of trust.
>
> *Pas Lechem*: "*necessity*" - Whether a man is forced in his deeds, without any free will. According to this outlook, there is not one righteous person in the world, because the righteousness is not attributed to him.
> "*righteousness*" - Or he performs his deeds through his own desire and free will, and therefore "*righteousness*" can be attributed to him.)

When he sees you lax in the service [of G-d], and turning towards the path of sin, he will try to convince you of the matter of necessity with powerful arguments drawn from Scripture and Tradition, in order to give you excuses, and he will say to you:
"If the Creator wanted you to serve Him, He would force you and make you zealous in this, for only what He decrees can occur. How can you stand up against His decrees or defeat His judgments? You can only do what He decreed on you to do, because all things occur through the Creator's decrees as written 'I am G-d who does everything' (Yeshaya 44:24)."

> (*Tov Halevanon*: If G-d wanted you to be a Tzadik (righteous person), He would have compelled you in this.
>
> *Pas Lechem*: "*He would force you and make you zealous in this*" - for some act of service which you want to refrain from doing, he will tell you that if the Creator wanted you to do this, He would force you to do it. And on some act of service which you do lazily and sluggishly, he will tell you that G-d would have made you zealous in it...
>
> *Pas Lechem*: "*How can you stand up against His decrees or defeat His judgments?*" - he specified two parts corresponding to things between man and G-d and things between man and his fellow man. Corresponding to sins between man and G-d, he wrote "*against His decrees*", i.e. G-d decreed and this thing came to be, therefore I was compelled to do the sin.
> Corresponding to sins between man and man, he wrote "*defeat His*

*judgments"*, that G-d sentenced that person to suffer on that matter through you. Therefore, you were forced to cause him pain.)

But if he sees you engaged in secular matters and occupations, he will tell you (the opposite): "be careful of laziness (of heart - *PL*) and sluggishness (of limbs - *PL*). Don't rely on anyone but yourself, because good and evil are in your hands and success and failure in accomplishment depends on you. Therefore, exert yourself with all your strength and work with all your ability and you will succeed in obtaining your desires of this world. Guard from damaging things with all your strength and you will be saved from them, as the wise man said "Thorns and snares are in the way of the crooked; whoever guards his soul will keep far from them" (Mishlei 22:5), and "A man's folly perverts his way" (Mishlei 19:3), and "from your own hands this came" (Melachim 1:9). And so the yetzer turns around the argument, sometimes he comes with necessity and divine decree and sometimes with justice and free will according to what he deems fitting for him to entice you (to evil - *PL*) and weaken you (to good - *PL*).

But if you wake up and put to heart what our Sages said "everything is in the hands of Heaven except the fear of Heaven" (Berachos 33b), you will exert yourself in religious matters in the way of someone who understands that according to his own actions in them will be his reward and punishment, as written *"He repays a man for what he has done; he brings upon him according to his ways"* (Iyov 34:11). And in secular matters, you will conduct yourself with the conviction that all of your movements and the course of your matters are bound to the decree of the Creator, and you place your trust on G-d on all of them, as written *"Cast your cares on the L-rd and he will sustain you"* (Tehilim 55:23).

(*Marpe Lenefesh*: see the gate of trust chapter 4. There you will find peace of mind (an explanation) so that these two things are not contradictory.

*Tov Halevanon*: He spoke of this at length in the fifth chapter of Gate 3. There he demonstrated that the foundation of faith is to believe that regarding things which are related to yira shamayim (fear of G-d, i.e. moral issues), free will is in a man's hands. While for things related to worldly matters, everything is bound to the decree of G-d.. only that it is beyond the power of our minds to grasp the depths of this secret and its full explanation.

*18 - WAIT UNTIL TOMORROW*

When the yetzer gives up trying to entice you in this way, he will come from a different angle. He will say to you: "that which you desire to fulfill of the service of G-d and to do it wholeheartedly for Him, you can do so after some time in the future. Even if you only have one day of life remaining, and you fulfill the service of G-d properly then before your death, you will have already earned everlasting reward and be saved from punishment. Don't you know the ways of repentance, and that the Creator will accept your repentance if you only serve Him wholeheartedly as is fitting and proper."

However, return to the correct argument, and answer him: "how can I wait until the last day of my life when I don't know when is the last day of my life? I would be similar to the story of the servant who trusted his king would never expel him all of his life, and then went off after the indulgences of this world, until the service of his master became a burden on him. Behold, suddenly he was summoned before the king to give an accounting and judgment on his work, and he did not have any answers or excuses and was sentenced to be expelled from the service of the king and from all of the king's cities. He left the king's presence poor and sorrowful in that all the time of his service to the king, he did not earn even one thing, when he could have done so. Thus he remained for the rest of his days, poor and destitute, sighing and miserable, full of sorrow and despised by all until the day of his death.

## 19 - INSTILLING ARROGANCE IN YOU

When the yetzer gives up trying to entice you in the ways we mentioned, he will try to do so by inducing in you haughtiness and pride and diminishing your humility.

> (*Tov Halevanon*: He will entice you to adopt the trait of arrogance.
> *Pas Lechem*: If he does not succeed in inducing in you arrogance, he will try nevertheless to diminish your humility.)

He will say to you: "you have reached the exalted levels, which the pious and righteous reached through your faithful heart and perfect deeds in the service of G-d. You are unequaled in your generation and singular among your contemporaries. It is proper for you to show your superiority over them, by being disgusted by them and despising them. Recall their faults, publicize the wickedness in their hearts, shame them and rebuke them for it, until they are humiliated and repent to G-d, and feel regret for their past. Thereby, you will follow the conduct of the prophets, as written "Son of man, describe the temple to the people of Israel, that they may be ashamed of their sins." (Yechezkel 43:10).

> (*Tov Halevanon*: *"You are unequaled in your generation and singular among your contemporaries"* - All human beings in your era are not worthy of you. All of them were created only to serve you and you give life to all of them through your religious deeds.
>
> *Pas Lechem*: *"by being disgusted by them"* - due to their little faith, *"and despising them"* - on their bad deeds. Both of these are in the heart. After this he will progress to the same two divisions verbally: *"Recall their faults"*, corresponding to their bad deeds, and *"publicize the wickedness in their hearts"*, corresponding to their little faith. And since the bad deeds reveal the wickedness in their heart, he specified that first.
> *"shame them and rebuke them for it"* - shame them generally by telling them *"be ashamed of your evil ways"*. Afterwards, rebuke them in the details to explain to them logically the disgrace of their deeds.
> Translator: Perhaps this also applies to every head of household, or business, etc.)

If you answer him: "how could I be disgusted and shame someone whose matters towards G-d in heart and mind I do not know? If externally he appears reprehensible, perhaps his inner being is not like his outward appearance. If the prophets shamed and rebuked their generation, they did this with the permission of the Creator who looked into their hearts and corrupt interior. But it is beyond my powers of wisdom and understanding to know what is in the hearts and the minds. Perhaps their inner heart which is disgusting in my eyes is much better than their outer appearance, and I don't even know it. Perhaps, their inner heart is better than mine in the eyes of the Creator.

And even if his appearance is bad, it is possible that the reason is because he is ignorant of his obligations to the Creator. Therefore he is more pardonable than me, because my knowledge is greater than his. For the Creator claims from a man only according to the extent of his wisdom. Therefore, I am more deserving to be considered reprehensible for my shortcomings in the Creator's service, despite my knowledge, compared to this man whose shortcoming is due to his ignorance. He rebels against G-d due to ignorance (of the greatness of G-d - *PL*) and error (in the correct deeds - *PL*), while I rebel against Him knowingly and deliberately.

It is possible, that the bad in him is revealed and visible while the good is hidden and concealed. For me it is the opposite. Therefore, he is more worthy of G-d's mercy and forgiveness than me. One merit of him outweighs many merits of mine, because no one observes it except G-d and no one praises him for it nor gives him any honor. But for me, it is the opposite. For my external appearance appears better than his.

Similarly, regarding sins, because one sin by me is equal to many sins by him since my sin is concealed and hidden, while his is visible and public. And due to other people shaming him for it, his punishment will be reduced, while for me, my reward is diminished due to my good deeds being known. He will be left with the full reward of his deeds in the next world, and will reduce his punishment for sin in this world due other's belittling him over his sins. As for me, I will be left with the full measure of my punishments in the next world.

(*Tov Halevanon*: Which is exceedingly more bitter and evil than any punishment imaginable in this world.)

Furthermore, if I exert my mind to search for the flaws of others and examine their bad traits, this will prevent me from examining my own flaws and lackings, which is something more useful for me, and for which I am more responsible for. My condition is like that of a sick man whose illness distracts him from the illnesses of others, and the healing of himself from the healing of others. Thus the yetzer will be smitten and broken before you.

(*Marpe Lenefesh*: As the sages said (Sanhedrin 19a): "first correct yourself, then correct others".

## 20 - INCITEMENT DURING PROSPERITY OR DIFFICULTY
If the yetzer's arrows do not hit you in what we mentioned, he will wait in ambush for you during your times of prosperity or times of difficulty.

When things are going according to your wish, he will say to you: "this is the fruit of your efforts, strategies, and wisdom. Therefore exert yourself more on your secular matters so that your success will perpetuate and you will reach a higher level. Receive these days with joy and enjoy them because soon you will be called by name (to die), and you will be forced to answer and will go to the darkness of the grave, a place where there is no wisdom, no movement, no pleasure, and no pain." He will even bring proofs of this from what the wise man said: "Whatever your hand finds to do, do it with your might; for there is no work, nor device, nor knowledge, nor wisdom, in the grave, where you are going" (Koheles 9:10) (but really, this verse refers to acquiring torah and good deeds not worldly things - TL).

> (*Tov Halevanon*: *"no pain"* - these are the words of the yetzer. But in truth, our sages said (Berachos 18b): "The worm is as painful to the dead as a needle in the flesh of the living". But he will tell you: "you do not need to be concerned about that time, rather, only about the time you are on the face of the earth".)

In your times of difficulty, he will bring to your mind the good life of the wicked, and the success of the nonbelievers, as written "The tents of bandits prosper, and those who provoke G-d are secure" (Iyov 12:6). He will say to you: "the difficulties you are going through are due to your having clinged to the service of G-d and His commandments. You are not capable of handling this due to the unbearable load and remote goal. If you had unloaded this from your heart and rested from it, you would have had joy from your situation as you see by the wicked. You can see from what scripture says: "with those near Me, I will be sanctified" (Vayikra 10:3), and "Only you did I love above all the families of the earth; therefore, I will visit upon you all your iniquities" (Amos 3:2), and many more like this.

> (*Tov Halevanon*: *"unbearable load and remote goal"* - it is with extreme difficulty that a man can escape from all sin. Hence, he is constantly being punished by them.
> *"due to your having clinged to the service of G-d"* - i.e. if you did not take on yourself the way of chasidut (piety) and perishut (asceticism), G-d would not have been so meticulous with you. You can see from what scripture says: "with those near Me, I will be sanctified" (Vayikra 10:3), that to those close to Him, He demonstrates His justice, and is more exacting with them.
>
> *Pas Lechem*: You are not capable of doing everything completely, since the goal is impossible to reach.)

## 21 - DIFFICULTY IN DOING GOOD AND PLEASURE IN DOING BAD

When he sees that you have taken on yourself to do something of the service of G-d, he will exaggerate its demands and attempt to scare you in order that you abandon it.

If you intend to fast, he will say to you: "be careful, this will weaken you and make you sick and prevent you from doing your secular and religious matters".

If this is regarding a voluntary prayer at night, he will attempt to convince you that sleep is more healthy than eating, and it guards and strengthens your health more than food and drink.

If this is regarding giving charity, he will picture in your mind financial destitution and put poverty before your eyes, and remind you of the suffering of poverty and lacking. Similarly with all the types of mitzvot and acts of kindliness, he will try to scare you and exaggerate the matter in your heart, in order to weaken your resolve.

(*Tov Halevanon*: "*he will picture in your mind financial destitution* - He will remind you of many people who lost their wealth, and will picture vividly in your mind their suffering, until your heart refrains out of fear. "*put poverty before your eyes*" - he will picture before you and imagine you as if you are walking naked and barefoot, begging for food, that this will happen if you lose your money.)

But if the thought of sin enters your mind, he will inflate (in your imagination) the pleasure it will bring and will try to make you forget its punishment and encourage you to do it (this time - *PL*) and tend towards it (that your heart tends and flames to do it in the future - *PL*).

Whenever you sense this, or similar to it, reply to him: Of all the suffering that came to me in the past, there is no trace of it left. It quickly passed and vanished, and the reward is mine forever. It will never fade nor end. One who fasts during the day and eats at night, is the same as if he didn't fast. His strength will return and his reward is reserved for him. And similarly one who rises for part of the night, and then sleeps, his alertness will return as if he never rose early, and the reward for his rising early and prayer will remain forever. And for the matter of charity, I have already explained this amply in the gate of trust.

For the matter of sins, you must put to your heart and contemplate in your mind how swiftly the worldly pleasures fade away afterwards, whether they are permitted or forbidden, and then you will remain with the disgrace and punishment due to them in this world and in the next. Thus the yetzer will be smitten before you and you will be zealous in doing good and sluggish towards all disgraceful acts.

(*Tov Halevanon*: "*whether they are permitted or forbidden*" - i.e. when the pleasure passed, then the permitted or forbidden are equal to you, and you have no more pleasure from the forbidden than from the permitted.)

## 22 - SADNESS IN DOING GOOD AND PLEASURE IN DOING BAD

When he will lose hope in enticing you in these ways, and you succeed in doing the religious activities which you undertook to do, he will strive to put worry in your heart (for future dangers - *PL*), and perpetuate in you a state of sadness (for past losses - PL). This is in order that you regret the good acts you did in the past, so that you will lose your reward and so that the Creator will not accept them.

But if you did a bad deed, he will strive to put joy and delight in your heart so that you will strengthen in this and be eager to do it again.

> (*Pas Lechem*: that you rejoice and enjoy the sin, and delight in the past for your striving to attain it.)

If you sense his deception, and stay alert for his many traps, you will guard from them and be helped from G-d to be saved from them. But if you do not sense his deception, he will knock you down and empty his arrows on you suddenly, as written *"until an arrow pierces his liver"* (Mishlei 7:23).

> (*Pas Lechem*: *"If you sense his deception"* - in that he places worry and sadness in your heart, *"and stay alert for his many traps"* - that he traps you by placing joy in your heart when doing a sin.
> *"he will knock you down suddenly"* - from the good deeds. *"and empty his arrows on you"* - his arrows refers to bad deeds.)

## 23 - WEAKEN TORAH STUDY

If you stand up to him despite all of this, and he will not be able to entice you in what we mentioned, he will try to remove you from the study of wisdom (torah). If he sees in you a zeal to study wisdom, he will say to you: "isn't it enough for you to know the torah as much as the great men of your generation (i.e. the important lay men, who are not wise in torah but are still considered wise due to their knowledge in other fields - *PL*)?

Don't you know that the torah is endless and has no final objective? Put your aspiration in knowing the elementals of faith and the foundations of the torah, and then learn what will make you esteemed with people, such as music and poetry, the depths of grammar, proverbs and famous sayings. Leave over the study of Jewish laws and the disputes of the sages in them. Do not enter into the study of the fundamentals of logical demonstration, comparisons, proofs, examining cause and effect, the connection between concealed wisdom and revealed wisdom, and other ways of reasoning because these subjects are deep and subtle. Rely on those who know the explanations of the tradition, even in matters which you can attain clarity through your own efforts, just like you rely on them for those matters which you cannot do so.

> (*Marpe Lenefesh*: *"the elementals of faith and the foundations of the torah"* - it's enough for you to study the main fundamental things such as Chumash, or the like, and halachic summaries.
>
> *Tov Halevanon*: *"the study of Jewish laws and the disputes of the sages in them"* - i.e. why should you exert yourself in the omek iyun hadinim (depths of talmudic investigation), and to decide with your reasoning between the disputes of the sages, and to insert your head between great mountains. What will you know that they didn't know?
> *"the connection between concealed wisdom and revealed wisdom"* - the wisdom of the reasons of mitzvot (Talmud), the wisdom of nature (science), astronomy, and other well known wisdoms, - all of them are connected and linked to the concealed wisdom, namely, the wisdom of Kabbala and inquiry. [Since they are all the handiwork of One Creator, therefore, they all originate from one wisdom, as written in the gate of reflection, ch.1 - ML] )

## 24 - JEALOUSY AND ARROGANCE

If you don't listen to him, and you exert yourself and strengthen yourself, he will shoot you with arrows of jealousy towards your friends. If they have acquired wisdom which you do not possess, you will begrudge them and look for faults in them. You will denigrate them and speak badly of them, as if they plundered your understanding and stole your wisdom.

If your wisdom is greater than theirs, he will try to make you look down on them on account of your superior understanding, and hate them due to their ignorance, and that you show this feeling to the common people. You will become haughty, and praise yourself for your wisdom until you claim that you know more than you do. In your inflated spirit, you will think you know everything and don't need to learn more. [When teaching,] you will be annoyed when others raise a question on your words. You will increasingly consider yourself a wise man. You will seek to honor yourself by exposing the ignorance of others, and glee in embarrassing your peers. Eventually, you will be divested of all the ethical teachings from the torah Sages regarding G-d and His torah.

If the yetzer's intentions to entice you in this angle of torah wisdom do not succeed, he will attempt to entice you from the angle of torah commandments. When you do a commandment of G-d, he will aggrandize and inflate it in your eyes, and make you haughty over it, and make the people of your generation appear contemptible in your eyes, so that it will be easier to be disgusted by them, and to humiliate and shame them, while really it is possible that in the eyes of G-d they are better than you.

If one of your peers is greater than you in some aspect of the service of G-d, and his acts are greater than yours, and he tries harder than you to come close to G-d. The yetzer will incite you against him and say: "any zeal by your peers in the service of G-d highlights your own deficiencies. Because, if it were not for this man, you would be in the eyes of men and G-d the most righteous of your generation. Denigrate him, envy him, hate him, seek out his faults, wait for his transgressions, watch for his mistakes and publicize them as much as you can, and belittle him for them. If you can spread false rumors about him to lower his esteem in the eyes of the public, do so."

Then answer him: "How could I be repulsed by someone who G-d loves, and denigrate one who the Creator deems praiseworthy. Is it not enough that I am lazy in not doing the service of G-d as zealously as him, that I must also hate one who serves G-d? This is certainly no way to repay the Creator for what I owe Him. Rather, it is my duty, out of love of G-d, to love those who love Him, and out of honor of G-d, to honor those who honor Him, as written and he honors those who honor G-d" (Tehilim 15:4). And you already know what happened to Miriam, as written: "Miriam and Aaron spoke against Moshe.." (Bamidbar 12:1), and what happened to Korach and his followers in envying Moshe and Aharon due to their closeness to G-d.

## *** CHAPTER 6 ***

Regarding watchfulness and guarding of one's thoughts, it is proper that you do not neglect watching over your thoughts, reflections, and musings of your heart. For most of the deterioration and rectification in deeds is due to nothing else but these and varies according to their deterioration and rectification.

> (*Pas Lechem*: According to the improvement of thoughts will be the improvement of conduct. Likewise, according to deterioration of thoughts will be the deterioration of deeds.)

As the verses say: "Guard your heart above all else, for it determines the course of your life" (Mishlei 4:23), and "for the imagination of man's heart is evil from his youth" (Bereishis 8:21), "For I know their imagination.." (Devarim 31:21), "for the L-rd searches all hearts, and He understands all the imaginations of the thoughts of every creation; [if you seek Him, He will be found to you, and if you forsake Him, He will abandon you forever]" (Divrei Hayamim 28:9), "Rather,[this] thing is very close to you; it is in your mouth and in your heart, so that you may do it" (Devarim 30:14), "And now, O Israel, what does the L-rd, your G-d, demand of you? Only to fear (revere) the L-rd, your G-d" (Devarim 10:12), and fear (reverence) is in the heart, reflections, and thoughts. Therefore, my brother, strive that all of your actions be devoted only to the blessed Creator, so that your exertion will not be for nothing, and your efforts not for falsehood, as written "Why should you weigh out money for that which is not bread and your toil without satiety?" (Yeshaya 55:2).

> (*Marpe Lenefesh*: Like one who does many undertakings and difficult jobs until he profits some silver and gold. Likewise, one who works hard in the field or the vineyard, and in the end has nothing to eat and be satiated due to various mishaps that G-d sends. Then all of his exertion and toil was for nothing, and his efforts for falsehood. So too, for one who does his religious acts not "l'Shem Shamayim" (for G-d). His exertion will be for nothing and naught, and he won't receive reward since his intent was for something else. Likewise, they said in the talmud (Yoma 72b): "Rava said to his disciples: 'I beseech you, do not inherit a double Gehinom'".) (i.e. work hard in this world and earn Gehinom in the next)

Do not neglect what I have aroused you to. For I have collected for you in this gate all the roots of the things detrimental to activities devoted to G-d, and from each root sprouts almost endless branches.

Therefore, you must guard from them to the utmost of your ability. Maybe then your acts will be complete before G-d and devoted wholeheartedly to His Name, and will then be pleasing and receive acceptance from the Creator. Conduct yourself in the service of G-d as you conduct yourself in your worldly affairs, where you choose the best option you can find and which will be far from potential damages, clean from falsehood, and clean of confusions. Since you do all this for this fleeting world, all the more so that you should do this many times over for matters of your final, permanent existence, and for what will bring you closer to G-d.

(*Pas Lechem*: Because the final reward is coming close to G-d, and likewise in this world, since G-d is far from the wicked...)

Strive with all of your strength that your deeds be pure even though they will be fewer. For it is better than if you exert yourself to do many acts which are not pure. Because a small amount of pure is much, while a large amount of not pure is little and useless. And all the more so, that your work, small and insignificant as it is, should not be impure (intention - *TL*) before G-d.

(*Tov Halevanon*: As they said explicitly: (Orach Chaim 1:64) *"better a small amount with (kavana) intent than much without intent"*. Even though it is small in quantity, it is large in quality and shine)

Be careful that the matter of your deeds to G-d won't be like that of a certain careless bird which the verse speaks of, which lays an egg on the ground and sits on it to warm it, whereby other living creatures damage the egg and no chick hatches from it, as the verse says: "For she leaves her eggs on the ground, and she warms herself on the earth. She forgets that a foot may crush them, and the beast of the field may trample them. [She is hardened against her young ones as though they were not hers; though her toil is in vain, she has no fear]" (Iyov 39:13-16), and the rest of the matter.

The wise man already praised a creature who has the opposite trait. It is industrious and hardworking for its interests in this world. He commanded us to observe it and learn from it, even though it is the weakest of the vermin, saying:

"Go to the ant, lazy one! observe its ways and become wise; she prepares her bread in the summer; [for she has no chief, overseer, or ruler; she gathers her food in the harvest. O lazy one, how long will you lie there;

when will you get up from your sleep?]" (Mishlei 6:6-9)

Behold, we have discussed a small part of a large matter. Let it not seem excessive in your eyes, and don't be discouraged by it. For according to the value and importance of a matter will be the corresponding potentially detrimental things.

> (*Pas Lechem*: i.e. lest, G-d forbid, you become discouraged from the service due to seeing my words and how many mishaps it is liable to and needs to be guarded from. On this, he countered - on the contrary, due to this you should cling to the service, because this is evidence of its great value, "For according to the value and importance of a matter will be the corresponding potentially detrimental things")

The value and importance of our investigation in this book is not unknown by he who understands. May G-d, in His mercy, place our portion among those who are complete with Him, and who endeavor for the sake of His great Name, Amen.

# ****** SHAAR HAKNIA - THE GATE OF SUBMISSION
## ******

# *** Introduction ***

(*Tov Halevanon*: Submission is the opposite of arrogance, that a person much habituates himself to be in lowliness of spirit and brokenness of heart, until he can eradicate this strange god which dwells in his heart. The masters of ethics already wrote, and the Rambam quoted them in his Shmonei Perakim introduction to Pirkei Avot: "Even though for all middot (character traits) it is proper for a man to go in the middle way. For example, to not be too hot-tempered nor too soft-hearted, not too stingy nor too generous, and likewise for all the character traits. When a man sees that he is tending too much towards one side, he should force himself to bend to the other extreme until his natural disposition stands on the middle way. The exception is arrogance, whereby one should not seek the middle way. Rather, one should tend himself always towards submission as much as possible. And like our sages said (Avot 4:4): "*Be exceedingly lowly of spirit...*")

## *** INTRODUCTION ***

Since our previous discussion dealt with the duty to devote one's acts wholeheartedly to G-d alone, and arrogance in the acts devoted to G-d was found to seize the person more swiftly than any other potential damager, and that its damage to these acts is exceedingly great, I deemed pressing to follow the discussion with that which will distance arrogance from man, namely, submission.

And furthermore, because it is clear to us that submission is the root of servant hood, and this trait of submission alone is what separates a servant from the traits of master hood.

(*Tov Halevanon*: that the servant submits to his master, since the primary matter of servant hood is that the servant submits to his master and does his will.

*Pas Lechem*: For servant hood and master hood are two opposites, and a man cannot be deemed a complete servant of G-d if he is not utterly removed from the trait of master hood. And this is accomplished only through submission since "*submission alone is what separates a slave from the traits of master hood*")

And also to come to acknowledge that G-d is singular in this attribute unlike the creations.

(*Tov Halevanon*: [the attribute] of master hood, in that He alone is divested of the trait of submission unlike any created being, that even though it may have some signs of master hood relative to that which is below it which submits to it, nevertheless it also has signs of servant hood due to its own submission to that which is above it. The only exception is G-d - it is not conceivable to attribute to Him any vestige whatsoever of the trait of submission. Therefore He is the Master of masters.)

As King David said: "Yours, O L-ord, is the greatness, and the power, and the glory, and the victory, and the majesty (in an absolute sense, unlike the creations which may have these attributes but only in a temporary or relative sense - *TL*) [for all that is in the heaven and in the earth is Yours; Yours is the kingdom, O L-ord, and you are exalted as Head above all]" (Divrei hayamim 29:11), and *"For who in the heavens can be compared to the L-ord? [Who] among the mighty can be likened to the L-ord?"* (Tehilim 89:7).

Furthermore, it is the nature of this trait (of submission) to distance a man from the grandiose, from presumption, pride, haughtiness, thinking highly of oneself, desire for dominion over others, lust to control everything, coveting what is above one and similar outgrowths of arrogance.

(*Pas Lechem*: i.e. besides that submission distances a man from arrogance as mentioned earlier, its nature is also to distance from *"grandiose, presumption, etc."* He specified six terms. Coveting is not a type of arrogance, even though it is an outgrowth of it. In addition to arrogance the sum totals seven. In truth, each one of these certainly has a specific instruction [to combat it]. These correspond to the seven traits which our sages counted that a man becomes proud of. Therefore, they said that these traits are good for the righteous because they don't become arrogant in them. Corresponding to these seven, Shlomo said seven "vanities" (Koheles 1:2) *"Vanity of vanities, said Kohelet; vanity of vanities, all is vanity"* [vanities plural counts as 2, hence 1+2+1+2+1]

*Tov Halevanon*: Submission is the bandage and medicine to excrete from a man the primary great poison hidden inside him, in his physical nature, and to expel from his insides the viper of his animalistic side - namely, arrogance, the head of all sicknesses of character traits, which requires one to bend himself greatly towards the ways of submission until he extracts this affliction from his heart)

It is now proper for us to clarify 10 things on the subject of submission.

1. What is submission?

2. How many divisions it divides into.

3. what brings to submission?

4. How should one conduct himself in it?

5. How one acquires it.

6. How the submitted should conduct himself.

7. When it is proper when is it not proper?

8. Does submission depend on good traits or the opposite.

9. If it is possible for a man's heart to contain submission and arrogance simultaneously.

10. benefits of submission in this world and in the next.

# *** CHAPTER 1 ***

- What is submission

Submission is lowliness of the soul, its bowing down and not thinking much of itself.

> (*Pas Lechem*: *"lowliness"* refers to one who is low from the beginning. *"bowing down"* refers to one who was erect from the beginning. Likewise, when the soul feels in itself that it raised and elevated itself a bit, it will hasten to bow and lower itself. *"not thinking much of itself"* is relative to others. Understand this.)

It is one of the traits of the soul (that can be acquired - Rabbi Hyamson). When it becomes established in the soul, its signs will appear in the limbs. Among them: a soft tongue, a low voice, humility at a time of anger, little exacting revenge when one has the power to do so. It was said about a certain king who told a man who was convicted and a whip had already been brought [for punishment]: "I swear by G-d, if I did not feel such a strong anger against you, I would have exacted a severe revenge on you." Then he pardoned him. It is said of him that he would say: "I don't know of any sin of others which are greater than mine".

> (*Pas Lechem*: *"soft tongue"* - he speaks soft words and supplications with every person.
> *"humility at a time of anger"* - even when he gets angry, he does not become brazen faced. This indicates he has acquired it a kinyan atzmi (in his essence). For when a person acts [with submission] at a time of non-anger, perhaps this is only incidentally by him, since even by arrogant people, sometimes one sees them acting humbly incidentally (temporarily).
> *"little exacting revenge"* - he said *"little"* even though it is proper for a man to completely avoid taking revenge as written: *"Do not seek revenge"* (Vayikra 19:18). Rather he said *"little revenge"* because of the example of the king that he brought, since certainly a king must show some revenge to instill fear, as Rabeinu Hakadosh exhorted us (Ketubot 103b) *"cast bile..."*, only that he should be satisfied with little as in the story, that he had the whip brought to scare him which served as a *"little revenge"*.
> *"I would have exacted a severe revenge on you"* - i.e. it was proper to exact a severe revenge on you according to your evil deeds. However, I am refraining from this since I sense in myself great anger, and anger stems from arrogance (see Shaarei Kedusha 1:2 - "arrogance and anger are the same trait, because a man becomes angry when his will is not being

done..."). Therefore, I am abstaining from vengeance in order to break my anger and arrogance.

*Manoach Halevavos*: *"who told a man who was convicted"* - Since my anger was so strong on you, I will not exact vengeance on you so as not to give room to anger, which is an ugly trait, and so I do not acquire a bad disposition in my soul through this. On the contrary, I will habituate myself to good traits, namely, submission and refraining from exacting revenge when I have the power to do so.

*"I don't know of any sin of others which are greater than mine"* - some texts render *"greater than my humility"*, which means: I don't know any sin which can outweigh and nullify humility on the day of judgment when the King of kings will put on scales the merits and sins [for each person, i.e. humility is a very great merit.])

## *** CHAPTER 2 ***

- How many divisions it divides into

The explanation of the divisions of submission is as follows. Submission divides into three categories.

(1) One category applies to human beings and many species of irrational animals. It is poverty of the spirit and patient bearing of harm it is capable of avoiding due to ignorance regarding the right ways to remove the harm. This sort of submission is found among foolish and ignorant people due to their little knowledge and weak understanding of their soul and its capacities. This is called submission in the way of common language only, but in truth, this is merely spiritual poverty and blindness due to stupidity that has overcome the soul and prevents it from seeing what could further its welfare, as written *"For You have hidden their hearts from understanding; therefore, it cannot raise itself"* (Iyov 17:4).

> (*Pas Lechem*: He does not know and recognize his soul's esteem, which is greater in level than other creations. If he knew and recognized his soul's esteem, he would not submit and bear everything like now. Because since he regards himself as base, and his level is low in his eyes, he bears everything with a good countenance. He is like the peasant who bears the smoke of the stove which stings his eyes and does not wonder about this since he thinks little of himself and says to himself "why should a nobody like me care about things like this? Am I a prince or an important minister?"... The patient bearing that one sees in them is due to spiritual poverty. That their soul deems itself lowly and of little worth.
> *"therefore, it cannot raise itself"* - since they have no intelligence, they don't recognize their soul's worth. Therefore they cannot raise their heart. Hence, their humility is animal-like humility.)

Rather, true submission is that quality which comes into being after an elevation of the soul, after rising above being similar to the animals, with their base traits, and after it has elevated itself from being of similar traits to the lower class of men. This elevation stems from having greater wisdom than them, greater esteem of one's soul than them, and clear knowledge of which traits are good and which are base. When submission and lowliness comes after this elevation - then it is a praiseworthy trait. Otherwise, it does not enter into the category of good traits and qualities of the soul, but rather among the disgraceful traits. For its submission is like that of the animals (who bear suffering out of ignorance of what can rectify that pain - *PL*).

> (*Pas Lechem*: *"This elevation stems from having greater wisdom..."* - this
> elevation and departure from associating with the previous things, the soul
> obligates itself to undertake due to its superior wisdom over them and
> superior quality of soul.
> *"When submission and lowliness comes after this elevation - then it is a
> praiseworthy trait"* - *"submission"* to G-d and *"lowliness"* in bearing
> [things He decreed].
>
> *Tov Halevanon*: *"after an elevation of the soul"* - i.e. separating from its
> physical and from the lusts of its animal side.
> *"after rising above being similar to the animals"* - above the base traits and
> pettiness.
> *"from having greater wisdom"* - Not out of arrogance rather only out of
> wisdom and nobility of soul, it is disgraceful in his eyes the conduct of the
> low people, and attaching oneself with the contemptible.)

(2) The second category - submission towards other human beings. If
because they rule over him, such as a prisoner in the hands of his enemy, or
a slave in the hands of his master; or because he lacks what they have and
greatly needs what they possess such as a tenant to his landlord or a poor
man who looks to the generosity of the wealthy man, or a student to his
teacher, or a substantial loan that one is unable to repay and he must be
submissive and lower himself before his lender, as written *"A rich man will
rule over the poor, and a borrower is a slave to a lender"* (Mishlei 22:7).

To this category belongs the submission of one who knows about himself
that he is falling short regarding the bounds (the torah set - PL) in matters
of this world and the next, and is ignorant of the proper path. When he
finds the prophet of his generation or righteous teacher or anyone else who
preaches the proper path (as the sages said: "accept the truth from whoever
said it" - *TL*), he will submit to him and lower himself before him (always,
to serve and minister him and tend to his needs - *TL*), as our teachers said:
*"serving (a wise man) is greater than learning by him"* (Berachos 7b), as
written: *"Elisha ben Shafat who poured water for Eliyahu"* (Melachim II
3:11), it does not say: *"who studied by Eliyahu"* but rather: 'who poured
water', this teaches that serving a Sage is greater than studying by him; and
also: *"his (Moshe's) attendant, Joshua, the son of Nun, a young man, would
not depart from the tent"* (Shmos 33:11). Likewise the wise man said
regarding the general masses: *"A rich man will rule over the poor, and a
borrower is a slave to a lender"* (Mishlei 22:7).

(*Tov Halevanon*: i.e. the verse is not referring only to a monetary borrower and a lender. Rather it is only a proverb on every thing whereby one person needs to associate with another person for some benefit.
*"serving (a wise man) is greater than learning by him"* - since *"service"*, which is the trait of submission brings to all the good character traits, and learning [torah] is included in it.)

This category of submission, proper though it may be, is not of universal character, since it does not apply to all human beings, nor does it apply at all times and in all places. Because, when the prisoner leaves his prison, or when the slave redeems himself, or the lender pays back his debt, or the student leaves his teacher's presence, or the poor man leaves the rich man's presence - it is no longer their duty to submit to them and to humble themselves and lower themselves before them.

(*Pas Lechem*: *"since it does not apply to all human beings"* - because there are many human beings in the world who never need [favors of] other people. Afterwards, he wrote that even those human beings who do need other people, this need does not last all of their days, for *"the prisoner..."*, and *"the slave.."*, and *"the lender..."*, all this was corresponding to what he said *"at all times"*. Afterwards, *"the student.."*, and *"the poor man..."*, corresponding to what he said *"in all places"*.
*"to submit to them, and to humble and lower themselves"* - *"to submit"* - to their command and to follow their discipline.
*"to humble themselves"* - in heart.
*"lower themselves"* - from the term *"to bow"* in practice, i.e. to grant them honor.)

(3) The third category: submission to the blessed Creator. This duty applies to all rational beings. They are obligated in it at all times and in all places. To this (category of submission) was our intent in this gate.

The submitted one is called in scripture: "humble", "low in his eyes", "modest", "broken", "low of spirit", "broken spirited", "crushed", "soft hearted","weak in spirit", "broken hearted", "bowing spirit".

(*Pas Lechem*: these are the opposites of the seven terms of arrogance mentioned earlier [in the introduction].)

When we will speak of the term "submission", in general, our intent is only in this third category which is the highest degree of submission.

One who has reached this level, the path to nearness to G-d and [worthiness] to stand before Him is not far off (but one who has not will never get there under any circumstances - *TL*). He will be accepted by G-d and be pleasing to Him, as written *"The offerings of G-d are a broken spirit: a broken and a contrite heart, O G-d, You will not despise"* (Tehilim 51:17).

(*Pas Lechem*: *"nearness to G-d...stand before Him...be accepted by G-d and be pleasing to Him"* - The intent of this three stage melitza (poetic phrase) is to allude to a peasant whose heart inspired him and he related to his friend saying: "aha my friend, oh how much my heart and soul longs and yearns to serve my king. Would that it were that he would allow me in the palace and that I could be among those who stand before him and minister unto him. But three obstacles prevent me. One, the road is exceedingly far away and unfamiliar to me. Two, even if G-d grants me and I will reach the palace courtyard, who knows if I will be accepted to be among those who stand before the king. Perhaps, they will immediately oust me forcefully and tell me that I am not fit and worthy for this. Three, even if perhaps I will be accepted and will stand to minister before him, how can I be sure that my service will be proper in his eyes and will accepted and pleasing before him?"

His friend answered: "I advise you, lower your ego, and bow your pride. Then everyone you will meet on the way will have compassion on you and will help you go from city to city until you reach the destination (royal city) you wish to go. When you get there, it will be noticeable from your face that your goal and intent is not out of lust for royal feasts or desire for dominion over others. The truth will lead for you the way, that your motive and desire is solely to minister your king. Certainly you will be found just and acceptable for this. Likewise, if your service is done with submission and humility, undoubtedly you will be found proper and pleasing in the eyes of the king." The analogy is clear.

## *** CHAPTER 3 ***

- In what does one submit

The circumstances which will bring a person to submission and a lowly spirit after he has become proud are ten.

(1) When his physical strength wanes in its normal power of movement due to either sickness or frail temperament or weakening constitution and he becomes submissive due to this, and he pleas to G-d and to human beings, as written *"And He submitted their heart with toil"* (Tehilim 107:12).

> (*Pas Lechem*: *"And He submitted their heart with toil"* - i.e. from *"toil"* which means sufferings, their heart becomes humbled.)

(2) When he is smitten by troubles or suffers poverty and he now needs people whereby he previously did not need them, and he becomes submissive to them (specifically - *PL*), and his spirit becomes too broken to be arrogant in his situation (to everyone generally - *PL*), as written: *"And it will be that everyone who is left in your house, will come to prostrate himself before him for a silver piece and a morsel of bread"* (Shmuel 2:36).

(3) When someone who is better off than him, will manifest his kindness towards him, he will make himself submissive towards him, as written *"Many will entreat the favor of the generous man"* (Mishlei 19:6).

(4) One who must pay back his fellow a debt but is unable to do so, and makes himself submissive before him as written *"If you do not have what to pay, why should he take your bed from under you?"* (Mishlei 22:27).

> (*Tov Halevanon*: In the previous chapter he brought the verse *"a borrower is a slave to a lender"* for this, because there he was speaking of the duty and that it is proper that the borrower be submissive. Here, however, he is speaking from the side of a cause which pressures him, submits his heart, and lowers his [arrogant] nature. Likewise for all the things in this chapter. Therefore he brought the verse *"why should he take your bed from under you?"*, which is a cause that breaks his heart.)

(5) One who is in the prison of his enemy - will make himself submissive

towards him and his spirit will stoop low, as written *"They afflicted his foot with fetters; his soul was placed in irons"* (Tehilim 105:18), and "if they be bound in fetters, and be held in cords of affliction; [Then He declared unto them their work, and their transgressions, that they have behaved themselves proudly. He opened their ear to discipline, and commanded that they return from iniquity]" (Iyov 36:8).

(6) A slave who does not have the ability to redeem himself (purchase freedom) from the hand of his master and becomes submissive towards him as written *"Behold, as the eyes of servants look unto the hand of their masters"* (Tehilim 123:2).

> (*Tov Halevanon*: *"does not have the ability to redeem himself"* - and he sighs from the work and suffers from it.
> *"and becomes submissive towards him"* - so that he lightens on him his yoke.)

(7) When saddening troubles and disasters befall a man, his spirit will break and his heart will submit, as written *"And that I also have walked contrary unto them, and have brought them into the land of their enemies; if then their uncircumcised hearts be submitted"* (Vayikra 26:41).

> (*Manoach Halevavos*: #2 earlier was referring to troubles or poverty through which he needs human beings and humbles himself to them. Here the author is referring to a trouble G-d struck him with, either through the system of nature or through the system of hashgacha pratit (divine providence) in such a way that human beings do not have the ability to save him from it, and through this, he will humble himself towards G-d, not to human beings.)

(8) When one makes a personal accounting and sees that he has rebelled against G-d despite G-d's goodness towards him, and how instead of praising Him for it, he has kicked. Then, he will become submitted, ashamed, and humiliated from the Al-mighty, as written *"O G-d, I am ashamed and blush to lift up my face to You, my G-d: [for our iniquities are increased over our head]"* (Ezra 9:6).

> (*Pas Lechem*: i.e. with the good itself that G-d has bestowed on him, he rebels against G-d, namely, with the physical limbs G-d granted him, the strength G-d gave him, the wealth G-d graced him with, and the like.)

(9) When the Creator rebukes him and humiliates him on having rebelled against Him, he will become submitted and terrified, as written on Achav *"Have you seen how Ahab has submitted himself before Me?"* (Melachim

21:29).

(10) When one senses the nearness of death, and the coming of his final day, and he contemplates the terror of death, and how he will be brought to trial and have to give an accounting, he becomes submitted and bowed down. He will think little of himself and will regret the passing of his days, and wasting of his life without having prepared provisions of good deeds to come before him for his journey to the next world, as written *"The sinners in Zion are afraid"* (Yeshaya 33:14).

(*Pas Lechem*: He will regret that many of his days have already passed for nothing, without benefit. And also his life wasted away, i.e. his natural strength has weakened without attaining anything.

*Marpe Lenefesh*: i.e. that a man submits himself on his own (by contemplating death). The author mentioned these ten causes through which a man becomes submitted, so that a man can choose the proper one, and not procrastinate submitting himself until terrible troubles and disasters befall him like the first cause (which is inevitable). Rather, let him submit himself by contemplating the eighth, ninth, and tenth. And likewise, he wrote this in the 3rd gate chapter 4 and in the gate of repentance chapter 6. See there and you will understand.)

# *** CHAPTER 4 ***

- how should one conduct himself in it

In which matters is it a duty to conduct oneself with submission and lowliness? I say it is one's duty to conduct himself with submission in seven relations.

(1) In business dealings with his contemporaries, and in good conduct with his fellow human beings, as I will explain later. On this the verse says: *"despised and disgraceful is he in his own eyes"* (Tehilim 15:4).

> (*Pas Lechem*: *"despised and disgraceful is he in his own eyes"* - all of that Psalm speaks of the conduct of a righteous man with other human beings, [such as:] *"works righteousness, etc.", "who does not slander with his tongue, etc.", "nor does evil to his friend, etc."* Behold the psalmist attributed everything to: *"disgraceful is he in his own eyes"*.)

(2) When meeting those who are wise in knowledge of G-d and of His torah, or pious men who are near to G-d (who do good deeds - *PL*), as written: *"Let the righteous smite me in kindness and reprove me"* (Tehilim 141:5), and *"The evil bow before the good"* (Mishlei 14:19).

> (*Tov Halevanon*: Let the righteous man crush me and the true prophet hurt me for all of his strikes and rebukes are a kindness.
>
> *Pas Lechem*: i.e. I yearn that the righteous person will reprove me harshly and break the malice in my heart, and I will consider this a kindness.)

(3) When one is praised for his good qualities, it is his duty to submit himself, and to reflect on previous sins and iniquities he committed, which the Creator knows about and yet keeps them secret, and holds back (retribution) from him so that he may repent from them. He should not rejoice in that his fellow men are mistaken about him (in considering him a righteous person - *TL*). Rather, let him mourn, since the Creator knows truly the wickedness of his deeds, and his neglect in fulfilling his duties to Him and from rendering thanks for His kindnesses, and he should submit in his heart as written: *"For I relate my iniquity; I worry about my sin"* (Tehilim 38:19).

> (*Pas Lechem*: *"When one is praised for his good qualities, it is his duty to submit himself"* - so that his spirit will not become proud, in that other

human beings are praising him.

*Tov Halevanon*: *"...and he should submit in his heart"* - lest he will be punished a greater punishment due to other people praising him.
"as written: *'For I relate my iniquity; I worry about my sin'"* - so too it is proper for this one to worry about his sins.)

(4) If other people speak badly of him, he should submit himself to the Creator, and thank Him for having opened his eyes to a few of his many shortcomings in order to chasten him and rebuke him, so that he will repent to Him, as written *"He opens also their ear to discipline, and says so that they return from iniquity"* (Iyov 36:10).

(*Pas Lechem*: *"to chasten him and rebuke him"* - To *"chasten him"* on things he knows are bad. To *"rebuke him"* to his face on things which he judges himself favorably. He wrote *"to chasten him and rebuke him"* corresponding to two aspects. One, so that he suffers from this, for the disgrace from other human beings is also considered sufferings (which atone). The second aspect *"to rebuke him"*, i.e. to clarify to him through human beings that it is reprehensible, and that perhaps he was mistaken until now and thought there was nothing wrong with it.)

(5) When the Creator bestows much good on him in this world, he should submit himself to G-d because of the heavy burden of gratitude he owes for them. He should also lower himself before Him out of fear (i.e. that he must fear - *TL*) that perhaps this good is for exacting retribution from him (i.e. punishment for his sins - *TL*). For when G-d sends great wealth to a person, it is for one of three reasons:
1. as a benefit granted by the Creator.

(*Pas Lechem*: that the Creator intends in this to bestow good to him.)

2. as a trial and a test to the person.

(*Pas Lechem*: A *"trial"* in financial matters consists either of bearing a large monetary loss for the Creator, or it takes the form of abstaining from a large profit. For this, the author used a double expression...)

3. for exacting retribution and to make him stumble.

(*Pas Lechem*: Also in this, there are two aspects. One, the wealth becomes a means of exacting retribution from him for his sin, as the sages said regarding one who incurred a [divine] decree of death (Midrash Koheles Raba 5:18) - that he becomes arrested by the government or a bandit murders him, and G-d sends him wealth so that he will be murdered due to his money. Two, sometimes a man mortally stumbles because of his wealth such as Korach who become proud of his wealth and sinned.)

Signs that the wealth is a benefit:
* If he is more occupied with fulfilling his duties to the Creator rather than with busying himself with his wealth.
* That the wealth causes him to increase his service of G-d.

(*Tov Halevanon*: the more G-d benefits him, the more he will increase strengthening in the service of G-d out of fear lest the benefits be greater than his service.)

* He does not set his heart on this benefit and does not place his trust in it, but spends it on fulfilling his duties to the Creator.

(*Tov Halevanon*: *"he does not set his heart on this benefit"* - he does not rejoice because of it.)

This is similar to how Iyov described how he would spend his wealth, how he would spend it for fulfilling his duties to G-d, and how he would not place his trust in it, as written: *"If I put my hope in gold, and to jewelry I said 'my confidence'"* (Iyov 31:24).

Signs that the wealth is sent as a trial and test:
* That the wealthy man is more occupied in his worries with guarding and increasing his money and in fearing potential financial losses than he is with fulfilling his debt of gratitude to the Creator for it.
* That he has nothing but perpetual worry from it or from managing it. Thus, the man is tested with the wealth and will need to give a judgment and an accounting (in the afterlife), of such a person it is said *"For all his days are pains and his occupation is vexation; even at night his heart does not rest (i.e. in the grave, he will need to give a judgment and accounting - PL)"* (Koheles 2:23).

(*Tov Halevanon*: *"Thus, the man is tested"* - This is the sign of a test. That G-d tests him on how he will conduct himself with this benefit in the service of G-d.
Translator: G-d tests a person in areas that he is weak, as explained in Gate #4 ch.3, namely, that if a person consistently passes the tests in one area G-d will stop testing him in that area.)

Signs that the wealth is for exacting retribution:
* That the wealthy man is so preoccupied with enjoying his money and deriving pleasure from it that he fails to pay his debts to the Creator and to

his fellow man (such as tzedaka, maaser, good deeds - TL) that he owes on account of it, and from rendering thanks to his Benefactor (G-d). He does not feel that he is obligated to serve G-d on account of it, as the verse says: *"And behold, joy and happiness, slaying cattle and slaughtering sheep, eating meat and drinking wine; 'Let us eat and drink, for tomorrow we will die.'"* (Yeshaya 22:13), and *"And there are harp and lyre, tambourine and flute, and wine at their drinking feasts; and the work of the L-ord they do not regard, and the deed of His hands they have not seen"* (ibid. 5:12). And this is a retribution disguised as a benefit.

(*Pas Lechem*: i.e. In truth, G-d's intent is for exacting retribution. Only that it appears to the eye as a benefit.)

But for the intelligent person, when good fortune comes to him and all his matters go smoothly according to his wish, he will submit himself, fearing that perhaps this wealth may have come from the Creator for exacting retribution from him, as written: *"riches kept by their owner for his harm"* (Koheles 5:12).

(Summary:
*Manoach Halevavos*: The sign that the wealth is a benefit, is that he is more occupied with fulfilling his duties to the Creator rather than he is occupied with his wealth. The sign that the wealth is a trial is the opposite of this, as he writes, *"that the wealthy man is more occupied with guarding his money, etc. than with his duties to the Creator"*. However, nevertheless, he is also occupied in his duties to the Creator a bit. But the signs that the wealth is a punishment is that the recipient of the benefit is not at all concerned about "paying back the debts to the Creator, etc., and to praise his Benefactor, etc."

Alternative explanation:
*Tov Halevanon*: If he fulfills his debts to the Creator properly it is a sign of a benefit.
If he has no benefit from it, since he is perpetually worried about losing money and amassing more money and also is not fulfilling his debts to the Creator properly, it is a sign of a test. In the future he will give a judgment and accounting on whether he paid his debts to G-d. G-d acts with forbearance towards him, and leaves the money in his hand so that he repents and it becomes a benefit to him...
If he is only preoccupied with eating, drinking, and rejoicing in pleasures, it is a sign of a retribution, that he is eating the reward of his good deeds in this world to be destroyed in the next world.)

(6) When one reads the torah and the books of the prophets, and he sees

the rewards and punishments set forth, and he becomes aware how much he has neglected to fulfill his duties to the Creator, he will realize that it is his duty to submit and lower himself before the Creator out of fear of His punishment, as written on Yoshiyahu *"And it was when the king heard the words of the scroll of the Law, that he rent his garments"* (Melachim II 22:11). The Creator then said to him *"Because your heart was tender, and you have humbled yourself before the L-ord, when you heard what I spoke against this place, and against the inhabitants thereof, that they should become a desolation and a curse, and have torn your clothes, and wept before Me; I also have heard you..."* (ibid. 22:19).

(7) When one is involved in an act of service such as giving charity, prayer, or mitzva whether voluntary or obligatory, or in rebuking others, he should not have in his heart any pride or haughtiness, but rather should outwardly and inwardly submit himself and be lowly before the Creator. This act should be like nothing in his eyes compared to the magnitude of what is his duty to G-d which is many times more than that deed (therefore, on the contrary, he should submit himself for his service is little relative to his duty - *TL*), as written "With what shall I come before the L-ord, bow before the Most High G-d?...[He has showed you, O man, what is good; and what does the L-ord require of you, but to do justly, and to love mercy, and to walk humbly with your G-d? (i.e. submission to G-d who observes what is concealed in a man's heart - *TL*)]" (Micha 6:6).

## *** CHAPTER 5 ***

- How one acquires it

The manner to acquire the trait of submission and the way to facilitate its acquisition is for one's thoughts and reflections to be set on seven topics:

> (*Pas Lechem*: *"thoughts and reflections"* - thoughts refers to simple thought, while reflection refers to [deeper] contemplation.)

(1) The root and origin of his existence is from a putrid drop (of human seed) and blood, after they became foul and stenchful. Afterwards, he was nourished from blood of tumah, all the days of his stay in his mother's belly. Afterwards, he exited, and was weak and fragile in body and limbs. Then, he advanced from stage to stage until most of his years have passed. Afterwards, he will become ill from old age until he completes his days (dies).

One of the wise men would say on this matter: "I am amazed at how one who has passed through the pathway of urine and blood two times can be proud and haughty?" Contemplating this or similar things regarding the nature of man necessarily brings humility, as king David said: *"O L-ord, what is man that You should regard him, the son of man, that You should consider him?"* (Tehilim 144:3), and *"Man that is born of a woman is of few days and full of trouble"* (Iyov 14:1), and *"But I am a worm and not a man"* (Tehilim 22:7), and *"How much less man, that is a worm? and the son of man, which is but a maggot?"* (Iyov 25:6).

> (*Marpe Lenefesh*: As our sages said: (Avot 2:1) "Reflect upon three things and you will not come to sin. Know from where you came...")

(2) When one contemplates the severity of the tribulations that befall a man in this world such as hunger and thirst, cold and heat, sickness, accidents, worries, which one has no assurance against until death. When an understanding person puts all this to heart, and he realizes how weak he is, how limited and helpless he is from protecting himself from all of this, he will recognize his predicament. He is not only similar to a prisoner in this world, but he truly is a prisoner! And so he will humble himself like the humbling of a prisoner who is placed in a dungeon, and who has no strategy or ability to free himself without his master's consent, as written: *"May the cry of the prisoner come before You"* (Tehilim 79:11), and *"Bring*

*my soul out of prison"* (Tehilim 142:7).

> (*Marpe Lenefesh*: Not that he is like a prisoner as an analogy or metaphor, but rather he is actually a prisoner. Since, behold, we can see that he is incapable of averting all the accidents, sicknesses, etc. which suddenly befall a man. If so, he is not in control of himself and not able to choose for himself just like a prisoner.)

(3) When one considers his fleetingness, and the swift coming of death, and the abrupt cutting off of his desires and aspirations at that time. He must leave all of his possessions, and abandon hope that he can take with him any of them as provisions or that any of them will be of use to him when he is in the grave. The countenance of his face has already dimmed (in his illness before death - *PL*), its appearance darkens. And his flesh (after death) will bring up worms, decay and putrid liquid. The signs of his physical beauty vanished and an increasingly rotten odor will exude from him, (until he will smell so awful that it will seem - *PL*) as if he had never washed or scrubbed or put on a good fragrance. When he puts this or similar considerations to mind, he will feel humble and lowly. He will not become arrogant. His heart will not arise and become high and proud, as written: *"Withdraw yourselves from man whose breath is in his nostrils, for in what is he to be esteemed?"* (Yeshaya 2:22), and *"men of low degree are but vanity, and men of high degree are but a lie; were they to be put on a scale, together they would equal nothing"* (Tehilim 62:10).

(4) When one contemplates on the service he owes to G-d for the benevolent goodness and abundant kindness bestowed on him, and he considers how much he has neglected the precepts and fallen short in their observance, both those which reason mandates and those which the torah commands, and how his pleas and excuses will be cut short when the day of reckoning comes (i.e. the day of death - *TL*) and he will be full of regret on the great day of assembly (i.e. the future great day of Judgment - *TL*). Then he will be submitted and his spirit will be broken, as written *"For lo, the day comes, glowing like a furnace, and all the audacious sinners and all the perpetrators of wickedness will be stubble. And the sun that comes shall burn them up so that it will leave them neither root nor branch, says the L-ord of Hosts"* (Malachi 3:19), and *"who can endure the day He comes"* (Malachi 3:2).

> (Translator: *"The future great day of Judgment"* when all who ever lived will be resurrected to stand trial and also to watch everyone else's trial, the latter G-d does to show everyone that He judged each and every person fairly.

*Marpe Lenefesh*: *"his pleas and excuses will be cut short"* - there in the next world, he will have no pleas and no excuses. Likewise, regret [and repentance] will not help at that time.

*"he will be full of regret"* - then he will regret the disgraceful deeds he did while alive when he will be punished for them. Then too, he will see the reward for the righteous and the punishment to the wicked and it will pain him, and his regret will not help since (Avodah Zara 3a) "One who toiled on friday (this world) will eat on Shabbat (next world); but one who did not toil on friday, what will he eat on Shabbat?")

(5) When one contemplates the greatness of the Creator and His infinite might, who observes one's outer and inner life. When one fixes his mind on this great theme and considers what our sages report regarding the impressive and awesome presence of the pious sages in previous generations, for example "he (Rav Sheshes) gazed his eyes on him and the man (died and) became a pile of bones" (Berachos 58a), or as it was said of Yonatan ben Uziel: "when he would expound the torah, any bird that would fly over him was instantly burnt."

And there is no doubt that the prophets were greater than them, and you will find that the prophets' strength melted and they bent their knees and prostrated themselves when they were visited by angels, as written by Daniel, Yehoshua, and many like them. And you will find in the books of the prophets that the angels bow and prostate themselves before the Creator, as written *"the hosts of the heavens bow to You"* (Nechemia 9:6), and *"Behold, He does not trust His servants and He casts reproach upon His angels"* (Iyov 4:18), and *"in His temple does every one speak of His glory"* (Tehilim 29:9), and *"And one cried unto another, and said, 'Holy, holy, holy, is the L-ord of Hosts'"* (Yeshaya 6:3).

(*Marpe Lenefesh*: *"When one contemplates the greatness of the Creator and His infinite might"* - How can one picture in his mind and put to heart the greatness of the Creator? When one fixes his mind on this great theme, namely, the great and wondrous awe on the sages and pious ones of the early generations and [even] the later ones. How great was their deeds! They were capable of resurrecting the dead and of killing whoever they wanted (by mere words), as reported in the Talmud and the zohar in numerous places. Likewise it is known of the wonders that the Arizal did, and likewise his disciples, and many others. When one then compares the greatness of these sages with that of the prophets such as Eliyahu and Elisha and other famous ones, and we see that the prophets were seized with fear and trembling when they were visited by angels (see Megila 3a), and as mentioned in the zohar when Moshe ascended to the spiritual worlds. If so, "what is man that You consider him?" (tehilim 8:4) How could he raise his head and be proud before an omnipotent and awesome King loftier than everything, and even while He is observing him always in his outer and inner life.)

And when one reflects what is manifested to our intelligence in what He created, such as the sun, moon, stars, the celestial spheres, and the earth and all that is in it such as minerals, plants and animals - this should be sufficient for anyone who has understanding and intelligence, as written *"How great are Your works, O L-ord! Your thoughts are exceedingly deep; A brutish man knows not; [neither does a fool understand this]"* (Tehilim 92:6), and *"all the nations are as nothing before Him"* (Yeshaya 40:17), and *"all the inhabitants of the earth are as nothing"* (Daniel 4:32).

When an understanding man considers his significance relative to all of humanity, and the significance of humanity relative to the earth, and the earth relative to the lunar sphere, and the lunar sphere relative to the cosmos, and that everything relative to the greatness of the Creator is as nothing, he will be humbled in his soul and will lower himself before the Creator, as written *"[when I contemplate Your sky, the moon and the stars..] What is man that You should be mindful of him?"* (Tehilim 8:5).

(6) When one reads the books of the prophets and he sees the great punishment meted out to the arrogant and proud and also G-d's great protection over the humble and the lowly. Regarding the arrogant and proud it is written: *"The lofty eyes of man shall be humbled, and the haughtiness of men shall be bowed down, and the L-ord alone shall be exalted on that day"* (Yeshaya 2:11), and *"For the day of the L-ord of Hosts shall come upon everyone that is proud and lofty, and upon everyone that is lifted up; and he shall be brought low"* (Yeshaya 2:12).

Regarding both types, it is written: *"The L-ord lifts up the meek: He casts the wicked down to the ground"* (Tehilim 147:6), and *"Though the L-ord be high, yet has He respect unto the lowly: but the proud He knows from afar."* (Tehilim 138:6), and it is said about the lowly *"the humble shall inherit the land"* (Tehilim 37:11), and *"the L-ord has anointed me to bring good tidings to the humble"* (Yeshaya 61:1), and *"With the lofty and the holy ones I dwell, and with the crushed and humble in spirit, to revive the spirit of the humble and to revive the heart of the crushed"* (Yeshaya 57:15), and *"Before destruction comes pride, and before stumbling [comes] a haughty spirit"* (Mishlei 16:18), and *"Before ruin, a man's heart becomes haughty, but before honor there is humility."* (Mishlei 18:12).

> *(Tov Halevanon: "The lofty eyes of man shall be humbled..."* - Our sages
> said: "whoever becomes arrogant, it is as if he pushed against the 'heels' of
> the Divine Presence, since it is written, 'The whole earth is full of His
> glory'. Says the Holy One: 'I and he are not capable of dwelling together..."
> (Berachos 43b). This is what the verse means: "the haughtiness of men
> shall be bowed down, and the L-ord alone shall be exalted on that day".
> When the arrogant who push against the heels of the Divine presence are
> destroyed.
> *"The L-ord lifts up the meek: He casts the wicked down to the ground"* - it
> is clear from this verse that the arrogant are called "wicked".
>
> *Pas Lechem: "and the L-ord alone shall be exalted on that day"* - Behold
> the verse ties the exaltedness of G-d to the lowliness of man, implying that
> pride of man is contrary to His greatness, and it is considered loathsome by
> Him.)

(7) When one observes the changing of people's situations in this world,
the swift changing of governments and rulers, and the passing of people
from one condition to another, and the fall of one nation promoting the rise
of another, while the end of all is death, as written *"Like sheep, they are
destined to the grave; death will devour them"* (Tehilim 49:15), he will
submit and will not pride himself on any worldly possessions, and he won't
place his trust on any matter of them, as written *"Praiseworthy is the man
who made the L-ord his trust, and did not turn to the haughty and those
who turn to falsehood"* (Tehilim 40:5).

> *Tov Halevanon: "people's situations"* - i.e. how honor and greatness does
> not last long. Rather everything changes, the proud are brought low and
> vice versa.
> *"the swift changing of governments"* - not only for small scale greatness,
> but even for great countries.
> *"the end of all is death"* - even during the time of a country's success, the
> success is not on an individual level, since every individual goes to his
> place and to the depths of a pit.

If a man's mind is never empty of these seven matters we mentioned, he
will always be humble and lowly. Humility will cling to his nature and will
not separate from him. When he clings to humility, all the snares of
arrogance, haughtiness, and pride will keep far from him, as we mentioned.
He will be saved from sin and from stumbling as written *"and that His fear
may be before your faces, that you sin not"* (Shemos 20:20). And our sages
said: "Reflect upon three things and you will not come to sin. Know from

where you came and where you are going and before Whom you are destined to give account and reckoning. From where have you come? - from a putrid drop. Where are you going? - to a place of dirt, worms, and maggots. Before Whom are you destined to give account and reckoning? - before the supreme King of kings, the holy One, blessed be He" (Avos 3:1).

# *** CHAPTER 6 ***

- How the submitted should conduct himself

The manners of conduct, which are proper for the submitted person to adopt, are ten.

(1) Knowledge of G-d, and of His good attributes, and the higher qualities He bestowed on man over other living creatures, as written *"You give him dominion over the work of Your hands; You have placed everything beneath his feet"* (Tehilim 8:7).

> (*Tov Halevanon*: i.e. the submission should not be out of poverty of spirit, due to ignorance of one's soul, but rather after an elevation of spirit, from rising above being associated with the animals, as written in chapter 2.)

When one recognizes the infinite greatness of the Creator and His exalted omnipotence and supreme wisdom, he will submit to Him and become humbled before Him. And he will learn from the verse: *"Do not glorify yourself before a king"* (don't be arrogant by showing your honor before a king - TL) (Mishlei 25:6) and draw the inference - how much more so before the King of kings, and the Master of masters, who is exalted beyond any likeness or comparison, as Chana said: *"There is none as holy as the L-ord, For there is none like You"* (Shmuel 2:2).

> (*Pas Lechem*: *"the infinite greatness of the Creator and His exalted omnipotence and supreme wisdom"* - these three things correspond to the three attributes ascribed to the Creator (in the Amida prayer), namely "HaGadol" (the great), "HaGibor" (mighty), "veHaNora" (the awesome). Hence, "the infinite greatness" corresponds to "HaGadol", "exalted might" corresponds to "HaGibor", and "supreme wisdom" corresponds to "HaNora", as written by Shlomo (Kings 3:28): "and they held the king in awe: for they saw that the wisdom of G-d was in him".
> Translator: See Jewish Meditation by Rabbi Aryeh Kaplan page 113 for some powerful meditations to do when saying these three attributes.)

(2) He should know the duties ordained by the torah and those which reason teaches us. He should read G-d's torah, and gain understanding in the wisdom derived from reason, the written law, and the oral law (talmud) so as to learn from there the conditions for humility, and the areas where it applies.

> (*Tov Halevanon*: i.e. in which circumstances is humility proper. This is

similar to what he explained in chapter 10 of the third gate that sometimes one must don the trait of arrogance.)

(3) To cultivate a broad heart (forbearance -TL) and ability to bear patiently words and deeds one hates, [and do so] for the Creator's sake, as written *"If I repaid the one who did evil to me, Or have plundered him who without cause was my enemy"* (Tehilim 7:5), and *"Do not say, 'As he did to me, so will I do to him; I will repay the man according to his deeds'"* (Mishlei 24:29), and our sages taught (Gitin 36b): "those who are insulted, but do not retaliate, who hear themselves humiliated and do not respond, serve (G-d) with love and rejoice [even] in suffering, on them the verse (Shoftim 5:31) says: "those that love Him will be like the sun when it goes forth in its might". The sages refer to this as *"Ma'avir Al Midotav"* (lets offenses pass and is forgiving).

(*Tov Halevanon*: *"cultivate a broad heart"* - this refers to the trait of savlanut (forbearance) for one who has a narrow heart is not able to bear any thing.
*"If I repaid the one who did evil to me"* - i.e. if I repaid with evil even to those people who did to me evil, even though human nature tends to make one take revenge from those who distress him.
Manoach Halevavot: a "broad heart" is the opposite of *"tzarut halev"* (lit: narrow of heart) and *"kotzer ruach"* (impatience of spirit), that one cannot bear any hardship or something hateful to him. He said one should cultivate a broad heart to bear that which is the will of G-d, even though one deems it hateful.)

(4) He should do good to others, speak well of them, judge them favorably, not speak of their faults, forgive them when they speak badly of him, even if they do not deserve this, as written *"Even in your thoughts, do not curse a king"* (Koheles 10:20) (i.e. even if no one hears, do not speak badly of a person - TL), and *"You let loose your mouth for evil, and you accustomed your tongue to deceit, you slandered your own mother's son"* (Tehilim 50:19). Regarding forgiving others who speak ill of him, the verse says: *"and Miriam and Aharon spoke of Moshe"*, and then *"the man Moshe was exceedingly humble"*, i.e. (the intent of the verse is to teach that - PL) he had forgiven them. Likewise, the wise man said: *"Also take no heed on all words that are spoken"* (Koheles 7:21), and adds *"For your heart knows that many times you too cursed others"* (Koheles 7:22).

And our Sages taught (Taanis 25b) that Rebbi Eliezer once (in a time of drought) became Chazan (cantor) and offered 24 supplications for rain and there was no response. Afterwards, Rebbi Akiva became Chazan and said only: "Our Father, our King..." and his prayer was accepted. A heavenly voice proclaimed "not because the latter sage was greater than the former, but only because he was 'Ma'avir Al Midosav' (lets offenses pass and is forgiving) while the former does not behave thus."

And it is said of a pious man who passed by an extremely foul smelling carcass of a dog. His disciples said to him: "how foul-smelling is this carcass!". He answered them "how white are its teeth!" And they regretted on having spoken disparagingly about the carcass.

If it is improper to speak disparagingly of a dead dog, all the more so for a living human being. And if it is proper to praise the carcass of a dead dog for the whiteness of its teeth, how much more so, according to this, is it a duty to praise a human being endowed with intelligence and understanding. His intent was to rebuke them, to not habituate their tongues to speak badly, as this will enter their nature.

> (*Pas Lechem*: i.e. certainly it is not reasonable to hold that speaking negatively about an animal's carcass is reprehensible, since the carcass has no perception and hence no pain from this. Rather, it was *"to not habituate their tongues..."*. And likewise, for the opposite, when speaking of its positive aspects...)

Likewise, when one habituates his tongue to speak good, it will become part of his nature, as written *"He who does not habituate/slander with his tongue"* (Tehilim 15:3), and it says regarding the opposite of this *"Your tongue devises mischief, [as a sharpened razor, working deceit], You love all devouring words"* (Tehilim 52:4), and *"What does it give to you, what does it increase unto you, O deceitful tongue?"* (Tehilim 120:3), and *"The words of a wise man's mouth are gracious; but the lips of a fool will swallow him up"* (Koheles 10:12)

> (*Pas Lechem*: *"You love all devouring words"* - this expression teaches that the matter [of speaking badly] becomes an acquired temperament - to love all corrupt speech, and the acquisition occurs through habit.
> *"What does it give to you..."* - since there is no benefit whatsoever from this, therefore it must be occurring only through habit.)

(5) There should be humility in all his worldly matters, whether they are public or private. In speech and in deed, when he is active or resting, his interior should not contradict his exterior, nor his hidden matters contradict his revealed matters. Rather his behavior should be weighed, proper, harmonious, and consistent - all going in the spirit of submission and

humility to G-d and also towards human beings. This should be in accordance with each person's merits (their wisdom and fear (reverence) of G-d - *TL*) and the good he benefits from them in religious and secular matters, as written *"Good is the man who is gracious and lends, who conducts his affairs with discretion"* (Tehilim 112:5). And our sages said: "be humble in spirit before all men" (Avos 4:12), and "Be submissive to an elder and courteous to the young" (Avos 3:12).

(6) That one's esteem be high and one's desire great for matters of the next world, that it should not be sufficient for him whatever comes his way, and he should not consider that what he does is enough. Rather, his good deeds, service, and efforts should be little in his eyes. He should always strive to reach a higher level, as the verse says of Yehoshafat *"And his heart was lifted up in the ways of the L-ord"* (Divrei Hayamim II 17:6), and let one always complain to himself that he is not doing enough of his torah duties to G-d and men. And he should seek help from G-d, and strengthen to add in the service and in good deeds, as written *"I pray that my ways be directed to keep Your statutes"* (Tehilim 119:5).

> (*Tov Halevanon*: That his spirit be esteemed in his eyes, and his soul be high, i.e. that he is a baal taava (insatiably desirous) for matters of the next world, that he always yearn to attain more and more acquisitions in matters of the next world. Because, if his spirit is lowly in his eyes and his soul is meek in matters of the next world, it will be sufficient for him a little good deeds and service and he will tell himself 'who am I that I should raise my heart to go in the matters of the Tzadikim?')

(7) That his deeds be little in his eyes, and that he should complain to himself over his shortcomings in the fulfillment of his religious duties to G-d and to his fellow men. He should pray to G-d for help and strength. For the sake of G-d, he should put aside all haughtiness, and renounce personal pride and dignity while he is performing any religious service, whether he is alone or among a crowd of people. As the verse said about Aharon, in his exalted status (as head priest), *"And he shall lift out the ashes"* (Vayikra 6:3). The Creator obligated him to take out the ashes every day in order to lower and remove pride from his heart. And similar to this by king David: *"and she saw the king David leaping and dancing before the L-ord; and she despised him in her heart"* (Shmuel II 6:16), and the rest of the matter, and also *"I will speak of your testimonies before kings, and will not be ashamed"* (Tehilim 119:46).

> (*Pas Lechem*: In the previous section, he wrote from the aspect of raising and lifting oneself to a higher level than the one he is currently in. Here, he

is writing from the aspect of mourning for his shortcomings and beseeching help from the Creator.)

(8) He should be contented with whatever means of livelihood present themselves, and with whatever he finds, because he regards himself (i.e. his lower soul which lusts for gratifications - *PL*) as insignificant and of little worth. He should accustom himself to abstain from gratifying bodily desires in order to be free to pay his duties to G-d for His many favors and great goodness towards him, as David said *"I will run the way of your commandments, for You will free my heart"* (Tehilim 119:32).

(*Pas Lechem*: Earlier in the psalm, King David wrote: "my soul clings unto the dust...", "my soul melts away for heaviness..", "remove from me the way of falsehood...", i.e. the way of physical lusts, and after he said all of these things and curtailed his desires, he then said that through this his heart will be free to "run the way of Your commandments")

(9) To exact vengeance from the wicked for the honor of the Creator. Let one not be enticed on account of his own practice of forgiving others in matters that only affect himself to also forgive them in matters of G-d, or to forgive those who speak against His prophets, or his pious and treasured ones. Likewise, let one not conduct himself in his personal way of forgiving others, when he sees a man oppressing another man. Rather, he should come to the rescue of the oppressed and help to free them from the hands of their oppressors, as written *"O house of David, thus said the L-ord; Execute judgment in the morning, and deliver him that is spoiled out of the hand of the oppressor"* (Yirmiya 21:12), and *"I broke the jaws of the wicked, and plucked the spoil out of his teeth"* (Iyov 29:17).

He should teach others the service of G-d, rebuke them and make them feel ashamed. He should exhort them on the good, and warn them on the evil forcefully and by word of mouth to the extent of his ability, and be swift to exact the punishment G-d commanded to administer to one who is guilty. He should not be humble or lowly in this, as written by Pinchas: *"Then Pinchas stood up and exacted justice, and the plague was stopped. It was accounted for him as a merit for generation to generation forever"* (Tehilim 106:30).

(10) He should speak little and in a low voice. He should laugh little. He should seldom take an oath in the name of G-d even if what he swears is true. No falsehood should come out of his lips. He should not sit in the company of men engaged in laughter and idle talk, nor delight in the

worldly things ignorant people delight in. He should act like this out of submission and lowliness of spirit, not out of arrogance and pride as the prophet said *"I sat not in the assembly of merrymakers, nor did I rejoice; because of Your hand I sat alone, for You filled me with indignation"* (Yirmiya 15:17).

(*Tov Halevanon*: *"not out of arrogance"* - [an example of arrogance:] not wishing to associate himself with those "lesser" than himself.)

## *** CHAPTER 7 ***

- When it applies and when it does not

The signs by which true submission is verified in a humble person are five.

(1) When he is intensely angry towards someone who reviled him, whether in word or deed, and he rules over his spirit, and forgives, despite that he has the ability to take revenge, and instead forgives him out of humility and lowliness - this attests to true submission.

(2) When he is struck with a severe financial loss, or some calamity occurs to one of his loved ones - if his calmness overcomes his shock, and he humbly accepts the Creator's decree, and justifies the Divine judgment - this attests to good submission and to his lowliness before G-d, as the verse tells of Aharon when Nadav and Avihu were killed (by a heavenly fire): *"And Aharon was silent"* (Vayikra 10:3), and David said: *"Be silent to G-d and wait patiently for Him"* (Tehilim 37:7), and *"Therefore the wise shall keep silence in that time"* (Amos 5:13).

(*Tov Halevanon*: i.e. at bad times, he will be silent and will not be questioning of G-d's ways.)

(3) When a deed he does becomes generally known, whether it is good or bad.
If it is a good deed and he is praised for it, he belittles the deed to the one who praised him, and he will consider in his thoughts that the deed is small and lacking in quality to be acceptable to the Creator due to his being obligated to do deeds many times more than this. And he will say to the one who praised him: "stop my brother, because compared to my sins, it is like a spark of fire (trying to extinguish) the sea, and even if it is worth something, how can I know if it is saved from the things which nullify a mitzvah (as described in Gate #5), and that the Creator will accept it from me, and will not return it to me, or throw it back into my face?, as written: "When you come to appear before Me, who requested this of you, to trample My courts?" (Yeshaya 1:12), and *"You shall no longer bring vain flour-offerings, it is smoke of abomination to Me"* (ibid 1:13).

(*Pas Lechem*: *"return it to me, or throw it back into my face"* - When a gift sent to a king is not accepted by the king, he returns it to the sender, and perhaps in his anger towards him, he may even throw it to his face.")

All the more so, if the praise is false, that he must reject it, and say to the speaker: "My brother, it is bad enough that I am lacking in fulfilling my obligations to the Creator, do not add to my discredit the iniquity of accepting praise for something I have not done, for I am aware of my sins and iniquities better than you are, as David said: 'For I know my transgressions..' (Tehilim 51:5).

If people speak of bad things he did (which are true):

He will admit his failings and will not seek false excuses to absolve and justify himself, as Yehuda said: "She has been more righteous than I" (Bereishis 38:26), and he won't attempt to shame the speaker and make him out a liar, nor condemn him for having exposed him, rather, he will say to him: "my brother, the amount of bad things you have observed in me is little compared to what you don't know about me and which the Creator has for so long kept hidden. If you knew the full extent of my bad deeds and transgressions, you would flee from me, fearing that the punishment of the Creator which they merit, would befall you too, as a poet once said: "if my neighbors could smell my sins, they would run away and keep far from me", and as Iyov said: *"Did I, like men, cover my transgressions, to conceal my iniquity in my hiding place?"* (Iyov 31:33).

If the bad thing that was said of him was false, he should say to the person who reported it: "my brother, I am not amazed that the Creator has saved me from doing that which you accuse me, since He has bestowed upon me so many benefits. What really amazes me, is that He allowed to remain concealed what is far worse and more reprehensible than that which you have told over about me. Stop my brother, and be concerned for your merits, that you do not lose them without your noticing it. For it is told of a pious man about whom someone spoke badly of, that when he heard of this, he sent a basket full of the choicest fruits of his province to the one who spoke badly of him and wrote to him: 'I have been notified that you sent me an offering of your merits, and I am sending you this gift in return' "

Another pious man once said: "Many people will come on the day of judgment, and when they are shown their deeds, they will find in the book of their merits, good deeds that they did not do, and they will say: 'we did not do these things'. They will be answered: 'they were done by someone who spoke badly of you'. Likewise, at that time, those who spoke badly of others will find that some of their merits will be missing, they will seek them, and will be told: 'you forfeited them when you spoke of this or that person'".

Similarly, some people will find in their book of sins, sins they did not do, and when they will protest saying "we did not commit these things", they will be told "these were added to the list of your misdeeds for having spoken of this or that person", as written: *"And return to our neighbors sevenfold into their bosom, their reproach with which they reproached You, O L-ord"* (Tehilim 79:12). And on this scripture warns us: *"remember what the L-ord your G-d did to Miriam on the journey"* (Devarim 24:9).

(4) When G-d bestows a special benefit on him such as exceptional wisdom and understanding, or great wealth, or honor from the ruling king, or other things like this which people commonly take pride in and become haughty on account of, and yet one remains in his humility as before and even increases in humility and lowliness before G-d, and honors and benefits other people, as written by Avraham who said: *"I am but dust and ashes"* (Bereishis 18:27) when the Creator praised him saying *"how can I hide from Avraham what I intend to do"* (Bereishis 18:17). And Moshe and Aharon said *"we are nothing"* (Shmos 16:7), and David said: *"I am a worm and not a man"* (Tehilim 22:7). (If one acts like this), it will clarify his interior and affirm his submission is true. The wise man said of this matter: *"If the spirit of the ruler rise up against you, leave not your place; for gentleness pacifies great offenses"* (Koheles 10:4).

(5) When the humble man rebukes himself, exacts the Creator's justice upon himself of his own initiative, and voluntarily submits to it, even though no human authority has the power to enforce it - this points to his true humility before G-d as well as his lowliness and submission to Him, as written: *"We have trespassed against our G-d, and have taken strange wives of the people of the land"* (Ezra 10:2), and *"they gave their hand to send away their wives"* (Ezra 10:19).

> (*Marpe Lenefesh*: i.e. he rebukes himself just like it was proper for the Creator to rebuke him, doing so before the Creator's punishment strikes him. Through this, he confesses and mourns his bad deeds and repents from them before the Creator's punishment strikes him. This is like the first group mentioned in Gate#6 (Gate of Repentance) chapter 6. see there.)

Through these situations and others similar to them will be fulfilled the signs of [true] submission to G-d and humility from the submitted and whether their heart is faithful in them.

## *** CHAPTER 8 ***

- does submission depend on good traits or the opposite

Is submission secondary to other moral qualities or are other moral qualities secondary to it? I answer this as follows:

> (*Marpe Lenefesh*: which depends on which? Is it due to a man possessing the other moral qualities that he can come to the trait of submission, or no, that submission is primary, and through it, he can come to the other moral qualities?)

It is well known to us, that the first prerequisite for the service of G-d is for one to divest himself completely from the trait of masterhood and leave it to G-d alone and that he accepts on himself all the traits of slavehood to the Creator.

> (*Marpe Lenefesh*: all the while that one has not shed completely all the traits of masterhood, arrogance, and grandeur, then how can he possibly serve G-d, since he is also a master and is therefore not fit to serve another?)

Because slavehood and masterhood are interdependent, one cannot exist without the other. A man cannot be called a slave if he does not have a master, and a master is not fit for this title until he has a slave. Neither one can precede the other whether by title or by relationship, similar to a buyer and a seller.

Hence, a human being's service of G-d can only exist when he assumes all the traits of slavehood, namely submission and humility before Him, shedding from himself all traits of masterhood, namely, self-glory, honor, splendor, pride and the like.

> (*Tov Halevanon*: "*a man cannot be called a slave...*" - The term "slave" here refers to a slave acquired with money as he says afterwards regarding a buyer and a seller. The reason is that for this type of slave, the term "slave" applies completely, and he has no trace whatsoever of masterhood because of the principle "whatever the slave acquires belongs to the master" (Pesachim 88b). Likewise, his master is a complete master. Because if this master was himself also acquired by a second master, then his slave would also belong to the second master. And it is known that the slavehood status of created beings is similar to that of slaves acquired with

money, as written: "Do you thus give back to G-d, Oh foolish and unwise people? Is He not your Father who acquired you? Has He not made you and established you?" (Devarim 32:6). Hence the term "master" cannot possibly apply to a man since it is not conceivable for a man to own a slave because he himself is already acquired by "the most high G-d, possessor of heaven and earth" (Bereishis 14:19) and therefore "whatever the slave acquires belongs to the Master". )

One of the wise men said: "Grandeur is the garment of the Creator. Whoever wishes to come into His presence in this garment will be pushed out. David said: *"The L-ord reigns; He is clothed in majesty"* (Tehilim 93:1).

(*Marpe Lenefesh*: All the worlds and levels from above to below are all garments to the Ein Sof (infinite essence of G-d). They are His praise and grandeur... Hence it is not proper for a human being to don the garment of his blessed Master.)

## PROOF THAT SUBMISSION IS FIRST AND FOREMOST

The believer cannot acquire [extra] piety until he [first] discharges his [basic] obligation, as written *"Has the L-ord as much desire in burnt offerings and peace-offerings, as in obeying the voice of the L-ord? Behold, obedience is better than a peace-offering"* (Shmuel 15:22).

(*Marpe Lenefesh*: A man must first discharge the primary and obligatory duty, namely, to fulfill all the commandments of G-d and afterwards he can add on to this, as he wrote earlier (Gate 5 ch.5), "these extra acts are not accepted until one first fulfills the obligatory duties".

*Pas Lechem*: One cannot truly ascribe any [extra] piety to a believing Jew before he first discharges his basic duty, i.e. it is incorrect to ascribe to him any extra measure [of piety] whatsoever before he first discharges his obligation in the obligatory duty.)

And he cannot succeed in fulfilling the [basic] duty until he undertakes the service of the Creator.

(*Pas Lechem*: Because if he does not have a strong mental picture of his servanthood fixed in his mind, why would he obligate himself in the service?)

And he cannot succeed in undertaking the service of the Creator until he first designates G-d alone with all the traits of masterhood and divests them from himself for His sake.

And he cannot succeed in this until he undertakes all the conditions of slavehood.

And he cannot succeed in undertaking the [conditions of] slavehood except through training to submit himself to G-d, and to humble himself and lower himself before Him, as we explained.

> (*Pas Lechem*: i.e. by habituating himself in submission and lowliness, etc. And since there is no extra piety before discharging his primary duty, and the discharging of the primary duty depends on picturing slavehood on himself (that he pictures that he is a servant of G-d), and slavehood depends on submission, if so, behold, submission precedes all good qualities, and all of them are secondary and stem from it.
>
> He specified three terms *"submit himself"*, *"humble himself"*, and *"lower himself"*. *"Submit himself"* due to G-d's greatness, *"humble himself"* due to G-d's benefits, both are in the heart, while *"lower himself"* is in action.
>
> Translator: Interestingly enough, the first halacha in the shulchan aruch (code of Jewish law) in the Rama brings the verse *"I have set G-d before me always, He is at my right hand, I shall not be moved"* Tehilim 16:8". The Chafetz Chaim explains this verse as follows (from Shem Olam part 2 ch.10): "the general principle, is for every good person to contemplate always how H-shem's presence fills the world, and that he is standing before G-d to do His will. This is what is meant by 'shivisi H'..', that 'I have constantly contemplated that I am standing before G-d to do His will", and this is what G-d said to Avraham - "Walk before Me and be Perfect.." (Bereishis 17:1), which means contemplate always that you are standing before Me." End quote.)

Hence, it follows that all moral qualities are secondary to the trait of submission, which is the head (in importance - *PL*) and beginning (in time - *PL*) of all of them. And it follows logically from this, that no piety can possibly exist in one whose heart is devoid of submission to G-d or has in it any trace of arrogance or pride.

Therefore the beginning of repentance is lowliness, humility, and submission, as the verse says: *"If My people, who are called by My Name, shall humble themselves, and pray, and seek My face, [and turn from their wicked ways; then will I hearken from Heaven, and will forgive their sin...]"* (Divrei II Hayamim 7:14), and *"They have submitted themselves;*

*therefore I will not destroy them, but I will grant them some deliverance"* (Divrei Hayamim II 12:7).

(*Pas Lechem*: since they have submitted themselves, I will not destroy them because submission is the beginning of repentance, and the beginning is half of the whole, and certainly they will complete their repentance.)

## *** CHAPTER 9 ***

Can submission and pride co-exist in the heart of the believer? I answer this as follows:

There are two categories of pride:
(1) A man's pride in his body (such as if he is tall, of good form and appearance - *TL*), and its conditions (such as his strength, beauty or the like - *TL*), or in all things that further his body's well being (such as his clothing, houses or other possessions - *TL*).
(2) A man's pride in his spiritual qualities - the wisdom used and good deeds he performed in the service of G-d.

Any pride which stems from bodily things distances submission from the heart. It is impossible for both to co-exist simultaneously since they mutually repel each other. For if a man takes pride in any secular thing, what brings him to this pride is:
* belittling the Source of this good (G-d)
* downplaying the value of this good
* little consciousness of how swiftly it can be taken from him or leave him. Rather, he will consider it that he himself is the creator of his good fortune, that he has acquired it with his own strength and ingenuity, as written about Sancheriv *"by the strength of my hand I have accomplished"* (Yeshaya 10:13), and about Nebuchadnezar *"Is this not the great Babylon, which I built for a royal palace with the strength of my power and for the honor of my glory?"* (Daniel 4:27), and Pharaoh *"My river is my own..."* (Yechezkel 29:3), and you already know what swiftly followed their boastful proclamations - the destruction of their kingdom and their land.

Pride in spiritual qualities divides into two categories, one reprehensible and one praiseworthy.

The reprehensible one - that a person prides himself on his wisdom or a righteous man on his good deeds. This causes the wisdom and righteousness to become magnified in his eyes (he thinks his wisdom and righteousness is much - *TL*), so that he is satisfied with what he has already accomplished, and thinks that it is enough for him the good reputation and praise he has achieved from his fellow men. This will cause him to look down on others, despise them, and speak badly of them, to belittle the wise men of his generation in his eyes, and glorify himself in the shortcomings and ignorance of other people. Our Rabbis of blessed memory call this: "one who seeks honor by putting down others (has no share in the world to come)". One like this will never be submitted nor humble.

> (*Pas Lechem*: *"This will cause him to look down on others"*, due to their little wisdom *"and despise them"*, due to their deeds which he deems reprehensible. These two are in the heart. And afterwards, *"and speak badly of them"* which is verbally.)

The praiseworthy one - the pride of the wise man in his wisdom or of the righteous man in his good deeds when it is an expression of his gratitude to the Creator for helping him greatly on them, and of his joy in them. When it causes him to improve and continue exerting himself in them, and to be humble to his colleagues, happy with their success, and concerned for their honor (if he sees their honor will be slighted, he will quickly rectify the matter - *PL*). To not reveal their failings and to speak good of them (against one who speaks badly of them - *PL*). To love them and judge them favorably, and to be careful of their honor (that they don't receive saddening things due to him - *PL*). All of his own good deeds will seem few in his eyes, and he will always exert himself to increase them. He will be humbled by his inability to reach his longing in them (his heart will be broken and mourning that he is unable to attain the wisdom and good deeds according to his desire - *PL*). He will lower himself before someone who he hopes will help him to increase in them. He will be grateful to G-d for having graced him with qualities and thanks Him for helping him to reach exalted levels.

This kind of arrogance (aggrandizing) is not detrimental to submission and does not repel it. The verse says of Yehoshafat *"And his heart was uplifted in the ways of the L-ord"* (Divrei Hayamim II 17:6), just the opposite - such pride helps humility and increases his submission as written *"In the wake of humility comes fear of the L-ord, riches, honor, and life"* (Mishlei 22:4). (humility leads to fear of G-d - *ML*)

### *** CHAPTER 10 ***

The benefits of submission in matters of this world and the next world are six things, three of them refer to matters of this world and three to matters of the next world.

For matters of this world:
(1) That one is happy in his portion. Because for one whom arrogance and pride have entered in him, the entire world and everything in it is not enough for his needs due to his inflated heart and due to his looking down with contempt on the portion allotted to him (he thinks he deserves much more - *PL*). But if he is humble, he does not consider himself as having any special merit, and so whatever he attains of the world's goods, he is satisfied with it for his sustenance and other needs. This will bring him peace of mind and minimize his anxiety. He will eat what is available and wears and dwells with what he can find. Due to his submission, even the minimum of the world's goods is enough for him. But for the arrogant - the entire world will not satisfy his lacking due to the pride of his heart and arrogance, as the wise man said: *"A righteous man eats to sate his appetite, but the stomach of the wicked shall feel want"* (Mishlei 13:25).

> (*Pas Lechem*: *"peace of mind and minimize his anxiety"* - peace of mind due to not desiring more than he attained and *"minimal anxiety"* from losing what he has because even if he loses some, he will be satisfied with the remainder.
> *"the stomach of the wicked shall feel want"* - whatever indulgences he fills his belly with will induce him to desire other things better than those, and there is no end to the matter...)

(2) The humble man can bear it when troubles befall him or when reverses in his affairs occur to him due to his lowliness and humble spirit.

> (*Tov Halevanon*: *"due to his lowliness and humble spirit"* - whatever befalls him, does not appear to him to be a decline from his level which is lowly in his mind.)

But for the proud man, his fear will be great (when troubles are near - *PL*) and his ability to bear will be little when hit by troubles because his soul is proud, his heart is haughty, and he is dissatisfied with his matters, as written by one who was in this way: *"How have you fallen from heaven, oh morning star? You (Nebuchadnezar) have been cut down to earth, You who cast lots on nations"* (Yeshaya 14:12).

(3) The humble man will find more favor in people's eyes. He is beloved by them, and will easily fit in with them and adopt their customs.

It was already said on a king who would hasten his steps when walking. He was asked about this and answered: "because it keeps me away from the way of pride, and also so I arrive more quickly to my destination"

A wise man was asked: "How were you able to become accepted as head of your entire generation?" He replied:
"Because I never met one of them that I did not see in him a quality in which he is greater than me. If he was wiser than me, I concluded that he must be more G-d fearing than me since his wisdom is greater than mine. If he had less wisdom than I have, I considered that on the day of Judgment, he will be held less accountable than I, because my transgressions were committed with knowledge and intent while his were committed in error.

If he was older than me, I would reason that his merits must be greater than mine since he came into the world before me. If he was younger, I thought that his sins were fewer than mine. If he was equal to me in age and wisdom, I would tell myself: maybe his heart is more devoted to G-d than mine, because I know of my past sins, but I don't know of any that he committed. If he was wealthier than me, I would think that due to his wealth, he likely served G-d more than me, in doing charities and helping the poor. If he was poorer than me, I would consider that he was more low and humble than me due to his poorness, and he is better than me. Due to this, I never ceased to honor all of them and humble myself before them."

> (*Tov Halevanon*: *"If he was wiser than me, I concluded that he must be more G-d fearing than me"* - and that is the purpose of it all, and this is all of a man as written "the fear of G-d is his treasure" (Yeshaya 33:6), and our sages, of blessed memory, said: (Kidushin 40b) "study [of torah] is greater for it leads to action"
> *"since his wisdom is greater than mine"* - and as they said (Avot 3:17) "without wisdom there cannot exist fear [of G-d])

Similarly, our sages taught "judge every man favorably" (Avos 1:6), "receive every person with a cheerful countenance" (Avos 1:15), and "Be very, very lowly of spirit" (Avos 4:4), and "One should always be flexible as a reed and not unyielding as a cedar. This is why the reed has merited to

have made from it a quill to write a Sefer Torah, Tefilin and Mezuzot"
(Taanis 20b).

(Manoach Halevavot: *"This is why the reed"* - i.e. to allude that submission
is a great root to torah, and one who adopts it is beloved by G-d. Therefore,
we write with it a Sefer Torah...)

(4) The fourth benefit, which is for matters of the afterlife, is that the
humble person is nearer to attaining wisdom, since he is drawn to the
Sages (his heart is drawn to their words - *PL*), he submits to them, and
frequently goes to them, as written: *"He who goes with the wise will
become wise"* (Mishlei 13:20). Our sages of blessed memory said: *"Let
your house be a meeting house for the sages; sit amidst the dust of their
feet and drink in their words thirstily"* (Avos 1:4). G-d will help him to
attain wisdom as written: *"The humble will He guide in justice: and the
humble will He teach his way"* (Tehilim 25:9). But for one who has a proud
heart, true wisdom will never endure in him, and he will never reach the
goal of clear knowledge. For he feels too important to go to the wise men
and torah sages, as written *"The wicked, through the pride of his
countenance will not seek..."* (Tehilim 10:4).

(5) The humble man hastens to do his religious duties with diligence and
zeal. He does not become arrogant because he fulfills them, and does not
take lightly any of them as our sages said: *"Be as scrupulous about a light
precept as of a grave one"* (Avos 2:1). But one who is proud procrastinates
from doing the service, due to his high heartedness and inflated spirit. He
does not sense this until he falls and becomes low, as written: *"Say unto the
king and to the queen, Humble yourselves, sit down: for your rule shall
come down, even the crown of your glory"* (Yirmiya 13:18), and *"Six things
the L-ord hates, and the seventh is an abomination of His soul; Haughty
eyes..."* (Mishlei 6:16).

(*Tov Halevanon*: He who makes himself proud is hated by G-d and G-d
reduces him to even less than his true level. This is like the allusion in the
Midrash (Bereishis Raba 65:11) "an analogy to a province who would call
themselves 'the giantons of the king'. A woman who had a midget son
arrived to some place and said 'my son is a gianton'. They replied to her: 'to
you he seems like a gianton but to us he seems like the midget of the
midgets.'" (end of midrash). At first they said she had a midget son, and
since she said he was a gianton, they reduced him more than his true status
and said he is among the midget of the midgets.)

(6) The service of the humble man is acceptable to G-d, as written: *"The*

*sacrifices of G-d are a broken spirit; [O G-d, You will not despise a broken
and crushed heart]"* (Tehilim 51:19). His sin is quickly forgiven if he
repents from it, as written: *"He who conceals his sins will not succeed, but
he who confesses and abandons [them] will obtain mercy"* (Mishlei 28:13),
and *"When men are cast down, then you shall say, There is lifting up; and
He shall save the humble person"* (Iyov 22:29).

FINAL WORDS

These ten roots (i.e. chapters - *ML*) of submission will clarify for you, my
brother, the remaining qualities of this important, supremely lofty virtue,
which I have not mentioned in this gate. Remember therefore what I have
called to your attention concerning this virtue. Place it before your eyes.
Ponder it always. Strive to acquire it. Be constantly checking it with your
soul and faculties (always sense and check if it is still with you - *PL*). Seek
the help of G-d in this. Plea to Him for it, in order that you be drawn closer
to Him and attain His favor. Perhaps He will (heed your request - *PL*) and
straighten you to this virtue, thereby preparing for you the path to Him, as
the pious would ask after their prayers: "O G-d, keep my tongue from evil
and my lips from deceit. Help me to be silent in the face of derision, and
let my soul be like dust to everyone."

(*Pas Lechem*: *"Plea to Him for it, in order that you be drawn closer to Him,
and attain His favor"* - beseech the virtue of submission from the Creator,
and your intent should be to attain it in order that through it you will draw
closer to the Creator and will obtain His favor.)

Be on guard against the imaginations of your heart, and enticements of the
yetzer (evil inclination) towards you that would mislead you to
haughtiness, arrogance, pride, lust for ruling, self-glorification and
domineering. The wise man already exhorted us as to the right road a man
should take in this world in saying: "Two things have I asked of you...
Remove far from me vanity and lies: [give me neither poverty nor riches];
give me my daily bread. [lest I become sated and deny, and say, 'Who is
the L-ord?' Or lest I become poor and steal]" (Mishlei 30:7-9).

(*Pas Lechem*: *"be on guard against the imaginations of your heart..."* -
because if a man lets loose the imaginations of his heart, automatically the
evil inclination will entice him to pride and haughtiness.)

Wake up my brother! Do not evade from healing the sickness of pride from
your soul and your traits with the medicines I have taught you. Let not
your observing of the masses' neglecting the healing their souls from this

disease stop you from doing so, in saying to yourself: "I will share the same fate as them". Because, if a blind man finds the potions which can benefit and heal him if he applies them, it is not proper for him to procrastinate using them and say "I will share the same fate of my blind friends". Anyone who heard him saying such a statement would scorn his words and ridicule his reasoning.

According to this, examine your soul, and exert yourself with all of your might to promote its well-being. Do not neglect what will benefit you in this world and in the next, lest you die without fulfilling your longing for exalted spiritual levels which you are capable of reaching, as the wise man said: *"The desire of a lazy man will bring about his death, for his hands refuse to labor"* (Mishlei 21:25), and *"By the fields of a lazy man, I passed and by the vineyard of a man without sense. And behold, thistles had grown all over it; nettles had covered its surface, and its stone fence had been torn down"* (Mishlei 24:30), and the rest of the matter.

(*Pas Lechem*: *"your longing for exalted spiritual levels"* - certainly it is in the nature of man to long and yearn to attain exalted spiritual levels)

May the Al-mighty teach us the path to His service, in His mercy and kindness. Amen.

# ****** SHAAR HATESHUVA - THE GATE OF REPENTANCE ******

# *** Introduction ***

Since our preceding discussion dealt with the subject of submission, which is the root and beginning of repentance, I deemed it fit to follow with a clarification of its essential parts and the ways to complete its fulfillment.

I will start with the obligation and necessity for repentance. For it is already clear to us through reason and scripture that a human being falls short in the fulfilment of his service to the Creator which he is under duty to perform.

Through reason:
By what we observe of man, his changing nature, his composition of different elements, his opposing natures (good/evil inclination - *ML*), his changing moods and emotions, the changing of circumstances which motivate his behavior. All this inevitably causes changes in his actions according to the state he is in, such as from decent to indecent, wicked to righteous, good to evil. For this it was necessary for the torah to restrain him (from evil) and guide him (to good).

> (*Pas Lechem*: the soul and the body are the basis of his composition, and they are diametrically different because the soul tends towards the spiritual while the body tends to the physical..
>
> *Tov Halevanon*: his nature changes, to love something and then afterwards hate it...His traits such as anger or contentment, etc. change in him according to his age, place, and habit ... and a human being's behavior follows his nature, traits, and [habitual] conduct)

Through scripture:
Among them, what the verse says: *"for the imagination of man's heart is evil from his youth"* (Bereishis 8:21), and *"the L-ord saw that the wickedness of man was great in the earth, and that every imagination of the thoughts of his heart was only evil continually"* (Bereishis 6:5), and *"a man is born as a wild donkey's colt"* (Iyov 11:12), and *"Behold, the moon has no brightness"* (Iyov 25:5) and *"how much less, man, who is a worm, and the son of man, who is but a maggot!"* (Iyov 25:6), and *"[How then can man be justified with G-d,] or how can he be clean that is born of a woman?"* (Iyov 25:4).

> (*Manoach Halevavos*: *"Behold, the moon has no brightness"* - some of the

commentaries on the book of Iyov explain this verse that it is an analogy, namely that the intellect of man which is from the soul, and the soul is referred to as a "candle", as in the verse "the candle of G-d is the soul of man" (Mishlei 20:27). Hence he is saying that the intellect does not illuminate in a man until he brings it out from potential to actual (through torah study) just like the moon does not illuminate in the beginning of the month until it receives its light from the sun.

*Tov Halevanon*: The early sages already said that a man's intellect receives light from the torah, just like the moon receives its light from the sun. This is what is meant *"behold, the moon"*, i.e. it is like the moon, *"which has no brightness"* - it does not illuminate on its own, because it is a dark mass. Only the sun grants it light. So too the intellect of man does not shine from the side of the physical body. Some commentaries explain the verse to refer to great men - that their righteousness will be shown to be null and void if G-d chooses to judge their deeds strictly.)

Since we have clarified the reality that man's actions fall short, it was out of Divine grace to man that the Creator gave him the capability of rectifying his mistake and of returning the loss of his service through repentance. G-d encouraged the matter and promised (its effectiveness) through his servants, the prophets. And He expanded the possible excuses (vindications) for the man who went off the path of His service, and promised us that He would accept these excuses from us, and desire in us quickly, even if we rebelled against His word and broke His covenant for a long time as written: *"And when a wicked man repents of his wickedness and performs justice and righteousness, he shall live thereby..."* (Yechezkel 33:19).

(*Marpe Lenefesh*: *"it was out of Divine grace to man"* - this means grace, favor, and mercy - that the Creator granted man the ability to repent, because according to [strict] reason, "the soul which sins shall die" (Yechezkel 18:20) as is the custom for [human] kings of the land (who execute those who rebel). Only that G-d desires in kindness... "for I do not desire the death of the wicked, says the L-rd G-d, but that he repents and lives"... and (Yechezkel 33:11) "Say to them: As I live, says the L-rd G-d, I do not wish for the death of the wicked, but for the wicked to repent of his way so that he may live. Repent, repent of your evil ways, for why should you die?")

Since tzadikim (righteous people) fall into two categories: (1) those saved from sin and iniquity, (2) those who sinned but repented. Since the vast majority of tzadikim are of the penitent (second type), therefore the psalmist opened with *"How blessed is he whose transgression is forgiven,*

*Whose sin is covered"* (Tehilim 32:1), and afterwards spoke of the first type.

And even though, those saved from ever sinning are on a higher level (than the penitent), since every penitent was a tzadik before he sinned, but not every tzadik was a penitent (i.e. the penitent must return to the state of tzadik, but the tzadik does not ever need the state of penitent to become a tzadik, therefore he is greater - *ML*). And David said of them *"How blessed is the man to whom the L-ord does not count in him iniquity"* (Tehilim 32:2), and the reason he mentioned them second is because they are few to be found in every generation, as written: *"If You, L-ord, should mark iniquities, O L-ord, who could stand?"* (Tehilim 130:3), and *"For there is not a just man on earth who does good and sins not"* (Koheles 7:20), and *"for (there is) no man who does not sin"* (Melachim 8:46).

Because of this our Rabbis instituted in the beginning of our (Amida) prayers the matter of repentance and forgiveness in saying *"harotze biteshuva"* (who desires repentance), and *"hamarbe lisloach"* (who abundantly forgives).

It is now proper for us to clarify ten matters on the subject of repentance:
1. What is repentance?
2. What are its parts?
3. What are the prerequisites of repentance?
4. An explanation of its essential elements.
5. the conditions for each element.
6. which things stir a man to repent?
7. which things are detrimental to repentance?
8. is the penitent equal to the tzadik who never sinned?
9. if it is possible to repent of every sin or not?
10. strategy to be adopted by one for whom repentance is difficult

In this, we will complete the various kinds of repentance and its obligations, by the fulfillment of which, with G-d's help, we hope to obtain forgiveness of our transgressions.

## *** CHAPTER 1 ***

- What is repentance

With regard to what is repentance, I say that repentance means that a man makes himself fit to resume the service of the Creator after he went out of it and transgressed against it, and to restore what he lost in it. This could be due to:

> (*Pas Lechem*: *"after he went out of it"* - out of the good.
> *"and transgressed against it"* - committed the bad
> *"and to restore what he lost in it"* - the mitzvot that were in his power to do)

* ignorance of G-d and of the matters of serving Him.

> (*Tov Halevanon*: *"ignorance of G-d"* - that he does not realize G-d's awesome greatness, hence he does not care about His commandments. Also, he does not know well the service, how and with what to serve Him.)

* his evil inclination had overpowered his understanding
* neglect of his duties towards G-d

> (*Manoach Halevavos*: i.e. it is not due to *"ignorance of G-d..."*, but rather due to not being mindful to watch over, think, and contemplate his duties...)

* associating with bad company who entice him to sin,
or other similar reasons, as the wise man said: *"My son, if sinners entice you, do not consent"* (Mishlei 1:10), and *"My son, fear the L-ord and the king; and meddle not with them that are given to change"* (Mishlei 24:21).

The withdrawing out of the service of G-d occurs in two ways, whether one (1) abandons and ignores what the Creator commanded us to do, or (2) one does what He warned us not to do, with the intent to rebel against his Creator.

If his withdrawing out of the service consists only in abandoning what the Creator commanded to do (but not in doing what He warned against), then the repentance for his shortcomings will be to exert himself in the proper acts and to cling to the roots of repentance which I will clarify in this gate.

If his withdrawing consisted of doing what the Creator warned against, the way to make up his failing will be in guarding from returning to do any form of this act, to endeavor to do its opposite, and to cling to the roots and conditions of repentance which I will clarify in this gate with G-d's help.

An analogy of this with regard to natural matters. A man became sick due to poor diet, whether because he refrained from eating food which promotes good health or because he ate something damaging to him and so ruined his health.

When his illness is due to starving himself from proper food, the way to bring him back to good health is for him to eat a larger amount than normal of proper foods, compatible with his nature, until he returns to proper balance. After he returns to his original balance, he can reduce his diet to normal amounts.

If his illness was due to habitually eating food harmful to him (ex. too much spicy food), the way of his healing would be to abstain from this food or others similar, and to habitually eat foods of an opposite nature and composition (ex. non spicy), until he returns to his original state. When his health is restored and he reaches a balanced state, he can eat foods midway both types of nature and composition (mildly spicy), and the verse already compares moral iniquities to bad food as written: *"But every one shall die for his own iniquity. He who eats the sour grapes, his teeth shall be set on edge"* (Yirmiya 31:29).

## *** CHAPTER 2 ***

- What are its parts

There are three kinds of repentance:

(1) One who repents because he does not have an opportunity (or the means) to repeat the transgression. But when he does find the opportunity, his evil inclination overpowers his understanding and he does not refrain from it. After he finishes the deed, he realizes the shamefulness of his act and regrets what he did. This person repented with his mouth but not with his heart, with his lips but not with his deeds, and he is guilty and deserving of the punishment of the Creator. Of such a person, it is written: *"Will you steal, murder, and commit adultery, and swear falsely,... And come and stand before Me in this house, which is called by My Name, and say, 'We are saved'...? Has this house, which is called by My Name, become a cave of thieves in your eyes?..."* (Yirmiya 7:9).

(*Pas Lechem*: Behold they regretted temporarily and prayed to be saved, but G-d scorns them for this in saying *"Has this house... become a cave of thieves in your eyes?"*. The intent is that the thieves are bandits who hold up travelers on the road. They stay in a concealed cave and from there run and plunder travelers. But when they sense a large crowd approaching them (to arrest them), and from far they sense that people are coming and searching for them - then they panic and flee swiftly to their hiding place. When they reach the cave and saved their necks, and call out *"we are saved"*. Then most of them regret their deeds in seeing how close they are to mortal danger. But afterwards after some time has passed, when their hearts' agitation and arousal has calmed down, they return to their villainous work. And all their days are back and forth.

*Tov Halevanon*: For example, one who transgresses in forbidden relations, after he finishes the deed and his desire and lust have passed, he feels the shame and disgrace of his transgression and regrets it, as the sages said: "the wicked are full of regret" (see Shevet Musar Chapt.25))

(2) One who repents in his heart and in deed. His understanding stands up to his evil inclination. He trains himself to discipline his inward being, and fight its lusts until he defeats it and restrains it from what is hateful to the Creator. But his inner being always desires to draw him to the opposite of the service of G-d, and longs to do transgressions. He exerts himself to restrain it. Sometimes he defeats it, sometimes it defeats him. This person is not complete in the way of repentance. It will not secure an atonement,

until he renounces the sins completely, as written: *"Therefore by this the guilt of Jacob will be atoned for, and this will be the full fruit of the removal of his sin: when he makes all the stones of the altars like chalkstones crushed to pieces, no Asherim or incense altars will remain standing"* (Yeshaya 27:9).

(*Pas Lechem*: i.e. that he is assured that he will not return to his folly under any circumstances, namely, after he destroyed the remnants of his abominations and no trace of them remains.)

(3) A man who has fulfilled all the conditions of repentance (as will be explained later), which means, has strengthened his intellect over his lusts, and habituated himself in making a personal accounting (see gate#8), fears his Creator (His punishment - *PL*), is in awe of Him (of His greatness - *PL*), contemplates the greatness of his sin and error, recognizes the infinite greatness of the One who he rebelled against and He whose word he transgressed, places his sins always before his eyes, regrets them and prays for forgiveness on them all the days of his life, until his final end comes - to the Creator, this person is worthy of being spared.

(Translator: *"places his sins always before his eyes"*, this is not in order to be sad over his sins, but rather in order to stay humble - Igeret HaTeshuva, Tanya)

## *** CHAPTER 3 ***

- What a man needs to know to repent

What are the prerequisites of repentance? I say on this, to be effective, repentance must be preceded by first understanding seven things:
(1) The penitent must understand clearly that he did a disgraceful act. Because, if this is not clear to him, and he is in doubt or ignorant of it, it is not possible for him to regret it and seek forgiveness for it, as written: *"For I know my transgressions, and my sin is ever before me"* (Tehilim 51:5)

> (*Tov Halevanon*: i.e. that he knows clearly that he did these things. This is to exclude where he is in doubt, that he does not clearly remember the act or the disgracefulness of it, or that he only remembers it partially...
>
> *Marpe Lenefesh*: I deemed proper to quote from the Orchot Tzadikim who brought the *"seven things"* of this book and expanded on them a bit. From his words the author's words will be properly understood. Here is the excerpt from Shar Teshuva there: After a man deliberates on repenting, he will not be able to do a complete repentance unless he puts to heart seven things. The first: That one knows and recognizes all of his actions... know my son that most people are not careful about devarim betalim (useless chatter), nor from looking at women and speaking to them without needing to. They are also not careful to pray with kavana (intent), and to speak [mundane things] in a synagogue, and from frivolity (sechok and kalut rosh), nor from giving tzedaka to those fitting to receive... and talmud torah, and likewise from jealousy, hatred, slander, arrogance, anger, and all the [bad] traits mentioned in this book...)

(2) He must understand the gravity of his sin and its disgracefulness, since if it is not clear to him that his deed was evil, he will not regret it nor take on the conditions of repentance for it. He will imagine that his act is like unintentional and that he will easily be able to justify himself, as written: *"But who can discern their own errors? Forgive my hidden faults"* (Tehilim 19:13).

> (*Marpe Lenefesh*: Even if he knows the transgressions he committed, he will not regret them if he is not certain of the evilness of what he did. If he thinks "so what if I benefited from this world without a beracha, or if I wasted time for torah study, it is not so bad?" He who thinks thus will not regret nor repent wholeheartedly. Rather one must think: "there is nothing worse in the world than one who doesn't care about the orders of the lofty

| King...")

(3) That he realizes the punishment the act obligates (the inevitable punishment which is already prepared for his transgression - *TL*). Because, if he does not know this, necessity does not bring him to regret it. But, if it is clear to him that he will be punished for it, he will regret it afterwards and seek forgiveness, as written: *"For after my return I have completely changed my mind, and after I had been brought to know myself (the punishments waiting for me) I smote upon my thigh"* (Yirmiyahu 31:18), and *"My flesh bristles from fright of You, and I dread Your judgments"* (Tehillim 119:120).

(*Marpe Lenefesh*: The penitent must know and believe from the depths of his heart that there are harsh and bitter retributions and punishments in the next world for the sins he committed. If he does not know this, he will not care to repent. But after the inevitability of the punishment is clear to him, then he will repent and regret it and beseech forgiveness for it from G-d.)

(4) He must realize that his sin is pending [retribution] and inscribed in the book of his sins. It is not subject to being neglected, forgotten, or overlooked, as written: *"Is it not laid up in store with Me, sealed up among My treasuries?"* (Devarim 32:34), and *"By the hand of every man He seals so that every man should know His deed"* (Iyov 37:7). Because if one thinks that since he has not been punished for it until now, therefore the sin is discarded and not pending for him, then he will not regret it nor seek forgiveness for it, as written *"Because the sentence of an evil deed is not executed swiftly; therefore, the hearts of men are fully set in them to do evil"* (Koheles 8:11).

(*Tov Halevanon*: "his sin is pending" - the sin is held for him. Justice demands that he be punished immediately for it, only that G-d withholds the punishment and waits until he repents or until his measure is up.)

(5) He must be fully convinced that repentance is the remedy for his illness, and the road to recovery from his evil deed and disgraceful conduct, and through it he will correct his error and recover what he had lost. Because if this is not clear to him, he will despair from obtaining the Creator's atonement and mercies, and he will not seek forgiveness for past wickedness, as written *"So have you spoken, saying: For our transgressions and our sins are upon us, and because of them we are melting away, so how should we then live?"* (Yechezkel 33:10), and they were answered by the Creator through His prophet: *"Say to them: As I live, says the L-ord G-d, I do not wish for the death of the wicked, [but for the*

*wicked to repent of his way so that he may live. Repent, repent of your evil ways, for why should you die, O house of Israel]"* (Yechezkel 33:11).

> (*Pas Lechem*: *"the remedy for his illness and the road to healing"* - Repentance is the remedy for the illnesses of the soul and it is the *"road"* which leads to *"healing"* from his evil deeds, i.e. to remove the acquired evil, which he acquired in his nature through habitual practice - namely, the longing to do evil, - that he will no longer do evil deeds in the future. These two expressions correspond to regret and abandonment of the evil deed. Understand this.)

(6) He must make a spiritual accounting (see Gate#8) with himself on the kindness the Creator already bestowed on him, and how he had rebelled against Him instead of being grateful for them. He should weigh the punishment of the sin in the next world against the pleasure (he got from the sin in this world), and the sweet bliss of the reward for good deeds he will get in the next world against the suffering he has [here] in doing them, as our sages taught: *"Consider the loss from doing a mitzvah against its reward and the gain from doing a sin against the loss it involves"* (Avos 2:1).

(7) He must strengthen himself greatly to be able to bear the suffering from refraining to do the evil he had been addicted to do, and firmly resolve inwardly and outwardly to renounce it, as written *"And tear your hearts, and not your garments"* (Yoel 2:13).

Only if these seven things are in the mind of the sinner, can repentance from his sins be effective.

# *** CHAPTER 4 ***

- its essential requirements

The essential components of repentance are four:

> (*Marpe Lenefesh*: i.e. if he is not perfect in these four components and conditions of repentance, he is still outside, and there is a breach in his repentance, as mentioned earlier.)

1. That he should regret the past sins he committed.

> (*Marpe Lenefesh*: that he regrets having transgressed the command of G-d.)

2. That he abandon and turn away from them.
3. That he confess them and beseech forgiveness for having committed them.
4. That he take on himself with heart and soul not to repeat them.

> (*Tov Halevanon*: To never repeat them and to not desire them in his heart. *Manoach Halevavos*: Even though he already said in #2 to abandon them. There the explanation is to abandon them now, but it is still possible that after some time he will return to doing them. Therefore, he added this 4th component *"to take on himself..."*)

1. Regret is a sign that the sin is disgraceful in his eyes, as written: *"He who knows will return and regret and leave a blessing behind him"* (Yoel 2:14). It is said of one who persists in his sins for a long time: *"no man repented himself of his wickedness"* (Yirmiyahu 8:6). We ourselves can see in relationships between human beings, that when one who wronged his fellow shows regret for having wronged him, this will be strongest the factor for his fellow's granting him forgiveness.

2. Abandonment (of sin) is a sign of his firm faith in reward and punishment, as written: *"The wicked shall give up his way, and the man of iniquity his thoughts, and let him return to the L-ord, who shall have mercy upon him, and to our G-d, for He abundantly pardons"* (Yeshaya 55:7). Of one who persists in his [evil] ways for a long time, the prophet says: *"For the iniquity of his covetousness was I angry, and smote him, and he went on forwardly in the way of his heart"* (Yeshaya 57:17). Similarly we can observe among human beings, that if one has wronged his fellow, and along with expressing regret, ceases to wrong him, then it will be proper to

forgive him and overlook the misdeed.

3. Beseeching forgiveness demonstrates submission and humility before G-d, and confession of one's sin is a ground for forgiveness, as written: *"he who confesses and renounces them will obtain mercy"* (Mishlei 28:13). Regarding the opposite of this, it is said: *"[Yet you say, Because I am innocent, surely his anger shall turn from me.] Behold, I will contend with you, because you say, I have not sinned"* (Yirmiyahu 2:35), and *"he that conceals his transgressions will not succeed"* (Mishlei 28:13). Similarly we can observe among human beings, that if one wrongs his fellow, and afterwards humbles himself towards him, and admits that he sinned against him and wronged him and beseeches forgiveness from him, and the fellow recognizes that he truly regrets the wrong he committed, the fellow will not refrain from forgiving him and will overlook the wrong-doing, and the grudge in his heart against him will be removed.

4. The resolution not to repeat [the sin] reflects his understanding of the wickedness of his deed and the gravity of his sin, as written *"If I have committed iniquity, I will do no more"* (Iyov 34:32), and *"Assyria shall not save us... nor will we say any longer to the work of our hands, you are our gods"* (Hoshea 14:4). Of one who acts in the opposite manner, it is written: *"Can the Ethiopian change his skin, or the leopard his spots? then may you also do good, that are accustomed to doing evil"* (Yirmiya 13:23). And similarly we can observe among human beings that when one who wronged his fellow takes on himself not to wrong him again, and demonstrates that he regrets and abandons his sin and confesses it, this will complete the grounds which lead to forgiveness and removal of his iniquity, and cancelling the punishment from him.

When the penitent combines these four components along with their conditions, which we will clarify [next chapter], the Creator will forgive the sinner his iniquity, and overlook his transgression. If it is a sin of the type which it is written: *"he will not hold him guiltless"* (Shmos 20:7), such as a false oath or adultery, the Creator will reduce his punishment in this world (to atone for his sin - *ML*) and show him grace in the Olam Haba (afterlife), and he will be included in the group of tzadikim (righteous), as written *"And a redeemer shall come to Zion, and to those who repent of transgression in Jacob, says the L-ord"* (Yeshaya 59:20), and *"If you return, O Israel, says the L-ord, to Me you shall return"* (Yirmiya 4:1), and *"thus says the L-ord, If you return, then will I bring you again, and you shall stand before Me"* (Yirmiya 15:19).

## *** CHAPTER 5 ***

The conditions of the (four) essential components of repentance are exceedingly numerous. I will only mention, of them, twenty conditions. Hence we will clarify five conditions for each of the four components. Through these conditions, the corresponding components will be complete.

(*Tov Halevanon*: The essential components are general principles, while the conditions are branches of them.
The conditions are exceedingly numerous since every penitent needs many tikunim (rectifications) according to the nature of the sin, the nature of the sinner, and the factors which led him to sin.)

Among the conditions for regret, the following five:
(1) To fear the imminent punishment of the Creator for the sins he already committed, and that his remorse intensifies due to this, as written *"Give glory to the L-ord your God, before He causes darkness, [and before your feet stumble upon the dark mountains, and, while you look for light, He turns it into the shadow of death, and makes it to deep gloom]"* (Yirmiya 13:16). (i.e. before troubles dim his eyes or that death strikes him - *TL*)

(*Tov Halevanon*: "the imminent punishment" - the sinner should imagine as if a sword is drawn out for him, and he is being taken immediately to the execution platform to be punished for his crimes.)

(2) He should be broken hearted and humbled before G-d due to his sins, as written *"If My people, upon whom My Name is called, will humble themselves [and pray and seek My presence and repent of their evil ways, then I shall hear from heaven and forgive their sin...]"* (Divrei Hayamim II 7:14).

(*Pas Lechem*: i.e. besides fear of punishment, through reflecting in his heart on G-d's greatness - he will regret. This is yirat haromemut [fear of G-d's greatness. #1 previously was fear of punishment.])

(3) He should change his clothing and adornments and show signs of remorse in his speech in his eating, and in all of his conducts, as written *"Because of this, gird yourselves with sackcloth, lament and wail [for the fierce anger of the L-ord has not turned back from us]"* (Yirmiya 4:8), and *"Let man and beast be covered with sackcloth [and cry mightily unto G-d, let them turn every one from his evil way, and from the oppression that is in*

*their hands]"* (Yona 3:8).

(4) By tears, lamentations, and mourning, the penitent should express remorse for the sin he had committed, as written *"Rivers of waters run down my eyes because they did not keep Your commandments"* (Tehilim 119:136), and *"Let the priests, the ministers of the L-ord, weep between the porch and the altar"* (Yoel 2:17)

> (*Marpe Lenefesh*: Because the eyes and the heart are the gates of sin - "The eye sees, and the heart desires, and then the body commits the deed" (Bamidbar Rabba). And the wise man wrote (Sefer Chasidim siman 9): "nothing stops desire like closing of the eyes")

(5) He should rebuke his soul and inwardly shame it for not having fulfilled his obligations to the exalted Creator, as written *"And tear your hearts, and not your garments, and turn unto the L-ord your G-d"* (Yoel 2:13).

> (*Tov Halevanon*: To shame and humiliate his soul for ingraining in his heart lusts and bad thoughts.
> *"And tear your hearts"* - to abstain from his soul's lusts, and to straighten the crookedness of his heart [by shaming and rebuking himself,etc.])

The conditions for renouncing (of sin) are also five, as follows:
(1) Abandonment of everything the Creator has warned against, as written *"Hate the evil and love the good"* (Amos 5:15), and *"...guards his hand from doing any evil"* (Yeshaya 56:2), and *"let the wicked abandon his way"* (Yeshaya 55:7).

> (*Tov Halevanon*: To completely renounce everything the Creator has prohibited, and to remove desire for them from his heart, and not yearn for them at all, just like one does not yearn for something very remote from him. For example, one who has a hundred silver coins will certainly not lust for 1 million gold coins because it seems unattainable to him. How much more so, to not desire for something the Creator has prohibited which should seem even more remote.)

(2) Abstaining from what is permitted if it might lead to what is forbidden in cases where one is in doubt whether they are permitted or forbidden. It is said of some of the pious, that they would refrain from seventy kinds of permitted things out of fear of taking one kind that is forbidden. This is like the Rabbinic fences which our sages commanded us, in saying *"make fences for the torah"* (Avos 1:1).

(3) Abandonment of sin while one has the ability and opportunity to repeat it, and that he refrains from doing it only out of fear of the punishment of the Creator, as written *"My flesh bristles from fright of You, and I dread Your judgments"* (Tehilim 119:120)

(4) That one abandons sin out of a feeling of shame from the Creator, and not out of fear of human beings or because one hopes for some benefit from them, or out of being ashamed of them. He should not be like those which the verse speaks of: *"with their lips they honor Me, but their heart is far away from Me. their reverence for Me consists of tradition learned by rote"* (Yeshaya 29:13), and *"Yehoash did what was proper in the eyes of the L-rd all the days that Yehoyada the priest instructed him"* (Melachim II 12:3, which implies after the death of Yehoyada, his teacher, he stopped doing what was proper).

(5) That one abandons the evil, a permanent abandonment - to not enter in his heart to repeat it. He should resolve in his heart and say in speech what the pious man said: *"if I have done iniquity, I will do so no more"* (Iyov 34:32).

The conditions for beseeching forgiveness are also five:
(1) The penitent should confess his sins, and realize their enormity in his eyes and in his heart, as written *"For our transgressions against You are many, and our sins have testified against us"* (Yeshaya 59:12).

(*Tov Halevanon*: *"realize their enormity"* - when he compares his puniness and insignificance relative to the loftiness of the King of kings, the holy One, blessed be He, which he transgressed against.)

(2) That he recalls them always, and places them before him, opposite his face, as written *"For I know my transgressions, and my sin is ever before me"* (Tehilim 51:5).

(3) He should fast by day and pray at night, the time when his mind is free and he is not distracted by secular matters, as written *"Arise, cry out in the night, [.. Pour out your heart like water before the presence of the L-ord]"* (Eicha 2:19). I will later explain the greatness of prayer at night, with G-d's help (Gate 10 chapter 6).

(4) That one pleas to G-d and constantly beseeches Him to atone for his sins, forgive him, and accept his repentance, as written *"Therefore, let every one who is pious pray to You at the time that You are found"* (Tehilim

32:6), and *"I acknowledged my sin to You, And my iniquity I did not hide; I said, 'I will confess my transgressions to the L-ord'; And You forgave the guilt of my sin"* (Tehilim 32:5).

(5) That one labors and exerts himself to warn other people of sins similar to his, and arouse them to fear the punishments incurred [by the sins], and remind them to repent from them, as written *"Perhaps G-d will turn and relent, and turn away from his fierce anger, that we perish not?"* (Yona 3:9), and *"I will teach transgressors Your ways, and sinners will return to You"* (Tehilim 51:15).

The conditions for resolving to not repeat what the Creator warned against are also five:
(1) To weigh an immediate pleasure which is fleeting and mixed (with pain - *TL*) against a future, constant and everlasting pleasure, pure with no darkness and without any mixture of pain. And to weigh an immediate, fleeting pain (in doing a mitzvah or in breaking his lust for a sin - *ML*), which is without permanence, against a future pain, which is everlasting and without interruption.

Regarding the pleasure (in the afterlife), it is written: *"And when you see this, your heart shall rejoice"* (Yeshaya 66:14), and *"the sun of mercy shall rise with healing in its wings for you who fear My Name. Then will you go forth and be rich as fatted calves"* (Malachi 3:20), while regarding the pain it is written: *"And they shall go forth, and look upon the carcasses of the men that have transgressed against Me: for their worm shall not die (i.e. everlasting - TL), neither shall their fire ever be quenched (i.e. without interruption - TL); [and they shall be an eternal abhorrence unto all flesh]"* (Yeshaya 66:24), and *"For lo, the day comes, that shall burn like a furnace, and all the audacious sinners and all the perpetrators of wickedness shall be stubble. And the sun that comes shall burn them up so that it will leave them neither root nor branch, says the L-ord of Hosts"* (Malachi 3:19). When the sinner puts this matter to heart, he will deem it proper to take on himself not to repeat his sin.

(2) He should put to heart the coming of his day of death, when the Creator will be furious on him for having neglected his duties, as written "Now who can endure the day of His coming (the great day of judgment - *TL*), and who will stand when He appears, for He will be like a blazing fire that refines metal" (Malachi 3:2). If he puts this to heart, he is bound to fear His punishment, and will resolve strongly not to repeat what will arouse the

wrath of the Creator on him.

(3) He should put to heart the days during which he turned away from G-d, and did not care about His service, in spite of His continuous goodness towards him during then, as written: *"For of old I broke your yoke, I tore open your yoke-bands, and you said, 'I will not pass'"* (Yirmiya 2:20), the explanation of *"I will not pass"* is: *"I will not take on Your service, and will not enter Your covenant"*, as if he said *"I will not pass in Your covenant"*, similar to the matter *"to pass you over the covenant of the L-rd your G-d"* (Devarim 29:11).

(4) He should return stolen things and refrain from sin, and from doing harm to any human being, as written: *"The wicked man shall return the pledge, he will repay the theft; [in the statutes of life he walked, not to commit injustice - he will surely live, he will not die]"* (Yechezkel 33:15), and *"If iniquity be in your hand, put it far away, and let not wickedness dwell in your tents; For then shall you lift up your face without shame"* (Iyov 11:14).

> (*Pas Lechem*: *"(1) return stolen things, (2) refrain from sin, and (3) from doing harm to any human being"* - he specified three expressions corresponding to the teaching in the talmud (Bava Basra 165a) "most are guilty of theft, few in forbidden relations, and all in evil speech", the latter's intent is solely to harm since there is no benefit...)

(5) His mind should reflect on the greatness of the Creator, whose word he rebelled against - casting off the yoke of His service (positive commandments), and removing the ropes of His torah (negative commandments), and one should rebuke himself and shame himself for this, as written *"Is this how you repay the L-ord, [you disgraceful, unwise people?! Is He not your Father, your Master? He has made you and established you]"* (Devarim 32:6), and *"Will you not fear Me? says the L-ord, or, do you not quake from before Me, for I made sand a boundary for the sea, an everlasting ordinance, which it cannot pass"* (Yirmiya 5:22).

> (*Pas Lechem*: *"Is this how you repay the L-ord"* - corresponding to reflecting on His greatness, *"you disgraceful, unwise people"*, corresponding to rebuking and shaming oneself, *"is He not your Father, your Master? He has made you.."* to clarify the matter in the way of debating [with oneself].
> *"Will you not fear Me?"* - also corresponds to reflecting on His greatness.)

In this, we have completed the requirements of repentance.

## *** CHAPTER 6 ***

- which things stir a man to repent

The stirring of a person to repentance occurs through one of four ways:
(1) It is stirred by a person's strengthening himself in the recognition of
G-d (His greatness -PL), reflecting on the constant goodness he receives,
and realizing of what is his duty in exchange for it of the service [of G-d],
of observing His commandments and of refraining from what He
prohibited.

He is like a slave who ran away from his master and then when he reflects
on the good his master bestowed on him, he will return to him of his own
free will to beseech his forgiveness for rebelling against him and fleeing
from his service. This kind of slave has chosen the right way and
understands the path which leads to his salvation (from punishment) - it is
proper to forgive him and accept him.

Of (a penitent) like him it is said: *"If you return, O Israel, says the L-rd, to
Me, you shall return, and if you remove your abominations from My sight
and will not wander; And you will swear by My Name in truth and in
justice and in righteousness, nations will bless themselves with you and
boast about you"* (Yirmiya 4:1)

The explanation is as follows: *"If you repent willingly before the
punishment comes on you, I will accept your repentance, and choose you
for My service, and if you remove your abominations from My face and you
don't move and you don't run away from My service, and you swear in My
name in truth, and your heart will faithfully return to Me, if you repent
with all the conditions (i.e. remove abominations of your own free will, etc
- TL) the nations will bless and praise themselves that: '(would that it were
that) we should be like you"*.
It is also said: *"return to Me and I will return to you"* (Malachi 3:7).

(2) When the Creator rebukes and humiliates him on his evil ways and
deeds, whether through the prophet of his generation, if he lives in the era
of prophecy, or from the Torah of G-d (i.e. the 2 strong rebukes there [in
parsha Bechukotai and Ki Tavo], and the other places of rebuke - *PL*), or
through a Rabbi who preaches to him on the service of G-d. And this is
grounds for a charge by G-d against all of humanity, since no generation is

ever without such a guide, as our sages said "Before the sun of Moshe Rabeinu has set (his death), the sun of Yehoshua his disciple had risen, before the sun of Eli set, the sun of Samuel rose, before the sun of Elijah set, the sun of Elisha rose. The day Rebbi Akiva died, Rebbi HaKadosh was born" (Kidushin 72b), and in this way it can be found in every generation and in every land, there is never an absence of a preacher who calls to G-d and His service, and teaches His torah.

A penitent stirred this way is like a slave who ran away from the service of his master. He then met another slave who was faithful to his master, who rebuked him for fleeing from his master, and advised him to return, and assured him that the master will forgive him. He reminded him of the abundant goodness and kindness that he had received. The slave returned and humbled himself to his master.

(3) When one observes the trials and severe punishments the Creator meted out to a person who followed the path he himself is following, in leaving G-d's service, and he will be reproved by it and return to G-d because he fears G-d's punishment and severe retribution. He is like a slave who ran away from his master. When he heard the punishment another slave like him received for running away, he became reproved by it and returned to his master pleading him to forgive him and pardon his sin before his punishment comes. Thus, the verse says: *"And let the land not vomit you out for having defiled it, as it vomited out the nations that preceded you"* (Vayikra 18:28).

(4) When the punishment of the Creator comes on him, in the form of some type of tribulation. Since he sensed (the message early), he awakened and got up from his slumber, and repented to G-d his sin. He is like a slave who ran away from his master, and the master dispatched an emissary to punish him and beat him for running away from his service. When the emissary reached him, he ran back to his master, confessing his sin and seeking forgiveness. On one like him, it is said: *"when your fear comes like a storm, and your calamity comes like a whirlwind; when trouble and straits come upon you; then they will call Me, but I will not answer; [they shall seek Me, but they shall not find Me; Because they hated knowledge, and did not choose the fear of the L-ord;]"* (Mishlei 1:27), and *"And when he was distressed, he entreated the L-ord his G-d, and he humbled himself greatly before the G-d of his fathers"* (Divrei Hayamim II 33:12).

| (*Tov Halevanon*: Even though repentance always helps, even after the

punishment comes, and even in lower levels than this, but that is from the aspect of the kindness of G-d, whereas this verse is referring to the aspect of *"wisdom"* [i.e. strict justice]...)

The most successful (in being spared from punishment - *PL*) and most accepted (for being considered henceforth a faithful servant - *PL*) is the one who repented to G-d in the first case (on his own). Below him in success and acceptance is the second case: he who did not repent until being alarmed by the Creator's rebuke; below them in success and acceptance is the one who did not repent until punishment inflicts those around him. Below him in acceptance and return is he who did not repent until punishment was inflicted on him and made him suffer.

(*Pas Lechem*: Here the author does not use the term *"success"*, which refers to being spared from punishment, since behold he was already inflicted with punishment, he suffered, and was purged of his sin. For this the author substituted the term *"success"* with *"return"*, which means that he heals from the wounds of his punishment and recovers to his former state.)

He is the furthest of the penitent and the least likely that G-d will accept his repentance and pardon his sin unless he repents to G-d, and demonstrates regret, abandonment, beseeching forgiveness in heart, speech, and movements, to an extent that will make him fitting to be pardoned and to accept his repentance and to overlook his sin.

(*Pas Lechem*: the other penitents, have their repentance accepted immediately, when they start to repent, unlike this penitent who is not accepted and pardoned until he fulfills all the conditions of repentance, and then he will be accepted by the blessed Creator.)

# *** CHAPTER 7 ***

- things detrimental to repentance

The things detrimental to repentance are very numerous. I have already mentioned most of them previously (these are all the things detrimental to wholehearted devotion to God and everything mentioned in Chapter 4 of Gate #5 - *TL*). Some additional detrimental things: complacency in doing the sin, which means persisting in doing the sin, and delaying to [resolve to - PL] abandon it. As long as this condition continues, it is not possible to repent.

There is a saying: "no sin is small if done persistently, and no sin is big if one beseeches forgiveness for it". The explanation: doing a sin persistently reflects one's disregard for the word of G-d, and that he regards His commandment and prohibition lightly, and so invites on himself punishment. Of such a person, it is said: *"But if a person should act highhandedly, whether he is a native born or a proselyte, he is blaspheming the L-ord, [and that soul shall be cut off from among its people]"* (Bamidbar 15:30).

Furthermore, persistence in sin, even though it is small, it continuously grows by his repeating it. While, for a big sin, when its owner beseeches forgiveness for it, and abandons it out of fear of G-d, it gradually reduces and shrinks until it is entirely erased from one's book of sins, and its owner is purged from it with repentance.

> (*Tov Halevanon*: For the biggest of sins, if he abandons it and beseeches forgiveness, it is not considered anything, whereas even the smallest of sins, when repeated many times, is considered extremely big.
> *"invites on himself punishment"* - invites death on himself.
>
> *Pas Lechem*: Even though the sin itself is small, nevertheless, the disregard of the Creator's honor which it demonstrates is big.)

You can see regarding a strand of silk how strong it becomes when it is doubled over many times, though it is made up of the weakest of material, namely the saliva of the silkworm. Consider the huge rope of boats. After a long time of use, the rope gradually wears out until it eventually breaks and the material returns to being the weakest of the weak.

Similarly for the matter of the smallness or largeness of sins, with regard to repeating them frequently or seeking forgiveness on them. Therefore, the verse compared them to a rope as written: *"Woe to those who draw iniquity with cords of falsehood, who draw sin as with cart ropes"* (Yeshaya 5:18).

It was already said: "do not look at the minuteness of what you committed, but rather look at the [infinite] greatness of He who you sin against."

(*Tov Halevanon*: i.e. even for the smallest of sins, if you persist in it, you are being light with the command and prohibition of the Creator. Know with Whom you are being light.)

Do not rejoice that others cannot recognize your hidden bad deeds, but rather it is proper to mourn because the Creator knows that which you are concealing, sees your hidden thoughts and revealed acts, and that He will remind you of them, more than you will remember of them, because you forget, but He does not forget. You will ignore them, but He will not ignore them, as written: *"Behold, it is written before Me [I will not keep silent, but will repay, even repay into their bosom]"* (Yeshaya 65:6), *"The sin of Judah is written with a pen of iron, and with the point of a diamond"* (Yirmiya 17:1).

(*Tov Halevanon*: *"but rather it is proper to mourn"* - since only the Creator knows of them, because then you will receive full punishment. For if people knew of them and shamed you for them, your punishment will already be reduced. This is similar to what the author wrote earlier in Gate#5 chapter 5 regarding when the evil inclination comes from the side of arrogance.)

Another detrimental thing: To return to the sin, after completing all the conditions of repentance from it, as written in its chapter: *"the word which came to Yirmiyahu...to proclaim freedom, that every man should let his manservant and every man his maidservant.."* (Yirmiya 34:8), and the rest of the matter.

Another detrimental thing also: That one assures himself that he will repent in his later years, and thinks he will refrain from sins after he is satisfied and has obtained his desires in them. He is like one trying to cheat G-d. Regarding him, the sages said: "one who says: 'I will sin then repent, I will sin then repent', will be prevented from doing repentance" (Yoma 85b).

In the Tochecha (rebuke) section I wrote at the end of this book, (I wrote): "O my soul, prepare many provisions, do not be scant while you are still alive and have the opportunity, because the journey before you (after death - *TL*) is exceedingly long (and you need much provisions for such a long journey - *TL*). Do not say tomorrow I will take provisions, because the day is closing and you don't know what the day may bring. Realize that yesterday will never return and all that you did was weighed, written, and accounted for. Don't say tomorrow I will do my duty, because the day of death is hidden from every living creature. Hasten to do every day's portion, because like a bird is driven from its nest, so too a man is driven from his place".

Another detrimental thing: That the penitent repents on part of his sins but continues in others. For example, he stopped from the sins between man and G-d, and repented on them, but did not stop from what is between himself and other men, such as theft, ona'a (overcharging money), or the like. On this it was said: *"if iniquity is in your hands - distance it far away"* (Iyov 11:14). And our sages said: "R. Adda b. Ahaba said: One who has sinned and confessed his sin but does not repent may be compared to a man holding an [spiritually] unclean reptile in his hand. For although he may immerse himself in all the waters of the world his immersion is of no avail unto him; but if he throws it away from his hand, then as soon as he immerses himself, immediately his immersion becomes effective, as it is said: "one who confesses and abandons them shall obtain mercy" (Taanis 16a).

The detrimental things we mentioned in previous gates of this book, all of them are also detrimental to repentance, and there is no need to repeat them in this gate.

## \*\*\* CHAPTER 8 \*\*\*

- the penitent and the tzadik

If the penitent is equal to the tzadik (righteous person). On this I say: (1) sometimes a penitent is equal after repentance to the tzadik who never sinned, (2) sometimes he is greater than the tzadik, and (3) sometimes the tzadik is greater than him even though he repented.

The explanation of the first case: That the lacking was in a positive commandment which does not carry the punishment of Karet (spiritual excision), such as tzitzit, lulav, sukka, or the like. When the person repents on them in his heart and in speech, and exerts himself to fulfill them, and does not repeat his neglect to do them, the Creator will forgive him, and he will be equal to the tzadik who never sinned in them. On such a penitent, it is said: "one who repents from a sin is as if he never sinned", and our sages said of them: (Yoma 86a) "one who transgressed a positive commandment which does not incur Karet (spiritual excision) and repented - he is forgiven right away, as written: 'return to Me and I will return to you' (Malachi 3:7)".

For the second case, where the penitent becomes greater than the tzadik, the explanation is that the penitent committed a minor sin of the negative commandments, such as one which does not carry the punishment of Karet, and afterwards fully repents with all the conditions of repentance. He places his sin before him and opposite his face, and always beseeches for forgiveness of it. He feels full of shame before the Creator, his heart penetrated by the fear of the punishment, his spirit is broken (i.e. his lusts - PL). He always submits and humbles himself before G-d, and the sin becomes a cause for his submission and for his endeavoring to fulfill his debts to the Creator. He does not become haughty in the least for his good deeds and they do not amount to much in his eyes. He does not glorify himself in it and guards from stumbling for the rest of his life - such a sinner, is the one who is greater than the tzadik who never sinned this sin or others like it. For the tzadik is not assured that his heart will not become proud and haughty for his deeds. It was said that "sometimes a sin is more useful to the penitent than all the righteous deeds of the tzadik, and sometimes a good deed damages the tzadik more than all the sins of the penitent". This applies when the tzadik turns his heart away from submission and grows pride, flattery (hypocrisy), and love of praise.

One of the righteous would say to his students: "if you were completely without any sins, I would be afraid for you, on what is worse than sin", they said, "what is worse than sin?" He answered, "pride and flattery". Regarding a penitent like this, our Sages said: "In the place where the penitent stands, the perfectly righteous cannot stand" (Berachos 34b).

> (*Pas Lechem*: *"pride and flattery"* - that he becomes proud of his deeds, even though in the beginning he did them l'shem shamayim (wholeheartedly to G-d). Through this he will come to the trait of flattery, to do it from the beginning hypocritically - to appear honorable and important in the hearts of those who see him. After this, he will love and endeavor that others praise him in speech.)

For the third case, (where the tzadik is greater than the penitent), this is where the penitent transgressed big sins of the negative commandments which carry the punishment of death by Beit Din or Karet from the heavenly court, such as Chilul H-shem (desecration of G-d's Name - i.e. causing others to sin - *ML*), false oaths, or others like these of the severe sins. The person afterwards repented from his evil path, and fulfilled all the conditions and requirements of repentance. In this case, forgiveness will not be granted until he receives suffering in this world with what he will be able to bear and so be cleansed of his sins. On this kind of penitent our sages said (Yoma 86a): "If he has committed a sin punishable by Karet or death through Beit Din, and repented, suffering cleans him and death completes the atonement, as written 'I shall punish their transgression with a rod, and their iniquity with afflictions' (Tehilim 89:33)", and *"certainly this iniquity shall not be atoned for you until you die"* (Yeshaya 22:14). Without any doubt, the Tzadik who never transgressed these types of sins is greater than the penitent in them.

## *** CHAPTER 9 ***

- repentance on all sins

Whether or not repentance is effective for all sins, I will answer this question as follows: Sins are of two categories.
(1) Sins between man and G-d only. For example, denying the existence of G-d, bad thoughts, bad interior, transgressing negative commandments which apply to the heart, and many of the commandments on the limbs, where the sinner hurts only himself, and his only sin is to transgress the commandment of G-d.

(2) Sins between man and his fellow. These have matters of oppression and wickedness towards other people, whether to their bodies, possessions or reputation. In these, the sinner combines two forms of affliction: one, for himself in rebelling against G-d and two in afflicting other people.

The sins which are between man and G-d alone, it is possible to repent on them during the whole of his lifetime, whenever he arouses himself from his lacking, and endeavors to turn away from his sin and repent to the Creator.

If possible, it is proper that his repentance from the sin be related to the sin he did. For example, if his sin was in the duties of the heart, such as maintaining a bad heart, evil thoughts, bearing a grudge, jealousy, hatred or the like, the proper repentance for this consists of cultivating a good heart and good thoughts, love of doing good to others, and forgiving them.

If his sin was in the physical limbs, such as eating what the Creator forbade to eat, forbidden relations, transgressing the Sabbath or the festivals, or false oaths, it is proper for his repentance to refer to the particular sinful act and also to the class the act belongs to. All the while, he should have intent of heart towards G-d. (i.e. not to become important in the eyes of human beings - *PL*)

(*Tov Halevanon*: Regarding each matter, to do whatever is possible. [Example:] For prohibited food, to afflict himself with fasting, with forbidden relations, to guard from [unnecessarily] looking at women or speaking to them, for Sabbath and festivals, to minimize his [useless] speech or strolling on the Sabbath, for swearing falsely, to not swear even for the truth.)

All this is possible for a man during his lifetime, if he lives long enough, and only if his intent is to repent and cleanse his soul of its sin before his Creator. Concerning such a penitent, the wise man said: *"If you are wise, you are wise for yourself, And if you scoff, you alone will bear it"* (Mishlei 9:12).

(*Pas Lechem*: *"if he lives long enough"* - i.e. to not procrastinate his repentance thinking he still has much time to live, since behold, the repentance needs a long time, therefore how can he push it off?)

But for the sins towards both G-d and man, it will be difficult to repent for several reasons:

1. He may not be able to find the person he oppressed, or the person died or moved far away.

2. The oppressor lost the money, and he is not able to return it to the oppressed.

3. Perhaps the oppressed will not forgive him for what he oppressed him or hurt him physically, or spoke badly of him.

4. The oppressor may not know whom he oppressed, or he does not know the amount of money involved. For example, if he oppressed the people of a city or a province, and he does not recognize them, and he does not know the amount of money he took from them wrongfully.

5. The forbidden money was mixed with a much greater amount of permitted money, and he cannot return it without incurring a much greater loss, as our sages said: "One who stole a beam and used it in the building of a palace. Beit Shamai says: 'dismantle the palace and return the beam', Beit Hillel says: 'he can return the value of the beam only, because of the enactment for the penitent' " (Gitin 55a) (which implies it is not a full repentance and it is better to return the beam itself only that there is a [rabbinic] enactment... - *TL*).

6. That the repentance becomes too difficult for him, such as when a person became accustomed to doing it until the bad deed attached to him and became part of his nature, and it will not be easy for him to abandon it, as written: *"they have taught their tongue to speak lies, and weary themselves to commit iniquity"* (Yirmiya 9:4), and *"Can the Ethiopian change his skin, or the leopard his spots? [then may you also do good, those that are accustomed to doing evil]"* (Yirmiya 13:23).

7. Spilling blood or killing the innocent, whether he killed them directly or whether he caused their deaths through slander, as you know of the matter of Doeg and the city of Kohanim, who caused them to be sentenced to death first through his slander, and later executed them himself, as written: *"Then the king said to Doeg, 'You turn around and attack the priests.' And Doeg the Edomite turned around and attacked the priests, and he killed that day eighty-five men who wore the linen priestly ephod"* (Shmuel 22:18).

8. One who causes his fellow to lose money on account of slander, his repentance does not avail until he makes amends with him, whether by paying him or by beseeching him with words and humbling himself before him to forgive him and pardon his wrong, as written: *"and those who ate the flesh of My people and did flay the skin from upon them...then they shall cry out to the L-ord, but He will not answer them"* (Micha 3:3).

9. One who had forbidden relations (punishable by Kores) and fathers a mamzer (illegitimate child) - the disgrace will never leave, and the wrong cannot be corrected, as written: *"For that is lewdness, and it is iniquity to be punished by the judges; For it is fire; it consumes to destruction"* (Iyov 31:11), and *"They betrayed the L-ord for they begot strange children"* (Hoshea 5:7).

10. One who habituated his tongue to lie and to speak of the faults of others, and to denigrate them. For he cannot remember all of what he said and all those who he spoke about due to the countless words, and forgetting the people he spoke against. It is all guarded against him and recorded in the book of his sins. On him it is said: *"And if he comes to see me, he speaks vanity: his heart gathers iniquity to itself; when he goes abroad, he tells it"* (Tehilim 41:7), and *"When you saw a thief, you are pleased with him, and you keep company with adulterers"* (Tehilim 50:18), and the rest of the matter. Behold, the verse equated evil speech with theft and adultery. So too, it is said *"they deceive (corrupt) one another and do not speak the truth; they have taught their tongue to speak lies, they commit iniquity until they are weary"* (Yirmiya 9:4).

11. One for who repentance will be extremely hard for him: he who enticed people with a false religion that he invented and influenced them to believe in it. He sinned and caused others to sin, the more people join his false beliefs, the more his sin will increase and be multiplied over, as the sages

said: "Whoever leads the masses in the right path will not come to any sin, but whoever leads the masses astray will not be able to repent for all the wrong he commits.. Yeravam ben Nevat, sinned and caused the multitude to sin, and so the sin of the masses is ascribed to him as it is written (I Kings 15:30) 'Because of the sins of Yeravam that he committed and that he caused Israel to commit.' " (Avos 5:18)

Included in this last category is one who is capable of bringing others to the good and steer the erring away from evil, but refrains from doing so due to hoping to receive money from them or due to being afraid of them, or being ashamed to rebuke them, and they went off, and he did not teach them the right way, as written: *"if you do not speak to warn the wicked, that wicked man shall die in his iniquity; and I will hold you accountable for their blood"* (Yechezkel 33:8).

# *** CHAPTER 10 ***

What strategy should be adopted by one for whom repentance is difficult? We will answer this question as follows:

One who has transgressed a sin for which repentance is difficult, the particular sin necessarily falls into one of two categories. One, that the sin is between him and G-d. Two, that the sin is between him and his fellow men, such as overcharging, various types of theft and trickery, violence, and oppression.

Whatever category it belongs to, if the repentance is difficult due to one of the factors we previously mentioned (last chapter) which cause repentance to be difficult, then, if the person takes on himself to fulfill the requirements of repentance with all its conditions to the utmost extent that is in his power and ability to do, the Creator will make his repentance easier. He will pardon what is hidden from him and not in his ability to do, and will give him a nearer exit for deliverance from his sin and allow him to absolve himself in this way (as will be explained).

If the sin is in the category of forbidden relations, which we mentioned, for one who fathers from an illicit relation (a mamzer), the Creator will wipe out his descendants (from the mamzer).

If it is from overcharging or theft of money, G-d will give him money to pay back his fellow and appease him so that the latter will forgive him.

If he hurt his fellow physically or damaged his possessions, the Creator will put in his fellow's heart favor and love until he forgives him for his sin towards him, as written: *"When the L-ord favors a person's ways, He will cause even his enemies to make peace with him"* (Mishlei 16:7).

If the oppressed is far away, the Creator will arrange their meeting, and the oppressor will humble himself before the oppressed and will be forgiven by him.

If he doesn't know the number of people he oppressed and the amount of money he took, the Creator will give him the opportunity to spend his money in some kind of public project, such as building a bridge, digging a well to benefit the public, or digging water pits in roads where water is scarce, or other similar things to benefit the public, until the project will serve the one he oppressed and also the one he did not oppress.

If the oppressed died, he should return the money to his heirs. If he hurt him physically or he spoke badly of him, he should confess at his grave with a minyan of ten Jews and he will be forgiven for his sin, as our sages on this matter said: "And if he had died, he should bring ten Jews and to stand by his grave and say: I have sinned against the L-ord, the G-d of Israel, and against this man, whom I have hurt." (Yoma 87a).

Repentance is not withheld from a sinner, rather the obstruction comes from his own wickedness and deceitful heart. But if he sincerely wants to draw near to G-d, the gate of repentance will not be closed before him, and no obstacle will prevent him from reaching it. Rather, G-d will open for him the gate of the just, and teach him the good path in His mercy and in His goodness, as written *"Good and upright is the L-ord: therefore will he teach sinners in the way"* (Tehilim 25:8), and *"from there you will seek the L-ord your G-d, and you will find Him, if you seek Him with all your heart and with all your soul"* (Devarim 4:29), and *"Rather,[this] thing (repentance) is very close to you; it is in your mouth and in your heart, so that you can do it"* (Devarim 30:14), and *"The L-ord is near to all who call upon Him, To all who call upon Him in truth"* (Tehilim 145:18).

FINAL WORDS

I have already clarified for you, my brother, some of the obligations of repentance, and I revealed to you some of the ways to return (to G-d). Now, there are grounds for a claim against you, and your escapes are gone. What will you answer tomorrow to G-d? - "I was ignorant (that I needed to repent)" - but you were not ignorant! Or maybe you will answer: "I did what I did, but I didn't know (how to repent)".

What will be your answer to this question? And there's no doubt that we will be asked. Prepare the repentance while (G-d) is still pushing off (your punishment, to give you an opportunity to repent). Know my brother that the answer to this question will not be acceptable with our words but only with our deeds. Think to yourself, make a personal accounting of how you can obtain favor from your Creator, know that only one who hastens will reach the good, and the fruit of not doing enough will be regret.

Wake up my brother from the slumber of your simplemindedness. Have mercy on your soul, which is the most important deposit of all the deposits the Creator entrusted by you. How long, and how much longer will you procrastinate in this? You have already consumed your days gratifying your selfish desires, like a base slave, now return and finish your remaining days following the desire of your Creator. You already know that the lifetime of a man is brief, and what remains of your life is still briefer, as our sages said: "the day is short and the workload is great" (Avos 2:15).

You have, my brother, a precious and exalted spirit. With it, you honored this fleeting and lowly world and you abandoned your end that you will be left with. Should you not lift up your spirit to think of that exalted place, the high abode, the place where the spirits which ascend to there will not be lowered from their exaltedness forever. Hurry, while the gates of repentance are open and the acceptance and atonement are still available, as written *"Seek the L-ord while He is found, call to Him while He is still near"* (Yeshaya 55:6).

Hurry my brother, hurry before the horror you dread comes, because you are not assured that you will live for even one more day. Examine yourself with a careful and weighed examination according to what is proper and possible for one like you.

> (*Marpe Lenefesh*: *"careful and weighed"* - i.e. that you carefully examine to do everything according to your physical and mental strength - to not overburden yourself thereby losing everything, as he wrote at the end of gate 10 - "Proceed slowly and thoughtfully in acquiring the good traits, according to how your matters allow you to bear. Beware of taking on too much, or too quickly, without moving gradually, lest you become lost, because too much oil in a candle is a cause to extinguish its light")

And he who wants to obtain the favor of his Creator will enter through the narrow opening through which the pious who bear in this world (in the service of G-d). All of us hope for the good. But only those who hasten towards it will reach it, who run towards it, as our sages said: "Be bold as a leopard, light as an eagle, swift as a deer and mighty as a lion to do the will of your Father in Heaven" (Avos 5:23), and David said: *"I hastened and delayed not to keep Your commandments"* (Tehilim 119:60).

> (*Tov Halevanon*: *"all of us hope for the good"* - i.e. even though all of us hope for the good, and each person yearns for [the bliss of] the afterlife - the matter does not depend on desire and yearning, rather one must hasten towards it and exert oneself to acquire it.)

Take counsel with your soul. Be ashamed to act with your Creator in a way that you would be ashamed to act with even a human being like yourself. For, you know that if you angered even a low ranking official of the king, you would not delay to humble yourself to him, and to plea to him to forgive you, so that he will not punish you, even though he has little power in this. All the more so if a high ranking officer were to be angry at you, and even more so if it was the king himself, that you would hasten to seek forgiveness from him, show remorse to him, and try to appease him out of your fear of being swiftly punished.

Yet you already know (from the gate of trust of this book), his helplessness of being able to do anything without the decree of the Creator, as the wise man said: *"A king's heart is like rivulets of water in the L-ord's hand; wherever He wishes, He turns it"* (Mishlei 21:1). All this despite that (he may never get around to punishing you due to) his reign ending, his kingdom being overthrown, his mind confused or distracted by his numerous matters, forgetting or overlooking you. This happens for revealed things, all the more so for hidden things. Despite your knowledge of all of this, you would not delay to seek from him a pardon to your transgression. You would rush to do that which will appease him and be acceptable to him.

My brother, how then can we not be ashamed of our Creator, who observes what is revealed as well as what is concealed of all our deeds and thoughts. He is not subject to forgetting nor overlooking anything. No matter can distract Him from another matter. None can escape from His justice, and there is no end to His reign? How can we turn away from Him, or delay humbling ourselves before Him and repenting to Him, while we don't know our final end nor the number of days we have been allotted.

If a man were to visit a village or province and announce to the people saying: "People, be prepared to go on to the next world, for one of you will pass away this month (be executed by the king - *TL*), but I will not reveal who it is". Is it not proper for each person to prepare for death, for fear he is that man?

And we can see that every month, death consumes a large number of the living. Surely it is proper for us to fear for our souls every month, at least for one day, and to reflect on our matter and provisions and final destination before we need them, as our sages said: *"repent one day before your death"* (Avos 2:10), and *"at all times let your garments be white"*

(Koheles 9:8, i.e. that you are clean of sin).

> (*Marpe Lenefesh*: *"repent one day before your death"* - hence repent today, since perhaps you will die tomorrow.)

With your superior intellect and recognition examine what you see with your own eyes, and it will be clearer to you than if you had only heard it from someone else.

> (*Pas Lechem*: Just like regarding the previous analogy which you heard from someone else regarding a person who "visits a village and announces, etc.", that certainly it is proper that you would need to ready yourself and prepare provisions, so too let it be clear to you through that which you see with your own eyes, that "death consumes etc".)

Do not push away that which your intellect and understanding [obligate you to do - PL], since it was already said: the Creator bestows many good things to His servants (wisdom, etc), if they accept them (use them to serve Him), they will gain. But if they refuse them (use them to rebel against Him), they will become grounds for a claim against them, and afterwards a reason to exact retribution against them.

The Creator did good to you. He bestowed you with wisdom, understanding, and knowledge. He gave you of them more than another. Be careful, and be careful - that they don't turn to become grounds for a claim against you.

He has already stirred you to the straight way (through this book), and taught you the path leading to your good, out of mercy for you, and to guide you gently. He didn't want you to continue in your foolishness (in pursuing the vain worldly lusts - *PL*), and continue in your rebelliousness, He conducts with you in the way of kindness as befitting Him, and out of pity and mercy for His creations, as written *"Good and upright is the L-ord; therefore does He instruct sinners in the way"* (Tehilim 25:8). He has already called you gently and with a soft language, and afterwards with rebukes and embarrassments, and finally threatened you with His punishment, in order that you repent to Him, and speedily return to His service.

Hurry my brother, and hurry to lend ear to Him. Listen to His voice, and cling to Him. Choose for your soul what your G-d has chosen for it (the bliss of the afterlife - *PL*). Desire for it what your Creator desired for it. Do not allow laziness to make you lax in it, because if your own soul is light in your eyes, then what else will be important by you?

(*Tov Halevanon*: All of a man's labor is for himself. And if in losing his soul he is silent, then what does he desire further in all of his deeds?)

Be careful lest the thoughts of your mind (evil inclination) entice you saying: "Now?! After my long protracted neglect of the service of G-d, and the passing of most of my days, how can I now return to G-d and seek His forgiveness?!"

(*Tov Halevanon*: i.e. is it possible that after my protracted wickedness and the passing of most of my days in sin that G-d will accept my repentance?! Because it is incorrect. For even one who transgresses all sins during all of his days, but repents in the last one - G-d will have mercy on him.

*Marpe Lenefesh*: What, after most of my days have been wasted in sins, how could I lift up my face to repent to G-d, lest and perhaps He will not accept me? Don't say this since all the prophets, and also Moshe Rabeinu, have already proclaimed, that G-d will accept us in [our] repentance, and there is nothing that stands in the way of repentance...)

You should reply to him (the evil inclination) as the prophet spoke of this matter: *"And when the righteous turns from his righteousness and does wrong.... All his righteous deeds that he has done shall not be remembered; in his treachery that he has perpetrated and in his sin that he has sinned, in them shall he die.... And when a wicked man repents of his wickedness that he has done, and does justice and righteousness, he shall save his soul alive; Because he considered, and turned away from all his transgressions that he had committed, he shall surely live, he shall not die."* (Yechezkel 18:24-27), until the end of the matter.

(*Tov Halevanon*: To teach you that everything goes by the end of his deeds. For even one who was righteous all of his days but sinned in the end - he will die for the sin he committed.)

The early ones already compared this to a man who had in his possession silver coins, and he needed to cross a big river, when he reached the river bank, he threw all the coins in the river hoping to slow its flow and walk over the coins, and he threw all of them except for one that remained in his hand, and the current was not stopped by the coins, when he saw this, he said to one of the sailors who happened to pass on the river: "take this coin which is in my hand, and take me through the river with your boat". The sailor did this, and the man reached his desire with the remaining coin that was in his hand. He accomplished more with that coin than all the coins he lost in the river, and it was as if he didn't lose anything.

Likewise, a baal teshuva (penitent) who wasted most of his life in things other than the service of G-d, if he repents at the end of his days, the Creator will forgive him for all of what happened of the bad deeds of all of his previous days, as written: *"None of his transgressions that he had committed shall be remembered against him; [for his righteousness that he had done he shall live]"* (Yechezkel 18:22), and *"None of his sins that he had committed shall be remembered against him; [he performed justice and righteousness; he shall surely live]"* (Yechezkel 33:16).

Let it not be too wearying, my brother, my exhorting you on guarding yourself, which you have neglected for so long to do. Because I am speaking not only to you but to myself also. Submit to the truth. Do not run away from it. Thank the Al-mighty who aroused you on that which you did not know, and let not the long hiding of other people be an excuse for you, because this is one of the distortions and snare of the yetzer (evil inclination) for people who are of weak understanding.

> (*Marpe Lenefesh*: do not bring a proof from wicked people who persist in their foolishness and wickedness and never even think of repenting. Perhaps they are even doing well and full of prosperity... take heed and guard yourself from bringing a proof from such blind and wicked people since this is a snare of the yetzer to entice you and others like you.)

May the Al-mighty place us among those who hurry towards him, who repent to Him wholeheartedly, in His mercy. Amen.

# ****** SHAAR CHESHBON HANEFESH - THE GATE OF SPIRITUAL ACCOUNTING ******

# *** Introduction ***

The author says: Since our previous discussion dealt with the essentials of repentance and its conditions, and making a spiritual accounting was one of those conditions, I saw proper to follow with a clarification of the matter of making an accounting with oneself, because this contains matters to arouse oneself for things beneficial in both worlds, as David, peace be unto him, said: *"I reflected on my ways, and turned my feet unto Your testimonies"* (Tehilim 119:59).

> *Matanas Chelko*: David would always make a cheshbon (accounting) where he should go, and he always decided that the best path to go is only the one which brings him to Torah.

It is proper for us to clarify six matters on the subject of the spiritual accounting.
1. What is meant by making a spiritual accounting with oneself?
2. If the accounting is equal for all individuals or not.
3. how many ways should one bring himself to an accounting?
4. What are the benefits of this accounting?
5. Whether the spiritual accounting is a constant duty.
6. Which activities should follow the accounting?

> *Matanas Chelko*: Behold, by servants of G-d, the term "Cheshbon HaNefesh" (spiritual accounting) usually means the accounting of their deeds to examine whether they were good or evil. Namely, that at the end of the day or the week, or the like, they make an accounting of the deeds they did or did not do, whether the mitzvot they did were done properly, whether they stood up to trials and did not fall into sin. Likewise, for their middot (character traits), whether they exerted themselves properly to correct them or they stumbled in one of them.
>
> However, in this gate, Rabeinu's explanation and intent is for a spiritual accounting of a different type. Namely, for careful accountings (cheshbonot) through which a person comes to feel in his soul and rouse his heart that it is his duty (mutal alav) to toil in the service of the Creator and that he is obligated to fulfill His commandments and words. For behold, a man could serve G-d like a soldier in an army, namely, that the Holy One, blessed be He, commanded and the man does what he is commanded to do. However, in this approach, there is not doubt that the Yetzer Hara (evil inclination) will find for the man many rationalizations and excuses for not doing the will of G-d. Thus, the explanation of "Cheshbon Hanefesh"

(spiritual accounting) here, is the considerations which obligate a man to do the service of G-d, blessed be He. A man must indeed make an accounting with himself why in truth he is under obligation to do the will of G-d and to what extent he is obligated to do so.

However, after he already did an accounting with himself that he must fulfill the will of G-d, then it is incumbent on him to make another accounting - whether he did so correctly and properly. But this is already a different type of Cheshbon (accounting), the accounting of "examining (pashpesh) his deeds and feeling (mashmesh) them out" (Eruvin 13b). But the "accounting of the soul" (cheshbon hanefesh) which Rabeinu speaks of is one which needs to precede this. For through it, a person connects himself (mitkasher) to the service of G-d, and furthermore, he even becomes zealous (energetic) to do the will of G-d and does all that is incumbent on him with joy.

In truth, the Gate of Spiritual Accounting is a small "Duties of the Heart". I am used to calling it "Kitzur Chovot Halevavot" ("summary of Duties of the Heart"). For it includes the whole book. In this gate one learns all the Cheshbonot (accountings) of Emunah (faith), gratitude, matters of trust, and all the duties (chiyuvim). For this is among the foundations of man's service in this world. In truth, really the entire book is all one big "Cheshbon Hanefesh" of how a man can attach himself (mitkasher) to the service of G-d, blessed be He.

In the 6th great assembly in the year 5740 (1980), the Vizhnitz Rebbe, author of "Yeshuot Moshe", Rabbi Moshe Yehoshua Hagar zt'l, proposed to those present the following undertaking: Since, there are 30 Cheshbons (accountings) in the Gate of Spiritual Accounting (brought in ch.3), and there are 30 days in the month. Thus, each person should take on himself to study one Cheshbon every day, and then review it again each month and delve deeper into it each time. Without a doubt, this is an excellent advice which yields great benefits.

## *** CHAPTER 1 ***

*- What is meant by making a spiritual accounting with oneself*

Spiritual account-taking means the deliberation of a man on his Torah and worldly affairs between his nefesh (bodily soul/emotional side/will) and his intellect, so that one may know what one has and what one still owes of his duties. (this will be clarified through examples).

> *Tov Halevanon*: The Torah and the world are like opposites, as they said (Berachos 61a) "Oy li mi yotzri, Oy li miyitzri" (Woe to me from my Creator [Rashi: If I go after my evil inclination], woe to me from my Yetzer [Rashi: if I don't go after my evil inclinations, he will weary me with thoughts/urges]).
> The proper way is for a man to go in the middle path between the Torah and the world, namely, that all of one's affairs in his worldly pursuits do not cross the bounds of the Torah's commandments and warnings. Since this is so, behold, all of one's days, a person needs to seek an accounting with himself between the Torah and the world - whether he trampled something of the Torah for a worldly benefit... The accounting is "between his nefesh (bodily soul/emotional side/will) and his intellect" because they are also antagonistic, as mentioned in Gate #3 ch.5 in the debate between them.

The prophet (Moshe) has already exhorted us on this in saying: *"Know therefore this day, and establish it in your heart that the L-ord he is G-d"* (Devarim 4:39), and David, peace be unto him, said: *"O taste and see that G-d is good"* (Tehilim 34:9) (i.e. examine well how G-d is good to us - TL), and *"know the G-d of your father and serve Him.."* (Divrei Hayamim 28:9), and *"be you not as the horse, or as the mule, which have no understanding"* (Tehilim 32:9).

It was said of one who did not examine his matters and did not account with himself on them: *"None returns it to heart, neither is there knowledge nor understanding to say"* (Yeshaya 44:19), and *"they remembered not His hand [nor the day when He delivered them from the oppressor]"* (Tehilim 78:42), and *"remember the days of old..."* (Devarim 32:7), and *"I remember the days of old [I meditate on all Your works; I ponder on the work of Your hands]"* (Tehilim 143:5), and *"I will get my knowledge from afar [and will ascribe righteousness to my Maker]"* (Iyov 36:3).

> *Tov Halevanon*: From these verses we learn that a man must consider

whether he has fulfilled his duty to the Creator for the benefits G-d has bestowed on him.

*Pas Lechem*: (on the verse "None returns it to heart, neither is there knowledge nor understanding") At first one must bring up and remember all the past matters that are forgotten from him, as if he calls up and returns a person who left him, and after this, one needs knowledge and understanding to do the spiritual accounting with his nefesh. But he did not look at his matters nor account with his nefesh.

*Matanas Chelko*: *"so that one may know what one has and what one still owes of his duties"* - on a deeper level, the primary Cheshbon HaNefesh is a matter of gratitude, as the Pas Lechem says: "how much has he paid back the Creator with his deeds, and corresponding to this, how much service he owes the Creator for the good He bestows to him." This is along the lines of the verse "Who has gone before Me that I should repay him" (Job 41:11). Thus, there is no claim of reward for mitzvot performed, for what does man do? If he puts a mezuzah on his doorpost, who gave him the house? If he puts tzitzit on his garment, who gave him the garment? Likewise for all things. Therefore, we are not speaking of reward, only debts.

Thus, the explanation of "what one has and what one still owes" is what he has of the gifts G-d gave him and the corresponding debts he is under duty to pay back G-d for them. This is also the explanation according to the Pas Lechem...

*"when he delivered them"* - one must contemplate that all these miracles were great kindnesses from G-d, and not as a reward for their deeds.. Contemplate very carefully and you will see with your mind's eye that G-d is good, and that you are living out of His goodness, not out of reward for your deeds..

*"Remember the days of old...* - this verse screams - "know the history of the world" in order to recognize the Creator of the world (the miracles, providence, etc. such as during the Exodus from Egypt). All these thoughts must obligate a man and stir him to do the will of G-d.

## *** CHAPTER 2 ***

*- If the accounting of all men is equal or not*

Whether or not the spiritual accounting of each person is equal, I will answer this as follows:

The self accounting for people in their religious and secular matters varies according to their level of perception, intelligence, and clarity of understanding. Every person is commanded to deliberate with his soul (i.e. bodily soul/instinct/will) as to what are his duties in the service of G-d, in accordance with his recognition of the favors of the Creator, whether collective or individual as the verse says: *"And know this day; for I speak not with your children that have not known, and that have not seen... but your eyes have seen all the great work of the L-ord which He did"* (Devarim 11:2-7).

The verse means to say, that the claim from the Creator on you is stronger and more evident than the claim on your descendants who did not witness the miracles of the Creator. For you witnessed them with your own eyes, and only you were bestowed these great favors and were spared from the plagues of Egypt, and of Korach (where all the Jews were guilty along with him - *TL*). But your descendants were not present, therefore you are more obligated to serve G-d on account of them.

Similarly, we can say for other individuals - that their obligation varies in accordance with their level of understanding and the amount of good bestowed to them.

> *Matanas Chelko*: i.e. there is no doubt that each person, without exception, is obligated to do the Cheshbon HaNefesh (spiritual accounting), and this Cheshbon is on the general good which every human being receives. One must also do an additional accounting on the special benefits that one receives personally, only that one is only obligated to do this Cheshbon according to his mental ability and recognition.
>
> *Matanas Chelko*: *"you witnessed them with your own eyes..* - with this Rabeinu answers the question as to why these verses were written in the Torah for all generations. The explanation is that even though G-d is speaking to them, the generation of the desert, but nevertheless, we see

from here the difference between the obligation of one who saw the matter first-hand versus one who merely heard about it. Although, those who merely heard are also obligated in recognizing this (favor), but the Holy One, blessed be He, claims more from those whose perception was greater..

It is incumbent on the believer to take account with his soul what are his duties to G-d, and to think through this in meticulous details to the utmost extent of his ability, and according to what he is able to grasp of it. Then, whatever one is capable of attaining in practice, he should make diligent efforts in it and exert himself, and that which is beyond one's ability to attain in practice - he should attain an understanding of it, and desire for it, as David, peace be unto him, said *"O that my ways were directed to keep your statutes!"* (Tehilim 119:5), and *"more to be desired are they than gold, than fine gold"* (Tehilim 19:11). and the Creator will judge him favorably (that he did not fulfill them - *LT*), and he should be on watch, for the time when he will be able to fulfill what is possible for him of his debts to the Creator.

Let him not try to find escapes for himself, treat this lightly (the personal accounting - *TL*), leave it, or ignore it (saying that he is not able to do it or that it is not necessary - *PL*), lest he be in total despair on the great day of accounting, as written: *"Whoever despises the word shall be destroyed by it"* (Mishlei 13:13).

## *** CHAPTER 3 ***

*- how many ways one should bring himself to an accounting.*

Regarding how many ways is the accounting of a man with himself on his duties to G-d, I say, that the ways of accounting in this matter are numerous. However, among them, I will expound thirty ways whereby it will become clear through them, what a man is obligated to his G-d, when he puts them to heart and takes on himself to reflect on them and remember them always.

### THE FIRST:
*(Obligation to serve G-d for creating him, elevating him over other creations, and taking care of his needs)*

> *Matanas Chelko*: Rabeinu already presented [this] in the Shaar Bechina (Gate of Examination). There he wrote on many matters regarding the goodness, loftiness, and wisdom of the Creator, blessed be He, whereby contemplating those things brings a person to do the will of G-d with joy, out of gratitude towards G-d for all these good things. The first few Cheshbonot (accountings) Rabeinu brought here are similar to those Cheshbonot but in a concise manner.

When a man reflects on his own matter, and considers the first beginning of his being, his emergence from non-existence to existence, from nothing to something, without his meriting any of this, but rather solely out of pure kindness of the Almighty, out of His benevolence and generosity. And when he will see with his understanding that he is more important in his matter, more exalted in level, and more elevated in form over the animals, plants, and inanimate objects, he will realize that he is under an obligation to thank his Creator, blessed be He.

> *Pas Lechem*: the phrase "emergence from non-existence to existence" refers to the formation of the drop (of seed) from blood which itself was formed from food. And it was still just a putrid drop, without human form, and afterwards its development and formation in the womb into human form. And still his existence was as nothing, removed from all assemblies, hidden from all eyes, until he was born and came into humanity - this is what he meant by "from nothing to something".

> *Translator*: This kindness is not just something G-d did collectively to

humanity, rather, even on a personal level, G-d did you a personal favor. ex. He could have made you a frog instead of a human being.)

Let him take a tangible illustration and imagine that when he was an infant, his mother abandoned him on the road, and a man passed by and saw him, and had pity on him, and took him in to his home, and raised him until he grew and his intellect matured. How greatly is he under an obligation to run to do his adopter's will and follow all of his commands and refrain from his prohibitions. (In short,) how much such a man is obligated to his benefactor! (i.e. even for things he did not explicitly command him to do but he knows that it is his adopter's will that he do them, he is under an obligation to do them - ML)

Likewise according to the Creator's protection of him, and providing for all of his needs, there should be a corresponding drawing towards His service and acceptance of His commandments. And the prophet already rebuked the Jewish people on this matter in saying: *"Is this how you repay the L-ord, you disgraceful, unwise people? (Is He not your Father, your Master? He has made you and established you)"* (Devarim 32:6), and Yechezkel elucidated this saying *"And when I passed by you, and saw you wallowing in your own blood..."* (Yechezkel 16:6), and the rest of the matter. (there this exact illustration is explained in more details - PL)

### THE SECOND:
*(debt to G-d for one's body)*
To bring oneself to an accounting for the great favor of G-d on him in composing his body and completing his form, his essence, and the anatomy of his limbs, taking him out of his mother's belly, and preparing his sustenance before this (the sustenance for the fetus in the womb - TL) and after this (his mother's milk - TL) - as fitting for him and according to the amount he needs. All this is a kindness of G-d on him. Let him think to himself, that if in his early creation he were lacking eyes or hands or feet, and a certain man was able to make them for him so that his body would be complete, how would he thank the man, and praise him, and be drawn to do his will, and cling to serving him. According to this one should correspondingly be drawn towards the Creator, who built his body and all of his limbs according to perfect functionality, as written *"Remember now that You made me like clay and to the dust You will return me"* (Iyov 10:9), and the rest of the matter, and *"For You created my reins, You covered me in my mother's womb"* (Tehilim 139:13).

*Tov Halevanon*: You alone made me and covered me in my mother's belly, a place where there is no light and nothing can reach there.

And *"For You drew me from the womb"* (Tehilim 22:10).

> *Tov Halevanon*: You drew me and extracted me. The previous verse was evidence on the wonder of the formation in the womb and afterwards (the second) on the wonder of birth.

> *Matanas Chelko*: in truth, our sages already decreed for us a place for this contemplation - every morning. For they decreed for us to recite the morning blessings whereby one considers and thanks the Creator for all these matters. The blessing "who made all my needs" is the first Cheshbon of Rabeinu. The second Cheshbon is "who opens the eyes of the blind" (pokeiah ivrim) and "who frees the bound" (matir asurim) - one needs to contemplate how things would be like if he did not have eyes. How would it be like if he had no legs - "who makes man's steps stable" (hamechin mitzadei gaver) - can a man move by himself? Is not everything from the Creator, blessed be He? One is under duty to think on this every morning, to recognize G-d's goodness and kindness. Through this contemplation, a man obligates himself and rouses himself to the service of G-d.

## THE THIRD:
*(debt to G-d for one's intellect)*

To observe and bring oneself to an accounting for the great favor of G-d on him for bestowing him with intellect and understanding and with many good, noble, and honorable traits.

> *Pas Lechem*: The term "good" refers to benefiting others... Among the traits in man, some are of the class "benevolence" such as generosity, some are of the class "noble" such as being content with little, and some are of the class "honorable" such as humility, since "who is honorable..." (Avos 4:1). I have given one example of each type from which you can extrapolate the rest.

Through these he has superiority over the irrational creatures (animals), as written *"Who teaches us more than the beasts of the earth, and makes us wiser than the fowls of heaven"* (Iyov 35:11). Let him imagine that if he were without intellect and understanding and a certain man came and helped him to attain them, and he afterwards understood the superiority he had gained over his previous state.

Would it be enough for him to thank and praise the man for the rest of his days to repay him for his help? How much more so the Creator, for who there is no limit to His favors on us (in the past - *PL*), and no end to His kindness towards us (in the future, since we also need His kindnesses in the future - *PL*), as written: *"Many, O L-ord my G-d, are Your wonderful works which You have done, and Your thoughts which are toward us: they cannot be recounted in order unto You: if I would declare and speak of them, they are more than can be numbered"* (Tehilim 40:5).

*Marpe Lenefesh*: Here is a quote from the book Orchos Tzadikim (shaar zechira): "Imagine if he were crazy or insane and would rip his clothes, how much would his affairs be ruined and he would be considered a complete nobody in people's eyes. And if a doctor came and cured him from his craziness and insanity, how fitting would it be to praise him for this, and all the more so for the Creator.."

## THE FOURTH:
*(debt to G-d for the Torah)*
To bring oneself to an accounting for the great favor of G-d on him for arousing him to what will bring him life in both worlds - the exalted and faithful Torah, to remove his blindness, root out his ignorance, enlighten his eyes, bring him nearer to the will of G-d, make known to him the truth of the existence of his Creator and what is his duty towards Him, and through which he will be successful in both worlds, as written *"The statutes of the L-ord are right, rejoicing the heart"* (Tehilim 19:8).

Let him imagine to himself after he recognized its worth, that if it had been unknown to him, and afterwards he met a certain man who bestowed it to him, would his efforts and abilities to pay him back be enough to convey his gratitude and praise? All the more so, for the Creator who rouses him to it (i.e. rouses his heart to toil in it - *PL*) and helps him to understand it and to fulfill it. The least debt of gratitude that we are obligated for it is to run to cling to His Torah, and that we hasten to accept the obligation of His commands and His prohibitions, as written *"I made haste, and delayed not, to observe Your commandments"* (Tehilim 119:60), and *"How I love Your Torah"* (Tehilim 119:97), and *"How sweet are Your words to my palate"* (Tehilim 119:103).

## THE FIFTH:
*(obligation to study the Torah beyond superficial)*
To bring oneself to an accounting for delaying coming to understand the book of G-d's Torah, and his being contented not to grasp its matters.

(*Pas Lechem*: man wants to be at rest and in tranquility instead of busy toiling to examine and grasp the depth of its matter.)

One would not act like this for a book that was sent to him from a king. If he had a doubt as to its meaning due to its unclear handwriting or words, or due to the depth of its matter, or its subtlety, or confusing mix of subjects or its enigmatic words. Rather, he would apply his whole heart and mind to understand its meaning, and would greatly pain himself until he understood its meaning.

> (*Marpe Lenefesh*: The book Orchos Tzadikim (Shaar Zechira) ends off: "Without a doubt, if there were in his city even the lowest of the lowest person who knew how to explain the part of the letter he did not understand, he would hurry to go to him and would not be embarrassed for this.)

If he does this to understand the words of a weak, mortal man like himself, how much more so is it his duty to do many times more than this until he understands the book of G-d, which is his life and his salvation (from eternal death - PL), as written *"For it is your life and the length of your days"* (Devarim 30:20). How did you permit yourself, my brother, to hide from it, and to content yourself from it with that which is readily familiar of its matter and revealed of its surface meaning, and you were lenient with (knowing) the rest.

> (*Manoach Halevavos*: The plain meaning and that which is readily evident of its matter is enough for you, and the other deep and hidden things, you are completely lenient in them and you do not at all apply your mind to understand them.
>
> *Marpe Lenefesh*: This refers to the secrets of the Torah, that you cast off behind you the profound matters of the Torah. In the Zohar this is expounded at length (Chelek 3, 152a): "woe to he who says that the Torah is only the plain meaning, because any wise man can also author chronicles and stories like these, and it's not for nothing that it is depicted: 'the Torah of G-d is perfect, it returns the soul...', and it's not for nothing that the Angels (spiritual beings) wanted to receive the Torah, rather certainly there is an inner side to it and great secrets on every letter and crown of letter..." see there.)

Can you see your own faultiness and lowliness in this?

> (*Pas Lechem*: The double expression (faultiness and lowliness): One, for being lazy in the study of the Torah. Two, for not being lazy in the letter of a flesh and blood king. This is like what the prophet said (Yirmiya 2:13): "For My people have committed two evils; they have forsaken Me, the spring of living waters, to dig for themselves cisterns, broken cisterns that

| do not hold water", and likewise for the following story...)

This is similar to the story of who it was said: *"But over the L-ord of heaven you exalted yourself, and the vessels of His House they brought before you, and you, your dignitaries, your queen, and your concubines drank wine in them, and you praised gods of silver and gold, copper, iron, wood and stone, which neither see nor hear nor know, but the G-d in Whose hand is your soul and all of your ways - He, you did not glorify"* (Daniel 5:23).

> *Matanas Chelko*: i.e. there is in this an aspect of idolatry, as if he bowed down to idols of silver and gold, G-d forbid, and not to the Holy One, blessed be He. For he did not have either a feeling or a mindset like this regarding the letter from a flesh and blood kind.
>
> In truth, this matter is brought in the Torah as written: *"these things which I command you TODAY shall be on your heart"* (Devarim 6:6). Rashi there brings the Sifri: "they should not be in your eyes like an old Diyutgama which a person does not take interest but rather like a new one which everyone runs to read. "Diyutgama" is a decree of the king issued in writing". end quote. This is the explanation of the word "today" - that the Torah was given to us today. This consideration can arouse in a man longing and clinging to the Torah, when he contemplates that the Torah is a letter from the King which grants him eternal life - "for it is your life and the length of your days" (Devarim 30:20).

## THE SIXTH:
### (obligation to not disobey G-d)

To make an accounting with oneself, when one feels that his tendencies are to rebel against the Creator and to break His covenant. Let him take account with himself and put to heart that all of what he perceives in the world with his senses - whether the foundations of the earth and its branches, or its elements and compounds, its higher (stars, planets) and its lower creations (i.e. physical creatures) - all of them exist by the word of G-d and guard His covenant (follow the laws of physics, etc).

Does one see anything leaving the bound of the service of G-d (being lazy in or not doing its purpose, which is its service - PL), rebelling against His word or breaking His covenant? If we would imagine in our mind that one of them would transgress the covenant of the Creator, no human would be left alive.

For example, what would happen if one of the elements would transgress the covenant of the Creator and change its nature, or that the earth would leave its center (its orbit around the sun), or that the waters of the ocean would spill over their boundary and cover everything on dry land. Would any man be left on the face of the earth?

More wondrous than this, regarding the organs of a man, if they were to rebel against the covenant of the Creator, and the organs whose nature is to move (ex. heart, lungs - *PL*) would be stationary, or the stationary ones (such as intestines - *PL*) would move, or that the five senses would not transmit the information they were commanded to transmit - one's formation would break down, his composition would disintegrate, and his normal ability to function would become null and void.

And how can a man not be ashamed to transgress the covenant of his G-d in a world which does not transgress the covenant of G-d, and do so with the help of limbs which G-d has commanded them to obey the man's wish and bear all the man's affairs, and these limbs do not transgress the Creator's covenant?

> (*Tov Halevanon*: How can one lift his face to use matters of this world for his own selfish pleasures against the will of the Creator? And since the matters of the world guard their purpose and do not change their nature which the Creator has set for them, how can one change the purpose the Creator set for him using the matters of this world?)

As an analogy, a king commanded a group of his servants to cross one of his ministers over a wide river with the utmost careful guarding to a specific place and during a specific time. Then, he commanded the minister to do to them during that time certain things. The servants fulfilled what the king had commanded them to do towards the minister, but the minister did not do what the king had commanded him.

One of the servants said to the minister: "you the minister who ignores the command of the king, would you not be afraid if one of us did like you and transgressed the command of the king to guard you, just like you transgressed while with us, thereby you would fall in this great river and die a grim death? Retract from your mistake by repenting and asking for forgiveness, because the king has commanded us to neglect guarding you if you transgress his command while with us." The minister woke up from his neglect (of guarding the king's command), and corrected his mistake.

Consider, my brother, if one of your limbs were to transgress the Creator's command in relation to yourself when you wished to use it. You know that the Creator stipulated in His faithful Torah that everything in the world is in your command and will obey your wish on condition that you serve Him, and (the opposite), that it (the world and everything in it) will go against your will when you transgress His word, as explained in Parsha Bechukotai: *"If you will go in My statutes..."* (Vayikra 26:3), and in other places.

(*Tov Halevanon*: Parsha Ki Tavo (Devarim 28) "G-d will strike you with 'techorim'...and you will become meshuga (insane)..", that the nature in his body will abandon its post and then many diseases will befall him)

*Matanas Chelko*: i.e. [the servants said:] if you don't do your part, we do not need to do our part. It is implied that this is included in what they were commanded... Man is the minister of the world. The entire world was given to aid and assist him. However, this was on condition... "If you will go in My statutes...", which are all the verses of blessings and curses written in the Torah. Rabeinu gives us a clear picture and simple analogy to fully understand the matter.

## THE SEVENTH:
*(to complete the conditions of slavehood to G-d)*
To bring oneself to an accounting to His G-d regarding assuming the conditions of slavehood, and to take on himself the obligation of masterhood due to His Creator (that one act towards G-d the way a slave is obligated to act towards his master - *ML*). We have noted most of the conditions in the third gate of this book. Let the seeker find them there.

*Marpe Lenefesh commentary*: To reflect in his mind whether he is fulfilling all the conditions that a slave is obligated to act towards his master, and to reflect if he also acts at least like this towards his Creator, who is our Master, our Creator, and our King as he wrote in Gate 3 end of chapter 5.

*Matanas Chelko*: until now, he mentioned various Cheshbons which are understood according to the Shaar Bechina (Gate #2), namely, that we are obligated to do the will of the Creator out of gratitude for the world and all the good the Creator does [to us]. Now he enters into a deeper Cheshbon - the concept of slavehood (hishtabdut)... that one is obligated perforce (even against his will). Not as if he is doing good or paying back good to G-d. But rather, he does out of slavehood, whose explanation is to do in such a manner that he is not serving out of his own volition, but because he is forced in the matter. This is a condition of slavehood, that the Holy One, blessed be He, is a Master over us, due to doing many good things to us always, as explained in Gate #3.

One should think of them when he realizes the constant favors of the Creator on him in preparing what is beneficial to him, having compassion on him, always providing him with the food he needs. Neither did G-d abandon him to himself (during his childhood - TH) when his understanding was weak in the proper way to conduct his affairs, and He bestowed him with wisdom, intellect, and understanding to conduct his affairs. Through them, he will know his debts to G-d, as David said: "I am Your servant; grant me understanding, that I may know Your testimonies" (Tehilim 119:125).

And when a slave recognizes (all the following traits from his Master - ML) the great favors from his Master on his soul and body, and all his movements, and that the Master watches over him constantly, and knows his revealed and hidden matters, and guards all of his movements, and binds them with his bonds and rules over them (that all his movements are bound to the will of G-d, like clay in the hands of a potterer, thus we are in His hand - ML), and (he also contemplates - ML) how the Master tests and checks him with what he granted him (free will, even though everything is in G-d's hands - ML) on whether to use his limbs and turn his thoughts towards his good inclination or whether he will turn them towards his evil inclination. And the slave considers the teachings of the Torah and its rousing as to what is the will of G-d and what is against it and will bring G-d's wrath upon him - (if the slave puts to heart all of this, then certainly - ML) he will use all movements of his body and all powers of his spirit for what will find favor in the eyes of his Master, and bring him closer to Him. He will remove the veil of foolishness from himself, and don the garment of awe and reverence from Him and love of Him, and he will desire what G-d wants - then the great good, and the great light from G-d will come upon him, as written: *"O G-d in the light of Your countenance they shall walk"* (Tehilim 89:16), and *"the L-ord will cause His countenance to shine on you and favor you"* (Bamidbar 6:25).

The main thing of all - is to complete the conditions of slavehood and to designate G-d alone with masterhood - that all this be wholeheartedly and faithfully (all that one does to serve G-d should be wholeheartedly and faithfully, without any outside interests - ML), and through this one's love of G-d will be wholehearted and likewise will be G-d's love towards him, as written: *"You have declared the L-ord this day to be your G-d...And the L-ord has declared you this day to be His treasured people"* (Devarim

26:17-18), and *"to make you supreme, above all the nations that He made"* (Devarim 26:19), and *"Then all the peoples of the earth will see that the name of the L-ord is called upon you, and they will fear you"* (Devarim 28:10).

> *Matanas Chelko*: *"wholeheartedly and faithfully"* - i.e. the intent here is not to do external deeds which demonstrate slavehood. Rather, one must feel slavehood in his inner being truthfully and faithfully. For the Holy One, blessed be He, knows what is in one's heart... then he will come to love G-d and also the Holy One, blessed be He, will love him.
>
> *"to make you supreme"* - G-d will elevate you higher and greater than everything [in creation].

The reason for this: it is known that the greatness of a slave in the eyes of men is according to the greatness of his master and according to his master's choosing of him, and bringing him close, and since the Name of the Creator is above and higher than all the high in the eyes of the nations, as written *"For from the rising of the sun even unto the going down of the same, My Name shall be great among the nations"* (Malachi 1:11), and the closest nation to Him, which is singled out for His service is the nation of Yisrael. Thus, it would be proper, according to this, that our level and glory be above the other nations.

> *Matanas Chelko*: *"the greatness of a slave in the eyes of men is according to the greatness of his master"* - for example, if we see a man dressed as a military general, adorned with badges, looking very important, we nevertheless still need to clarify which army he leads and which country he belongs to. For it is possible that he merely leads some small faraway country at the end of the world, whereby he would not be important at all. For the greatness of a general is measured by the country, people, and king who appointed him... For example, if the president of the USA granted him this power and appointed him, he represents the USA and there is in this importance. But if he represents some remote African tribe, even if he wears important clothing, it means nothing.

The reason for *"that the Name of the L-ord is called upon you"* (Devarim 28:10), is that we were called "the nation of G-d", "the nation of the Almighty", "the priests of G-d", "the servants of G-d", "the slaves of G-d", "the sons of G-d", and other titles similar to these of words depicting special treasured status and special choice. But "they will fear from you", is for the honor of the Creator and awe of Him, as written *"Who would not fear you, O King of nations?"* (Yirmiya 10:7), and like the verse says of what in the future we will attain of closeness to the Creator, and being singled out for His service *"One shall say: 'I am of the L-ord'"* (Yeshaya 44:5), and therefore the importance of a person to the Creator is according to the person's closeness to Him and serving of Him.

> *Matanas Chelko*: *" 'they will fear from you', is for the honor of the Creator and awe of Him"* - for example, for one who has an American passport, it is possible that they will fear him more than one who has a passport from a small country such as Congo. For perhaps, he is a friend of the president (or an important official) of the country and he loves him and will protect him. Thus, the fear is from the fear of the master. Likewise regarding the matter of the Creator...
>
> Thus the Nations will fear the Jewish people because they are servants of G-d, and the nations have fear of G-d, blessed be He. Therefore, according to the strength of our slavehood towards the Creator, so too will be the fear of the nations towards the nation of G-d, and they will fear harming us... And according to the extent of slavehood we have towards the Creator, so too will He guard us and make their hearts fear harming us..

Therefore, my brother, bring yourself to an accounting on this matter and do not be swayed by your evil inclination. Do not consent with your base desires when using your intellect and understanding in this (accounting - PL) . Put to heart the Creator's observing your making an accounting with yourself in your inner thoughts and let your intent be for the sake of His Name. Carefully think through it for His honor, out of shame of His observing you on it, as written *"The L-ord knows the thoughts of man, that they are vanity"* (Tehilim 94:11).

## THE EIGHTH:
*(obligation to serve G-d sincerely)*
To bring oneself to an accounting in what one is obligated regarding devoting one's heart to G-d alone.
The devotion of heart is in two ways:
One: wholehearted devotion when declaring the unity of G-d, as we explained in the beginning of this book.
Two: wholehearted devotion to G-d alone when doing an act of the next world (i.e. a mitzvah), whether it is an act one is obligated to do or it is an optional act, as we explained in gate 5 of this book.

Some of the essentials of acknowledging the unity of G-d are:
* to acknowledge that there is no other god besides Him
* to not associate Him with any image, form, measure, movement, nor any kind of physical representation, nor any kind of state whether purposeful or

incidental (see Gate 1).

* to believe that there is no beginning to His being and no end to His existence.

* to know that He is [absolutely] One and there is nothing which is one like Him, and there is no creator other than Him, and no maker besides Him, and likewise for His other Names and attributes (see Gate 1).

> *Matanas Chelko*: when we speak of slavehood to G-d, blessed be He, this is because He is the Ribono Shel Olam, i.e. the L-ord of the whole universe, and Master of all the worlds. Therefore, one must serve Him. This is the point in this cheshbon. One must contemplate on every Hishtabdut (undertaking) that he does, that it be done to G-d [alone]. When we say every morning "Shema Yisrael, the Eternal is our G-d, the Eternal is One" and accept His Unity on the whole world and the four directions and that He is One, one must be aware afterwards when fulfilling His commandments all day that it is for Him... And in the Shulchan Aruch (O.C.231): "our sages said: 'let all your deeds be for the sake of Heaven', that even mundane things such as eating, drinking, walking, sitting, rising, talking, and all bodily needs, etc. should all be directed towards serving your Creator...". This is the Cheshbon before doing a deed, to have intent for His great Name.
>
> (Translator: saying to oneself generally "l'shem shamayim" before doing things helps in this. It is also important to think of some specific intent such as "to be healthy in order to serve G-d" when eating. see the book Shaarei Orah by Rabbi Avigdor Miller, sec. l'Shem Shamayim for powerful words on this.)

Some of the essentials of wholehearted devotion to G-d alone when doing a religious act:

* to not have intent when doing it other than for the sake of His great Name, not out of love of praise from men, not out of hope to get benefit from them, not out of fear of them, not to bring some benefit or prevent some damage in this world or in the next, as our sages said: *"Be not like servants who minister unto their master for the sake of receiving a reward, but be like servants who serve their master not upon the condition of receiving a reward"* (Avot 1:3).

You can observe this, my brother, with how human beings conduct themselves regarding friendships. When one senses that his friend's heart is not sincere with him, and all the more so a master regarding his slave - he will be angry with him and will not desire his deeds, even if he exerts himself to the best of his ability and appears sincere externally, and even though a man needs his friend and needs his help.

All the more so for the Creator, that all the created beings need Him, and He has no need nor benefit from them. He can see into their hearts and their innermost secrets. How can we expect Him to desire in us with what we would not expect our friends to desire in us with, despite their ignorance of our inner deception and of our little wholeheartedness towards them?

(*Pas Lechem commentary*: How can we want that our conduct towards G-d be in a manner that we would not be happy with if our colleagues conducted themselves towards us like this? And even if it is possible to say an excuse on our friends, that their heart is not sincere towards us because they do not know if our heart is also sincere towards them, and certainly if our hearts is in truth not sincere with them. And even so, we nevertheless become angry with them for this (despite that we are not sincere with them). This is what he meant by "despite their ignorance, etc". All the more so, if we conduct ourselves with G-d like this.)

*Matanas Chelko*: for example, he loves mister so and so and is his friend because that person has connections to someone or some place. Thus, in truth, he does not love him at all. Likewise, for a slave, even if he does everything and does more than needed, but when the master perceives that the slave is doing only for himself, all of the master's grace towards the slave will disappear and he will be angry with him. For this is not service of the master but service of oneself!..

When the understanding person will reflect on this matter, he will feel disgrace and shame before the Creator, and will rectify his inner self, and devote his heart to G-d alone when declaring His unity, doing one of His commandments or learning His Torah, and he will do it with exertion and zeal, as David said: *"I will run the way of Your commandments, for You will broaden my heart"* (Tehilim 119:32).

*Matanas Chelko*: *"he will feel disgrace and shame"* - in truth, one needs to feel shame when he serves not for G-d's sake (shelo lishma).

## THE NINTH:
*(intent in prayer and mitzvot)*

*Matanas Chelko*: this cheshbon (contemplation) is among the fundamental teachings (min HaChidushim HaYesodiim) of Rabeinu in the matter of the service of G-d. We need to study it in-depth.

To bring oneself to an accounting that one's acts and exertion in doing the various religious activities in the service of G-d be at least as much as what one would do if his (human) king would request of him to do for some physical activity. Surely, one would not hold himself back in the least from exerting himself fully and to the best of his ability [for the human king].

> *Matanas Chelko*: this Cheshbon (contemplation) is on how he would exert himself, watch over and be meticulous in all sorts of deeds which a flesh and blood king had commanded him to do.
>
> And in Pesachim 75b: (regarding the prohibition of bringing coals which make too much smoke for the incense offering) "For that you don't need a verse, [to prohibit it] since before a flesh and blood king, one would not do this, how much more so before the King of kings, the Holy One blessed be He." end quote.

If it were an act requiring investigation, thought and counsel, he would apply all of his heart, understanding, intellect and perception to work on it with the utmost care and zeal.

If he came to praise and thank the king for some good or some favor he received from him, whether he would transmit the message of gratitude through a song or poem whether it be oral or written - he would not refrain from all sorts of eloquence, metaphors, analogies, embellishments whether true or false (such as Melachim 1:31, "may the king live forever" - *ML*), that it is possible to say of him. And if he could praise him with all of his limbs and his inner and outer being he would do so. If he could move heaven and earth and everything in them to praise and thank him in order to show the king his good feelings towards him, he would do so, in spite of his being a mere weak human (like himself - *PL*), small and of swiftly passing days.

> *Pas Lechem:* All this is due to his great desire that he wishes and hopes that the king will perceive his good heart and wholeheartedness towards him.

According to this the intelligent person should conduct himself in the service of G-d. When he does anything of it.
Every act of service to G-d must necessarily fall into one of three categories.
(1) Duties of the heart alone. It was our intention to clarify them in this book.
(2) Duties of the heart and limbs together, such as prayer, Torah study, praise and psalms to G-d, study of other wisdoms (needed for Torah such

as astronomy or gematrias - *PL*), instructing others to do good or refrain from evil, or the like.

(3) Duties of the limbs alone, whereby the heart has no participation, except for the intent to G-d at the beginning of the act, such as (dwelling in a) sukkah, lulav, tzitzis, mezuza, guarding the Sabbath and the festivals, charity, or others similar where distraction of the heart by other things does not damage the act.

> *Matanas Chelko*: *"except for the intent to G-d at the beginning of the act"* - Rabeinu writes here a great foundation (Yesod Gadol). The intent of "lishma" (for G-d), whereby one does a mitzva for G-d's sake (l'shem Hashem) - this is before doing the act. Afterwards, the act can continue onwards. There is no need for intent "lishma" every second after this. For example, one who needs to do an act of kindness, certainly, in the beginning he should have intent to do it "lishma", i.e. that he is doing the mitzva l'Shem Shamayim (for G-d's sake). But afterwards, at the time of doing the act of kindness, he need not think thoughts of lishma and devekut (clinging) to G-d. Then, one needs only to help and be kind to his fellow.
> This is unlike the second category. For there, one also needs intent of heart all the time he is engaged in prayer or Torah, etc., unlike this [third] category.

However for the duties of the heart, one is obligated to empty his heart from thoughts of this world and its distractions, and to focus his heart and mind to G-d alone at that time, as it was said of one of the ascetics who would say in his prayer to G-d: "my G-d! The sorrow I have for You nullified all my other sorrows, and the worry I have from You (from my sins which distanced me from You - *PL*), distanced me from all other worries".

> *Manoach Halevavos*: The sorrow and worry that I have in my heart due to You nullifies from me all other sorrows and worries of the thoughts and distractions of this world.

Through this, G-d will accept his act and desire it, of these our sages said (Berachot 13a): "mitzvot need kavana (intent)".

If one is engaged in a religious act of the category involving both the heart and the limbs together, such as prayer or praising G-d - he should free his body from doing any worldly or other religious act, and clear his heart from all thoughts which distract him from the matter of the prayer (even thoughts of Torah - *MC*). After he has cleansed himself, and washed from any filth or dirt, and distanced from any bad smell or the like, then he

should put to heart:
1. to Whom he has intent to pray to.

*Matanas Chelko*: first and foremost, he must prepare himself for prayer with the consideration of to Whom he is about to pray.

2. What does he seek from it.

*Marpe Lenefesh*: i.e. his needs, sustenance, health which are all in the hands of G-d to give or withhold.

*Matanas Chelko*: *"what does he seek from it"* - i.e. the explanation of the words. These two matters are laws brought in the Shulchan Aruch O.C.98:1 "the person praying must have intent in his heart for the explanation of the words he utters with his lips and to also have intent that it is as if the Shechina (divine presence) is opposite him" end quote.

One who enters the synagogue, dons tefilin, opens the prayer book and begins to pray - does he realize he is speaking to someone? Without this, it is not called prayer, but merely "reading a Sidur (prayer book)", and as Rabbi Chaim HaLevi's work on the Rambam (Hilchot Tefila) establishes that the intent of "standing before G-d" is a requirement (me'akev). Without it, it is not an act of prayer. For by definition, prayer is speaking to the Holy One, blessed be He. (see there). Without recognizing and feeling this intent, it is not prayer but rather merely 'occupying oneself' (mitasek b'alma).

The difference between a small child in school and an adult praying is only in the kavana (thought) - the thought of to Whom he is praying and that he is now speaking to the King. This is what Rabeinu wrote that even after cleansing his body and mind from all thoughts, it is still not yet prayer until he has intent constantly before Whom he is praying.

*Matanas Chelko*: the Path of the Just writes (ch.19) that the most difficult matter in prayer is that one is speaking to another. He writes there: "he is actually (mamash) standing before the Creator, blessed be He, engaging in a give and take with Him, even though a man's eye does not see Him. You will observe that this is the most difficult for a person to form a true image in his heart because his senses do not at all aid in this" end quote.

Behold, if we tell someone to hold a telephone to his ear and speak as if he is speaking to someone, he will not be able to do this. But when he calls his friend, he is able to speak to him on the phone for hours even though he does not see his fellow standing before him and merely speaks to a piece of plastic. Nevertheless, he can do this. This is only because he feels his fellow is listening and hears him. Perhaps this is the reason for the

invention of the telephone - to teach us [tangibly] that it is possible to speak
with another even though one does not see who it is. From there, he can
learn a lesson regarding prayer. Namely, that even though he does not see
the Holy One, blessed be He, nevertheless, he can feel that He listens and
hears his prayer.

And as the "Path of the Just" continues there: "However, he who is of
sound intellect can establish in his heart the truth of the matter, with a little
contemplation and attention, how he comes and quite literally engages in a
give and take with G-d, blessed be He, pleading before Him, and
beseeching Him, while G-d, blessed be His Name, lends ear to him, gives
attention to his words, just like when a man speaks to his fellow and the
fellow attentively listens to his words".

3. With what he will speak before his Creator, of the words and the subject
matter of the prayer.

*Marpe Lenefesh*: These are the words and matters of prayer one speaks
with to the King of kings. When one puts to heart these three introductions
before his prayer - even after all this, maybe, he will have proper kavana
(intent) in his prayer.

Know that the words one is forming with his tongue are like the shell and
the meditation on the words is like the fruit, (or) that the uttering of the
prayer is like the body, and the meditation is like the soul.

*Matanas Chelko*: "body..soul" - if we were to compare a prayer to a man or
animal, the prayer (meditation) is the "life spirit", the primary thing, while
the words are just the physical body.

When one prays with his tongue but his mind is distracted in a matter other
than the prayer, his prayer will be like a body without a soul, or like a shell
without a fruit, because his body is present but his mind is not with him in
his prayer. Of like him, scripture says: *"For as much as this people draw
near with their mouth and with their lips do honor Me, but their hearts are
far from Me, and their fear of Me is a commandment of men learned by
rote"* (Yeshaya 29:13).

*Matanas Chelko*: the explanation is that it is not that the prayer is on a low
level, or that it is not so good. But rather, it is waste (pesolet) and nothing.
A body without a life spirit is nothing!

*Marpe Lenefesh*: In the sefer Chasidim (Siman 46): "To habituate oneself in
kavana (intent), to do this small habit before prayer, or any blessing, to
pause a bit before and not allow any thought or hirhur (musing) to take

hold in his mind, because if one gives a place to laziness, even for one second, or for any thought whatsoever - he is already ensnared in the trap of the yetzer, and he will continue and overpower him...", see there.

An analogy was further said on this regarding a slave whose master came to his home. The slave ordered his wife and children to honor him and do everything for him, but he himself left to engage in merriment and laughter, and refrained from serving his master personally, and from trying to honor him and doing what is proper to him. The master became angry with him and did not accept his honors and service, and he threw everything back to his face.

Likewise for one who prays, while his heart and mind are devoid of the matter of prayer, G-d will not accept the prayer of his limbs and tongue.

| *Matanas Chelko*: since the essence of the person himself is not there.

You can see from what we say at the end of our prayers: "May the words of my mouth and the thoughts of my heart find favor before You O G-d..." And when a man (is distracted and) thinks of any matter in the world, whether it is permitted or forbidden, and afterwards he finishes his prayer and says "imrei fi vehegyon libi lefanecha" (may the words of my mouth and the thoughts of my heart find favor before You), is this not a great disgrace, that he claims to have spoken to his G-d with his heart and mind while his heart was not with him, and afterwards he asks G-d to accept it and favor it from him?

He is similar to one of whom it was said "as a nation that pretends to show righteousness..." (Yeshaya 58:2), and our sages said: "a person should estimate himself - if he thinks he is capable of having intent in heart, he should pray. Otherwise, he should not pray" (Berachos 30b). And Rebbi Eliezer said when he was about to die, among the things he commanded his disciples - "when you are praying, know before Whom you are praying" (Berachos 28b). And scripture says: *"prepare yourselves to greet your G-d, O Israel"* (Amos 4:12), and our sages said: *"When you pray do not make your prayer a form of routine but a plea for mercy and supplications"* (Avot 2:18), and *"When my soul grew faint upon me, I remembered the L-ord: and my prayer came to You to Your Holy Temple"* (Yona 2:8), and *"Let us lift up our heart with our hands unto G-d in the heavens"* (Eicha 3:41).

PURPOSE OF PRAYER

You should know, my brother, that our aim in prayer is only the longing of the soul to G-d, its submitting before Him, elevating its Creator, praising and thanking His Name, and casting all of its needs on Him.

*Tov Halevanon*: The praises and psalms with which we exalt and elevate our Creator along with the acknowledging of His many kindnesses on us are in order that we humble/submit ourselves greatly in picturing His greatness and to what extent we are obligated to serve Him....we pray to Him on our needs and troubles even though nothing is hidden from His eyes, and He knows our needs better than we do, and He provides sustenance to all living things according to its deeds and according to what His wisdom decreed. Nevertheless, we pour our prayers to Him in order to feel our great need for Him and to place our trust in Him, as the author writes later in number 18.

*Marpe Lenefesh*: The matter of prayer is in order that a man humble/submit himself before the Creator...this is the primary mitzva of prayer...therefore a person can pray in any language and for all matters, as long as his intent is to submit himself before the Creator and to request his needs...

*Matanas Chelko*: "*casting all of its needs on Him*" - this is a great foundation (yesod) in prayer. Likewise, other Rishonim (early sages) wrote this in the way of pshat (plain meaning). The matter of prayer is that a man changes through it. Namely, even if he prays and asks for his needs or to be saved from some trouble or the like, it is not as if he is trying to change G-d's mind through this. Only that he is changing himself through the prayer and thus incidentally the trouble will be removed or he will find salvation. For he is already a different person, not the same one on whom the decree or trouble was decreed upon.

For example, one who became ill and prays to G-d to heal him. Is it conceivable that if he prays properly, G-d will reconsider and regret what he decreed? Rather, the explanation is that since the man prays and humbles himself before his Creator, blessed be He, and draws closer to Him through his prayer, through his words and trust that only G-d has the power to save him, and G-d alone is the healer of all flesh; if through this, he draws closer to G-d, behold, he is already a different person, not the same one upon who a decree of illness was decreed [and therefore the decree is no longer needed]....

*Matanas Chelko*: the matter still requires explanation for one who is sick in such a way that he is unable to pray for himself. Such as a person in the hospital unable to speak. How does the decree become annulled from him?

But this also needs to be understood according to Rabeinu's foundation that a person changes himself. [Answer:] for example, if the sick man could give over to the public a lecture of Mussar from his hospital bed through a microphone, and his words would help the public improve their ways, and due to him, they pray better and change themselves as before.

This great merit is credited to the sick man. So too here, even if the sick man cannot speak, but since others pray for him, and through their prayers, they improve, this is a great merit to the sick man. Thus, automatically, it is found that such a decree cannot be decreed on a man with such [great] merits.

We must still clarify the following. According to this, let whoever needs a salvation or healing just study mussar and through this he will change himself. Why then does he need specifically prayer? But this is not difficult. For even though, certainly he should study mussar, nevertheless, prayer has special segulot (abilities) and wonders. This is the path our forefathers set and its matter and effect is lofty as Rabeinu wrote here "longing of the soul [to G-d]". Through it, a man draws closer to the blessed Creator and perfects himself in the trait of Bitachon (trust) "casting all of his needs on Him."

And since it is difficult for the mind to remember all of this, it was necessary for our sages to arrange a written order of the matters which most men need. This demonstrates to them their great need for G-d and their need to submit to Him on account of them. These are the matters of prayer which were ordered and arranged, so that the person can greet his Creator, and not be ashamed in approaching Him, and to see in the prayer matters which bring to humility and submission before G-d.

And since the thoughts of the heart change rapidly, and these thoughts do not hold firmly due to the swift arising of thoughts that flash through the mind, it is difficult for a person to arrange his prayer.

*Pas Lechem*: The mind does not have the power to hold onto one position and meditate on some thing and this is due to the great swiftness of thoughts and ideas which constantly pass through a man's heart one after the other.

*Matanas Chelko*: how much more so for our generation, where a man cannot concentrate his mind and thought on one matter for more than a minute and a half. Consider how if one wants to focus his thoughts on some difficulty in a sugya (talmudic topic) he is learning, and instead of looking at the Gemara or book, his eyes roam around the room. How much time

can he concentrate his mind on the kushya (question) before outside
thoughts enter his mind and distract him?

For this our Sages composed the prayer with fixed words, to place them on
a man's tongue, because the thoughts of the mind go after and are drawn
after the words one utters.

Therefore the prayer has fixed words and subject matters. For words need a
subject matter (i.e. words need to express a subject matter, otherwise they
are meaningless - *PL*). But a subject matter of thought does not need
speech, if it is possible to arrange it in orderly fashion in the heart. For the
subject matter is the essence of our devotion and the chief aim to which
our attention should be directed.

*Pas Lechem*: through the words, it becomes easier for a man to have intent,
since the words rouse the intent, and the intent follows them...and since our
primary purpose for uttering the words is to arouse the heart, therefore we
find that the heart is the main purpose.

You can see what the sages said regarding a time of difficulty: "a man who
experienced a seminal emission should say the blessing in his mind and not
utter the words, neither before (the shema) nor after it" (Berachos 20b),
and they permitted one to pray a short version of the (amidah) prayer
(under some circumstances). And if the uttering of words was the main
purpose of the prayer, it would not have been permitted for us to reduce
them under any circumstances.

Therefore, my brother, rectify the subjects of your prayer in your heart, so
that it will be consistent with your words, and let your intent in both be
only to G-d. Keep your body free from any movements and restrain your
senses and thoughts from dealing with any worldly matter while you are
praying.

Compare i.e. bring for yourself a proof and comparison of what you would
do to your (human) king when you are engaged in thanking him, praising
him, and lauding him for his good deeds, in spite of his ignorance of your
thoughts. All the more so for the Creator who watches your external and
internal being, who observes what is visible in your life and what is
concealed.

It is a wonder (how one can imagine that he has fulfilled his duty of prayer
by praying without intent - *PL*), since prayer is like a trust and deposit the

Creator entrusted you with, since he gave over its matter in your hands and your domain. Nobody can watch over it except Him (unlike the other mitzvos where people can see and watch over and pressure their observance, but nobody can see prayer except G-d, therefore it is like a deposit He entrusted you with - *PL*)

> *Matanas Chelko*: relative to other Mitvot, prayer is unique in that it is between oneself and G-d. For even in Mitzvot between man and G-d, since they contain some form of physical action, he has "fear of flesh and blood". This is as Rabbi Yochanan ben Zakai blessed his disciples before his death and gave them an advice for fear of heaven (Berachot 28b) saying: " 'may it be that the fear of Heaven be upon you like the fear of flesh and blood'. His disciples replied: 'only that much [and no more]'? He answered: 'would that it were (halevai)!, know that when a man is about to sin, he first asks himself 'can any human see me?'" end quote.
>
> For example, in the mitzva of Tefilin, if a flesh and blood king would decree to don Tefilin, there is no doubt that he would fear not fulfilling this decree. Likewise, regarding the fear of other people. If it became known to his peers that he does not put on Tefilin, he would certainly be embarrassed from this. On this it says: 'I hope no human will see me'.
>
> All this is because it is something which depends on an act. But prayer is not like this. There is nobody who knows whether he has intent of heart or not. Therefore, regarding prayer, there is no "fear of flesh and blood", only "fear of Heaven". For a man can come to the synagogue and shake his body during prayer (pretending to be intently praying). Thus, prayer does not have any aspect of "fear of other people" so that a man will learn to fear Heaven through this. Furthermore, it is not shayich (possible to be) shelo lishma (not for G-d's sake) in prayer. Even though, it is possible for one to come to the synagogue shelo lishma and pretend he is praying. But for the actual prayer itself, if he has proper kavana (intent), it is all only lishma (for G-d's sake).

If you pray like the Creator commanded, you will have fulfilled your duty of faithfulness, and He will accept it from you. But if you are not faithful in it, in your heart and tongue, you will be considered among those who betray the trust G-d placed on them, and the verse says of them: *"for they are a very inverted generation (i.e. their hearts and intents are opposite of what comes out of their mouths - TL), sons in whom is no faith"* (Devarim 32:20), while for those who are faithful the verse says: *"My eyes shall be upon the faithful of the land, that they may dwell with Me"* (Tehilim 101:6).

DUTIES OF THE LIMBS

If one engages in the duties of the limbs alone such as (dwelling in a) sukka or (taking a) lulav, or other things we mentioned earlier (Sabbath, festivals, mezuza, etc.), it is an obligation to precede the intent to G-d before doing it, so that the root of his act is to heed the commandment of the Creator, to elevate, to glorify, to thank Him, and to praise Him - for His great favors and great kindnesses on him.

*Pas Lechem*: The beginning is the root of every act, therefore the wise man said: "the beginning is half of the whole".

And so he will attain the ultimate purpose of the service, at its beginning, during its performance, and until its completion. That he will do them (1) due to reverence of G-d, (2) desire to fulfill His will, and (3) to keep away from what will bring the wrath of G-d on himself.

*Marpe Lenefesh*: i.e. that if he does not do it, there will be on him anger and punishment from the Creator. If at the beginning, middle, and completion of the act, there will be these three things... - then he will do it with passion and zeal until he completes the mitzvah wholly.

As David said: *"to do your will, O G-d, I desired"* (Tehilim 40:9), and one should imagine to scrutinize himself with the analogy I preceded at the beginning of this way regarding speaking with a (human) king, and that he should ever keep this on his mind - then he will find zeal in his limbs for the acts of service, with G-d's help, as we introduced from the words of David "I considered my ways (i.e. my ways with people like myself, namely, the previous analogy, and through that... - *PL*), and turned my feet to Your testimonies; I made haste (behold - zealousness - *PL*), and delayed not, to observe Your commandments" (Tehilim 119:59).

## THE TENTH:
### (the watching of the Creator)
To make an accounting with oneself regarding the Creator's watching his outer and inner life. That G-d sees him, remembers all of his deeds and all of the thoughts that go through his mind, whether good or bad. And therefore, one should fear Him always, and make efforts to rectify one's public and private life to be in accord with G-d's will.

*Marpe Lenefesh*: To always remember that G-d watches him and knows what is visible in a man's life and what is in his heart, in his concealed and in his innermost being...as the Rambam ends off his book the "Guide for the Perplexed" (Chelek 3 ch.54) and the Shulchan Aruch starts off with it in the Ramah, on the verse: (Tehilim 16:8) "I have placed G-d before me

| always" - this is a great general principle..etc

Let one make the following analogy to himself: If a man was watching him and constantly observing his every movement, would he do something that would cause the man to be disgusted by him? And all the more so, if the man was a benefactor of him, and all the more so, if the man was his master, and all the more so if the one watching him was his Creator. How much greater is his duty to be ashamed (from transgressing His word - *PL*) and embarrassed (from being lazy in His service - *PL*) before Him, and to be careful to refrain from rebelling against Him, and to hurry to His service, and to try to obtain His favor and love.

Furthermore, it is known to us that we adorn ourselves with the best clothing we can when going out to greet our kings, high officials, or great men of our generation because they observe our exterior appearance, as written *"for one may not enter the king's gate dressed in sackcloth"* (Esther 4:2), and *"So Pharaoh sent and called Joseph, and they rushed him from the dungeon, and they shaved and changed his clothes, and he [then] came to Pharaoh"* (Gen.41:14). According to this, we are obligated to adorn ourselves in the service of G-d in our exterior and in our interior for G-d, because He observes us equally in both respects at all times, since if we believed in our minds that the (human) kings were able to look at our interior just like they can see our physical exterior, we would not delay to adorn our interior in a way that they would wish us to do.

You can observe that for the majority of men, the main reason they occupy themselves to study and teach the fields of wisdom is only in order to become great through them in the eyes of the kings. And likewise for many portions of the laws/culture of the kingdom, for the people are commanded to obey the laws of their king (and they are afraid for their necks of transgressing his laws - *TL*).

| *Manoach Halevavos*: Much of the laws and customs/culture are adopted by the masses due to their love of the king and fear of him, since most are commanded to follow the culture and religion that their king (society) follows.

Surely, regarding G-d, it is more fitting and more obligatory on us to adorn ourselves in His service in our inner thoughts, heart and limbs, since He watches them and contemplates them continuously and nothing can distract Him from some matter, as the verse says *"I am the L-ord who searches the heart; I test the reins"* (Yirmiya 17:10), and *"the eyes of the L-ord are in every place, beholding the evil and the good"* (Mishlei 15:3), and *"the eyes of the L-ord, that run to and fro throughout the land"* (Zecharya 4:10), and the verse says regarding the awe one should feel regarding the watching of the Creator: *"Be not rash with your mouth, and let not your heart be hasty to utter a word before G-d; for G-d is in heaven, and you are upon earth; therefore let your words be few"* (Koheles 5:1), and *"The L-ord looks down from heaven upon men"* (Tehilim 14:2).

> *Matanas Chelko*: *"I am the L-ord who searches the heart.."* - the intent is not that G-d has the ability to search and examine or that He does this from time to time. Rather, "I am the L-ord who searches the heart - always". Every second, he knows and examines what is in a man's heart.
>
> *"The L-ord looks down from heaven upon men"* - in truth, this cheshbon (consideration) is the first Halacha in the Shulchan Aruch (Orach Chaim 1:1, Rama):" 'I have placed G-d before me always' (Tehilim 16:8) - this is a general principle of the Torah and of the virtues of the righteous who walk before G-d". end quote. This is a simple matter, but it is hidden from us. For when a man understands that the Holy One, blessed be He, is looking straight at him, at his deeds and in his heart, immediately, he transforms to a different person, and does only that which the Holy One, blessed be He, wants from him.
>
> [the Rama continues there:] "For the way in which a person sits, moves around, and carries out his daily activities while he is alone in his home is not the same way he would engage in these activities while standing before a great king. Furthermore, the way one speaks while amongst those in his home and the conversations he partakes with his relatives is not the same manner in which he would speak while in the presence of a mortal king. Surely when one considers in his mind that the mighty King, The Holy One blessed be His Name, where the whole world is filled with His glory, stands before him and sees his deeds...[immediately the fear and the proper awe of G-d will descend upon him and he will always be abashed before G-d...]"

When this matter returns in the thoughts of the believer at all times, and the believer will make an accounting with himself on this always, then the Creator will be with him in his inner realm, he will see G-d with the eye of his intellect, and will fear Him always, and glorify Him, and reflect on His works (i.e. in nature. see gate 2 - *PL*), and examine His deeds in governing His creations, which testify to His greatness, exaltedness, wisdom, and power.

> *Pas Lechem*: *"when this matter returns"* - he used the term "returns", since it is impossible to tell a person to think on this always without any

interruption, since many thoughts must pass through one's mind such as Torah matters, prayer, business matters, etc. Rather, the intent is that one should put this to mind only from time to time, that this thought be with him leaving and returning always.

When one does this diligently, the Creator will grant him peace from his sadness and calm his heart from fear of Him.

*Marpe Lenefesh*: he will no longer be sad due to lack of money or other needs. And likewise, he will no longer fear coming to sin, since G-d will be with him...

*Pas Lechem*: If until now his service was in sadness...from now on, it will be with joy, and if until now he was always afraid of stumbling in the trap of sin, from now on he will be assured of not sinning again.

And the Creator will open for him the gates of His knowledge, and reveal to him secrets of His wisdom, and G-d will put His attention to guide and lead him, and He won't abandon him to himself and his (limited) ability, as the entire psalm 23 says: *"The L-ord is my shepherd; I shall not lack.."* (Tehilim 23:1), until the end.

*Matanas Chelko*: on this Rabeinu added more chidushim (novel teachings). Namely, his emotional state will change completely. He will feel that he is always walking with the Master of the world. I.e. not only will he think on matters of fear of G-d, but rather, the Creator will be with him in his inner being, and he will feel that he is with Him always. This is the meaning of "the qualities of the righteous who walk before G-d" which the Ramah (in Shulchan Aruch) referred to, that he walks always with the thought and feeling that the Holy One, blessed be He, is with him right now and that it is always so. Such a person lives in a different world, in the world with the Master of the world...

*"He won't abandon him to himself and his (limited) ability"* - the Holy One, blessed be He, will make him into almost a Malach (angel). He will conduct Himself with him outside the natural order (supernaturally)...

*"as the entire Psalm 23..."* - the level of king David was "though I walk through the valley of the shadow of death, I will fear no evil; for You are with me".
And also "Your rod and Your staff, they comfort me" - he was always with the Creator, and G-d conducted Himself with him always for the good. A person sees this with his own eyes.

*Translator:* - I have also found that studying nature with proper outlook is extremely beneficial, especially, today when the divine wisdom is being revealed to such a vast extent, it is hard to fail to see the awesome, bottomless divine wisdom.

And he will be on an exalted level, among the levels of the Chasidim (extremely pious), and a high level among the Tzadikim (righteous), and he will be able to see without his physical eyes, and hear without his physical ears, and speak without a tongue (he will be able to speak to others without a physical tongue - ML), and he will sense things without his physical senses, and be able to picture them without need for a [physical] comparison.

*Tov Halevanon*: All this refers to deep, Divine matters, close to the level of Ruach HaKodesh.

*Marpe Lenefesh*: he will see with his Ruach Hakodesh (holy spirit) things happening far away that a man is not capable of seeing with his physical eyes, and will see them with his mind's eye since he has purified his physicality to the extent that he fulfills the verse (Tehilim 16:8) "I have placed G-d before me always".

*Matanas Chelko*: he progresses further in the level of "Ein od Milvado" (there is nothing but G-d - Devarim 4:35) as the Nefesh Chaim explained from the Rambam's Moreh Nevuchim regarding the level of "Ein Od Milvado". How does one attain this level? He starts from the thought of "I have set G-d before me always", and afterwards becomes diligent in the level of Yirah (fear of G-d). For since, G-d sees everything, he must fear Him.

Afterwards, he must adorn himself and his mind since G-d observes him always. And since he understands that G-d looks at him every second without any interruption whatsoever, from now, behold, he walks always with the intent and thought that G-d is with him, and he already feels and recognizes the presence of the Creator of the universe, until he reaches the level of "Ein Od Milvado".

For, "I have placed G-d before me always" is a level every person can attain. In truth, every person feels thoughts of "I have placed.." during times in his life. When he contemplates deeper and diligently into this, he can attain the higher level of "Ein Od Milvado" until he no longer needs to exert and force himself to this. Rather, he has a true feeling that G-d is with him always. And therefore, no creature has any power to harm or help him at all. Rather, everything is from the Creator of the world. When a man adorns his thought and transforms to such a different person, the Holy One,

blessed be He, conducts Himself with him in this way, until He does for
him things which are supernatural.

He will not dislike any situation nor will he prefer another situation other
than what the Creator chose for him.

> *Tov Halevanon*: due to his strong trust in G-d, since everything G-d does is
> for the good...and he knows that whatever happens to him is a decree from
> G-d who knows what is good for him better than he does.

And he makes his will like G-d's will, and his love, what G-d loves. He
will cherish what G-d cherishes (clings to G-d's traits, ex. merciful - *TL*),
and what is disgusting to him is what is disgusting to G-d. Of like him, the
wise man said: "Blessed is the man that hears me (the Torah), watching
every day at my gates (this hints at one's constant accounting with himself
- *TL*), waiting at the posts of my doors" (Mishlei 8:34), and "For
whosoever finds me (the Torah) finds life, and shall obtain favor of the
L-ord" (Mishlei 8:35).

## THE ELEVENTH:
*(regular accounting of one's deeds)*

> *Matanas Chelko*: this is much closer to the familiar explanation for
> "cheshbon hanefesh" (spiritual accounting) we are used to using. But this
> too, is only in order to activate in oneself the will and desire to the service
> of G-d with greater strength.

To make an accounting with oneself regarding one's days which have
already passed whether he was engaged in the service of G-d or the service
of his own yetzer (evil inclination, ex. selfish desires, wasting time).
He should apply to himself the following illustration: Let him imagine that
a king gave him money to spend for certain purposes, and he commanded
him not to spend any of the money for anything else. The king informed
him that at the end of the year, he would make an accounting with him and
will not forgive him in the least of it. Is it not proper for the man to make
an accounting with himself at the end of each month of that year to see
how much of the money was spent and with what he had spent it (and if he
sees that he already spent more than what is proper, he can rectify it in the
remaining months - *TL*)? And likewise so that he will be careful with the
remaining money and the remaining time before the time of accounting
suddenly comes and he is ignorant of what he may claim and what may be
claimed from him?

*Pas Lechem* - then he will not know what debts other people owe him and what debts he owes other people, like the common way of all business dealers, who are mingled and entangled with each other.

Alternatively, "what he may claim and what may be claimed from him" refers to between him and the king - Tov Halevanon.

*Matanas Chelko*: *"so that he will be careful with the remaining money"* - i.e. even if the yetzer hara (evil inclination) tricked him until today and he did not do the cheshbon (accounting). But from now on, he should begin to arrange this cheshbon. For on each and every day there is an accounting.

Similar to this illustration, my brother, you should check with yourself, if you can, each and every one of your days, and make an accounting with it concerning your service of G-d, which is a duty incumbent upon you. And if you have neglected doing this (daily accounting) in the days of your life that already passed, at least do the accounting with yourself for your remaining days. Do not continue neglecting due to your previous neglecting, nor continue overlooking due to previously overlooking it. For before G-d there is no neglect, nor overlooking nor forgetting.

*Matanas Chelko*: *"do not continue..."* - do not think "since I refrained from doing the cheshbon until now, I will refrain from it also in the future". This is foolishness. For even if he comes to the world of truth and he will be able to give an accounting for just half of his days, this is better than one who does not have in his hands anything whatsoever.

*Tov Halevanon*: i.e. do not continue neglecting in thinking that you can continue neglecting making your accounting with the Creator since you see that He did not punish you right away for the previous sin, as if your affairs are hidden from His eyes, and therefore you would like to continue your deeds. Likewise, do not think G-d overlooks, and that He already overlooked your previous sins and He will continue overlooking more.

It has been said: "Days are like scrolls, inscribe on them what you wish to be remembered by". And scripture says: *"Be you not as the horse, nor as the mule, which have no understanding"* (Tehilim 32:9). It was said of one who prolonged his time of neglect to make a personal accounting *"also old age was cast into him, yet he knows not"* (Hoshea 7:9).

*Matanas Chelko*: *"days are like scrolls"* - every day is a blank page in the book and you can write on it whatever you wish. It is like a diary. Do not write on the paper what you will in the future be ashamed of.

*Translator*: See Marpe Lenefesh commentary for a mystical explanation on this.


## THE TWELFTH:
*(the pursuit of physical)*
To make an accounting with oneself at a time when one's heart is excited and diligent for worldly matters, applying himself fully with his utmost ingenuity and maximum ability, and to weigh this against one's laxness in matters of his final end, and his straying from the service of his G-d.

Then he will see and feel that his thoughts for matters of this world are the highest of his thoughts, and his aspiration for this world is the higher of his aspirations. For all the various types of possessions will never be enough for him in the least. On the contrary he is like a fire, the more wood is added, the more it increases flames, and all of his heart and intent will be drawn to it (this world - *PL*), day and night. He will not consider anyone a close friend except one who helps him in them, and no one a friend except he who leads him to them. His eye will be to the times it is good to buy, and the times it is good to sell. And he will observe matters of the selling rates for the whole world. He investigates where they are cheap and where they are expensive, and when they go up and when they go down. He will not refrain from travelling to faraway places. Neither heat, nor cold, nor stormy sea, nor long desert roads - all this out of his hope to reach the end of his desire but there is no end to it.

It is possible that all of his efforts will be for nothing, and he will not attain anything except a long suffering, exertion, and toil. And even if he attains some of what he hoped for, perhaps he will not get any benefit from it but instead will only guard it, manage it, and protect it from potential damages, until it will go to he who G-d decreed it should go to, whether while he is still alive, as written: *"at mid life he will leave it"* (Yirmiya 17:11) or after his death, as written: *"they will abandon their fortunes to others"* (Tehilim 49:11).

The wise man already warned us against zeal and exertion for amassing wealth, as written: *"Labor not to be rich: cease from your own wisdom"* (Mishlei 23:4), and he spoke of the calamity found in it, in saying *"Will you set your eyes upon that which is not? for riches certainly make themselves wings; they fly away as an eagle toward heaven"* (Mishlei 23:5), and the other wise man (King David) taught us and permitted us to make efforts in earning money for our basic needs only, in saying: *"If you eat the toil of your hands, you are praiseworthy, and it is good for you"* (Tehilim 128:2).

And likewise, the pious man asked G-d to give him his livelihood only in the basic amount, and to distance him from wealth which leads to the luxuries, and from poverty which leads to loss of morals and Torah, in saying: *"Two things have I asked of you; Do not give me poverty nor wealth, provide me with my food portion"* (Mishlei 30:7), and the rest of the matter. Like him, we find our forefather, Yaakov, who asked G-d only for his basic needs, in saying: *"If G-d will be with me, and He will guard me on this way, upon which I am going, and He will give me bread to eat and a garment to wear"* (Gen.28:20).

Wake up my brother! Look at the deficiency of that which you hurry and pursue - to maintain your body in its natural state. Your association with it will only be for a short time (relative to the long afterlife - *TL*), it will not be spared from pain (the body will never be free of pain - *TL*, see Gate #10 which says the body always has a desire or worry, etc) and it will not be saved from troubles while you are attached to it. If it eats too much, it will become sick. If it eats too little, it will become weak. If you clothe it more than it needs, it will become uncomfortable, and if you leave it naked, it will be pained. Furthermore, its health and sickness, its life and death are not according to your will and not in your control, rather everything is directed by your Creator.

Where is the superiority of your soul over your body? And the exaltedness of its world over the body's world, its rising above (after death) while the body descends below, its spirituality versus the body's physicality, its unchanging nature versus the body's changing nature, its eternal existence versus the body's deteriorating and disappearing existence, its simple form versus the body's composite elements, its pure essence versus the body's baseness, its wisdom and understanding versus the body's beastliness, its tendency for the virtuous traits versus the body's tendency for the disgraceful traits.

If you conduct yourself in this kind of zeal and effort for the rectification of your body, in spite of its lowliness and baseness, and despite your weak capacity to save it from damage or to benefit it, how much more is it your duty to conduct yourself with this zeal and effort for the rectification of your soul, which is so important and which you will be left with (forever), and which you were commanded to guide its matter, and to look into things which will rectify it in acquiring wisdom and understanding, as written: *"Buy the truth, and sell it not"* (Mishlei 23:23), and *"Get wisdom, get understanding"* (Mishlei 4:5), and *"How much better is it to get wisdom than gold! and to choose understanding rather than silver!"* (Mishlei 16:16), and *"So shall the knowledge of wisdom be unto your soul"* (Mishlei 24:14), and *"If you are wise, you shall be wise for yourself"* (Mishlei 9:12), which means that the spiritual acquisitions are yours. No one can ever steal them from you, unlike what occurs by physical acquisitions.

See, my brother, what is between the two things, and what is between the two matters. Turn away from the luxuries of your world, and exert yourself in what you need for your final end. Do not say: "I will share the fate of the fool" (who does not make this accounting). Because more will be claimed from you according to your higher level of understanding, and your punishment will be greater. The accounting demanded of you for your neglect will be stricter. Do not rely on a claim which you will have no grounds for, and do not rest assured on a plea which will be used against you and not for you.

The discussion to complete this subject is too lengthy, let it be enough for you what I have aroused you on it, and taught you according to your understanding. Contemplate my words, and understand my allusions. Investigate them in the book of the Torah of G-d, and the words of our sages. You will see their explanation from the verses, from logic, and from Tradition (oral law), with G-d's help.

## THE THIRTEENTH:
*(not to waste time)*
To make an accounting with oneself regarding that one's wisdom is greater than his deeds, that one's recognition (of his duties) exceeds his efforts in the service of the Creator, and that one's capabilities exceeds what he is actually paying back to the Creator, [in return] for His many favors to him.

> *Matanas Chelko*: our sages said: "he whose deeds is greater than his wisdom, his wisdom endures. But he whose wisdom is greater than his deeds, his wisdom will not endure" (Avot 3:9). One must do a cheshbon on whether his deeds are in line with his wisdom or not. This is a cheshbon which rouses him and obligates him to do this...
>
> It is known of the Netziv that when he published his book he said over that as a child, he did not succeed in his Torah studies. His parents wanted him

to leave yeshiva and study a trade. He cried on this and from then on began to learn with great diligence until he eventually became a great Torah scholar and merited to publish his commentary on the Sheiltot and other books. He said that without this, when he reached the Heavenly Beit Din, they would have claimed from him: "where is the commentary on the Sheiltot? Where is the HaEmek Davar commentary on the Torah (which he wrote)?"

Behold, Teshuva (repentance) helps on everything, even on Bitul Torah (wasting time that could have been used Torah study). But it does not help for what he needed to do and learn. Even if he did Teshuva on Bitul Torah, he would still not have published through this the commentary on the Sheiltot... My master and teacher, Rabbi Elyah Lopian z"l would say even though it says "let your garments be always white" (Kohelet 9:8), and by going through Gehinom, one's garments become white from the filth of sin, but nevertheless, the missing buttons are not placed on his garment. Thus, a man is roused through this cheshbon.

Let one imagine the analogy of a slave whose master gave him land to sow, and gave him the seeds according to what he needs. The slave planted part of the seeds and used the rest for his own use. When the master checked the land, he found part of it was not sown. When he asked the slave on this, the slave admitted his lacking in this matter, and the master made a calculation based on what the slave claimed he sowed of the seeds in the land, and checked the land to see how much was sowed. He then investigated how much produce grew from the land (to see how much produce each seed makes), and then claimed from the slave the rest of the seeds by charging him to pay what the land would have produced from those seeds - his pain was great and his trouble was multiplied.

*Tov Halevanon*: Based on the produce that grew from the field, the master calculated how much produce would have grown had the slave planted all the seeds and claimed the whole amount from him. According to this, the more the ground was fertile and blessed, the more he will be claimed for the loss of potential produce. So too by a man, the more his ability and recognition is greater, the more he will be claimed for loss in the service of G-d.

*Matanas Chelko*: the master did two accountings with the slave. One, that which he used the seeds for his own use instead of the master's. Two, what would have grown if he had done what was incumbent on him to do.

Likewise, my brother, it is proper for you to make an accounting with yourself for what the Creator has graced you with to understand Him and

His Torah, and how much strength and ability He has given you to pay back what you owe Him. Then check with yourself what you have actually done and imagine that you are in judgment for all of this, and being taken into account for it (by G-d - *PL*), and all the more so while receiving prolonged and constant benefits from the Creator.

It is proper for you to endeavor with all of your strength, and exert yourself to the best of your ability to pay Him back, and to bring your deeds equal to the level of your wisdom (that your deeds correspond to the wisdom you are capable of - *TL*), and your exertion to the level of your recognition. And let all your extra toil (beyond what you need to toil for your worldly needs such as earning a basic livelihood) be spent doing according to your level of wisdom. Do not get involved in the luxuries of this world, lest you will weaken from paying your Torah debts. G-d has given a person strength according to what he needs for his Torah and his worldly (needs). One who spends any of it for the luxuries, which he can do without, will be lacking (in strength) that he will need for the necessary things.

Do not absolve yourself with "if only" or "maybe", saying "if only I would reach such and such a level of education or money, then, after that I would pay everything that I am obligated of the service of the Creator", or other similar answers, because they are false claims. One who relies on them will veer away and one who leans on them will fall. This is the greatest mistake of the "deposit takers", which I mentioned to you in (chapter 6 of) the Gate of Trust.

Be careful lest you take it for yourself as an excuse, because then you will be just like any other sinner who claims this, and you already know that this claim does not save a person from punishment, as Shlomo said regarding a thief: *"Men do not despise a thief, if he steals to satisfy his soul when he is starving, but if he be found out, he shall pay sevenfold"* (Mishlei 6:30). Even though his dire situation is clear, and necessity brought him to steal the money of others, even so, he will not be spared from punishment and the fine of Kefel (double payment). How much more so for other sins.

*Tov Halevanon*: If a man commits some sin, certainly no claim or excuse will absolve him from the punishment, like the thief which he brought as an illustration, that even though desperation pushed him to steal, nevertheless he is obligated to pay Kefel (double), and if he cannot pay, he will be sold (by the Beit Din as a slave for 6 years to repay) for his theft.

*Pas Lechem*: even though one should not degrade him so much for this ugly deed, since he has a valid, obligatory excuse, namely, to "feed his soul when he is starving", even so, if he is caught, he will pay sevenfold - behold we see from here that an excuse does not save a person from punishment.

*Matanas Chelko*: so too for all matters, one cannot claim: "if I were not a baal taava (person of strong desires), I would not have sinned". Or "if this trial were not sent to me, I would not have stumbled". Because it is for this that G-d gave you the desires and the trial - in order that you strengthen yourself and stand up to the test!

Instead, make this procrastination time into a bounty (use it properly), while you can still pay back your daily obligations to the Creator, and do not procrastinate doing today's service until tomorrow, lest it will be too much of a burden for you to pay back, assuming that you reach tomorrow and are among its (living) men. Worse than this, if your end comes, your excuse will be cornered, and your claim will be halted, because this world is like a market fair which crowds together and then disperses. He who did business and profited is joyful, but he who lost money regrets. Therefore, the wise man said: *"And remember your Creator in the days of your youth, before the days of calamity come..."* (Koheles 12:1).

## THE FOURTEENTH:
*(the spider web)*
To make an accounting with oneself when feeling love, closeness, or devotion towards someone who one thinks loves him, as written: *"As in water, face reflects face, so the heart of man to another man"* (Mishlei 27:19).

*Tov Halevanon*: Just like in water, when a person looks on it with a friendly face, it will reflect to him a friendly face. So too, for the heart of a man, if he is in good will towards his fellow, then his fellow's heart will also be in good will with him.

*Matanas Chelko*: this is human nature.. when a person feels love from his fellow, he too will love him back in return. This is so even if he does not recognize the person. If the person merely shows him love and grace, he too will feel love back towards him... one needs to do this cheshbon when he feels this love [from another person] as Rabeinu wrote "when feeling love..", how G-d bestows so much love to him and gives him so much... and to say to himself "how much more so should I feel love towards G-d on all the good He did and does with me, which are far more than what this man gave to me and loves me". Thus through feeling love towards this man, he can reach love of G-d...

I saw a beautiful point in the book "Ohr Yahel" (end of vol.3): " 'you shall love the L-ord your G-d' (Devarim 6:5) - how much should a Jew rouse himself to love his G-d with all his heart and soul when he sees the wondrous love of G-d towards him. This itself that the Holy One, blessed be He, requests love of Him and commands him "love Me" - is it conceivable that a powerful and awesome king would seek the love of a peasant sheep herder? But everything will make sense when we realize that the peasant is the king's son, who wound up in a lost and faraway village. The prince's blood and soul is from the royal lineage. Therefore, his father falls on his neck and asks of him - "love me!". All this is but an analogy and metaphor so that we may understand the greatness and preciousness of Yisrael, the connection between them and their Maker - "you are sons to the L-ord your G-d"! (Devarim 14:1).

And all the more so, if this person is an important official or a ruler, and still more, when one sees signs from the person such as drawing him close, promising (to help him), or benefiting him and doing kindness to him without needing anything from him in return - then nothing will distract him from remembering his love for the person. He will not hold back any of his ability for the person but rather will use his full capacity to fulfill his friend's command and do his service, and in his gratitude, he will volunteer of himself, of his money, and of his sons to pay the person back.

Since one does this for a weak creation like ourselves, how much more so are we obligated many times more to our Creator, who told us through His prophet that He loves us, as written *"Not because you are more numerous than any people did the L-ord desire in you and choose you, etc."* (Devarim 7:7). And in addition to telling us of His love we saw signs of His love for us, and His help to us, both in the present and in the past, and His drawing us to Him and promising to us for every generation, as written: *"And yet for all that, when they are in the land of their enemies, I will not cast them away, neither will I abhor them, to destroy them utterly, and to break my covenant with them; for I am the L-ord their G-d"* (Vayikra 26:44), and *"For we are slaves, and in our servitude our G-d has not forsaken us"* (Ezra 9:9).

*Matanas Chelko*: there are times when a person feels this love from G-d, such as when he merits to make a "simcha" (joyous occasion) in his family. At such times, he should not merely say "Baruch Ha-shem that I merited this". But rather, he should strive to feel that G-d is giving him a kiss, and thus, he should also kiss G-d back with feelings of love... every feeling of love is a fulfillment of the mitzva to love G-d, even if it is only for one

| second.

More on this matter: it is evident that for a person who was the friend of our fathers and our forefathers, we are obligated to recall this love by honoring him and treating him with love, as the wise man said: *"your own friend, and your father's friend, forsake not"* (Mishlei 27:10). And the Creator reminds us of the bris (covenant) of our forefathers and His providence over us due to them, and in order to fulfill His covenant with them, as written: *"But because of the L-ord's love for you, and because He keeps the oath He swore to your forefathers"* (Devarim 7:8), and many more like this.

If we do not place our trust in Him, and do not rely on His kindness nor move ourselves to love Him and cling to His service, nor pour our prayers to Him - how crude is our nature (for not having any stirring in our hearts to love Him - *PL*), how stiff-necked (for not clinging to His service - *PL*) and of little faith our we (for not praying to Him - *PL*), and how strongly we resist going after the truth!

> *Matanas Chelko*: these are words of mussar (rebuke) that a person speaks to himself. How crude, weak, etc. if one does not reach love of G-d after G-d shows him so much love...

We do not recall His love for our fathers and forefathers nor do we pay back the Creator's love and providence for us, nor for His promises and for drawing us close to Him do we do His service, nor for His great goodness and kindness to us do we listen, nor on account of His creating us and benevolent guiding of us do we feel abashed (before Him in prayer - *PL*).

Wake up my brother from this slumber. Roll away from your heart the curtain your yetzer (evil inclination) has spread over you, until he separated you from the light of your understanding, like a spider who weaves a web around the window of a house, and when it persists in this, it will thicken the web and block the light, until the light of the sun is completely prevented from penetrating inside the house. In the beginning, when first spun, the web is extremely weak and thin, but as the matter (of weaving) persists more and more, it will strengthen and thicken, eventually completely preventing the light of the sun's rays from penetrating it and entering the house.

Similarly is the work of the yetzer in your heart. At the beginning of the matter, it will be extremely weak, and will not prevent you from seeing the truths. If you sense it at that time, and drive it out of your heart, it will be an easy matter. But, if you treat the matter lightly and neglect it, the work of the evil inclination will strengthen and he will prevent the light of your intellect from reaching you, and then it will be difficult to remove its (evil) effects from your mind.

> i.e. even what you know intellectually to be true will be blocked and prevented from reaching your heart, and therefore won't affect your actions. Like Eisav who knew much of the truth intellectually in his head but could not bring the knowledge to heart due to blockage between the mind and the heart - Lev Eliyahu.

Therefore hurry to save your soul, and plea to G-d to help you drive him off of yourself. Work hard and exert yourself, then you will be illuminated with the light of wisdom, and you will perceive the truth of things with your mind's eye.

> *Tov Halevanon*: When you strengthen yourself, and toil hard on this - then you will be illuminated with the light of wisdom.

The early ones already compared the acts of the yetzer on a man with different analogies based on verses, in saying: "And there came a *wayfarer* unto the rich man, and he refused to take of his own flock and of his own herd, to prepare for the *guest* that had come to him; but took the poor man's lamb, and prepared it for the *man* that came to him" (Shmuel II 12:4), at first he was termed "wayfarer" and then "guest", and after that progressed to "man".

Similarly, it is written: "Happy is the man that *walked* not in the counsel of the wicked, nor *stood* in the way of sinners, nor *sat* in the seat of the mockers" (Tehilim 1:1), at first "went", then "stood", then "sat", and many others similar.

Commune with your soul, my brother, on this and on similar ideas to it, and force it to do that which will be its salvation, because the wise man already said of those who neglect the duty of reflection: *"Evil men understand not justice"* (Mishlei 28:5).

> *Tov Halevanon*: Men who are used to iniquity and [bad] toil - it becomes their nature, until they do not understand the truth, similar to the analogy of the spider web the author mentioned.

## THE FIFTEENTH:
*(preparing for the journey)*

To make an accounting with oneself when preparing provisions before needing them, without knowing whether he will live until the time that he will be able to benefit from them. Likewise, when one needs to go on a long journey, he will prepare matters of his journey many days in advance: he researches which merchandise he will be able to sell at the place he is going, and then prepares what he will ride on, and what he can of provisions and company (he tries join a good company of travellers - *PL*), and which stations he will stop along the way, and similar to this, despite not knowing what the Creator decreed for him on all of this nor how long he will live.

In this way, my brother, we are obligated to be prepared for the appointed time, and to prepare for the faraway journey to the other world, which we have no escape from, and no refuge from (rather, everyone ends up there - *MC*), and to think on the provisions (i.e. what provisions are important there - *MC*), and with what we will greet our Creator on the great day of accounting which scriptures says of it: *"For, behold, the day is coming, it burns as a furnace; and all the proud, and all that work wickedness, shall be stubble; and the day that comes shall set them ablaze, says the L-ord of Hosts, that it shall leave them neither root nor branch"* (Malachi 3:19).

How can we ignore this when the journey is constant, (i.e. we can see every day people dying and making the journey - *TL*, another explanation: "every day we are getting closer to it, and losing vitality due to aging" - *PL*), and the displacing is forever, and the road is long, and the resting place is faraway. (see Marpe Lenefesh commentary for a mystical explanation) Why do we not put to heart to remember our end, and do not think of the provisions we should make for our final abode? We occupy ourselves with a fleeting world, and abandon the everlasting one. We occupy ourselves with the ailing of our bodies, and forget our spiritual ailments, we occupy ourselves with the service of our evil inclination, and abandon the service of our Creator, we serve our base desires and do not serve our G-d.

*Pas Lechem*: We busy ourselves with saving our bodies from ailments and maladies while forgetting to heal the ailments of our souls. The author specified three points (1) "spiritual ailments" corresponding to faith and character traits, (2) "our evil inclination" corresponding to the lust for bad things, through the enticements of the yetzer, and (3) afterwards said that even without the empowering of the yetzer, human nature tends towards the "base desires"...and on the base desires that a person has pleasure in and rejoices in, he later says "And to this drunkenness...", since wine arouses enjoyment and rejoicing in a man's heart..

Alas to this confusion! How so universal it is (in that it applies to virtually every person - *TL*)! And to this drunkenness, how strong it is!, as the verse says: *"for their eyes are shrouded, that they cannot see, and their hearts, that they cannot understand"* (Yeshaya 44:18), and *"ye that are drunken, but not with wine, that stagger, but not with strong drink"* (Yeshaya 29:9).

*Matanas Chelko*: this cheshbon is so evident. But when one learns it, it does not make an impression. Only through contemplation and study with emotion (hitpaalut) time after time, then after 20 times, with proper nigun (melody) in order that the words enter the heart - then fear will seize his heart properly in a good and beneficial manner.


## THE SIXTEENTH:

*(reflecting when seeing sudden death)*
To make an accounting with oneself on the lengthy amount of time he survived in this world, and to put to heart the approaching of his end, and the coming of death on him, at a time when he sees that other living things, whether of the speaking (human beings) or otherwise (the animals), die suddenly without foreknowledge, nor even any hint, and (to put to heart) that there is no time that a person can be assured that it is not his time. It does not refrain from coming any month of the months of the year, nor any day of the days of the month, nor any hour of the hours of the day. It does not come only in old age, sparing the middle aged, or the young men, the young girls, the children or babies, rather it befalls all the living at all times, in every stage, and in every place.

*Matanas Chelko*: one must think: "perhaps this will happen also to himself". For a man is not assured of life. This is not like that person which the Zohar speaks of (Parsha Nasso) saying: "a man walks in this world and thinks it is his and he will remain in it for all generations". On this it is written: "better to go to a funeral then a party.. and the living will put to heart" (Kohelet 7:2). When one goes to a levaya (funeral procession) to accompany the dead he should contemplate: "this dead person also thought he would live forever, and it did not turn out like this. If so, I am also not assured". The Chafetz Chaim would say: "why does this not make such a strong impression on a person?" He explained that it is because a person is so very strongly used to being alive that he thinks certainly there is a "club of dead people" and he is not part of that club. But in truth, this is blindness from the power of the evil inclination.

A person should imagine to himself as if a king had placed a deposit in his charge, and did not specify the time when to return it. And the king commanded him to be ready for his return at all times, so that he will not go to another city and will be available at the time the king will claim it from him. Is it conceivable for him to dwell outside the city of the king while the deposit is still in his hands?

> *Marpe Lenefesh*: The analogy is that a man must have intent to cling to the Creator, and that if he momentarily forgets Him, it is as if he is outside of G-d's place.

Some make the following analogy: One should imagine himself as if he has a debt to pay with no fixed payment date, expecting every moment to be called for payment. He will not be at peace until he pays it back.

> *Pas Lechem*: The analogy is that a man must fulfill his debts in the service of G-d while he is still alive, and since his lifespan is unknown, it is like a debt without a fixed time of repayment.

When a man considers his long stay in the world, and remembers that many of his friends journeyed to the other world before himself, at a time when they had strong expectations to be in the company of the world (they did not put death before their eyes like himself, but instead their intent was to build and invest in matters of this world - *TL*), and one does not see any advantage in himself (whether in age or build - *PL*) that would obligate his living longer than them - his hope in this world will diminish, and he will consider his end. He will think on his provisions for the time of his journey, and will commune with himself before the day of accounting (death - TL).

One of the wise men said: "one who precedes death before him rectified himself".

> *Pas Lechem*: He who pictures in his imagination and thinks always on death - we are certain that this man rectified himself.
>
> *Tov Halevanon*: One who precedes before himself the matter of death, and places it before his eyes always, rectifies himself
>
> *Manoach Halevavos*: One who sees his fellows die before him and contemplates on the matter of death, he will rectify himself.

And the wise man said: *"the heart of the wise is in the house of mourning"*

(Koheles 7:4), and *"It is better to go to the house of mourning, than to go to the house of feasting; for that is the end of all men, and the living will lay it to heart"* (Koheles 7:2), the intent of "the living" is he whose heart is living, namely, one who understands and realizes. It is also written: *"Man is like vanity: his days are as a shadow that passes away"* (Tehilim 144:4).

> *Matanas Chelko*: this cheshbon and the previous one are very powerful. The matter is that a man needs to contemplate his own death. Especially, when he hears of one who died or when he goes to a house of mourning. People don't want to think these thoughts because it brings to sadness and they don't want to feel sad thinking of their own funeral. But the idea is only to contemplate that a man does not live forever.
>
> For example, if a person stands on his field and is lazy in working it, and his friend sees him and tells him "work your land while the sun still shines. In a few hours, the sun will set and you will not be able to work". Will the owner of the field reply: "don't remind me of the night. Right now the sun is shining!" Certainly, not. Rather, he understands that his friend's intent is that there is a limit and end to the time he can work. So too, regarding thinking on the day of death. One must do [good] while he still has the ability, while he is still alive, and he must prepare provisions for the journey.
>
> The Yetzer Hara (evil inclination) always tries to distance these thoughts from people. Rabbi Itzele would say (Shaarei Ohr 70): "when a young man dies, people ask how he died and what killed him. Why do they want to know how he died? What difference does it make? Rather, they want to attribute the matter to some cause of nature in order to rest assured that this will not be their fate. For example, if he hears a man died suddenly from a heart-attack. For psychological reasons, a person tells himself: "thank G-d, my heart is healthy", i.e. that heart attack will not happen to me. Or when he hears someone died from a certain illness, he tells himself: "thank G-d, I don't have that illness". Thus, he calms himself like this. But the truth is not so. Rather, when a man dies, all those who hear must tell themselves that they too will die in the end." This is the cheshbon here.

## THE SEVENTEENTH:
*(benefits of solitude)*

At a time when one sees himself tending towards association with people and enjoying their company, he should reflect on the benefits of solitude, and separation from people, and with the evil resulting from being in the company of fools without necessity.

*Marpe Lenefesh*: When a person feels himself desiring and longing to sit with people and enjoying their company, and he thinks it is a good thing for him and an enjoyment, let him reflect in his mind on how many benefits there are in solitude and separation from people and how many bad things come about from being in the company of fools. And the author will now list them, one by one.

*Matanas Chelko*: - it is natural for people to love to be with others and friends. But one must contemplate that there are a few detriments in joining the company of people of the foolish type, which are most people, for they do not live with cheshbon.

However, certainly there are times when one is forced to associate with others, even fools. Namely, when there is a necessity and need for this. But otherwise, there is no need for this and one should separate and be in solitude.

The evil of their company:
(1) Excessive talk (i.e. one of the evils is that one habituates himself to talk useless speech - *TL*), "so and so said", "it was said on so and so", long winded confusion without purpose, and the wise man said: *"In the multitude of words there lacks not sin, but he that refrains his lips is wise"* (Mishlei 10:19) (since useless speech leads to slander, frivolity, disputes and of course - wasting the precious time - *PL,ML*). One of the wise would say: "safeguard the superfluous of your words, and muzzle the superfluous (movement) of your tongue".

(2) Speaking of people, recalling their bad deeds, and mentioning their faults. The verse says of this matter: *"You sit and speak against your brother; you slander your own mother's son"* (Tehilim 50:20).

(3) Falsehood and lies. On this the verse says: *"wickedness in its midst"* (Tehilim 55:12), and *"I hearkened and heard, but they spoke not aright"* (Yirmiya 8:6).

*Manoach Halevavos*: it is the normal way for groups of people who are sitting idly to discuss falsehood and lies. Likewise, it progresses to all of the following.

(4) False oaths and useless oaths. The Creator said of them: *"for the L-ord will not exonerate one who takes His Name in vain"* (Shemos 20:7), and one of the pious said to his disciples: "the Torah permitted us to make an oath in the Name of the Creator for truth, but I advise you not to swear

neither to what is true nor to what is false, rather say only 'yes' or 'no' ".

(5) Arrogance and frivolity, and to put down some of those present, and to laugh with them, and I already designated a gate in this book on the subject of distancing oneself from this matter, namely, the Gate of Submission.

(6) Absence of fear of G-d in one's heart at a time when one mingles with people and converses with them (since one is not free to strive in fear of G-d - *TL*), along with little chance of being spared their damaging his business affairs and talking of him.

> *Pas Lechem*: since one may divulge his private dealings with them and afterwards they will be able to use the information to damage him financially or talk to others of his faults which he revealed to them.

> *Marpe Lenefesh*: All these groups he mentioned, they are those "four groups who do not greet the Shechina in the next world" (Sotah 42). They are the groups of flatterers, liars, jesters, and speakers of lashon hara (slander). And all of them are dependent on speech, and are called "evil". And it is written: "You, G-d, do not desire wickedness, evil will not dwell with You" (Tehilim 5:5). And here is an excerpt from the book Reishis Chachma (Shaar Hakedusha perek 12): "One who fixes his place in the street corners for useless conversation and idle talk, is called a jester (letz). Since he was capable of learning Torah at that time but refrains from doing so. He is called a jester (letz), since he is like a man who the king told: "count gold coins for one hour, and all that you count will be yours", but he sits idly.

> This man jests from the king's gold coins and they are lowly in his eyes. Is there frivolity greater than this? So too, one who is idle from learning Torah after he understood the great reward for toiling in Torah - he is a real (mamash) jester... and even those who learn Torah must be careful from idle speech, since if words of frivolity enter his heart, correspondingly, words of Torah will spill out of his heart, etc.". He ends off: "whoever wants to distance from sins should distance himself from the company of the wicked", see there for more.

(7) Flattery and love of acquiring a name for oneself, to become proud over them, and to try to be important in their eyes by demonstrating what he knows of the various branches of wisdom and deeds, whether or not he actually knows them.

> *Pas Lechem*: Through his enjoyment of their company, he will crave to acquire a name among them, and this will bring him to try to appear

pleasing to them in his deeds.

*Matanas Chelko*: because he wants to find favor in the eyes of others and to be loved by them, he flatters them and tells them that they are not doing evil. And he also becomes arrogant saying that he knows things which he does not really know and becomes a liar. All this results from joining the company of other people.

(8) The obligation to command others on the good and warn them against evil, which the Creator commanded us in saying: *"you shall surely rebuke your neighbor"* (Vayikra 19:17).

We are obligated to warn against evil in three ways: One, forcibly hitting someone by hand (physically), as Pinchas did in the case of Zimri and Cozby. Two, to verbally protest, as Moshe did in saying to the wicked man: *"Why strike you your fellow?"* (Shemos 2:13). Three, in one's heart, as David said: *"I hated the congregation of the evildoers, and with the wicked I shall not sit"* (Tehilim 26:5).

If one can protest forcibly (and it will help) but refrains, this will be considered a lacking on his part. If it is difficult for him to protest forcibly, let him protest with words. If he cannot protest with words, it is his duty to do so in his heart.

Therefore, we are obligated to rebuke the wicked, in any event, since the common people are not free from shortcomings.

*Pas Lechem*: If you ask, on the contrary, this very reason obligates us to join their company and to put an eye on their deeds in order to know their faults and rebuke them, which would be impossible if one kept a distance from them and remained ignorant of their deeds, because then one would be unable to fulfill the mitzva of rebuke. On this he said, this is incorrect since either way - if they will heed his words and he can effectively rebuke them, even if he does not know the details of their misdeeds he can speak general public words of mussar, thereby fulfilling the mitzva of rebuke. And this is what he meant by "rebuke the wicked in any event", i.e. even without knowing anything. And don't say "how can I rebuke without knowing anything? Maybe it is for nothing?" On this he added that rebuking the masses is needed at all times since "the common people are not free from shortcomings".

But when one is alone, undoubtedly, he is absolved of the mitzva of commanding others to good and warning them from evil. And it is difficult to fulfill G-d's command, and to fully discharge one's obligation in this mitzva (unlike rebuking the public which is easy - *PL*), as the sages said: "it is a wonder if there is someone in this generation who accepts rebuke" (Arachin 16b), and others said: "it is a wonder if there is someone in this generation who knows how to give rebuke" (ibid).

(9) Loss of clarity of thought and intellectual understanding, and strengthening of the yetzer (evil inclination) while in their company and camaraderie, and learning from their bad traits, as the wise man said: *"a companion of fools shall be corrupted"* (Mishlei 13:20), and therefore our sages said: *"conversing with children and sitting in the assembly houses of the unlearned (amei haaretz) takes a man out of the World (To Come)"* (Avot 3:14).

> *Matanas Chelko*: *"strengthening of the yetzer"* - in the end they will influence him to do evil things.
>
> *"sitting in the assembly houses of the unlearned"* - for they annul him from fear of Heaven and bring him to many sins as before.

The general principle: Most sins cannot be completed without two people, such as illicit relations, corrupt business practice, false oaths, false testimony, all sins which depend on speech. All these cannot be completed without the company of others and by mixing with them.

But solitude and separating from people is a means to be saved from all of the sins we mentioned, and it is one of the strongest things which bring one to good traits, and it was already said that the pillar of a pure heart is love of solitude and choosing to be alone.

Therefore, my brother, be careful lest the yetzer deceive you and embellish in your eyes the company and mingling with people, and lest he entice you to yearn for them at a time when you feel lonely in solitude.

Afterwards (after you listen to my words and learn to love solitude - *PL*), be careful lest the musings of your heart deceive you, telling you that the company of sages who know G-d and His Torah, and the mixing with great men is detrimental to the matter of solitude, and takes away from the benefits of being alone. Rather, in truth, this is the complete separation and the perfect solitude. Furthermore, to frequent men who excel in good deeds and in Torah has much greater benefits over the benefits of solitude.

*Manoach Halevavos*: and likewise the Talmud states (taanis 7a): "a sword (death) on those who learn Torah in solitude".

And the wise man said: *"He that walks with the wise shall become wise"* (Mishlei 13:20), and *"hearken your ear, and hear the words of the wise"* (Mishlei 22:17), and it was said of one who refrained from being with pious men:: *"A scorner loves not one that reproves him: neither will he go to the wise"* (Mishlei 15:12). And the sages, of blessed memory, said: "The gathering together of the wicked is bad for them and bad for the world, but for the righteous, it is good for them and good for the world. The dispersing of the wicked is beneficial for them and beneficial to the world, but for the righteous, it is bad for them and bad for the world" (Sanhedrin 71b). And they said: "Let your house be a meetingplace for the sages and sit amidst the dust of their feet and drink in thirstily their words" (Avos 1:4), and *"Then they that feared the L-ord spoke one with another; and the L-ord hearkened, and heard"* (Malachi 3:16).

## THE EIGHTEENTH:
*(the elevation of man)*

To make an accounting with oneself when one feels himself becoming arrogant and proud, and (as a result) overly ambitious in this world - to then contemplate one's significance in the creation (before being elevated by G-d), among the lower and the celestial creations. Then one will understand his puniness and lowliness among the works of the Creator, as I clarified on this matter in the sixth gate of this book.

> *Marpe Lenefesh*: In chapter 5 of the gate of submission and in introduction to Gate #3 he explains that man is "lacking and weaker than the animals in three things..." (and much less than the angels with respect to wisdom.. - MC) see there.
>
> *Matanas Chelko*: when a man sees his matters of this world succeeding, he feels in himself greatness and pride, and he wants to succeed more and more. All this comes from the Yetzer Hara (evil inclination) who entices him to think thus. Instead of thinking of his puniness and lowliness on account of G-d's great kindness towards him, he feels grandeur and that he deserved everything. At that time, a man needs to "contemplate one's significance..."

Afterwards, reflect on the Creator's granting greatness to man, that he made him ruler over the animals, plants, and natural resources, as written

*"You (G-d) give man dominion over the work of Your hands; You have placed everything beneath his feet"* (Tehilim 8:7), and He made known to man the statutes of His Torah, and established him (to understand) what will further his welfare of the upper and lower wisdoms of this world.

> *Matanas Chelko*: *"the Creator's granting greatness to man"* - i.e. the qualities of man. For in certain matters he is greater even than the angels since he has free will, and this is solely due to G-d's granting this to him. He did not earn this of himself.

And G-d elevated man further by permitting and desiring his praise and gratitude, and to [allow man to] call to Him during difficulties, and to answer his prayers in difficult times, and chose in him (i.e. G-d chose man to minister unto Him - *PL*), and appointed him over His creations (to rule over them - *PL*), and transmitted to man secrets of His might (the keys to wisdom - *PL*), and made miracles through His treasured ones (the prophets of Israel - *PL*), besides what would be lengthy to recall of the hidden and revealed favors, whether physical or spiritual, general and specific, of His kindness and goodness towards us.

> *Matanas Chelko*: the main principle (Yesod) is: the more kindness a man receives, the more he needs to humble himself. There are some people that even though they don't say "my power and the strength of my hands have produced this good for me" (Devarim 8:17), but nevertheless, when G-d sends them good, they are prone to think they deserve this due to their qualities. This cheshbon that one must do is to think that even though I do not deserve anything, and all I have, and that I am a human being, and even a Jew, and that I understand of G-d's holy Torah - all this is only due to the kindness of G-d and His goodness towards me. With this thought, he can humble himself before G-d, blessed be He.
>
> In Tehilim (8:7): "You give him dominion over the work of Your hands; You have placed everything beneath his feet". But earlier there it says: "what is man that You should remember him, and the son of man that You should be mindful of him?" (Tehilim 8:5) - he deserves nothing, and nevertheless, "You give him dominion.." For man is the master of the creation...
>
> *Matanas Chelko*: In the morning blessings, we say "who made for me all my needs" when putting on shoes. What is the connection between "all my needs" and shoes? The Vilna Gaon explains (Imrei Noam) that shoes demonstrate man's dominion over the world... a man slaughter's an animal, eats of its meat and makes shoes with its skin - this is ultimate dominion and this is what the verse hints to us: "You give him dominion over the

> work of Your hands; You have placed everything *beneath his feet*" (Tehilim 8:7)... Thus the way to be saved from pride in this is by thanking G-d for this, out of understanding and realizing that if G-d did not do this, he would not have had any dominion whatsoever.

See, my brother, how little is your worth and how unimportant is your matter, and yet, how much the Creator has elevated you, even though He has no need for you and (just the opposite, see) your great need for His providence. Don't waste this glorious crown He has crowned you with, and the exalted status He has elevated you to in this world, and the great reward He has hidden away for you in the next world when you cling to His service and to thanking Him.

Let not the Creator's elevating you, of what I recalled to you, of his kindnesses and favors, be reason to become proud in your status, and haughty in your spirit, and to glorify yourself due to the kindness of the Creator towards you by thinking that you deserve it, and that you are worthy of it, and that it is befitting you.

Rather, cling to the traits of submission, humility, and lowliness which is fitting for you to cling to when you admit to the truth of your worth among the creations of the Creator, as a weak, unimportant, and petty slave is obligated to do when his master elevates him and places him inside his inner circle of treasured ones out of pure benevolent kindness - he is obligated to humble himself and to see himself as he was in his original status, before his master's kindness towards him, and not to become proud before his master, nor haughty due to reaching greatness and importance, and not to request his own needs to his master in a habitual way (to think: since he gave me until now, he is obligated to continue doing so always - *ML*) . Rather, he will leave his matters to his master and trust in him and in his kindness.

It was said of one of the tzadikim (righteous) who would say after his prayer: "My G-d, I was not persuaded by my intellect to stand before You due to ignorance of my puny worth and little understanding of Your greatness, that You are high and exalted and I am insignificant, disgraceful, and petty to ask of You and to say before You praises and exaltations, or to sanctify Your holy Name using the words of the holy angels on high. Rather, I was persuaded to do this in that You have elevated me by Your commanding me to plea before You, and have given me permission to praise Your great Name according to my understanding of Your glory, so that I can demonstrate that I am serving You and that I humble myself before You.

You know what is beneficial for me, and how to guide me. I mentioned to You my needs, not in order to arouse You on them but rather so that I feel my great need for You and my trust in You. If, in my ignorance, I ask of You something, which is not beneficial for me, may Your exalted choice override my choice. I have already submitted all of my matters to Your decrees, which endure, and to Your supernal guidance, as David, peace be unto him, said: *"O L-ord, my heart was not haughty, nor were my eyes raised on high, and I did not pursue matters greater and more wondrous than I"* (Tehilim 131:1).

## THE NINETEENTH:
*(disasters of the world)*

To make an accounting with oneself in that the Creator has spared him from the disasters of the world, its sufferings, the various diseases which strike people, the calamities which befall them such as imprisonment, hunger, thirst, cold, burning, lethal poisons, dangerous animals, leprosy, insanity, paralysis, or the like - all the while knowing that they are fitting for him and he deserves them due to his previous sins and iniquities before the Creator, and the greatness of what occurred in the past, of his rebelling against G-d, and disrespecting His words, and leaving his duty of thanking and praising Him, and turning away from His service, and neglecting repentance and confession before G-d for his prolonged rebellion despite G-d's continuous favors and constant good towards him.

> *Pas Lechem*: *"they are fitting for him"* refers to refraining from doing good, that just like he strays from His service, so too it is fitting that G-d removes His providence and protection from him, and he winds up prone and liable to all troubles and damages, like a target to an arrow. And for not refraining from evil and actually sinning, he wrote "and he deserves them", that he deserves all these things due to his sins, unlike for refraining from good which the term "deserve" is not correct since punishment is not meted out for positive commandments (Menachos 41a).

> *Pas Lechem*: *"due to his previous sins and iniquities"*: - Due to being comfortable, with a full stomach, and unrestrained in his deeds, it is fitting that he be captured and "imprisoned" in "hunger and thirst" (measure for measure). And for rebelling against his Creator and kindling His anger, it is fitting for him "burning". And since his words and mitzvot were cold and indifferent, he deserves "cold". And since he did not exert his mouth and throat with thanks and praises, it is fitting for him to chew and eat poisons.

And for removing the yoke of His service, it is proper that the animals' natural fear of him be removed and the "dangerous animals" rule over him. Likewise leprosy comes from the rebellion of the order of health, and for neglecting to repent and confess and not reflecting with himself and regretting, it is proper "insanity", and that his limbs stop serving him (loss of senses) as he brought earlier in way #6 the analogy of crossing the minister over the river. You the reader, put to heart to analyze each corresponding to the other and you will understand his words.

*Matanas Chelko*: *"leaving his duty of thanking and praising Him"* - even for neglecting to thank and praise G-d for all the good, he deserves punishment.

Sometimes bad things happen to families and they come to ask why this happened and what should they do. He who has fear of G-d should certainly do a spiritual accounting on what he needs to do then. But in truth, one does not need to do big things. Even through a small thing he can be saved from the trouble.

During the time I was with Rabbi Shach zt'l, when many people came to him seeking his valuable advice on what they need to do to be saved from their troubles or in order to bring blessing to their lives. To all of them, he said that they should bless the Grace after Meals from a *Siddur* (prayer book) or *Birkon* (prayer paper) and to say it with kavana (intent). He said that most troubles come because people don't give thanks to G-d as they are obligated to do. The [only] blessing of thanks which is Biblical is the "Grace after Meals" (Birkat Hamazon). Therefore, through thanking and praising G-d on all the good He gives - who "gives sustenance to the whole world in His goodness", one gives strength to G-d, so to speak, to bestow good to a man and save him from his troubles.

When the intelligent man will look and contemplate how the Creator tests people with the troubles of this world we mentioned, and that he was saved from them, and spared from their tumults, even though he deserves them - his praise will increase for the favors of G-d on him. And he will hurry to repent and seek forgiveness for his past sins and iniquities which the Creator has concealed for such a long time (from his angels of wrath so that they do not punish him - PL), and he will run to cling to the service of the Creator, out of fear of them (the punishments he deserves) and so will avert them, as written: *"If you will diligently hearken to the voice of the L-ord your G-d... I will put none of these diseases upon you, which I have brought upon the Egyptians"* (Shemos 15:26), and *"the L-ord will remove from you all illness, and all of the evil diseases of Egypt which you knew, He will not set upon you, but He will lay them upon all your enemies"*

(Devarim 7:15), and one of our early pious ones would say to his disciples: "see, the serpent does not kill, rather it is sin that kills" (Berachos 33a), and David, peace be unto him, said: *"You shall tread upon the lion and adder: the young lion and the serpent shall you trample under foot. Because he has set his love upon Me, therefore I will deliver him"* (Tehilim 91:13).

## THE TWENTIETH:
*(acquiring and spending money)*

To make an accounting with oneself if he has wealth, in the manners he acquired it, and the ways he spends it, and whether he is fulfilling his obligations to G-d with it (such as tefilin, tzitzit - *PL*), and paying his debts to man (such as charities, favors - *PL*) according to how much he has, and not to think that the money will be for him alone (that the Creator gave him this money only for himself and his own enjoyment - TL, alternatively, not to think that he cannot do without it - *MH*). Rather, to know that it is by him like a deposit - it will remain by him for as long as the Creator desires that it be in his hand, and afterwards He will transfer it to someone else when He wishes.

When the rich man contemplates this, he will not fear the damages time brings on him. If the money stays by him, he will thank the Creator and praise him. If it is lost from him, he will bear His judgment and accept His decree. It will be easier for him to use it and spend it in the service of G-d, to do good with it, to return deposits people entrusted him with, and return money he took unjustly, and not to covet another man's wealth nor disrespect a poor man due to his poverty. And it will be a strong cause to help him acquire good traits and to refrain from the bad traits, as written: *"Honor the L-ord from your wealth, and from the first-fruits of all your produce"* (Mishlei 3:9), and *"He that has pity on the poor lends to the L-ord; and that which he has given will He pay him back"* (Mishlei 19:17).

## THE TWENTY FIRST:
*(on Divine help)*

> *Matanas Chelko*: now Rabeinu brings a great foundation (yesod) in the service of G-d, and just how far man's free will goes. He writes an awesome principle (chidush).

Accounting with oneself on the extent of his capability in the service of G-d and to train oneself in it, and be diligent in it, and to hasten and be zealous in doing it until it becomes habit to him, and afterwards to endeavor to do more than what was within one's ability, and to long for it in his heart, and desire it in his thoughts, and to plea to G-d with a faithful and genuine heart and mind to help him and strengthen him for what is above his current ability in understanding (Torah) and in good deeds.

*Matanas Chelko*: *"on the extent of his capability.."* - this includes all his powers: His spiritual powers such as to study [Torah] according to his strength and ability, and to delve deeply into the Torah according to his intelligence and ability to grasp, and to designate time to study. Likewise, his physical powers: to do acts of kindness and to exert himself in the general service of G-d according to the bodily powers he has been blessed with and to push himself according to his powers.

*"to hasten and be zealous in doing it.."* - to push himself and strive to concentrate all his powers and even more than he thinks he can do until he becomes so used to it that it becomes second nature to him.

*"afterwards to endeavor to do more.."* - this seems impossible. For according to above, this person is already doing all that is in his ability to do and he has also habituated himself in this. How then can he do more? But the chidush (idea) in this is that in truth, the Creator can grace him with additional understanding in Torah and increase his intellectual powers and understanding. He can also increase his bodily powers so that he can learn more and likewise send him his livelihood abundantly so that he does not need to exert himself so much to attain his sustenance and through this he will be more free to learn and to do acts of kindness with others. But Rabeinu explains when a person can hope to this and how it is done.

*"to plea to G-d with a faithful and genuine heart"* - i.e. that he has will and desire to increase his ability, and that he prays to G-d to help him and strengthen him in order that he will truly be able to increase in the service of his Creator. There is a condition in the matter. Namely, that he wants and prays for this out of a faithful heart. Not so that others will honor him through this. But solely in order to truly draw close to G-d, blessed be He, through the increase in his service.

When one perseveres more and more in this, the Creator will fulfill his request, and open for him the gates of His understanding, and strengthen his intellect and limbs, level by level, to fulfill the commandments on a higher level, above and beyond his abilities, as written: *"I am the L-ord your G-d, Who teaches you for your benefit, Who leads you by the way you should go"* (Yeshaya 48:17).

*Matanas Chelko*: *"level by level.."* - one must go in stages and not try to jump to a lofty level in one step. Let us give a small example from which we can apply to other matters. One who feels he must sleep ten hours at night. There is no question that through this he is limited in the amount of hours he can learn and serve his Creator. Therefore, he can hope that G-d will grant him the ability to learn and serve more, and to pray on this. Then "the Creator will fulfill his request", and he will find that he can guard his health through sleeping only eight hours a day. Afterwards, it is possible that he will desire to increase more in the service of G-d, and the Creator will grant him his request so that even 6 hours of sleep will be enough for him. With this example, he will be able to ascend the ladder, level after level properly.

It is like this for all matters and all powers of man. For example, one who learns a Tosfot and strains himself to understand the depth of matter, and nevertheless, he is unable to understand the matter properly. He can pray to G-d to "open for him the gates of His understanding". And even though he does not fulfill the mitzva of talmud Torah through his prayer and request, nevertheless, through his desire and prayer, he can come to a greater grasp and understanding in Torah and to ascend in the levels of his service. In any case, it seems from Rabeinu's words that through this way it is possible to increase, whether in one's bodily powers or mental and intellectual powers.

This is not just for talmud Torah. It is also so for fulfilling the mitzvot. For example, one who gives tzedaka according to his ability and he wants to give more than his ability. He can desire and pray that G-d will bestow to him alot in order that he can distribute more to tzedaka. But one must remember the condition of Rabeinu. One should not hope to this unless he seeks it in a "lishma" (for G-d, i.e. a mitzvah) manner, "with a faithful and genuine heart".

*"I am the L-ord your G-d, Who teaches you for your benefit..."* - Rabeinu writes that in truth we find this also in other matters. Not just Torah and mitzvot. The explanation is that because everything comes only from the Creator, blessed be He. And just like he granted him those powers he already has, so too, He can grant him more, whether in understanding or in deeds.

The analogy of this regarding learning the skills of a trade and learning mathematics : When one who learns a trade, in the beginning, he will do only parts of it according to his understanding and less than his ability. When his understanding of the trade strengthens and he persists in it, the Creator will enlighten him to the general principles of the trade and its fundamentals and he will be able to deduce new branches which were not taught to him by other people.

Similarly in learning mathematics: The master of geometry cannot teach his student the theoretical lessons in abstract concepts. Rather, he will first teach him concrete geometric drawings as Euclides organized them in his book of mathematics. When the student understands well, and desires to grasp its branches with diligence and interest, the Creator will help enlighten him on the subject, and establish his general understanding, and then he will be able to bring forth from this wondrous forms and fine works which appear almost divinely inspired.

So too in other fields of wisdom: The student will find when he exerts his mind in the wisdom, that he will feel a higher spiritual power which no human being has the ability to give him, on this the sages said: "the wise man is greater than the prophet" (Bava Basra 12a), and Elihu said: *"But it is a spirit in man, and the breath of the Almighty, that gives them understanding"* (Iyov 32:8).

> *Matanas Chelko*: man can build giant skyscrapers, but he cannot build thoughts. For they come only from G-d. When we examine this more we will see that it is so. For what is thought? Behold, even in Torah matters, when a man has a difficulty in a sugya (Talmudic topic) and he wants to delve deeply in it in order to resolve it, what does he do? He sits and ponders (meharher). What is pondering? He thinks and ponders on the question he has until the answer or idea "falls" in his head. This is from G-d. So too, for all matters. In truth, it should not be possible at all to think "my strength and the might of my hands.." (Devarim 8:17) on any matter, though people still think so, because "behold, the thought fell in my head and not in the head of another person". Understand this.

Through this, it is proper for you, my brother, to understand that the primary intended purpose in the mitzvot which involve the body and the limbs, is to arouse our attention on the mitzvot of the heart and mind, because they are the pillars of the service and they are the roots (and foundations) of the Torah, as written: *"You shall fear the L-ord, your G-d, worship Him, and cleave to Him.."* (Devarim 10:20), and *"Rather,[this] thing is very close to you; in your mouth and in your heart to do it"* (Devarim 30:14), and *"And now, O Israel, what does the L-ord, your G-d, ask of you? Only to fear the L-ord, your G-d, to walk in all His ways and to love Him, and to worship the L-ord, your G-d, with all your heart and with all your soul"* (Devarim 10:12).

And because this is beyond a man's normal power (that the commandments of the heart are beyond the normal powers of a man - *PL*), and it is not possible for him until he separates from most of his animalistic desires, and forces his base nature, and takes control of all his movements, [therefore] the Creator has made him serve with his body and limbs with what he is capable of doing, until it will be easy for him to fulfill them.

Then, when the believer engages in them with his heart and mind, and exerts himself to the best of his ability, G-d will open for him the gates of spiritual qualities, and he will attain with them what is beyond his ability, and he will serve G-d with his body and soul, with his outer and inner being, as David said: *"my heart and my flesh cry out for the living G-d"* (Tehilim 84:3).

> *Matanas Chelko*: i.e. a man does not have the power to change his heart. Only through his flesh, namely, by performing the mitzvot through his limbs, G-d will grant him fear in his heart. This is the explanation of the verse brought earlier "And now, O Israel, what does the L-ord, your G-d, ask of you? Only to fear the L-ord, your G-d.." (Devarim 10:12). Even though, fear in the heart is not in man's hands. But the explanation is: do the acts of mitzvot, and through this, I, G-d, will implant fear in your heart. This is what Rabeinu wrote earlier, that man needs to do what is incumbent on himself, and afterwards, G-d will grant him what is beyond his ability.
>
> Hence, according to this, whoever is more meticulous in the mitzvot receives more fear of Heaven. It is not like people think, that through fear, a person is more meticulous in them. Rather, the opposite, as before, because the fear is also from Heaven. And even though our sages said: "everything is in the hands of Heaven except for the fear of Heaven" (Berachot 33b), this means, that a man needs to have a will for [attaining] fear of Heaven. Only the will is in his ability. And when he has the will to [attain] fear, he will do what is incumbent on him to do in order to receive the fear, namely, the mitzvot.
>
> However, since even doing the mitzvot is against the will and nature of man, therefore, a man needs to study mussar in order to come to be meticulous in the mitzvot. The Chazon Ish writes (Emuna U'Bitachon ch.4 ot.8-9) that meticulousness in mitzvot and observing the laws in the Shulchan Aruch brings a man to fear [of G-d] and to rectifying his character traits, see there. But one needs to study mussar in order to come to this.

This was already compared to a man who plants trees and digs in their roots. He cleans the soil from rocks, thorns, and weeds, waters it when needed, fertilizes it, and afterwards he hopes that G-d will cause fruits to grow. But if he neglects working the land and supervising its needs, it is not proper for the Creator to give him fruits from them.

> *Matanas Chelko*: in the order of nature itself, G-d demonstrates the order of this unfolding. For a man needs to do only the preparations and works, and afterwards, the matter is not in his hands, and he does not know if the soil will produce fruit, or what their quality and quantity will be. This is already only in G-d's hands.

Likewise for one who strives to do actions for the service (of G-d), if he exerts himself with diligence and zeal to do what is in his power to do - G-d will help him to accomplish what is beyond his ability, namely, the divine fruit and the glorious good from G-d on His treasured ones and His beloved ones in this world, as our sages said: "whoever fulfills the Torah in poverty will fulfill it in wealth" (Avot 4:9), and the wise man said: *"For to a man who is good in His sight, He has given wisdom and knowledge and joy"* (Kohelet 2:26).

Our sages said (Talmud): "Torah brings to action, action brings to watchfulness, watchfulness brings to zeal, zeal brings to abstinence, abstinence brings to cleanliness, cleanliness brings to purity, purity brings to piety, and piety is greater than all of them, as written *'then You spoke in prophecy to Your pious ones'* (Tehilim 89:20)".

But if one neglects from doing what is within his ability, and is lax in doing what is within his power, the help and assistance from G-d will distance from him, as written: *"G-d is far from the wicked"* (Mishlei 15:29), and *"your sins were separating between you and your G-d"* (Yeshaya 59:2).

> *Matanas Chelko*: *"your sins were separating between you and your G-d"* - this is a great principle in the service of G-d - he who does what is in his ability, G-d will grant him more. But when he does not do what is incumbent on him, G-d will take away from him what he has. Likewise the Rambam writes in Hilchot Talmud Torah 3:13, see there and in Hilchot Teshuva 9:1.

## THE TWENTY SECOND:
*(to love for others what you would love for yourself)*

To make an accounting with oneself regarding his joining with people for furthering the general welfare, such as plowing or harvesting, buying and selling, and other societal matters which people help each other in - that he loves for them what he would love would happen to himself, and that he hates for them what he would hate would happen to himself, and that he has compassion for them, and saves them, according to his ability, from what would damage them, as written: *"love your fellow as you love yourself"* (Vayikra 19:18).

> *Pas Lechem*: To consider and see to it, that one loves and is joyous with what would bring them good in these matters. That one yearns that they will attain good in these things, just like one would love and wish and yearn that one attains these good things for himself.

Let one apply in this the following analogy: A group of people travel to a distant land on a difficult journey. They need to stop in several stops along the way, and they have many animals loaded with heavy loads, and the men are few, each one has many animals he must unload and reload frequently. If they will help each other in loading and unloading, and their desire is for the peace of all and to lighten each others' burden, and that they equally share the load of helping each other - they will reach the best results (their conduct is the best possible - *PL*). But if their opinions differ and they do not agree to one plan, and each one exerts to further only his own interests - most will become exhausted.

In this way, my brother, the world is burdensome on its inhabitants, and their work and exertion is many times more difficult. For each one wants his portion to be for himself alone and that he has more than his allotted portion (more than what he needs).

And because they desired more than their proper portion, and seek from it even what does not belong to them, therefore the world withholds from them their portion in it, and does not produce for any of them even their portion in it. Therefore, they are not content with it, and there is not even one who does not complain (for failing to attain superfluous things - *PL*) and weep over it, and because they seek the superfluous in food, they were prevented even from the basic necessities except through tremendous toil and great exertion.

If, however, their basic needs were enough for them, and their exertion was equal and for the benefit of all, and that they were equal in their interests, they would succeed in their world and attain even more of their desire in it. But not only do they not help each other in their worldly interests, but they weaken each other, and each one prevents his fellow and weakens his strength, until not one of them reaches his desire and attains his lusts.

Therefore, my brother, exert yourself, to acquire faithful and pure friends to be your helpers in your Torah and worldly matters (that their love to help you be without personal interests - *PL*) . (How is this done?) When your heart is whole with them, and your heart is pure towards them, and that they are precious to you like yourself (since "just like water reflects a face so too does the heart of a man reflect another" Mishlei 27:19 - *TL*), if you find among them some worthy of this.

Do not reveal your private matters except only to a very select few among them, as Ben Sira said: "let many be your friends, but reveal your secrets to only one in a thousand" (Ben Sira 6:6)

> *Pas Lechem*: strive not to anger any person, so that many will be your friends, but nevertheless, do not reveal your secrets except to one in a thousand which you have tested and verified that he is a faithful friend.

And the wise man said: *"Ointment and perfume rejoice the heart: so does the sweetness of a man's friend by hearty counsel"* (Mishlei 27:9).

> *Matanas Chelko*: after Rabeinu taught us that a man needs to acquire many friends, we may mistakenly think that one must be equal with everyone, and everything one has, he must give and share with others. This is not so. In truth, this was the view of the Communists. In Pirkei Avot (5:10) "one who says what's mine is yours and what's your is mine is an ignoramus". He is not a wicked person but an ignoramus. This is the opposite of the Torah view. The Communist view is that there is no ownership and no possessions to individuals. Rather, everything belongs equally to the community. However, in the Torah we find concepts of personal property, that a man is indeed the owner of his property. Rabbi Yerucham Levovitz of Mir clarifies as follows (Daat Chachma U'Mussar Vol.1 pg.175): "The depth of the matter of properties and ownership, is that there are things which are "mine", and this is the matter of 'the world was founded on kindness' (Tehilim 89:3). But if a man does not have any ownership in things which belong to him, it is impossible for him to do kindness with others. Then the man no longer has any individuality and he loses his identity. This is the mistake of the Communist view. All the individuality and identity of a man is lost through this type of life". end quote. see there. This we can see even today. The Russian children who grew up in the times when the communists ruled, are not able to smile and laugh. A man's possessions builds him. Not because of what he possesses, but because he is able to give and do kindness to others. Without this, he is not a man.

## THE TWENTY THIRD:

*(seeing G-d in nature)*

To investigate all that exists in the universe, from the smallest creations to the largest, and the superior qualities human beings have in the world, and the levels of the creations below and above, and the arrangement of the heavenly spheres, the movement of the sun, the moon, the stars, those stationary and those which move, the falling of the rain, the blowing of the wind, the emergence of a baby from the womb, and other wonders of the Creator, which are more wondrous, more subtle, more apparent (yet) more mysterious which teach on His perfect wisdom and power, and His good guidance, and all encompassing grace, His mercy, and His abundant providence over His creations.

> *Matanas Chelko*: Rabeinu mentioned a few examples from the whole world, in the heavens and earth, of the things that we call "nature". In truth, they are wonders of the Creator. Behold, if a man contemplates even a single drop of rain, he can see how wondrous it is... contemplating the wisdom in nature brings a man to be in wonder at the wisdom of the Creator and also to understand His beneficence...

Do not be deceived due to seeing them so frequently, and being used to them for so long, that you abandon being in wonder of them, and abandon contemplating them, and that it is inevitable that your previous knowledge of them cause you to make light of them due to habitually seeing them and observing them since your childhood.

In this way, we find most of the common people and many of the important men on this matter - that they are in wonder when seeing something they are not used to seeing such as a solar or lunar eclipse, thunder and lightning, comets, earthquakes, hurricanes, or other similar phenomena, but they are not in wonder of the movement of the spheres and their orbits, such as the sun, moon, and stars, the sunrise and sunset, the rain, blowing of the wind, or the like of the things that exist with them, and that they see constantly. Similarly, they are in wonder when seeing the sea, its waves and storms, and the creatures in it, yet they don't wonder at the flow of rivers, drawing of underground springs, and other things like this, which are continuous (around them) day and night.

Therefore, it is proper for you, my brother, to investigate all of what the Creator created, whether you are used to it or not, whether you have already seen it or not. Let not your foolishness entice you, that after you were foolish in your childhood and did not contemplate these matters when you first saw them, that you also do not contemplate them now in your adulthood and time of strong recognition, clear heart, and mature understanding. Rather, look at them and contemplate them, as if you never saw them, and imagine to yourself that you were blind before you contemplated them and afterwards your sight was restored and you could see them and contemplate them.

See my brother, that the fool is like a blind man, and when he becomes intelligent, he will be similar to a blind man whose eyes were healed and can now see, as the verse says on Adam and Eve: *"the eyes of both of them became opened"* (Bereishis 3:7), though we know that they could see before this.

> *Pas Lechem*: Do not think that I was advising you to imagine something false, because in truth it is indeed so, that the fool is like a blind man.
>
> *Matanas Chelko*: without contemplation, a man is literally blind to these things. Only when he begins to contemplate, it is as if his eyes were opened to see for the first time. For in truth, it is indeed the first time he opened his eyes to see.
>
> *"the eyes of both of them became opened"* - this is as before, that even though Adam and Eve were not blind. But nevertheless, since they were used to their situation of being naked, they did not contemplate this. But after, they did contemplate, it was considered as if they literally opened their eyes. Thus, it is clear from the verse of the Torah, that when a person grasps a new knowledge, it is considered as if he was blind before this and was now granted the sense of sight. Rabeinu learns from this verse, that without thought and contemplation, one is considered a blind man.

Do not hide yourself from contemplating them, and from investigating all of them - then you will see the truth of the matters, and will recognize some of the wonders of the Creator, which you have long been ignorant of and blind in, as one of the wise men said: "the hearts of the wise have eyes, they can see what the ignorant cannot see", as the verse says: *"Have you not known? have you not heard? has it not been told you from the beginning? have you not understood from the foundations of the earth?"* (Yeshaya 40:21).

> *Pas Lechem*: Not only should one examine the wonders of the Creator which appear infrequently, but also one should examine and contemplate that which a man sees all the time, from the smallest creations to the biggest, and from all of them, he will be able to perceive the wisdom,

compassion, and governance of the Creator, which no words can convey. Through this, a man can habituate himself and to fulfill the verse (Tehilim 16:8) *"I have set G-d always before me"*, since *"how great are your deeds, O G-d, You have made them all with wisdom"* (Tehilim 104:24)...

## THE TWENTY FOURTH:
*(child's eyes)*

That you make an accounting with yourself and claim from yourself on all matters which have been established in you regarding knowledge of G-d and His Torah, and the words of the ancients, and the metaphors of the wise, and the contents of prayers, which you started learning in your childhood and youth. For the picture of a complex matter by one whose understanding is weak is not like the picture for one whose understanding is strong, and the more a man increases understanding, the more he will increase clarity.

Therefore do not be content with what has been formed in your mind in the beginning of your learning of the difficult matters, and the deep reasons. Rather, it is proper for you to start at the age of mature intellect and understanding to examine the book of G-d and the book of the prophets, like someone who never learned one letter of them. Habituate yourself to expound and clarify them, and to contemplate their words and structure, and what you can of their interpretation, and what is to be understood literally and what is not, and what is visible and what is concealed, and what is possible to compare to other areas and what is not.

> *Matanas Chelko*: here Rabeinu writes a great principle: if a man does not go back and contemplate and study anew what he already learned in his youth - he will remain with the same childish and weak understanding as he had in his youth...

Similarly do for the prayers and praises, study their words and their intended message, so that when you speak them before your G-d, you will understand the words you are uttering, and what your heart seeks in the matter. Do not conduct yourself in this like the custom of the days of youth, that you pronounce whatever words follow (without understanding the words), and in whatever way you follow (without proper pronunciation, as the children pray - *ML*), without understanding the matter, and we have already dealt sufficiently with this matter (in #9 and #18).

Similarly do for the words of the sages and the words of the oral tradition, that you contemplate them and judge them favorably (for what appears strange to you, do not lay the error on them, G-d forbid, but rather consider that their understanding was greater than yours - *PL*). Do not be satisfied with the clarity you had when you first learned them, rather claim from yourself to be like one who starts learning it. What you understand, recall it and work it through (even something which appears correct without a doubt, recall it to work it through further, so that maybe you will grasp more on the truth of it - *TL*).

What you are now in doubt about its explanation (even after the re-examination), and which you were not in doubt in your youth, investigate after it from the wise men of your generation, then you will see of the secrets of the Torah and the secrets of the prophets and of the sages which was impossible for you to grasp from the learning of your teachers at the beginning of your studies.

Let not arrogance deceive you, to think that your perception did not increase from what it was in your youth, and that what passed into your mind then will not change and become strange in your mind now, because this is an enticement of the yetzer (evil inclination) on you, to weaken your resolve to examine and investigate the truth of the matters, and to imagine to your eyes that you are a completely wise man and lack nothing of what you need, as the wise man said: *"The lazy man is wiser in his own eyes than seven men that can answer reasonably"* (Mishlei 26:16).

> *Tov Halevanon*: One who is lazy from in-depth investigation is wiser in his eyes than multitudes who investigate and back up their words with truth and reason.

> *Matanas Chelko*: - a man refrains himself from reviewing and studying all these things. And even though certainly the primary cause is laziness, just like for all matters which are "sit and do not do" (shev v'al taase) but Rabeinu wrote an additional reason deep in man's soul: *"let not arrogance deceive you..."* for if a man attains a new understanding or deepens more, he will need to admit the truth, that before this, he was not so wise, and the arrogance prevents him from saying and thinking so.

And: *"Have you seen a man wise in his own eyes? there is more hope for a fool than of him"* (Mishlei 26:12), and *"the wise man's eyes are on his head but the fool walks in darkness"* (Koheles 2:14), which means that he looks at the beginning of his matters, and what passed over him of the matters of his Torah and worldly matters, and examines them, and understands the good and the bad of what has happened to him, and strengthens the good and repents from the bad.

But the fool ignores all of this, as one who walks in the darkness of night on a long road. He does not look at what has passed, since if he turns his head what he sees will not be clear to him, rather all of his attention is only on what is in front of him, on this it says: *"but the fool walks in darkness"* (ibid), and *"Then I saw that wisdom excels folly, as far as light excels darkness"* (Koheles 2:13).

> *Tov Halevanon*: The fool's aim is only to traverse the road and he is not interested in looking behind him.
>
> *Matanas Chelko*: *"the wise man's eyes are on his head"* - Rabeinu gave us a novel insight (chidush) in the explanation of this verse. For generally, we explain it in the manner of "who is wise? he who sees what will be born" (Avot 2:9). Namely, that already in the beginning of the matter, he foresees and understands the end of it (the future consequences). But Rabeinu explains "the wise man's eyes are on his head" to mean "on the beginning", i.e. the wise man always goes back to the beginning of the matters, to see what there is to learn and delve deeper. He learns from experience with what happened to him and to others. Through this, he strengthens and adds in the good and turns away from evil. Therefore, in all matters of Torah study, the wise man is always prepared to go back and review his lesson, perhaps he will grasp matters and points that he did not discover previously.
>
> *"but the fool walks in darkness"* - the fool conducts himself in the opposite manner. He does not go back to the beginning of the matter. Therefore, he does not learn from the past. Due to this, it is considered he is walking in darkness. The fool continues with his ideas and knowledge which he has acquired, without going back and looking whether his ideas and views are right and correct, or whether he needs to understand the matters anew in a different way, or in a deeper manner, in order to understand them fully. This is the difference between the wise man and the fool.

## THE TWENTY FIFTH:
*(fire and water)*

To make an accounting with oneself for being sunk in love of this world and strengthening its lusts over the love of Olam Haba (the next world), and to make efforts to remove the love of this world from one's heart, and strengthen the love of Olam Haba over it, by contemplating what will be one's end from both worlds and what will be one's final condition from both abodes, and to try to remove the love of this world from one's heart and to maintain the love of Olam Haba in it always.

*Matanas Chelko*: logically, we should love Olam Haba more than this world, since it is known to us that it is more essential than this world. But behold, we can see that it is not so. For the yetzer hara intensifies our lusts and love of this world, and we don't have so much love of Olam Haba. Therefore Rabeinu writes to us an advice: "to try to remove the love of this world from one's heart and to maintain the love of Olam Haba in it always".

This requires contemplation without which it is impossible to attain anything. The only advice for this is what our sages have advised us: "look at 3 things and you will not come to sin: know from where you came, - from a putrid drop; and where you are going - to a place of dirt, rot, and maggots; and before whom you are destined to give a judgment and accounting, before the supreme King of kings, the Holy One, blessed be He" (Avot 3:1) end quote.

Rabeinu's words here revolve more on looking "where you are going..". For Olam Haba is only an abstract concept to us. We do not have any picture or photo of it, as the prophet said (Isaiah 64:3) "no eye has ever seen..." And even after the metaphors of our sages to describe to us that it is an eternal world or the like, nevertheless, the love of this world with all its bodily lusts nevertheless still overpowers all our grasp which the words of our sages convey.

Therefore, Rabeinu writes that one must first distance love of this world by looking at its end. For in the end, everything goes to "a place of dirt, worms, and maggots". And even this needs the power of mental imagery - what is "dirt, worms, and maggots"? Behold, when we see a dead animal or bird lying on the road, exuding a rotting stench with many creatures crawling all over it - at that time one needs to contemplate that this is "a place of dirt, worms, and maggots" which our sages depicted to us.

When a man contemplates this, he will find that all benefits of this world are "pleasures of an hour" (taanuge shaah). For example, one who eats something sweet, he enjoys it for a few minutes and afterwards the pleasure passes. If a person were to tell his friend that this world is so good and wonderful, for we can suck on candies and sweets, there is no doubt that he would be considered a lunatic! Every intelligent person knows and understands that for the pleasure of a second, it is not proper to call the place where the pleasure is experienced a "good and wonderful place".

So too for all pleasures of this world, such as a nice car or a luxurious vacation, or anything else which causes the non-Jews to love this world, and which they enjoy and desire so much - behold in the end of the matter, the pleasure and enjoyment ends and afterwards nothing whatsoever is left.

Therefore, our sages said one must look at this world in its entirety and to appreciate what are the important things in it. One who contemplates this and looks from the present to the past on matters of this world, will see that nothing tangible remains in his hand from all his matters. But when he merits and comes to Olam Haba, the world which endures forever and ever - and he will look back on this world and the time he was there, all his lifetime will seem like a minuscule point of time relative to the eternal days of Olam Haba, and in the end of the matter, what resulted in those pleasures of this world was nothing but dirt, worms, and maggots.

We must emphasize again that without contemplation, it is impossible to uproot love of this world from one's heart and to love Olam Haba. During the study of mussar, one needs to use the power of mental imagery. Due to the many sins in our times, this is difficult for us. Not only because of laziness (even though it is indeed one of the reasons), but because today we have vivid photos of everything in the world. Therefore we think only on what is possible to see with an actual picture and photo. In previous times, when they did not have pictures and photos of every thing, they needed to close their eyes and contemplate to see with their mind's eye in order to make the matters tangible. Therefore, they used to also contemplate on these matters.

They used to employ the power of mental imagery also for matters of Olam Haba, contemplating with their imagination and mental imagery, and delve deeply into what the Talmud states in Berachot 17a: "a favorite saying of Rav was: Olam Haba is not like this world. In Olam Haba there is no eating nor drinking nor procreation nor business nor jealousy nor hatred nor competition, but rather the righteous sit with their crowns on their heads deriving enjoyment from the radiance of the Shechina (Divine presence)." end quote.

They would picture to themselves how this pleasure of "deriving enjoyment from the radiance of the Shechina" was far vastly greater than the pleasures of this world. For it is a pleasure which comes straight from the Creator, blessed be He. Through this, they would be disgusted with this world and would love Olam Haba.

However, today that we have so many pictures and photos, we are not used to employing this power. Thus automatically, we are lazy to contemplate also on matters of Olam Haba despite that we have no picture or photo of it.

Rabeinu wrote that without contemplation, it is impossible to attain any mental impression. Let us take an example. Behold, our sages told us that Olam Haba endures forever and ever (Kidushin 39b) - "a world which is all good, a world which is all-enduring". When Rabbi Simcha Zissel wanted to picture to his students the matter of eternity, he would say:

Imagine to yourself that one person took a box full of small seeds. A bird came and took one seed in its mouth and flew high and far away. After one full year, the bird returned a second time and took another seed and flew away. Likewise, for every year. Afterwards, imagine to yourself that the entire room is full of seeds and once a year the same bird came and took in its mouth one seed as before. Afterwards, imagine to yourself that the entire planet was full of these seeds. Contemplate in your mind how much time it would take until all the seeds were taken away by the bird. Doing this is already a certain grasping of eternity. end quote.

One needs to broaden and expand one's mind through the power of imagery, as before, and to compare this eternity against the seventy years of our life in this world (Tehilim 90:10). Behold, there is no comparison between the two.

Rabbi Eliyahu Dessler z'l explained the matter with additional contemplation such that every person can understand the matter properly. Behold, our sages said: "one pleasure (korach ruach) in Olam Haba is more than all the life of this world" (Avot 4). Thus, our sages gave us a picture so that we may contemplate Olam Haba and weigh the two against each other. This world versus Olam Haba. What is the meaning of the expression: "all the life of this world"?

Rabbi Dessler explains (Michtav M'Eliyahu Vol.1 pg.4): "I wish to reveal what I merited to hear on this from my master and teacher, Rabbi Tzvi Hirsh Broide, z"l. He explained that the matter of "all the life of this world" is as follows. Let us imagine that we concentrated into one second all the hours and seconds of happiness and enjoyment that a man has experienced throughout his entire life and we concentrate all this into one second (for this is the power of imagination). Next stage.

Note that it is impossible to properly grasp the picture immediately. One must picture it in stages. From one stage to the next until the picture is complete and whole. In this way one builds the power of the picture. Through stages, the picture can affect the person properly.

Next, imagine all the happiness and joy that all your friends and acquaintances ever experienced throughout their lives... And likewise, to add all of this into that one second and give it all to that one man as before. Is it possible to imagine the level of enjoyment this man will feel at that moment? But let us continue further.

Let us include into that second and give to that man all the happiness and pleasure experienced by all people of the entire city throughout their lives. And even more than this, we will include all the happiness of all inhabitants of the country and all other countries on the planet. i.e. all the good of the world for one entire generation. We will concentrate all that into one second and give it to that man.

Even with all this, it is still not "all the life of this world". For it is only of that generation. Rather "all the life of this world" means that we include all the happiness of all the generations from the beginning of the creation until the last generation, i.e. all the good of this world without exception. We will give it all to one man and concentrate it all into one second.

Behold, there is no greater pleasure than this anywhere. This second of pleasure is so great that it is already impossible to imagine. And even so, a pleasure of Olam Haba is bigger than this. And what is "korat ruach"? (mentioned earlier - "one pleasure (korach ruach) in Olam Haba is more than all the life of this world")? On this Rabbi Dessler continues: "the level of korat ruach" was explained by my teacher:

"Imagine the great banquet of a great joyous occasion in the palace of a king. (no doubt all kinds of foods and delicacies are found in the banquet hall of a king). A poor man passes there (who is very poor) and takes a whiff of the odor from the banquet when he passes by the street from outside and he derives enjoyment from the pleasant odor. This is the level of "korat ruach". Likewise in Olam Haba, if a man does not merit to Olam Haba itself, and he is permitted to pass from the outside and derive enjoyment only from the good smell of Olam Haba prepared for the righteous - this is the meaning of one who has a korach ruach in Olam Haba. end quote.

This is but a tiny portion of the reward and joy experienced by the righteous in Olam Haba. And this whiff is better and more enjoyable than all the life of this world as before. When one contemplates this, his knowledge and mind begins to explode, of course, for the good, and he begins to understand the greatness of the life of Olam Haba. But without mental imagery, a man has no idea or grasp of it whatsoever.

*Translator*: one should not forget the other half of that mishna also: "one hour of repentance in this world is greater than all the life of the world to come". i.e. not only is one hour of repentance greater than the blissful life of olam haba but greater than "ALL" the life of the world to come! If a person realized the tremendous opportunity that lies in his hands while he is alive here, he would love this world also in the proper way (based on Ohr Yahel). Namely, love this world for the unique opportunity it gives to serve G-d instead of loving its transient pleasures.

One of the wise men already said: "just like fire and water cannot coexist together in one container, so too the love of this world and the love of the Olam Haba cannot coexist together in the heart of the believer". They also said: "this world and the next world are like two jealous wives (of one husband), when he shows a liking to one of them, the other one gets angry.

*Tov Halevanon*: that if he thinks to please one of them, the second one, who is jealous of her, gets angry.

*Matanas Chelko*: *"fire and water"* - in this Rabeinu gives an insight (chidush) which a man does not want to believe. The Yetzer Hara tries to seduce a man that he can love also this world and also Olam Haba. A man will tell himself "certainly I love Olam Haba, but I also have love for this world." But it is not so. Rather, if he has love of this world, it will extinguish the fire through the water. But if he has love of Olam Haba, the waters will dry out through the burning heat of the fire.

*"two jealous wives"* - a man thinks: behold I can love this world and immerse in its pleasures and afterwards, I will immerse myself in matters of Olam Haba. But it is not so, for when one loves one of them, the other gets angry like two jealous wives. And when one draws one close, the other gets angry. So too, he who loves one of these two worlds, the other world resists that love. This adds to the first analogy. For the first analogy of fire and water, one of them causes the other to disappear. But here, it makes strife and even hatred towards the other. So that if a man loves this world, he will not find any pleasure or love of Olam Haba. And when the love of Olam Haba strengthens, his connection to love of this world weakens. This is like a poor destitute man who has nothing to eat until he sustains himself by walking around the city to find whatever he can from the trash heaps. Afterwards, he was given an important source of livelihood. From then on, what he previously esteemed to be important [from the trash heaps] becomes disgusting and despicable in his eyes. So too, for the matter of love of this world and Olam Haba.

My teacher, Rabbi Elyah Lopian zt'l would say that he once heard a woman say: "I know that this world is hevel (vanity), but I want a little hevel." So too by us, we know that everything is hevel but nevertheless we want a bit of hevel. But this is only because we don't feel what we are losing in the future, in Olam Haba.

*Translator* - try to tell someone who just ate a big steak to repent.

Likewise, my brother, both your soul and body need management and thought.

The strengthening and rectification of the soul is through habituating it with morals and wisdoms, and to guide it with words of wisdom, and to teach it the good traits, and refrain from the bodily lusts.

The strengthening and rectification of the body is to provide it with various types of good, tasty food and drink which are suitable to its nature, and to wash it with warm water, and to supervise its benefits and needs constantly.

If your thoughts will be on the needs of your body, and you place all of your attention on it - you will neglect the improvement of your soul. Likewise, if you turn your attention to rectifying your soul by focusing all of your attention on it - you will neglect much of the needs of your body.

Therefore, the proper way is to strengthen your eternal soul over your fleeting body, and that you focus attention on your soul and worry on its needs, but without neglecting the matters that are very necessary for your body, thereby overburdening it and weakening it, as this will be a means to make both weak. Rather, give your body the food it needs to maintain its functioning, and give your soul of the wisdoms and morals more than its ability to take.

*Manoach Halevavos*: i.e. the yearning and desire for wisdom and mussar should be more than your ability, so that through this you will exert yourself with your little ability and afterwards G-d will help you to reach more than this.

*Tov Halevanon*: this means to say, more than what you imagine now that your intellect is capable of, because since the soul is spiritual, it can increase for you much wisdom which you cannot imagine, its ability is unlimited, and it is possible to reach with it very exalted levels when you endeavor in this.

*Matanas Chelko*: it seems from Rabeinu's words that a person must not neglect his body (health). Rather, he must conduct himself in every matter in a measured and weighed manner.

On this the wise man said: *"Be not overly righteous...why should you bring desolation upon yourself? Be not overly wicked, and be not a fool; why should you die before your time?"* (Koheles 7:16), and *"It is good that you should take hold of this, and also from this you shall not withdraw your hand"* (Koheles 7:18), which means:

*"Be not overly righteous"* - Do not be extreme in the ways of the righteous who separate from this world, lest you become ruined.

> *Marpe Lenefesh*: to be like the first category of ascetics mentioned in chapter 3 of the Gate of Separation, which left civilization and dwelled in the wilderness.
>
> *Matanas Chelko*: even though one needs to strengthen love of Olam Haba over love of this world, the intent is not that one should not benefit at all from this world and not be involved in it. Rather, one needs to weigh with the scales of righteousness and take from the world only what he needs.

*"Be not overly wicked"* (ibid), Likewise, do not be extreme in the ways of the wicked who strengthen after this world, and you indulge in base desires more than the amount fitting for your religious and secular needs.

> *Tov Halevanon* - since this weakens the intellect, like the previous analogy with the two wives.

*"why should you die before your time"* (ibid), this refers to the death of the soul, in being overpowered by the base desires, and drowning in the sea of physical pleasures.

> *Tov Halevanon*: The soul drowns due to excessive physical pleasures, like a man drowns at sea, the physical pleasures are like a torrential flood relative to the spirituality of the soul.

Rather, hold on to the balanced path. Strengthen on your final end (Olam Haba) and do not abandon this world (your body's health - *TL*), because from it you will take provisions for the eternal world, and it is like the passageway to the place of rest, as our sages said: *"This world is like a corridor to the future world. Prepare yourself in the corridor that you may enter into the palace"* (Avot 4:16).

This is the path of the early pious ones who feared G-d.
He said: "Do not be overly wise", since wisdom has a fixed limit which cannot be crossed. The explanation is that all the various branches of wisdom which lead to the service of G-d, guarding His commandments, or

demonstrating His wisdom and power - this category is permitted to us, and it is our duty to investigate it, as written: *"Behold, the fear of the L-ord is wisdom"* (Iyov 28:28), and *"the fear of the L-ord is the beginning of wisdom: and the knowledge of the holy ones is understanding"* (Mishlei 9:10), which means knowledge of G-d, and also: *"The fear of the L-ord is the beginning of wisdom"* (Tehilim 111:10), and *"The wise men are ashamed, they are dismayed and taken; lo, they have rejected the word of the L-ord; and what wisdom is in them?"* (Yirmiyahu 8:9), and all that is a wisdom outside of this way we mentioned - it is forbidden to study it and investigate after it. Therefore he said: *"do not be overly wise"*.

But as for foolishness and frivolity he warned us against the smallest amount of it, therefore he said: "do not be foolish", and did not say "do not be too foolish", because even a small amount ruins much of the good qualities, as written: *"Dead flies make the ointment of the perfumed fetid and putrid; so does a little folly outweigh wisdom and honor"* (Kohelet 10:1).

> *Pas Lechem*: A little foolishness is heavier than, and outweighs all of the wisdom and honor and it nullifies them.

## THE TWENTY SIXTH:
*(fearing a mortal king)*

> *Matanas Chelko*: this cheshbon is truly very simple, just like many other cheshbons. However, without contemplation, we will not grasp even one of them.

To make an accounting with oneself that when one is under the commandment of a king, he fears being punished if he transgresses the king's command, yet one does not trouble himself about the commandments of G-d, and does not fear His punishment if he transgresses His command.

How could he neglect to consider the difference between the two commands and the two matters, and not understand the weakness of a mortal king in enforcing his decrees, his possible delay in administering punishment to him, his limited ability to see him, and his many distractions (with other affairs), and (despite all this - *TL*) the wise man already said: *"fear G-d and the king, my son"* (Mishlei 24:21), and *"the fear of a king is as the roaring of a lion: whosoever provokes him to anger sins against his own life"* (Mishlei 20:2).

How can an intelligent man not be abashed of his G-d, whose decree cannot be overturned, who watches over him always. He cannot be distracted. He cannot be prevented (from enacting His decree) by anything, and yet one does not fear His judgment? How can one rebel against His word when he knows that G-d is watching his inner and outer being. How can one not repent for his past by saying to himself: "how long have I rebelled against His word, while He continues delaying punishing me. I will seek His forgiveness before He destroys me from this world, or afflicts me in the next world", this is what David said: "The wicked, in the pride of his countenance will not seek (to repent - *ML*); G-d is never in his thoughts" (Tehilim 10:4).

*Matanas Chelko*: even though in our times, we do not have a king who commands us. But we have laws of the country and police officers and the like. Due to them, a person acts properly. For example, regarding the traffic laws when driving a car on the road, it happens often that a person drives his car faster than the law permits and then he suddenly sees a police car and immediately begins to slow down and drive according to the law. Behold, he thought he could drive fast and was not concerned for the law, but immediately when he sees someone that has the ability to punish him, he becomes a different person.

For then he feels that those who can force him to obey the law are able to see him. At the time he sees the policeman, he should contemplate - am I not foolish! I believe with complete faith that G-d sees me always, every second, and He commanded me to guard the mitzvot and not transgress His will, and I know that there is reward and punishment on everything. I should conduct myself as if the policeman is standing before me at all times! This is the matter of *"I have set G-d before me always"* (Tehilim 16:8). The Shulchan Aruch (1:1, Rama) claims this level from every Jew as written there:

"the verse states, *'I have set G-d before me always'* (Tehilim 16:8). This is a great principle in the Torah and is a paramount attribute of the Tzadikim (righteous people) who walk in the way of G-d. For the way in which a person sits, moves, and carries out his daily activities while he is alone in his house is not the same way he would engage in these activities while standing before a great King. In addition, the way one speaks while amongst those in his home and the conversations he has with his relatives is not the same manner in which he would speak while in the presence of a mortal king. Surely when one considers in his mind that the mighty King, The Holy One blessed be His Name, whom the whole world is filled with His glory, stands before him and sees his deeds, as it states: 'If a man will conceal his secrets, will I not see it?, says the L-ord'; immediately the fear and the proper awe of G-d will descend upon him and he will always be embarrassed before G-d..." end quote.

This example [of the policemen] is very relevant to our matter. For all the traffic laws are instituted for the good of the man himself and also for the good of other people driving on the road. The transgression of the law is itself the punishment. Such as if he goes and drives on the wrong side of the highway against the flow of traffic. It is very likely that through this, he will be killed or he will kill others, or at least there will be injuries, and he can really cause a great calamity. Thus, the traffic laws are for his good and one who transgresses them will be punished by the transgression itself. Hence, there is no benefit from transgressing. So too, l'havdil, regarding the mitzvot of the Creator. The sin itself damages, and one must make a cheshbon that no benefit whatsoever results from transgressing the mitzvot of the Creator.

*Matanas Chelko*: *"how can one not repent for his past"* - this is the claim. How is it conceivable that he not repent for all his previous deeds. Even though, he knows all the previous cheshbon, that G-d sees everything, and is not distracted by other matters, and the punishment is certain to come if he does not repent. Therefore, one must rouse himself to repent.

As we explained in other cheshbons, Rabeinu is emphasizing to us, that one should do these cheshbons at the times when different things happen to him, as he writes here "when one is standing in the commandment of a king" - at that time, it is incumbent on him to implant fear of Heaven in his heart, and to come and repent through this cheshbon.

According to our example, when a man drives a car and suddenly sees that all the cars are beginning to guard the traffic laws, and he wonders about what just happened. Afterwards, he sees police lights and realizes this was caused by fear of punishment from the police. He should then understand that this came to teach him mussar in this cheshbon of Chovos Halevavos, and he should tell himself: "G-d is showing me tangibly the foundation of 'I have set G-d before me always'". For if everyone is afraid of flesh and blood, even though it is only a slight doubt whether they will be punished and perhaps he will not even see me, or will be distracted, etc. as before. And nevertheless, they improve their ways on the road and drive according to the law, all the more so, do I need to fear from the King of kings, the Holy One, blessed be He.

*"the wicked...G-d is never in his thoughts"* - the wicked man who is arrogant does not seek G-d to repent to him. This due to only one reason - for G-d is not in his thoughts. He does not put to mind that G-d sees him

always. The summary is that due to his arrogance, the wicked man lacked the foundation of "I have set G-d before me always".

There is a famous story about the Vilna Gaon who took on himself to wander in exile. He travelled to places where he was not recognized and his name was not known. One time, he travelled in a wagon when suddenly the wagon driver stopped his horses and wanted to steal straw from a nearby field to feed his horses. He told the man riding with him: "stand guard and let me know if there is someone that sees what I am doing". The Vilna Gaon agreed, and when the wagon driver began to steal straw, the Gaon screamed: "someone is looking!". The wagon driver ran back to the wagon and began to drive. Afterwards, he saw that no man was there. "who was there that was looking at me?" He asked. The Gaon replied: "Wasn't the Master of the World looking?"

## THE TWENTY SEVENTH:
*(bearing suffering)*

To make an accounting with oneself when trouble strikes him, whether physically, financially, or any of his other matters. He should receive everything from his G-d with joy, and bear it as one who accepts the judgment of G-d and not bear it as one who is angry on His decree.

*Matanas Chelko*: *"bear it"* - the term "bear..accepting" (Sevel), means patient bearing, bearing a yoke, that a man bears on himself some yoke. He can either bear and accept this yoke wilfully or against his will, with joy or with anger. For example, a man bears on himself the yoke of earning a livelihood. Every day, he runs from morning till evening in many different exertions, to call others and arrange sales between buyers and sellers. Even so, since he makes a large profit, he bears this yoke with joy and does it willingly. Thus, Rabeinu writes that every bad and difficult thing which is sent to a man, he should receive it and accept it wilfully and with joy, not angrily. For anyways, he has no choice in the matter and is forced to bear it.

As written *"And I will wait for the L-ord, that hides His face from the house of Jacob, and I will hope unto Him"* (Yeshaya 8:17) (I am waiting and bearing His hiding and *along with this* I am hoping to Him that He will save me - *PL*), and he should not be like the one the verse speaks of: *"and it shall come to pass that, when they shall be hungry, they shall fret themselves, and turning their faces on high, curse by their king and by their god"* (Yeshaya 8:21).

Know, my brother, that for the ten trials which G-d tested Avraham our forefather with, we would not be praising Avraham for standing up to these trials, if it were not the case that he had received everything from G-d willingly and with a good heart, as written: *"And found his heart faithful before You"* (Nechamia 9:8).

> *Matanas Chelko*: *"we would not be praising Avraham"* - for he was forced to bear these trials and he had no free choice on this. For the case was that G-d tested him with them. Thus all his praise was solely that he accepted them and did them wilfully and with joy...
>
> We must emphasize the matter of emunah (faith) here. Behold Avraham could have said or at least felt that G-d does not appreciate him properly for jumping into the fiery furnace for his faith. On this (kind of self-sacrifice), the Rambam writes that "there is no higher level than this" (Sefer HaMitzvot, Mitzvah 9). For no reward was given to him for this act of self-sacrifice. On the contrary, G-d sent him difficult trials as if He was not happy from Avraham's service. And all the more so [he could have doubted G-d), after every trial. But Avraham did not think like this nor feel like this. Rather, he was only completely faithful and bore all that was given and sent by G-d, and his love of G-d did not diminish for this. This is what we have to learn from Rabeinu's explanation of the verse. For Avraham already demonstrated his love of G-d (at Ur-Kasdim), only afterwards did G-d test him in his levels of this love, whether he would be faithful and firm in it.

As for the generation who left Egypt, they were deserving of condemnation and rebuke in the desert only because they became angry and their hearts were not good with G-d and His prophet (Moshe).

As written: *"But they flattered Him with their mouth, and lied unto Him with their tongue, but their heart was not right with Him"* (Tehilim 78:36). Many times they would show themselves grudging and rebelling against G-d and breaching His covenant, as we find them constantly desiring to return to Egypt, or the like.

> *Tov Halevanon*: even though they accepted everything that came to them and did not sin with their tongues, nevertheless their hearts were always grudging against G-d and not desiring in His decrees but were like one who is forced to accept against his will...and with their lips, they expressed their bad hearts and thoughts, that they did not desire in G-d and in His decrees.
>
> *Matanas Chelko*: by the generation who left Egypt, it was the opposite [of Avraham]. For G-d already showed them His love towards them in taking them out of Egypt. Afterwards, He tested them whether they would return back this love. Even though it appeared that from G-d's side, His love was

not as strong as it was at the time of the Exodus, for He sent them difficult trials now in the desert. All this was in order to test them. Thus, that which Avraham succeeded in the ten trials, many of them [of the generation of Egypt] did not succeed.

Good bearing is a good character trait but one who bears (begrudgingly) out of force does not receive any reward for it, and he does not attain forgiveness (atonement) from it.

*Matanas Chelko* - the drawing close and distancing from the Master of the world, the ups and downs of man, generally speaking, are measured by the amount that a person bears difficult things during his life. Whether he bears them with joy or the opposite. If he is only forced in them and he accepts them not wilfully, he does not receive any reward for them nor forgiveness of sin.

People are used to saying "let my suffering be a kapara (atonement) for my sins". But it is not necessarily so. For only if he accepts the sufferings willingly and with joy will they bring forgiveness for his sins. This is what Rabeinu writes here. Only if when sufferings comes he says: "Ribono shel Olam (Master of the world), I accept these sufferings which I understand that through them my sins will be atoned for, therefore, I accept them with joy". Then he will have forgiveness (atonement) through them and will also receive reward for them. But one who kicks at sufferings and does not accept them wilfully and has claims against G-d - through this, he loses the opportunity given to him from Heaven, and cannot hope to reward and forgiveness through them. Everything depends on man's approach and outlook...

Consider, my brother, the difference between the two types of bearing suffering, and contemplate the different consequences between them (that the first results in forgiveness of sins and reward, while the other anger/frustration and begrudging - *PL*).

*Matanas Chelko* - one must make a simple cheshbon. For either way, he is forced to bear the suffering and difficulty. The difference is only in his reaction and outlook. Therefore, even logically, one should accept them with love.

You will see that the matter of bearing (suffering) divides into three categories:
1. Bearing it in serving G-d.

*Marpe Lenefesh*: bearing all types of hard work to fulfill the service of G-d.

2. Bearing it so as not to rebel against Him.

*Marpe Lenefesh*: to bear whatever comes to him so as not to rebel against G-d, as written in Shema: "And you shall love the L-ord...", which the sages expounded: "even if He takes your life".

3. Bearing from the afflictions of the world.

This third category subdivides to two parts:
one: Bearing for a loss (being struck by a loss in his money or his children or relatives - *TL*)
two: Bearing for lacking of something he loves (that one cannot attain his desires or lusts - *TL*)
Either way, it is possible this trouble came in the way of punishment, and through it you will be forgiven for a sin you committed or that G-d wants to bring you to a test and trial, and through this the Creator will increase your reward.

*Tov Halevanon*: For a virtuous man, G-d brings him to a test in order that the good in him can come out from potential to actual, and then through the actions he will attain purity and illumination of the soul far more than if his righteousness did not come into actual action and remained as potential. Through this, his reward will increase. This is the matter of all the tests of the Torah.

*Pas Lechem*: *test and trial* - He used the two terms "test" and "trial" since that which comes to purge his traits and humble his heart is called a "test", while that which comes to demonstrate his virtue and love of G-d is called a "trial".

*Matanas Chelko*: *in the way of punishment, and through it you will be forgiven for a sin* - if you accept it with love. Then you will merit full reward in Olam Haba for bearing suffering in this world.

*"or... increase your reward* - these two reasons for which G-d brings sufferings and difficulties on a man in this world - either he is paying for them in the way of punishment due to his sins, or they are in order to increase his reward. And that which the Talmud says (Berachot 5a) "if one sees sufferings coming upon him, let him examine his deeds". This is referring to a different category of sufferings which Rabeinu is not dealing with. These sufferings are coming to rouse him to repentance, while Rabeinu's words are regarding sufferings coming as a kapara (atonement) after he already did Teshuva (repentance).

The Talmud says (Yomah 86a): "if one transgressed sins warranting karet (early death from Heaven) or death by Jewish court and he repented, repentance and Yom Kippur suspend [the heavenly punishment] and sufferings complete [the atonement]". end quote. One needs to accept these sufferings on himself. But most sins that a man does are not of Karet or unintentional Karet, but are only [simple] "negative commandments". Therefore, most of his sufferings is in the way of punishment or to rouse him to repentance. Therefore, he should examine his ways to know which sin he committed and the Teshuva he needs to do. This is also a kindness of G-d to rouse a man to this.

Whichever way it is of these two ways, it is proper for you to receive what comes to you from G-d willingly and with good acceptance, as King David said: *"all the ways of G-d are kindness and truth unto those that keep His covenant and testimonies"* (Tehilim 25:10), because the trouble that befell you, if it is to forgive your sin - it is a "truth", and if it is the beginning (of a test) in order to give you in exchange for it good reward for bearing the test - it is a "kindness", therefore it is never other than truth or kindness.

*Pas Lechem*: He used the term "beginning" regarding a test only, since for the suffering which comes from a sin, man is the one who starts it, but that which comes as a test - G-d is the initiator.

If you contemplate well these matters, the result of your bearing will be good, and your reward for it is assured.

Therefore, my brother, do not neglect to check your thoughts constantly in this matter, and then your ability to bear properly to G-d will be strengthened, and it will be easier for you when harsh pain and bitter suffering weighs on your heart, to demonstrate your good acceptance of the decree of G-d, and that you find consolation in Him (when you reflect on the above, it will be a consolation and a medicine for your pain and bitterness - *TL*) , and that your trust is on Him, as written: *"Strengthen yourselves, and He will give your heart courage, all who hope to the L-ord"* (Tehilim 31:25).

*Marpe Lenefesh*: When troubles come on him, chas v'shalom, he should accept them with a good heart and with joy, as our Sages said (Berachot 60b): "a man is obligated to bless on the bad with joy, just like he blesses on the good with joy". For even though the bad already struck him and he has no escape from it, it is not the same if he receives it with love and says to himself "everything G-d does is for the good, and the bad is for my good, either it is to bring forgiveness for my sins or it is yisurim shel ahava (sufferings of love, see Gate of Trust ch.3)".

If he truly thinks this - he is forgiven for his sins as will be explained. On the other hand, if the bad is a burden and a hassle to him, and he is like one forced to bear it, because he has no escape from it, then since it is against his will, he may also come to complain on G-d's traits, as written: *"A man's folly (i.e. his sins) crushes his way, and his heart is angry with the L-rd"* (Mishlei 19:3). And even though he bears it, he gets angry and complains. With this you will understand well the author's words. And like our sages said Berachot 5a: "Rava said: If a man sees suffering coming on him, let him examine his ways...", as above (i.e. G-d is trying to atone for him on the sin he committed). And Rava said in the name of Rav Huna: "whoever G-d desires in, He will crush him with sufferings, as written 'G-d desired to crush him..' (Isaiah 53:10)... but on condition he receives them with love...

## THE TWENTY EIGHTH:
*(total acceptance)*

*Matanas Chelko*: this cheshbon is a continuation and increase of the previous one. There Rabeinu explained the verse: "all G-d's ways are kindness and truth" (Tehilim 25:10). That everything done to man is either in the way of punishment to atone for his sins or in the way of increasing his reward in the future. On this Rabeinu adds depth to the matter.

Making an accounting with oneself if, after putting his trust in G-d, giving himself over to Him, his money, his children, and all his matters to G-d's service, then his matters change and the Creator decrees for him something which is against his wishes.

*Matanas Chelko*: i.e. he did only that which is the will of G-d and was also moser nefesh (self-sacrificing) in this. Furthermore, he gave his money and children towards this - everything for the will of G-d, and despite all this, the Holy One, blessed be He, decrees bad things on him and things which are against his wish befall him such as health or financial troubles, to such an extent that a man wonders to himself and questions - "why did the Almighty do this to me??". At such a time...

He should think to himself: A man gave his friend a house or a field as a gift, and then the recipient of the gift thought in his mind to demolish it and rebuild it differently or to change it from its original manner. Is it right for the donor to mourn what the recipient did, and to grieve for changing it from its original state, after he had already given the house or the field?

Same for you, my brother, if you have given yourself and your possessions to G-d, do not mourn His acting on you as He desires, and conducts Himself towards you as He wishes. And even if it does not appear good to you, nevertheless it is proper for you to be at peace on Him, and rely on His perfect guidance and the judgment of His decree. Do not regret on having given to Him what you think was yours, and do not show anguish for His decree on you - and all the more so being that you are one of His creations, and He is your Maker and the provider of your sustenance, and guides you in what is good for you in your inner and outer matters, even if you don't understand the matter, as written: *"I taught Ephraim also to go, taking them by their arms; but they knew not that I healed them"* (Hoshea 11:3).

*Matanas Chelko*: *Do not regret on having given to Him* - i.e. don't regret on the good deeds and service of G-d that you did since now you have no benefit from them. For example, if he gave money to charity and afterwards his financial situation becomes difficult, and the Yetzer Hara (evil inclination) incites him to regret the good deed and say it was not worth doing. G-d forbid to say or even think like this. For "one who regrets past good deeds loses his reward for them" (see Kidushin 40b).

*Pas Lechem*: That which you considered yourself a Baal Bitachon (one who places his trust in G-d) during the good times is worth nothing, but now when your circumstances change reflect on the above analogy.

*Matanas Chelko*: there is to explain the matter according to what Rabeinu Yonah writes (Mishlei 3:6 and 3:26). There are two matters of Bitachon (trust in G-d), two levels. The first is that a man believes everything is in the hands of Heaven, and he trusts in G-d and not in man. He does not trust in his own might and ingenuity, and he does the will of G-d without worrying on anything. On this type, it is written: "trust in G-d and do good" (Tehilim 37:3).

However, there is a higher level, namely, that a man tells the Master of the World - "Ribono Shel Olam (Master of the world) - do to me what as You wish. I have no opinion or will. Rather, I will be like "clay in the hands of the potter". This is so whether regarding health of the soul and body, or whether his livelihood will be abundant or tight. On this David said: "my soul is to G-d.." (Tehilim 130:6). This is the level of Mesirut Nefesh mamash (real self-sacrifice), where a man has no questions on G-d. Rather, he accepts everything. This is the level of "[you shall love G-d] with all your heart, with all your soul, and with all your might" (in the Shema). Rabeinu's words here are referring to this level, where a man gives his soul to G-d to do with it as He wishes... Not because he recognizes that G-d knows better what is the best thing for him, but rather, because he nullifies his opinion and will to G-d's, blessed be He. This is mesirut nefesh (real self-sacrifice)...

This is the addition to the previous cheshbon. Not only should a man receive everything willfully and with joy. But sometimes a man who serves G-d properly thinks that certainly G-d will grant him good and kindnesses, and if it is the opposite, he comes to think that it appears G-d is angry with him and it seems He is not happy with his deeds. He must accept this too willfully for this level is that a man is moser nefesh to the Holy One, blessed be He, to do to him as He wishes.

## THE TWENTY NINTH:
*(greatness of the soul)*

To contemplate the superiority of the soul over the body, and to realize that some men are greater than other men, until one man can be worth as much as a thousand men, and to know that this superiority is not due to superior qualities of his body, but rather due to the higher degree of his soul, as was said to David: *"but now you are worth ten thousand of us"* (Shmuel II 18:3).

Even for women who are distinguished by physical beauty but are deficient in spiritual qualities, then not only is their beauty not pleasing, but it becomes ugly, as the wise man said: *"as a gold ring in a pig's snout, so is a beautiful woman from who (moral) sense has departed"* (Mishlei 11:22), and *"Charm is deceitful, and beauty is vain: but a woman that fears the L-ord, she shall be praised"* (Mishlei 31:30).

According to your understanding of the greatness of your soul over your body, it is proper for you to exert yourself in her rectification and in her salvation, so that she may stay with her L-ord who observes whether she is bright or darkened (by sin), worthy of praise or of blame, whether she has chosen good or evil, and whether she tends to reason or to lust. (the soul is being personified here - Rabbi Moses Hyamson zt'l)

Therefore tend to her matters always, more than you tend to the matters of your body, and know, that it is easier to heal your body from the worst of the diseases that befall it, than it is to heal the soul from the sickness of the yetzer (evil inclination) when he overpowers it, as the wise man said: *"The spirit of a man will sustain him in sickness; but a wounded spirit who can bear?"* (Mishlei 18:14) (if the soul is well, it can support a sick body. But if the soul is sick, it can bear nothing - Rabbi Moses Hyamson zt'l), and *"above all things guarded, watch over your heart"* (Mishlei 4:23).

> *Matanas Chelko*: *"more than you tend to the matters of your body"* - i.e. since without a doubt the Holy One, blessed be He, measures a man's importance solely according to the greatness of importance of his soul, therefore, a man needs to inspect and work on his soul and examine its needs more than matters of the body.
>
> *"it is easier to heal your body..than to heal the soul"* - i.e. one needs to guard the soul from illness, namely, to not do things through which it will darken and become foolish (metamtemah), or even things through which the soul will not be able to attain the qualities and perfection that it alone can attain. On this Rabeinu wrote this simple cheshbon, that it is easier to heal oneself from an illness of the body, than to heal the soul if it has become foolish and tameh (spiritually impure) through sin. Therefore, when doing this cheshbon, a man should contemplate and be watchful ahead of time to not make his soul tameh and foolish... for then it is almost in the category of "that which is crooked cannot be made straight" (Kohelet 1:15).
>
> *"than it is to heal the soul from the sickness of the yetzer"* - as an analogy, bandits captured the king's city and took control of what enters and leaves the gates of the city. Is it conceivable that they will allow messengers informing the king of what has happened and how to defeat the bandits? Surely, the bandits will block them. So too, when the Yetzer has captured a man's heart, he will not allow thoughts of his defeat to pass through his heart - *Ohr HaChaim parsha Ki Teitze.*

## THE THIRTIETH:
*(stranger in a strange land)*

The thirtieth and concluding accounting - to make an accounting with oneself regarding the conditions which a foreigner in this world (must accept on himself - PL). He should consider his status in it like that of a stranger who came from a faraway land and did not know even one of the inhabitants of the country he came to, and not one of them knew him. The king of the country had pity on him in that he was a stranger, and instructed him in that which will further his welfare. He provided him with his daily sustenance, and commanded him not to rebel against his laws, and not to transgress his commands. And he informed him of the benefit and reward if he obeyed him and scared him with the punishments (he would receive if he disobeyed him), appropriate for the time and place.

And the king warned the immigrant that a time will come when he must leave there (suddenly, and that he should always be prepared for this journey - *TL*), but he did not reveal to him when this time would be.

Among the conditions he is obligated in:
1. Submission and humility, and to abandon arrogance, and to distance from pride and haughtiness, as written in this matter: "And they said, 'This one came to dwell with us, and now he is judging us (as if he owns this place - *MC*)?'" (Bereishis 19:9).

> *Matanas Chelko*: a man who comes to a different country and is a stranger there, he does not at all think to become haughty. Rather, humility/submission is naturally fixed in him. So too in this world, one needs to feel thus... It seems the Torah set a specific holiday to review and learn this important principle, namely, Sukkot, where our sages said: "leave a fixed dwelling and go in a temporary dwelling" (Sukkah 2b). This is the teaching of Sukkot, to feel that this world is a temporary world (and in Pesach one needs to feel and emphasize the slavery and suffering, etc.). If a person lived with this outlook, that here is not his place, it would be easier for him to fight the evil inclination.

2. To be prepared for the journey and for moving on, and to not become comfortable and settled in, as written: *"The land shall not be sold permanently: for the land is Mine; for you are strangers and sojourners with Me"* (Vayikra 25:23).

> *Matanas Chelko*: this is one of the laws of the Torah so that a man will feel that the land is not his and he will not be so attached to it, and will know and recognize that he is but a stranger in this world.. Behold it is clear from the Torah itself that the foundational outlook in life in order to refrain from sin and not become entrenched in worldly matters is to feel like a stranger in this world.

3. To investigate the ways and laws of the country and what one is obligated to the king, as David said: *"I am a stranger in the land; hide not Your commandments from me"* (Tehilim 119:19).

4. To love another stranger like him, to help and aid him, as written: *"you shall love the stranger"* (Devarim 10:19), and *"But the stranger that dwells with you shall be unto you as one born among you, and you shall love him as yourself; for you were strangers in the land of Egypt"* (Vayikra 19:34)

> *Pas Lechem*: And since all the strangers help each other, certainly they will attain the collective benefit.

*Matanas Chelko*: Rabeinu's intent is also regarding "love your neighbor as yourself" (Vayikra 19:18). We see in truth a deep psychological matter regarding travellers which we don't find by people who live in fixed homes. When two people who have no connection to each other and don't normally speak to each other while in their city, travel on the road together, they become friends a bit. Since both are on the road, not in their homes, they feel like strangers and draw closer to each other. We also find that people who travel together don't have as much jealousy and strife like there is when they are fixed in their homes. The reason for this is because they need each other and also encourage each other.

One who contemplates this will recognize that jealousy and strife common to people comes from the feeling of permanence and arrogance that they have when in their land and home. But when they travel on the road, they all have one goal - that the journey pass safely and that they reach their destination without harm to their body and money. Therefore, they don't have so much differences of views and divisiveness of heart which disrupts them.

For this reason, when people feel the matter of being a stranger, namely, that all people are strangers and travellers in the road of this world, then, jealousy and strife diminishes between them. For all of them focus their strength and minds towards the journey to Olam Haba. And things which other people are very meticulous about due to thinking themselves permanent dwellers and citizens in this world, these things do not take up any room by them. For in their mind, they are on the road to eternal life. A small example: one who goes on the road is not concerned if his shirt is a bit wrinkled, unlike when he is in his house or city.

One needs to contemplate that the Holy One, blessed be He, created the world in such a way that a man can understand the concept of being a stranger in order to understand that we are only strangers in this world and to live like this always.

5. To hasten and be quick to cling to the service of the king of the land, because he has no friend who can intervene with the king on his behalf if he transgresses the service. His matter is opposite that of the answer the Shunamit gave when the prophet asked her: *"you have been careful for us with all this care; what is to be done for you? would you like to be spoken for to the king, or to the captain of the host?"* (Melachim II 4:13,), she answered "I dwell among my people", she meant to say: "my people and my family will speak to him on my behalf in the time of need". This is not so for a stranger. Rather, he is as written: *"I looked on my right hand, and*

*beheld, but there was no man that would acknowledge me: refuge failed me; no man cared for my soul"* (Tehilim 142:5).

> *Matanas Chelko*: when a man travels on the road, he is careful that all his matters be in order according to the laws of the country that he is travelling to. For example, that his passport be valid, and likewise for all matters which he knows that if he does not attend to them ahead of time, they will stop him at the border and request of him valid papers, and he will have no one to rely upon. But a citizen and fixed resident in his country trusts that if he transgresses one of the laws, his family or friends will come to assist him. Unlike the stranger who does not trust thus for he does not know anyone who can help him. Therefore, he does not trust in himself and is careful to guard all the laws of the country.

6. To be satisfied with whatever food he gets, and with whatever house and clothing he can find, and to conduct himself in all his manners on subsistence level and not to exert himself (for amassing luxuries).

> *Tov Halevanon*: to exert himself to earn only what is enough for himself, since he dwells in a land which is not his, to who will he leave all the fruits of his toil at the time he will depart from there?

7. To prepare for the journey and to consider what provisions he will need on the way.

8. That it be big in his eyes, a small favor someone does to him, and that he extends praises to someone who benefited him.

> *Tov Halevanon*: since one is a stranger in the land, a little favor someone does for him feels like a great kindness, similar to what Ruth said: "Then she fell on her face, and bowed herself to the ground, and said to him, Why have I found grace in your eyes that you should take knowledge of me, seeing that I am a stranger?" (Ruth 2:10)

10. To bear patiently any evil that befalls him, and monetary damage that strikes him - due to being broken and humble of spirit and due to being weak to prevent it from occurring.

Therefore, my brother, take on yourself the conditions of being a stranger in this world, because you are in truth a stranger in it.

> *Tov Halevanon*: your matter in this world is the true, most extreme state of being a stranger, more than any possible state of being a stranger in the world; here you are by yourself and all alone, no one can help you or

redeem you from the time you came to this world until the time you will leave it, as will be explained.

The proof that you are a stranger and all alone in it is that during the time you emerged into the realm of existence and were formed in the belly of your mother - if all human beings in the world were to exert themselves to hasten your formation for even one second or delay it for one second, or to assemble one of your limbs to another one, or to release one from another, or to try to form one of your limbs whether of the external (limbs) or internal ones (internal organs), or to grant movement to a limb which normally cannot move, or to grant rest to a limb which normally moves (ex. heart, lungs), or to advance the time you exit your mother's womb before the time decreed for you, or to delay it for the time to blink an eye, or to make the matter of birth easier for you or harder - they would not be capable of affecting you on this (unless G-d decreed so).

Likewise, after you entered this world, no human being is capable of bringing you sustenance without the help of G-d. No person can make your body larger or smaller. If you could imagine that no one were left in the world except you, and that the entire world was yours alone, this would not increase by even a mustard seed (tiny amount) the sustenance that would reach you until the end of your days.

Similarly, if the population of the world would double many times over, you would not be lacking even a mustard seed of what was decreed for you, no less and no more.

*Matanas Chelko*: this is a contemplation regarding a man's livelihood - that everything comes solely from G-d, blessed be He, and whether he is alone in the world or among many people, his livelihood is still given to Him by the Creator, blessed be He, in an exact manner. In truth, this thought should bring joy to man. For through it he recognizes that he does not need the help of others. For everything comes solely from G-d, blessed be He.

So too, none of the created beings (human or otherwise) are capable of benefiting you nor of harming you, and not one of them is capable of adding to the days of your life nor of decreasing them, likewise for all of your traits, your nature, and your good or bad deeds (which depend exclusively on your own free will - *TL*).

If so, what connection is there between you and other creatures? Or, with which kinship are you related to them or they related to you? Are you not in this world just like a stranger to whom its inhabitants however numerous can bring no advantage and whom their small number cannot harm him (since he has no help from them - *TL*). Are you not in it like a lonely, solitary individual, who has no association except with his Master, and no one to have compassion on him except for his Creator?

> *Marpe Lenefesh*: Since there is no person in the world, even amongst your friends and relatives who are capable of benefiting you in any way or of harming you, rather everything depends on the will of G-d. If so, are you not in this world like a total stranger?
>
> *Manoach Halevavos*: ...since what use is there for relatives if you have no benefit from them?...

Therefore, my brother, devote yourself to G-d's service alone, just like He alone created you, guides you, provides for you, and that your life and death are in His hands alone.

> *Marpe Lenefesh*: That you do the service of G-d for G-d alone, without any interests or thoughts for anything else, just like He is alone in managing you.

Place His written and oral Torah before your eyes, hope to His reward and fear His punishment, take on yourself the conditions of being a stranger which I aroused you on for all the days of your life in this world and you will reach the bliss of Olam Haba, as the wise man said: *"[My son eat honey for it is good, and the honeycomb which is sweet to your palate;] So shall the knowledge of wisdom be unto your soul: when you have found it, then there shall be a reward and your hope shall not be cut off"* (Mishlei 24:14).

> *Marpe Lenefesh*: Just like honey is sweet to your palate, so too, put to mind to make wisdom sweet to your soul, and through this, your end will be good, and your hope will never be cut off.

## SUMMATION

These, my brother, are thirty ways, among the ways a man should make an accounting with himself before G-d. When you think to yourself on them, and you bring yourself to judgment on them, then their light will rupture through, and their illumination will surround you. Reflect on them constantly.

> *Tov Halevanon*: by reflecting much on them, your understanding on their matters will deepen. Like the nature of truth, the more one contemplates it,

the deeper one understands it and it comes closer to the heart.

Review them in your mind all the days of your life. Do not be satisfied with my short discussion on them, and my mentioning them in a concise manner, because each matter, when it is clarified and explained properly, will expand many times over from what I mentioned.

> *Tov Halevanon*: Even though he wrote them briefly, they comprise many matters and branches which can be understood by each person according to his intellectual power and the brightness of his soul.

I merely aroused attention them, and recalled them to their seeker in a concise manner. I did not speak much on them, so that this book will not become too lengthy, and go out of my intent for it, which was to arouse and teach (concisely, as the sages said (Pesachim 3b): "one should teach his students in a concise manner" - *ML*).

Place them opposite your eyes, and before your vision. Establish them in your heart and in your mind - then when you review them, you will see in them, what you did not originally see, of hidden secrets and spiritual mussar (mussar which penetrates the mind and the soul - *TL*).

Do not think that when you examine them, and arrive at an understanding of the meaning of the words, that you have already grasped the full concealed matter, because you will not reach this from them until after you put your thoughts on them diligently and with exertion many times and over a long time.

Straighten yourself through them, and straighten others with them, you will reach the great reward from G-d, as written: *"And the wise will shine like the brightness of the sky, and those who bring the multitudes to righteousness like the stars forever and ever"* (Daniel 12:3), and the wise man said: *"But to them that rebuke shall be delight, and a good blessing shall come upon them"* (Mishlei 24:25).

> *Tov Halevanon*: those who rebuke others on their wickedness, the delight of G-d and the blessing of G-d will come to them, and certainly for one who rebukes himself for his wickedness, his reward will be greater and more intense.
>
> *Matanas Chelko*: it seems from Rabeinu's words what was said in the introduction - that in this gate is mentioned all the foundations of the service of G-d. Therefore, the more one reviews them and studies them, the

more he will find in each one more insights and foundations in depth and breadth of the service of G-d and all the obligations of man in this world. Thus Rabeinu claims from us to study and review this gate. For it includes the entire Torah, and all matters of the service of G-d, whether the foundations in the Gate of Examination(#2) or the Gate of Trust (#4), and all of them in a practical manner, until a man can reach lofty levels and great closeness to G-d, blessed be He.

*"after you put your thoughts on them diligently and with exertion many times and over a long time" - Ohr Yahel v.3 Vayera pg.41* - on the verse: "I am but dust and ashes" (Gen.18:27), the Ibn Ezra explains: "I was dust and will return to dust".

What is the chidush (novel insight) here? Behold, every sane person knows that he is dust and will return to dust.

The explanation is that we are used to thinking a great and whole man is one who has attained new wisdom which other people don't know. Therefore, when we want to attain wholeness in middot (character traits) or outlook (deot), we search for new insights in books or seek advice which contains novel or interesting ideas. All this is a total mistake.

For a man, whose soul is "hewn" from under the Kisei Hakavod (throne of glory), [potentially] grasps and understands vastly more than the Chayot and Ofanei HaKodesh (holiest angels), who are below the Kisei Hakavod, as explained in tractate Chagiga.

But because man's soul is incarcerated in the dark house of the body - which is the dark and obscuring physical - so that it blocks all light from reaching this holy soul. One should truly fear that he not remain in the bottom level of the pit, G-d forbid.

In any case, we learn that all man's work is not to contrive new ideas (chidushim) in his soul, which he did not know previously until now. But rather, it is to remove the disgrace of the prison (cherpat beit haasurim) which he sits inside, and to remove the dark ropes of the physical obscuring him. Then automatically, he will understand and feel what he already knows, in his nefesh, ruach, and neshama (soul, spirit and higher soul).

Likewise, what our sages said: "look at three things... know from where you came and where you are going..." (Avot 3:1).

Is there anyone who does not know this already? Rather, it is as we said - a man is only asked to know what he himself already knows. That is to say, to feel in his senses what his intellect knows. One does not need anything else more than this. This is everything!

However, this work is exceedingly much more difficult than to think of new insights (chidushim) in some matter. We see that despite all our toil in Torah and fear, we are far away from this as heaven is to earth.

Behold, every person utters with his mouth always that he is but dust and will return to dust, and that man is destined to die, and this world is futile of vanity of vanities (hevel hevelim), etc., etc., but nevertheless, day and night he does not stop from being occupied in this worthlessness (hevel), and he plunges his soul deeper in this abyss - with all his limbs and senses, from the soles of his feet to the top of his skull - every day more and more, as the verse says: "and they went after vanity and themselves became vanity" (Yirmiyahu 2:5).

That is to say, he goes after the vanity until he himself becomes a piece of vanity. This is a wonder! For even an animal will not eat something harmful to itself, and every intelligent person will distance and flee from something which can cut short the wick of his brief life on this earth. But regarding eternal life, which he himself knows that if he does not put an eye on his ways, he is liable to be destroyed forever and ever, G-d forbid. But nevertheless, he proceeds confidently in his way - the way of his habits, like a horse rushing in - only evil all day!

We must say "nimshal k'behemot nidmu" (he is compared to the silent animals - Tehilim 49:13). For an animal perception has taken root in his heart and in the depths of his soul - there is no calculation or understanding, "A man walks in this world and he thinks that it will be his forever, and that he will remain in it for all time" (Zohar Nasso 126).

But we must know that this awesome physical power which deceives human beings in this world is not tangible. It is but lies, darkness and blindness, concealing the truth from being seen. One need not push away the falsehood with his hands and banish it. For falsehood has no real existence.

Rather, when a man illuminates himself with the intellect of truth he possesses, automatically, the darkness will leave and the falsehood will run away. Likewise, king David said: "take my soul out of confinement to give thanks to Your Name" (Tehilim 142:8), for the soul is imprisoned inside the walls of this awesome prison, namely, man's body. But when the prison is removed and the soul goes out free, it no longer has anything blocking and preventing it. It is then entirely ready to stand before G-d and thank His Name. This is the meaning of "take my soul out of confinement to give thanks to Your Name".

The Torah says: "It is not in heaven, that you should say, 'Who will go up to heaven for us and fetch it for us, to tell [it] to us, so that we can fulfill it?' Nor is it beyond the sea, that you should say, 'Who will cross to the other side of the sea for us and fetch it for us, to tell [it] to us, so that we may fulfill it?' Rather, [this] thing is very close to you; it is in your mouth and in your heart, so that you can fulfill it" (Devarim 30:12-14).

There is room to contemplate here, if one wants to show his fellow something placed on his table, why the need to first tell him that it is not in the heaven? On the contrary one should tell him he need not move even one step to reach it.

Rather, the Torah teaches us here the fundamental principle we mentioned. For the truth is so obvious and clear that it is in your mouth and heart to do. But the falsehood hides and distances it far out until the heavens and the end of the sea. Thus before removing the obstruction, i.e. while the darkness covers the land, it appears in the heaven and beyond the sea. But after removal of the veil of falsehood and revealing of the truth, behold it is clear before you it "is very close to you".

We learn from all this that regarding Avraham Avinu who said: "I am but dust and ashes", it is correct that there is no real chidush (novel idea) in the matter. But the great difference is in this we said - that by Avraham Avinu it was chiseled as truth that he truly said before the Holy One, blessed be He, who is truth and whose seal is truth, i.e. that he felt in all his limbs the "I am but dust and ashes". This is the great difference between his declaration and ours, like the distance between "heaven.. and beyond the sea" to "in your mouth". This was the lofty level of humility of Avraham Avinu, the giant of giants... (see there for more)

## *** CHAPTER 4 ***

*- the benefits of the accounting*

The benefit the spiritual accountings we mentioned yields are the results which the soul develops after:
* attaining a clear grasp in the 30 ways of spiritual accounting we mentioned
* understanding their matters (their surface meaning - *PL*)
* understanding their actual form (their inner meaning - *PL*)
* understanding the truth of their obligation (to clarify through reason that it is indeed true that one is obligated in them - *Lev Tov*)
* the yearning of one's soul to undertake them, according to one's understanding of them and establishing of them in one's thoughts.

> *Pas Lechem*: That the soul yearns and accepts to undertake them on itself. This depends on one's understanding of them, and according to the amount of understanding will be the corresponding yearning.

> *Tov Halevanon*: Establishing of them in one's thoughts means returning to them and reviewing their matters in one's thoughts, time after time.

> Note: Rabbi Yosef Shalom Elyashiv zt"l would say: "The primary review which brings benefit is review whereby one learns the matter again anew (od paam mechadash es ha'inyan). This takes alot of time, though it is quicker than the first time, but it takes time. But the toeles (benefit) is davka (specifically) from reviews like this" (from the book: HaSod on Rabbi Elyashiv chapter 2)

Then, my brother, there will develop in your soul a sublime and lofty result, (1) you will learn from it all the good character traits, and you will reach through it to all the treasured things, namely, (2) purifying the essence of the soul from the obscurity of foolishness, and (3) you will dispel the darkness of doubt that is in your heart.

> *Tov Halevanon*: The darkness which brought the doubts in your emunah (faith) which are stuck in your heart.

You already know that (when learning mathematics), according to the correctness, number, and proper order of the fundamental principles will be the resulting clarity and mastery.

Likewise, for preparing a medication in the field of medicine, the benefit of the medication, and the potency of its effect will be according to the potency of the herbs, which the medication consists of.

> *Matanas Chelko*: one who wishes to become a pharmacist must first know how medicines are made. But this is not possible until he first acquires much knowledge in chemistry and other branches of science, so that he will know how to combine medicines in the proper way. Thus he must first study many preliminary things and fundamentals in the matter.

Likewise for the field of engineering, called in Arabic, Il-Handasa, according to the number of fundamental principles learned in the desired field will be the resulting quality and usefulness of the knowledge.

> *Matanas Chelko*: *"Il-Handasa"* - i.e. architecture/engineering. One needs to know the constitution of all relevant materials and the amounts needed to combine them, and also the properties of the materials, such as how much weight it can bear. Only after he masters all these things and other areas can he begin to use this trade to design beautiful buildings or the like.

So it is with many things. For example, a leverage scale cannot be designed without prior knowledge in engineering, mechanics, mathematics and weights.

Likewise for the astronomers' measure called in Arabic, Itztrolab, it cannot be designed without prior understanding in engineering, geometry, astronomical movements, and area of the earth.

> *Matanas Chelko*: likewise for the service of G-d, one needs to learn how to fight with one's evil inclination and how to trust in G-d, and in matters of mitzvot between man and his fellow and between man and G-d. There are many preliminaries and fundamentals.

So too, for this matter requested from the soul, it will not be possible for you, my brother, until you first bear accepting what I have aroused you in of the spiritual accountings with yourself in this gate and in the other gates, and are diligent in acting on them.

> *Tov Halevanon*: do not be wearied due to the lengthiness of the introductions, because this is the way of truth. It cannot be clarified except through many introductions due to the depth of its matter.

> *Matanas Chelko*: this is the explanation of "Cheshbon HaNefesh" (spiritual

accounting) - to give to the soul the knowledge and powers it needs in order to build the "machine" which it can use afterwards in the service of the soul.

And when you do this with a faithful heart and a pure soul, your mind will become illuminated. You will see the path to all of the exalted qualities, and the yetzer (evil inclination) will not have a way to reach you and entice you, and you will reach the status of one treasured by G-d. A new, strange, supernal sense will arouse in you, unfamiliar to you of all the senses you are used to knowing, as the wise man said: *"A man's wisdom makes his face to shine, and the boldness of his face is changed"* (Koheles 8:1). Then you will perceive the great matters, and you will see the deep secrets, with your pure soul, pure heart, and strong faith. You will not part from a permanent joy in this world and in the next, due to the magnitude of what you observed and the greatness of the secret which was revealed to you, with G-d's help.

I saw proper to give you an analogy, which will clarify for you a bit of what I have mentioned to you: Imagine that you are in a place, above this place and behind you is a wondrous image (and an object is blocking you from seeing it - *PL*), and there is no way for you to see it with your eyes, and gaze at it with your sense of sight. A certain person told you that when you make a sheet of metal and polish it until the darkness is removed, and you anoint it with various potions for a long time (some kind of metal mirror - *PL*), and then you place it opposite your face (like a periscope - *MC*) - then you will see the above picture that was previously hidden to you, and you will be able to gaze at it and to enjoy its pleasant appearance and radiant beauty.

*Matanas Chelko*: but the condition here is only if you polish it time and time again until it becomes very, very, shiny, and you remove the blackness from it. Only then will you be able to see the beautiful form in its radiant beauty and all its colors so that you enjoy it properly.

The high picture, which you have no way to gaze at with your eyes, is the wisdom of the Creator, and His power, and the beauty of the upper world whose form and quality is hidden from us. The sheet metal is the soul of man, the polishing is the guiding it in the wisdoms and the intellectual and Torah morals. The anointings are the thirty ways of personal accounting, which I have mentioned to you.

*Matanas Chelko*: *"the beauty of the upper world whose form and quality is hidden from us"* - the intent is knowledge of G-d and grasping the wisdom and ability to know and understand that which is happening in the upper worlds.

*"the anointings are the thirty ways of personal accounting"* - and according to how much one anoints and polishes and shines the soul, so too, will he increase to see more and more in the upper worlds.

Behold, in truth this is also the levels of prophecy as our sages said (Yevamot 49b): "all the prophets looked at G-d, blessed be He, with a dim "aspelakria" (mirror) while Moshe Rabeinu, who saw G-d "face to face" (Devarim 34:10), saw with a clear "aspelakria". The matter is an analogy to understand the levels of their seeing. The "aspelakria" is a mirror (Keilim 30:2), and the Rambam explains (Shmonei Perakim ch.7) this matter that any bad trait in a man causes a separation barrier between himself and the Holy One, blessed be He. When there are no evil traits, there is no barrier and man clings to Him, blessed be He, and it is possible to see G-d through a clear mirror like the level of Moshe Rabeinu. It is written "the man Moshe was humbler than any other man on the face of the earth" (Bamidbar 12:3). This means Moshe had rectified all his traits until the final one which is the "I" of man, the trait of Humility. Therefore, his soul was pure to such an extent that there were no separation barriers between him and his Maker, and he would speak to the Master of the world, face to face, like a man speaks to his fellow.

Rabeinu writes that this blessing is a situation that every man can reach. Therefore, every polishing and every shining by doing the mitzvot and rectifying the character traits, purifies and illuminates the soul of man more and more, until he merits to reach additional levels from the Creator, blessed be He. Throughout the generations, and even in our generation there were men who reached lofty levels up to Ruach Hakodesh (holy spirit). But it is impossible to come to the level of prophecy since there is no Temple today.

When you put them to your heart, and establish them in your thoughts, your soul will cleanse, and your intellect will illuminate, and all types of hidden matters will picture in your mind, and you will see true forms with open eyes, and the gates of virtue will open, and the separation veil over your eyes which separates between you and between the wisdom of the Creator will be removed from you. And G-d will teach you supernal wisdom and beneficial acts and will grant you Divine powers, as written: *"And the spirit of the L-ord shall rest upon him, the spirit of wisdom and understanding, the spirit of counsel and might, the spirit of knowledge and of the fear of the L-ord"* (Yeshaya 11:2), and *"But it is a spirit in man and the breath of the Al-mighty that gives them understanding"* (Iyov 32:8), and *"If you seek her as silver and search for her as for hidden treasures; Then shall you understand the fear of the L-ord, and find the knowledge of G-d"* (Mishlei 2:4-5).

# CHAPTER 5

*- whether the spiritual accounting is a constant obligation*

Whether this accounting is a constant duty on a man or only at some times but not at others, I say in response to this question as follows:

This accounting is a duty on a man according to his intellectual ability and level of understanding, at all times, with every blink of an eye, and if he can, with every one of his breaths, in order that he not part from awe, fear, and shame-facedness of the Almighty, may He be exalted, who constantly observes him.

> *Marpe Lenefesh*: There is no hour or second that a man is not involved in one of the thirty accountings. Whether he is alone, or with people, or learning, or praying, or engaged in worldly matters, or in talking. Every act one does or thought one thinks, one can put to heart one, two, or more of the accountings that he remembers at that time and place. Examine and you will see.

> *Pas Lechem*: (on the words "awe and fear") Awe refers to something far away, while fear refers to something close by. So too picturing G-d's loftiness, according to how distant it is from our ability to understand Him brings "awe". While picturing the verse "the entire world is full of His glory" and the nearness of His providence on us brings "fear".

> *Matanas Chelko*: *"with every one of his breaths"* - our sages said (Bereishis Raba 14:9) on the verse "may every neshama (soul) praise G-d" (Tehilim 150:6) - on every breath (neshima) praise G-d". It seems this is Rabeinu's intent, that always, on every breath, one needs to make a cheshbon, and the "I have set G-d before me always" is needed on every breath.

> If one asks: "if one needs to do a cheshbon every second, there will be no time left to learn Torah and do mitzvot". But the answer is that certainly when a person is doing a mitzva there is no need to do the cheshbon. For the cheshbons come to rouse a man to toil in Torah and mitzvot. This is the effect that results from them and their purpose... thus that which Rabeinu writes on "every breath". This refers to times when he is not toiling in clinging to G-d, namely, Torah study and fulfilling the mitzvot. Then he needs to make these cheshbons always to return him to clinging to G-d. (see there).

Let one learn from what G-d has commanded a king (of Israel) in saying:

*"And it will be, when he sits upon his royal throne, that he shall write for himself this Torah on a scroll...And it shall be with him always, and he shall read it all the days of his life [so that he may learn to fear the L-ord, his G-d, to keep all the words of this Torah and these statutes, to do them]"* (Devarim 17:18), and *"This book of the Torah shall not leave your mouth; you shall meditate therein day and night [in order that you observe to do all that is written in it, for then will you succeed in all your ways and then will you prosper]"* (Yehoshua 1:8). And also (to every Jew in the Shema): *"And these words, which I command you this day, shall be on your heart"* (Devarim 6:6), and *"you shall bind them for a sign upon your hand, and they shall be Totafos between your eyes"* (Devarim 6:8). And He reinforced the matter in the chapter of Tzitzit in saying: *"this shall be Tzitzit for you, and when you see it, you will remember all the commandments of the L-ord to perform them, and you shall not wander after your hearts and after your eyes after which you go astray"* (Bamidbar 15:39), and then *"So that you shall remember and perform all My commandments and you shall be holy to your G-d"* (Bamidbar 15:40).

> *Matanas Chelko*: *"from what G-d has commanded a king"* - the king specifically, since he is the "heart of all Israel" as the Rambam writes (Hilchot Melachim 3:5). He must conduct himself with a heavy head (not frivolous) - that all his thoughts be clinging to G-d and His Torah every second. Due to this, a sefer Torah must be with him everywhere he goes. In truth, this is so for every man. For it is written "this book of the Torah shall not leave your mouth; you shall meditate therein day and night" (Yehoshua 1:8). From there it seems that one must be clinging to G-d always.

What is there left, on the matter of arousing us on the spiritual accounting of remembering the Creator that He did not arouse us in?!

According to this, my brother, it is proper for you to conduct yourself, in habituating the accounting with yourself before G-d every hour and every moment.

Do not consider small in your eyes any good (any small mitzva - *TL*) that you do for His Name, even a word, or a gazing of the eye, because a little bit from you is a lot by Him, and likewise, for the matter of sins.

> *Matanas Chelko*: do not say: what worth or value is there in one word of rousing oneself or one looking at the greatness and wisdom of the Creator?.. And in Nefesh HaChaim (Shaar 1:13) on the verse (Amos 4:13) "For lo, He forms the mountains and creates the wind, and declares to man what is his speech" (after man's death, G-d shows him the effects of his

words in the mystical worlds). Here is an excerpt:

"he exhorts man here, that due to his being in this lowly world, he does not
see or grasp the building and destruction, G-d forbid, that occurs above in
the mystical worlds due to each and every word of his. He may even think
to himself: 'what importance is there to a word or simple speech that it
should affect anything in the world?'. But he should know faithfully that
every word and [even] light speech which he utters is never lost and does
not go to waste" end quote.

These words were said on a word and light talk. All the more so, that an
action or deed makes a vast effect above.. thus there is no concept of "small
thing", every second of cheshbon is a big matter.

*Marpe Lenefesh*: sometimes a man refrains from doing a good deed
because the thing seems small in his eyes, such as a mitzva with a word, or
looking at something for the sake of G-d. He thinks it is not worth anything
in the eyes of G-d, and he says to himself, 'if so, why should I do it?' On
this he wrote: 'Do not consider small in your eyes any good'. And here is an
excerpt from the Chassid on the chapter "Yesh Nochalim":

"know that the commandments and warnings which appear very small and
insignificant, and people are indifferent to them - they stand over the
heights of the universe. It is impossible to imagine their measure or
examine their effect by (limited) human intellect. It cannot be grasped
except by true, holy, supernal sages who the light of G-d shines on. And
every mitzva, even the smallest of the smallest, has a power and root in the
divine chariot (kabala terms), from which the matter emanates down to the
physical world. When one fulfills the mitzva, the corresponding supernal
power is aroused in his root above, and there they are illuminated without
limit, and he adds power and might to the Pamalya shel Maala (heavenly
domain).

And if he does a sin, whether in speech or in deed, thereby strengthening
the power of the "Samech-Mem" and his helpers (the forces of
evil/impurity), he arouses the power of tuma and klipa of that matter which
is aligned to him in the chariot of tuma. Therefore, G-d has commanded us
specifically on these commandments and warnings and not on others. And
likewise for all the Rabbinical commandments, which are also in this way,
etc.... And let one imagine as if he is actually toiling in the corresponding
matter on high, because even though he is a small creature, G-d has granted
him power to arouse supernal powers on high.

This is what is meant by the verse "the portion of G-d is His people,
Yaakov the rope of His inheritance" (Devarim 32:9), which means that G-d

has granted of His honor to them, and He blew into their nostrils the soul of living spirit. And the part is attached to the whole, like a rope whose one end is tied to a high place and the second end is down below - one who grasps the end below and pulls it with all of his strength - he moves the other end above. And this is what they said in the mishna (Avot 2:1) "be careful of a light commandment just like for a severe one". End of excerpt.

A familiar analogy for this is the movement of the sun's position in the sky. When it moves one meter (if the sun's rays shine through a small hole to the ground, then when the dot moves one meter on the ground - *TL*), the astronomical distance covered is many, many kilometers, likewise for the movement of the shadow in the astrology tool.

Do not consider big in your eyes the acts that you do, even if you do them with intent for His Name. Because, if you make an exact accounting, you will see that for even a little bit of the smallest favors He has done for you, all the combined good deeds of all the inhabitants of the world doubled over would not be enough to pay Him back for it.

> *Pas Lechem*: since all of the good deeds do not add any benefit whatsoever to Him. Nevertheless, you should know that in truth, a small act from you, He considers it as a lot. But from your perspective it should be the opposite - that even a big deed should not be big in your eyes, even if it is done for His Name, without any blemish or outside interest.
>
> *Matanas Chelko* - even though one must consider every small act as big, but a man should not tell himself, if so, I have many good deeds. On this Rabeinu says: "Do not consider big..."

Therefore, do not neglect from doing your accounting between you and your Creator, on the great favors He has done for you, and His great kindnesses with you each and every day. If your heart does not turn to this during the day, let it be at night. If the entire day (and night) has passed, complete it the second day, as our sages said: "repent one day before your death" (Avot 2:10), and "Let your garments be white (clean) always" (Koheles 9:8).

> *Matanas Chelko* - "*every day*" - at first Rabeinu wrote that in truth, one should do the cheshbon without any interruption, on every breath. But since in practice, it is impossible to conduct oneself like this always. Therefore, he writes that at least, do not neglect doing the cheshbon every day. And if one did not do it one day, let him do it at night or tomorrow. But to live without cheshbon is to live without clinging and without rousing to fulfill the Torah and mitzvot which G-d commanded us to do... However, this

cheshbon is not done at the time one learns Torah or fulfills mitzvot. Only at times one is not involved in these things. For then, one needs to arrange a cheshbon in order to remain clinging to the Creator and His service, blessed be He. On this, he brought what our sages said: "repent one day before your death", which implies one needs to do a cheshbon every day.

# CHAPTER 6

*- which actions should follow the accounting*

What actions need to follow the accounting with oneself?

> *Matanas Chelko* - i.e. since the cheshbon is done with one's intellect, therefore one needs to know what is the l'maase (practical action) that comes out of these cheshbons.

I say, this will be from a man according to the purity of the essence his soul, and according to what his soul received of the lights of truth which reach it from G-d, blessed be He.

> *Matanas Chelko*: i.e. it depends on the purity of the man's soul who did the cheshbon and how much light he received from the Creator, blessed be He. Behold, Rabeinu's view has already been clarified (in this gate and gate#4) that everything one attains in Ruchnius (spiritual) and especially in actions is not in his hands. Rather, it comes solely from Heaven. There is nothing in man's hand except the will (and resolve) to do. The resulting act depends only and solely on the will of the Creator. Therefore, there is no room for this question and the answer is obvious.
>
> But Rabeinu added depth to the matter, that even after all the cheshbons a man does, the effect that a man attains from the cheshbon depends on the purity of one's soul, and how much light he already received and attained. According to this, he can beseech G-d to grant him an impression and rousing. For one must understand and believe that the thought of "my strength and the might of my hands" in spiritual matters is mamash (literally) equal to the thought "my strength and the might of my hands" in physical matters. Man's free choice is only regarding the matter of the will, as Rabeinu wrote many times, that one needs to have a strong and powerful will. But after all the cheshbons and his will and rousing to the service of G-d, even the rousing itself depends solely on the will of the Creator. This is Rabeinu's intent in these words.

Because when the intellect of one who reflects on this accounting is pure, and he will understand the intent and desire in it, and he does it for G-d alone - he will attain the favor of the Creator who will help him to do His commandments, teach him by the light of truth which distances the ways of doubt from his heart, and will illuminate him with the light of wisdom so that his intellect will be bright, and his inner and outer being will be purely devoted to G-d, and he will be similar to what Iyov said: *"I put on righteousness and it clothed me; like a coat and a turban was my judgment"* (Iyov 29:14).

And then his soul will quiet, and his thoughts will calm from the worries of the world and its desires, and he will rejoice in the service of the Creator, and will delight in what he gazed of the secrets of wisdom and its lights. He will feel fortunate on what has reached him, of knowledge of the truth of the lower world and the upper world, and the good plan of G-d, and His conduct, and the fulfillment of His decrees on His creations, as David said: *"The righteous rejoice in the L-ord, and shall take refuge in Him"* (Tehilim 64:11), and *"let the heart of them rejoice that seek the L-ord"* (Tehilim 105:3), and *"Thus says the L-ord: Let not the wise man glory in his wisdom, neither let the mighty man glory in his might, let not the rich man glory in his riches; But let him that glory be in this - that he understands, and knows Me"* (Yirmiya 9:22-23).

> (*Marpe Lenefesh*: (on the words "and he will rejoice in the service of the Creator") this is the main thing in the service of the Creator as written: "because you did not serve the L-ord your G-d with joy..." (Devarim 28:47), and likewise for many verses the author brought down in countless places. And I already wrote that the Arizal merited Ruach Hakodesh, and the rest of his levels because he was [extremely] joyous in doing his mitzvot and service. Thus it is written in the (Assara Maamerot number 3 and 4) Shl"A)

And this is the highest level in the knowledge of G-d, because one who truly knows Him will cling to His service and to fear of Him, according to the knowledge in his heart and mind, and he will fulfill the duties of the heart and limbs without effort and without hassle, but rather with desire and craving (in the mind - *PL*), and zeal (in the limbs - *PL*), as David said: *"I made haste, and delayed not, to observe Your commandments"* (Tehilim 119:60), and on this the wise man said: *"Happy is the man that finds wisdom, and the man that gets understanding"* (Mishlei 3:13), and *"Happy are they that keep justice, that do righteousness at all times"* (Tehilim 106:3).

> *Pas Lechem*: "without effort" refers to the duties of the heart, that it won't be for him an effort and an exertion on the heart, while "without toil" refers to the duties of the limbs, because an act which causes sadness is called "toil" (amal), as written: "it is a toil in my eyes" (Tehilim 73:16).

May G-d place us among them, and enter us among their ranks, in His mercy, Amen.

*Matanas Chelko*: i.e. may G-d include us among those who merit Siyata d'Shmaya (divine help) and success in fulfilling the will of G-d. From Rabeinu's ending, it seems that in truth, the primary service of man is in doing the cheshbons that he wrote in this gate. His free choice is only in the will as before, and the explanation of "will" is to do cheshbons and devise strategies which will obligate and rouse him to do the will of G-d. In doing this, he fulfills the mitzvah of "you shall choose life" (Devarim 30:19). And every attainment and effect he merits, whether in knowledge or action, is only what G-d granted to him.

Therefore, Rabeinu stepped out here with special emotion. For in truth, practically speaking, this gate is the primary one of the book. All his other words [in the book], depend on siyata d'shmaya (divine help) relative to the things he explained in this gate which depend on rousing oneself, and this is done through Cheshbon HaNefesh (spiritual accounting).

# ****** SHAAR HAPERISHUS - THE GATE OF ABSTINENCE ******

# *** INTRODUCTION ***

Since our previous discussion dealt with the accounting of a man with himself, and abstinence from this world's interests was one of the ways of such accounting, I deemed it proper to follow with a clarification of the various types of abstinence, and which forms of abstinence are a duty for men of torah (religious people) to adopt. For this furthers the improvement of one's religious and secular pursuits and brings peace of mind and of body in both worlds [here and hereafter].

It is proper for us to clarify seven matters on the subject of abstinence.

1. What is general abstinence and why do human beings need it?
2. The special abstinence for the followers of the torah, and the need for abstinence by them.
3. The classes of abstainers as determined by their type of abstinence.
4. The conditions of special abstinence.
5. The kind of abstinence which is in accord with our torah
6. What the torah and the books of the prophets tell us on abstinence
7. The difference between the early ones and between us regarding abstinence.

## *** CHAPTER 1 ***

*- What is abstinence generally and why do human beings need it*

Regarding what is general abstinence (i.e. the kind of abstinence which all human beings adopt - *LT*), and why do human beings need it, I will answer this question as follows: Abstinence is a term which connotes many matters. The term is commonly used but the true matter is a hidden secret. When the cloak is removed, and the seal is broken - its hidden matter will appear, and its purpose will be revealed.

> *Pas Lechem*: the author has specified two expressions corresponding to two things which cover and hide from a man the true nature of a thing until he brings himself to contemplate on it:
> The first: the veil of the physical which obstructs the clear thinking of the soul until he willfully contemplates and reviews it over and over in his thoughts. This is the meaning of: 'the cloak is removed'. Because the physical is like a thick garment, a fur cloak which conceals the light of the soul, as written *"You have clothed me in skin and flesh"* (Iyov 10:11).
>
> The second: Pursuing unnecessary enjoyments, which is like a tight seal, which shuts and locks one away from reaching the benefits of abstinence. On this he said: 'the seal is broken'.
> And corresponding to both he then said 'its hidden matter will appear, and its purpose will be revealed' - which means that the true purpose and goal of abstinence will be revealed to him.

The plain meaning of abstinence is to bridle the inner lusts and to refrain from something, that one has the ability and opportunity for due to a reason which obligates this. It is said: "the abstainer is one who has the power but does not use it".

The reason which obligates bridling the inner lusts divides into two categories:
1. That which applies to human beings [collectively] and many of the other living creatures (animals abstain from excessive eating, mating, etc. which damages them - *TL*)
2. That which applies specifically to men of torah (Jews).

General abstinence is that which is practiced for the welfare of our bodies and to keep our secular matters in good order. Examples are: the practice of kings in instituting laws of the land, the regimen prescribed by doctors for the healthy or the sick, the practice of every intelligent person to bridle his lusts for food, drink, marital relations, clothing, speech, and his other activities and pleasures.

The abstinence which applies specifically to men of torah (religious people) is that kind which the torah and reason teaches on for the benefit of the soul in the Afterlife, as I will explain later on with G-d's help.

The need for abstinence in its general sense is due to what I have already introduced in the third gate of this book. Namely, that the Creator's purpose in creating mankind was in order to bring difficulties to the soul and test it in this world so that it purifies itself and attains the form of the holy angels, as written *"If you walk in My ways, and if you keep My charge, you, too, shall judge My house, and you, too, shall guard My courtyards, and I will give you a place to walk among these that stand (i.e. the angels)"* (Zechariah 3:7).

Divine wisdom necessitated the testing of the soul [by union] in physical earthen bodies which can grow and gain mass through eating foods suitable for it. G-d then implanted in the souls of human beings a desire for the foods appointed to its body in this world in order to sustain and maintain them during the time of their union.

G-d also implanted in human beings another power. Through this, a man longs for marital relations, so that a human being should procreate another individual to take his place. The Creator granted him reward for these functions, namely, the pleasure in this.

G-d instituted on man an inclination which drives him to eat, drink, engage in marital relations, and partake of other pleasures and relaxations, which further the welfare of his body, as written: *"also he has set the world in their heart[...that every man should eat and drink, and enjoy the good of all his labor, it is the gift of G-d]"* (Koheles 3:11-13).

But when this inclination predominates over the understanding, and the soul is drawn to it, the man turns to the excesses which bring to his detriment and to the destruction of his body (excessive indulgence/lusts ruins a man.. and as the Rambam writes: 'heavy eating is like swords to the body - *PL*). It is necessary because of this, a measure of abstinence from pleasures and relaxations, in order to balance his tendencies, and that his affairs be in proper order in this world, so that he will be considered praiseworthy in them, as written: *"A good man shows favor, and lends: he will guide his affairs with judgment"* (Tehilim 112:5).

Since it is necessary for human beings to practice abstinence which will further their welfare in this world by taking from it only what is necessary, it follows that there should be in this world complete ascetics which separate and cut themselves off completely from secular occupations. So that all of mankind can learn from them on abstinence, each person according to his need, and according to what is fitting for his customs and tendencies.

> (*Marpe Lenefesh*: i.e. since there are many human beings whose [bad] practice has become ingrained in them as second nature. They indulge excessively in pleasures, whether in food and drink, or in bad and disgraceful character traits, until this led them to many bad things such as ruining health, or even premature death, and they deem themselves incapable of refraining from them. Therefore, G-d put in the hearts of some human beings to become complete ascetics. This ascetic from such a trait, that ascetic from that trait, etc. until he has become completely separated from it. Thus, everyone can learn from them virtue, and to see with their own eyes that they are capable of forcing their nature in whatever matter to the middle way. Similarly, there are many different trades and sciences in the world, and there are countries which excel in certain skills or resources over all others, so that they will all benefit from each other.)

It would not, however, further the welfare of mankind if everyone would practice asceticism like them, because this would lead to the abandonment of civilization and to the end of the human race, and the verse already said: *"He did not create it to be a deserted but formed it to be inhabited"* (Yeshaya 45:18).

Abstinence is one of the cornerstones of the world, and the need of human beings for it is just like their need for other sciences and trades in which some nations excel over others, for the benefit of all of mankind. Each class takes from the world according to its needs and what is suitable for it. It would not further the welfare of the world if everyone devoted themselves to only one field and no others, because the general welfare of the world is furthered by the cultivation of all fields, as the wise man said: *"also He has set the world in their heart"* (Koheles 3:11), and *"everything has a time and place..."* (ibid 3:1).

We have explained, with this introduction the concept of general abstinence and the need of human beings for it. So that they may order their affairs in this world through it.

# *** CHAPTER 2 ***

*- The special abstinence for men of torah*

What is the special abstinence and what need do men of torah have for it? The Sages are divided as to its definition.

Among them, one said abstinence is the renunciation of all that distracts one from (fulfilling the service of - *PL*) G-d.

Another said: to be disgusted by (vanities of) this world and curtailing desires.

Another said: abstinence is tranquility of the soul and curbing its tendency for idle imagination.

> (*Tov Halevanon*: to curb the thoughts of the heart and tendencies which are "only evil since one's youth" (Gen.6:5), from all the lusts and desires which oppose the (spiritual) soul.

Another said: [Abstinence means] Trust in G-d

Another said: To limit oneself to wear only basic clothing of whatever material, and likewise to eat only enough to survive and push off one's hunger, and to abhor everything else.

Another said: Abandoning love of company of human beings and to [instead] love solitude.

Another said: Abstinence means gratitude for the good and bearing difficulty patiently.

Another said: Abstinence means to deny oneself all leasures or pleasures of the body except for what one's nature requires and that one cannot live without, and to remove everything else from the mind.

> (*Tov Halevanon*: To remove from oneself what is not necessary since this distracts one's soul.)

This last definition is closest to the abstinence prescribed in our torah, and is better than all the other definitions we mentioned.

The need for the torah observant to practice abstinence is as follows:
The torah's aim is to make the understanding rule over and prevail over all
the lusts of the [lower] soul.

> (*Marpe Lenefesh*: *"rule over and prevail over"* - i.e. there are lusts that one
> cannot do without, such as desire for food and marital relations, for
> preservation of the human race. On this he wrote: *"rule over"*. Some lusts
> are not needed at all. On this he wrote *"and prevail over"* - to nullify them
> completely.)

It is well known that the overpowering of lust over the understanding is the
beginning of all sin, and the cause of all that is reprehensible. The people
did not incline towards (the lusts of) this world until they had turned away
from the torah. Then the evil inclination enticed them to abandon
cultivating the world of their salvation. And thus, they turned away from
the path of their forefathers who limited themselves to what was necessary
and in the amount that was necessary, and who were contented with what
was sufficient for their livelihood.

The inclination enticed them by making hoarding and increasing worldly
possessions seem beautiful, by making indulgence in worldly pleasures
seem desirable, and by inducing pride in owning worldly possessions, until
they sank in the depths of its seas.

> (*Marpe Lenefesh*: Just like one drowning in the sea cannot come out, so too
> them, since (Avot 2:7) "more possessions, more worries"
> *Pas Lechem*: The worldly enjoyments which storm up a person's heart are
> like a stormy sea, while the worries and pains that result from excessive
> indulgence are like waves of the sea.)

The evil inclination then forced them to suffer the pain of [being tossed by]
its waves. This world rules over them and stops up their ears and shuts
their eyes. There is not one of them who does not occupy himself with
indulging in its pleasures whenever he can reach it and an opportunity
presents itself. This is his torah and his religion, until he is led completely
astray from his G-d, as written: *"Your own wickedness shall correct you,
and your backsliding shall reprove you... [know that it is evil and bitter
that you have forsaken the L-ord your G-d]"* (Yirmiya 2:19).

Included in this class of people, is also one who has been denied that
pleasure, but his mind is set on it, his soul longs for it and lives for it, and
he heartily pursues it night and day, as written: *"He devises mischief upon
his bed; he sets himself in a way that is not good"* (Tehilim 36:5).

Both these classes are drowning (in the sea of desires and lusts - *TL*), each in his matter, and yet they are cut off and weary from ever reaching any good out of it. They are losing in their business trade (trading an eternal world for a fleeting world - *PL*). Their soul is diminished, and their choice is bad.

> (*Pas Lechem*: their outlook is confused, what they see as good is bad and vice versa, as in: *"woe unto them that call evil good, and good evil; that change darkness into light, and light into darkness"* Yeshaya 5:18)

They are foolish in their exchange, as written: *"They exchanged their Glory for the likeness of an ox eating grass"* (Tehilim 106:20).

> *Tov Halevanon*: In normal business trade, one who exchanges something for another must know the worth of what he is giving and what he is getting for it. Who is foolish that receives in exchange something which he does not know its worth, and even more so if he does not even know the worth of what he is giving away. [How much more so if] he loses something infinitely valuable for something which is not worth anything.
> *"They exchanged their glory for the likeness of an ox eating grass"* - Just like the worshippers of the golden calf exchanged the service of G-d for the service of the golden calf, so too they exchange the service of G-d for possessions of gold and worldly pleasures.

The incessant call of habit overpowers them. They exert themselves and take pride in their business trade, in which they are losing (since they sell the next world for this world), and which never ceases to distract their minds from the resulting vanities, and to entrench in their hearts its never-ending desires. The more they become embroiled in this world, the more they distanced themselves (from the truth - *PL*); and the further they distanced from the light of truth from which they parted due to their association with the evil inclination, and the more the darkness engulfed them, and the (love of the lusts of this - *PL*) world grew on them.

The striving for its improvement became embellished in their eyes, and they ingrained themselves in it to the destruction of their understanding. The more this world was improved, the greater was the destruction of their understanding, until they considered its evil ways to be good, and its straying to be right, and they turned this into a statute and a moral outlook.

Parents then bequeathed this outlook to their children, their teachers aroused them in it. The masses were commanded to follow it. Their nobles vied with each other on it, until the evil inclination became firmly entrenched in them and they filled their homes with vanities. What had been strange to them became familiar to them, while the right way became strange to them. Whoever was contented and refrained from pursuing the superfluous, they considered him to be neglecting his duties.

Each one of them, did as he saw his fellow do. One who only took of this world what was sufficient for himself was called lazy. One who delayed to accumulate of it was considered a slacker. One who was contented with only what he needed was considered a weakling, while he who surpassed this amount was regarded as an industrious man.

And they praise themselves and pride themselves in it (in reaching material possessions - *PL*), and on its account they befriend, become angry, and congratulate each other. And in order to benefit from it, they appoint their bellies as their god, fine clothing as their torah, and houses in strong condition as their ethics.

> (*Pas Lechem*: sometimes, they befriend each other to help each other attain more, sometimes they get angry with each other, and afterwards make amends - everything according to what appears to them will be beneficial in attaining more.
> *"bellies as their god"* - the main purpose of creation is for man to serve his Creator, and to put his heart and all of his aspirations to this always, as written: "all my aspirations are to You" (Tehilim 87:7). But instead they worshipped their bellies and put all of their thoughts and aspirations to it...)

They went astray in the depths of folly, moving in the course of idleness, laden with burdens of lusts, and claiming the reward of the worshippers (of G-d) while committing the acts of the transgressors, and the levels of the righteous with the conduct of the wicked, as our Sages said: *"they commit the sins of Zimri and seek the reward of Pinchas"* (Sota 22b).

Since the evil inclination has brought most of the men of torah (Jews) as far as we have described, it is necessary to stand up to it with the special abstinence which we have described at the beginning of this gate. With the help of abstinence, we should hold firmly against the evil inclination until reaching the proper torah way for religious and secular pursuits.

Therefore it is necessary for there to be among the men of torah, special individuals, bearers of the special abstinence, who take on its conditions, and thereby benefit the other men of torah who turn and tend towards the animalistic lusts of the evil inclination. Thus these special people are the doctors of souls to the religion.

They bring healing to those who stray from the good traits and tended towards the disgraceful traits. Then the evil inclination has prevailed over their understanding, and when their occupation with increasing the superfluous of the world distracts them from the things essential in their religion.

If a man with a sickness of faith or who is sick with doubts comes to them, they will hasten to heal him with their genuine wisdom.

If it is one fleeing from the service of G-d (one who recognizes his Creator but rebels against Him due to the overpowering of the lusts on him - *TL*), they will return him to it and reassure him in it (that he will be able to return and that it is not too hard for him - *PL*).

If it is one burdened by his sins, they will reassure him of the forgiveness of G-d when he repents from his sins.

If it is one who has forgotten G-d, they will remind him. If a tzadik (righteous person), they will praise him (to encourage him). If one who loves G-d, they will love him (to encourage him - *ML*). If one who magnifies G-d's omnipotence, they magnify him. If he sins, they will exhort him to repent immediately. If he is physically sick, they will visit him and if they have more than they need of the world, they will bestow to him of it. If some trouble befalls him, they will come to his assistance.

In this world, they are similar to the sun which shines its light on the world, above it and below it, since it illuminates what is above it and what is below it, of the celestial spheres and planets.

So too they shine on this world as written: *"G-d said, If I find in Sodom fifty righteous men within the city, then I will spare all the place for their sake"* (Bereishis 18:26). And: *"Therefore He said that He would destroy them, had not Moses, His chosen, stood before Him in the breach to turn away His wrath"* (Tehilim 106:23), and in the next world, as written *"The fruit of the righteous is a tree of life"* (Mishlei 11:30), and therefore Devorah said: *"they that love Him shall be as the sun when it goes forth in its might"* (Shoftim 5:31).

You will find that this conduct of abstinence was practised by the prophets and the early pious ones in previous generations as clearly explained in their books, and as I will expound further in its proper place, with G-d's help, blessed be He.

## *** CHAPTER 3 ***

*- The classes of abstainers*

As to how many classes the abstainers are divided, I will answer this question as follows.
As we introduced, abstinence from this world is due to one of two reasons, one is religious and the other is secular.

Those who abstain due to religious reasons. They are the true genuine abstainers and are divided into three classes.

1) Men who went after the highest extreme of asceticism, to be like spiritual beings (angels, i.e. non-physical beings). They renounce everything that distracts them from G-d. They left civilization to dwell in the deserts, the wastelands, and the high mountains, places where there is no companionship and no acquaintance. They eat whatever can be found, vegetation growing on the soil and leaves of the trees. They dress in worn garments and raw wool. They take shelter in the rocks. Their fear of the Creator drives away fear of the created beings.

> (*Marpe Lenefesh*: they are so absorbed with the fear of G-d, that they have no fear whatsoever of flesh and blood. Because of this, they put themselves in danger to go off to deserts (i.e. the wilderness), a place where there are dangerous animals. For the fear of not being able to serve G-d in their homes is, for them, greater than the fear of the created beings.
> Translator's note: It must be that we are talking about someone who was given special permission from upstairs since it is forbidden to put oneself in danger and rely on a miracle, as brought earlier in the Gate of Trust Chapter 4: "Either he will die, and it will be considered as if he killed himself, and he will be held accountable for this just as if he had murdered another human being...")

Their delight in love of G-d distracts them so much that they do not think of the love of human beings. They are content with whatever sustenance G-d reserves for them, and they do not expect anything from human beings.

This class is the furthest extreme of all the classes from the middle way prescribed by the torah. For they renounce worldly interests completely and the torah does not bid us to give up social life entirely, as we have introduced earlier from the verse *"He did not create it to be a waste but formed it to be inhabited"* (Yeshaya 45:18).

2) The second class, men who went in the middle way of abstinence. They are completely repulsed with the superfluous things of this world, and undertake to bridle their lust in them.

The superfluous things are of two types:
One: superfluous things which are outside of a man and separate from him, such material things as food, drink, clothing, and dwelling.

Two: superflous things which cleave to a man whose causes are not outside of him, such as: [superfluous] speech, laughter, relaxation, leisure, watching or listening useless things, and useless musings.

This second class has renounced all things that are "superfluous", but did not deem it fit to withdraw from society. They stayed to provide their bodies with its minimum need, as is their duty. They exchanged the deserts and mountains with confinement in their homes and solitude in their dwelling. They attained both matters (abstinence and establishing the world - *PL*) and reached both portions (this world and the next world - *PL*). They are closer to the middle way of the torah, than the previous class.

3) The third class consists of those who walk on the lowest level of abstinence. These separated themselves from the world in their hearts and minds. But they associate outwardly with other people in the rectification of the world, such as plowing and sowing. They also actively toil with their bodies in the service of G-d. They realize that a man is being tested in this world, and that he is like a prisoner and a stranger in it, taken from the world of spirits and brought here.

(*Marpe Lenefesh*: They understand what G-d wants from man, and why He created him, namely, to test him in this world to benefit him in the next world.)

They are repulsed by the (pleasures of this) world and by its wealth, and they long for the next world.

They wait for death (where the soul returns to its Source of life, for them this is not death but eternal life. It is only called death due to its appearance to the [physical] eye - *TL*), and yet they guard themselves from death (danger). They prepare provisions (torah and good deeds) for the time of their journey, and they consider with what will they arrive to their final abode before their departure. They take from this world, the minimum of their food needs (the minimal possible - *TL*), yet they do not neglect anything of taking and carrying provisions that will be good for their final end, according to their ability.

This class is the closest to the correct balance and right way which is in accord with the torah than the other classes we mentioned. (since the intent of the torah is that the world not be desolate - *ML*).

## ABSTINENCE IN SECULAR AFFAIRS

Those who practice abstinence in order to secure worldly benefits. Their abstinence is in their limbs but not in their minds and hearts. These fall into three classes:

1) Those who abstain from some of their lusts or pleasures in order to gain a reputation for abstinence, in order to receive praise for their faith and piety, so that through this method they will obtain their full lusts.

They are hypocritical in faith and in abstinence. Doing so, in order that men should trust them, deposit their money by them and reveal their secrets to them. so that they will be able to harm them. They are the worst class of all human beings. They are the furthest removed from the truth, and more disgraceful than anyone else. Of such people, scripture says: *"Their tongue is a deadly arrow; It speaks deceit; With his mouth one speaks peace to his neighbor, But inwardly he sets an ambush for him"* (Yirmiya 9:7).

2) The second class: Those who obtained a small amount of wealth. When they see how swiftly money is lost and circumstances change, and combined with their little trust in G-d, they pain themselves by eating little and abstaining from their lusts (to save their money). They then claim that abstinence has pushed them to live like this.

But after true inspection, what really brought them to this is their great love for this world, their zeal to increase of its wealth, their worry from poverty, and their little satisfaction with what they have obtained from this world. Of such people, the wise man said: *"a man whom G-d has given riches and property and honor, and his soul lacks nothing of all he desires; [yet G-d gives him not power to eat of it, but a stranger eats it: this is vanity, and it is an evil affliction]"* (Koheles 6:2).

3) The third class: Those who are not capable of making enough money and have only acquired enough money to live in the poorest of circumstances. They deemed proper to maintain their self-respect and subsist with whatever food they can obtain rather than having to stand to ask and embarrass themselves to beg from other people. They restrained their desires by bearing constant hunger and by covering themselves with basic clothing. They do this in order to avoid receiving charity and to not be ashamed of asking help from others, thereby becoming disgraced. But, they claim to be doing all of this out of asceticism.

If you wish to test the true motive of one who claims to practice abstinence, whether he is doing this for religious or secular improvement, test them with the conditions for perfect abstinence which I will mention, and you will with G-d's help, discern whether they are genuine ascetics or only pretending to be so.

## *** CHAPTER 4 ***

*- The marks of special abstinence*

The marks of the special abstinence are as one of the pious declared:
The [genuine] ascetic:
* His joy is on his face, and his sorrow is in his heart.

> (he receives every person with joy, but his heart is as Koheles 7: "the heart of the wise is in a house of mourning" - TL
> *Translator*: Another explanation even if he has some sorrow in his heart, he nevertheless greets every person with joy - Rabbi Nachman Bulman z'l)

* His heart is exceedingly broad.
(to receive much wisdom, since there is nothing which troubles his heart, unlike the common person, full of lusts, his heart is constricted from receiving wisdom, since the thoughts of desires occupy a place in his heart and trouble him - *PL*)
* His soul is exceedingly lowly.
(from lusting anything - *PL*)
* He does not bear a grudge.
(he does not guard hatred towards anyone who did bad to him, since to him, even for the entire world and everything in it, it is not worth bearing a grudge on anyone, namely, to find him culpable of wrong and hate him for it - *PL*)
* He does not covet.
(He does not desire to take any possession of any person - *PL*)
* He does not speak negatively of anyone.
(since he abstains from lusts, all the more so, he does not have imaginary honor. Why then would he talk negatively of any person? For this is only due to lust for honor, namely, to elevate himself by putting down another - *PL*)
* He does not discuss anyone.
(since he does not desire to speak negatively of others, why should he speak of them? - *PL*)
* He abhors being honored.
(if others want to elevate him with some honor, he is abhorred by it and does not accept it from them, as told by Gideon when the Jewish people asked him to become their leader, and he strongly refused - *PL*)
* He hates dominion over others.

(He hates to be appointed over them and command them on his service, as written by Samson, who never asked one Jew even to move his staff from one place to another - *PL*)

* He is calm and collected.

(he does not hasten to answer before he is settled and clear in his mind - *PL*)

* He remembers well.

(since he does not have many thoughts of desire in his heart, which overpower the masses who lust, therefore he remembers the things which he puts his mind to - *PL*)

(alternatively, He remembers his spiritual accounting always - *TL* see Gate 8)

* He admits the truth.

(since honor and victory over others is worth nothing to him, why should he deny the truth? - *PL*)

* Has much shame.

(if something happens which is proper to be ashamed for, he is very ashamed, unlike the masses which due to their stormy hearts after lusts and pursuing after them, they are forced to act brazenly against each other. 'This one says it is all mine, and that one says it is all mine'. Therefore, the trait of shame diminishes and weakens by them - *PL*.)

* Avoids damaging.

(it is unlikely that any man will be damaged by him - *TL*)

* If he laughs, it will be little.

* If he becomes angry, he will not be wrathful.

(even if he gets angry, he will not hold a grudge, rather he will be quickly appeased or if he shows anger outwardly, he will not be angry in his heart - *TL*)

* his laughter is a mere parting of the lips.

(he does not fill his mouth with laughter - *PL*)

* his asking is in learning.

(he does not ask things of any man, since through his abstinence he is content with what he has. Only if he needs to learn torah from a man greater than him, will he ask him to teach him - *PL*)

* His wisdom is extensive and his humility is great.

* His resolve is strong.

(when he resolves in his mind to do something, he does not retract. Since he deliberated whether or not to do it with peace of mind. Unlike the hasty who errs in his view and lacks resolve, and one cannot rely on his words - *PL*)

* He is neither hasty nor foolish in his actions.

* His arguing is polite, his reply is courteous.
* He acts righteously when angry.
(does not punish completely as the person deserved. Also included in this is unlike the masses, whose nature is that when one gets angry with someone, he cannot then have mercy towards someone else. But the righteous can be angry with this person, and have mercy on another simultaneously, each matter in its proper place - *PL*)
* He is compassionate when entreated.
* His friendship is sincere.
(his love for another is pure without self-interest and deception - *TL*)
* His resolution is strong.
(if he takes something on himself - *TL*)
* His covenant is faithful.
* He desires in the judgment of the Creator. (joyful in suffering - *TL*)
* He rules over his evil inclination.
* He does not speak badly about one who harmed him.
* He does not occupy himself with what is not useful.
(one who occupies himself with something of no benefit - this is due to love of recreation, which does not exist by the ascetic - *PL*)
* He does not become joyful in the downfall of his enemy.
* He does not remind to anyone a wrong which that person had done him.
* He troubles others lightly but helps them much.
* His gratitude is great at a time of bad.
(when many bitter evils befall him, he thanks and praises G-d, as our Sages say: 'just like one praises on the good, so too he should praise on the bad' - *TL*)
* His bearing is patient at a time of financial loss.
(when some financial loss strikes him, he patiently bears it and does not question G-d's judgment - *TL*)
* If he is asked from, he gives. If he is robbed, he will forgive.
* If others refuse from him something, he will nevertheless volunteer.
(even if others refrain from doing good to him, nevertheless he volunteers and seeks their good, and pays back good in return for their bad - *TL*)
* If they keep him at a distance, he will nevertheless bring them close (be friendly to them).
* he is softer than butter, sweeter than honey.
* He exhorts others to adhere to the truth.
* He speaks righteously.
(since to do righteousness and kindness is ingrained in a person's nature if it were not for the lusts - *PL*)
* He relinquishes his desires, and looks forward to his final day.

(not only does he leave the lusts physically, but even in his heart he renounces them and forgets them - *PL*)

* What he says, he does.

(unlike the masses where after a promise, when a desire later clashes with the request he will retract from his word - *PL*)

* He is wise.

(since desires dull the mind - *PL*)

* He is energetic.

(he is zealous in his deeds unlike the desirous person who is lazy since the lust for comfort and leisure overpowers him, besides the great and many lusts which he cannot obtain which cause him constant distress and his limbs are heavy on him, and therefore he is dismayed in many of his matters and acts sluggishly - *PL*)

* His soul is noble.

(he does not debase himself with low deeds, unlike the desirous whose famished desire for obtaining his lusts brings him sometimes to humiliate himself to do base things to reach his desire - *PL*)

* His covenant is agreeable.

(when he agrees with someone to do something, certainly it is an agreeable and proper thing unlike the lustful who sometimes enter an agreement to do bad and disgraceful things - *PL*)

* He is powerful in the land.

(for he only fights for truth, and the truth endures. Therefore, he has a reputation as a powerful man who wins - *PL*)

* He is free of all that is blameworthy.

* He is a helper of the poor and a savior of the oppressed.

* He does not expose what is hidden nor reveal a secret.

* His troubles are many, but his complaints are few.

* If he sees good, he will mention it, if he sees bad, he will cover it.

(if he sees something good in a man, he will tell others and praise him for it. Likewise for the opposite, when he sees something bad in another, he will conceal it and won't reveal it to anyone - *PL*)

* He is pleasing in his manners and pure in his heart.

(everyone likes him and his heart is pure with all - *PL*)

* His company is a joy, his absence, a cause for sorrow.

* Wisdom purges him.

(the study of wisdom has purged and purified him of all traces of bad traits - *PL*)

* Humility has embellished him

(the humility in him makes him appear handsome and noble in the eyes of the public - *PL*)

* He is a mentor to the wise.
(even the wise benefit from him, that if some thing is forgotten by them, he will remind them, since all of his desire is to benefit others - *PL*)
* He is a teacher to the ignorant.
* Every act of others he considers purer than his (due to his lowliness - *PL*).
* Every person he considers more pure than himself.
* He is aware of his own lacking.
(if he is lacking in some good deed, he knows and recognizes his lacking - *PL*)
* He remembers his iniquity.
* He loves G-d and chases to do His will.
* He does not take revenge for any wrong done to him.
* He does not keep his anger long.
* His company is with those that remind him [of his duty to G-d].
(he joins always with G-d fearing men who tend to remind a person and encourage him in the service of G-d - *PL*)
* He sits with the humble.
(when there is some assembly, he sets his place among the humble due to his great lowliness - *PL*)
* He loves men of righteousness, and is faithful to men of truth.
* He helps the poor, is a father to orphans and a protector to the widow, and shows respect to the needy.

To these marks (of a true ascetic) should be added that he undertakes all the duties of the heart we mentioned earlier in this book and which I do not need to repeat them so that this treatise does not become too lengthy. Take note for yourself.

# *** CHAPTER 5 ***

*- What kind of abstinence is in accord with the torah*

> (*Tov Halevanon*: In the previous chapter, he mentioned the marks of abstinence in a general sense, to distinguish between abstinence which is for G-d and abstinence which is hypocritical. Now he returns to explain the ideal kind of specific abstinence which is in accord with the torah.)

Regarding what kind of abstinence is in accord with our torah, I will answer this question as follows: The abstinence recommended by the torah is on three fronts:
1) When engaged with business relations with other people and when engaged in social interactions with them.

2) In matters which relate to ourselves alone and do not affect other people, with respect to the function of our physical senses and movements of our limbs.

3) In matters which relate to ourselves alone and do not affect others, with respect to our inner being - our traits, our thoughts, whether good or bad, that are hidden in our hearts. All these I will explain in a concise manner as well as I can, with G-d's help.

## SOCIAL ABSTINENCE
The proper abstinence to adopt in association with other people is as follows:
* To receive them with a cheerful countenance and to exhibit joy when meeting them; at the same time, cultivating humility, gentle speech, and a lowliness of spirit towards all of them.

* Showing them mercy, graciousness, and compassion. Relieving them of their troubles, speaking good of them, doing kindness to them without expecting any benefit from them, and abandoning all thought of receiving anything of what belongs to them.
* To help them with what can further their religious or secular welfare, and to teach them the way which G-d approves.

* To patiently bear their difficult words, and to pour out one's words before G-d and not before them (that we speak our troubles before G-d and not

hope for help from human beings - *TL*).

\* To keep away from gatherings that assemble for eating, drinking, and merrymaking, and avoid anything in association with them that would lead to rebellion against G-d, or going out of the bounds of modesty, traditional morality, or the like.

## ABSTINENCE IN THE SENSES AND LIMBS

What is proper for us in the second type of abstinence, namely, that which relates to ourselves alone and involves only our physical senses and limbs. This is divided into two categories.

The first refers to what is forbidden to us. These are the prohibitions [negative commandments in the torah].

The second refers to what is permitted to us. These are all the things permitted to us of all the permitted enjoyments.

Both categories subdivide to three divisions.

(Regarding the negative commandments:) Everything that is forbidden to us necessarily falls into one of three classes.
1) That which is in a person's nature to desire these things, such as forbidden relations, theft, taking interest, eating or drinking of forbidden foods.

2) That which is neutral in a person's nature, namely, that he does not desire nor abhor it, such as wearing shatnez (mixtures of linen and wool), sowing Kilaim (diverse seeds together), eating meat and milk together, eating forbidden fat, and many more like this.

3) That which is in a person's nature to abhor and be disgusted by these things, such as eating from an animal carcass (treifa), eating blood or various types of creatures which a man would not want to eat even if these were permitted, such as the eight species of rodents and reptiles (Vayikra 11:29-30), or others like this.

It is proper for you, my brother, to train yourself in abstinence to abstain from all that G-d has forbidden to you until you reach a level that you are equally disgusted by what your nature desires as by what your nature abhors, so that forbidden relations or obtaining things in a forbidden manner (such as through theft, oppression, or interest, or the like - *PL*) seeking to honor yourself through lowering someone else, or holding him in contempt, which, by nature, are things people swiftly desire - should be as repellent to you as eating mice, blood, or reptiles, which your nature abhors and which your soul hates.

> *Tov Halevanon*: *"equally disgusted"* - that it be equal to you, that which the Creator has prohibited, even though it is not disgusting to you, just like something which is disgusting to you by nature. For you will habituate your nature and draw it according to the commandment of the Creator. Because since the Creator has forbade them, certainly, it is proper that they be much more inconceivable to you than what your nature abhors. For [your nature] stems from the powers of your body while the commandment of the Creator is from the powers of your soul.
>
> *"honor yourself through lowering someone else"* - seeking that your fellow be lowered in order that you be honored.

When you reach this level of abstinence from prohibited things without needing to force your nature and without resistance from yourself, you will belong to the class of those saved from sin and stumbling which the verse says of them: *"no mischief shall befall the righteous"* (Mishlei 12:21).

> *Marpe Lenefesh*: even though it was originally against your nature, if you habituate yourself many times to force your nature, you will reach the level where you will no longer need to force your nature.
>
> *Tov Halevanon*: until you are not pained in abstaining from this, and you no longer need to force your soul [which tended] to desire this thing.

Similarly the permitted things fall into one of three categories.
1) Taking food whereby one does not do so with intent for deriving pleasure, but because one cannot live without it, and one has no other remedy (for his hunger) besides this.

2) Taking permitted food in the way of 'overlooking' (beyond what is necessary), (that one 'overlooks' on himself by taking more than the necessary - *PL*) for mere enjoyment, but not to excess or unbridled over-indulgence, in order to compliment the minimum necessary. For example, eating good bread with decently prepared dishes, and drinking good wine in moderation, and likewise for one's clothing, home, and other requirements.

3) Taking much indulgence of the permitted pleasures. This distance a person (from all good qualities - *PL*) and leads him to also indulge in the

prohibited pleasures, besides the distraction it brings from fulfilling his duties to G-d, as written *"Lest he drink and forget that which is decreed"* (Mishlei 31:5)

Thus, it is proper for you, my brother, to strive with all of your ability to practice abstinence from the permitted pleasures until they become equal in your eyes to the prohibited pleasures for fear lest you abandon your torah and neglect your duties. You already know what the torah commanded a Jewish king in saying:

*"Neither shall he have many wives to himself, [lest his heart turn away]"* (Devarim 17:17), and it says *"he shall not have many horses"* (ibid 17:16). Furthermore, it says: *"Did not Solomon king of Israel sin by these things?"* (Nehemiah 13:26), even for him, the women caused him to sin, despite his exceedingly powerful intellect, vast understanding, and greatness. Hence, [how much more so for you] according to your understanding, take heed and guard your soul and abstain (from all unnecessary enjoyments, even those permitted - *LT*) that will distance you from fulfilling the commandments of G-d.

[At least] do so in your heart and mind, if you are unable to free your body to matters of the next world due to being so fully preoccupied with providing for your livelihood and maintenance, as our Rabbis mentioned on many (great men) who would toil in matters of this world while being separate from it (in heart and mind), such as Aba Chilkiya who would work hoeing the ground (Taanis 23a), Shammai in construction work, and Hillel who would earn his livelihood by chopping trees and selling the wood (Yoma 35b).

Let not your wholehearted abstinence prevent you from working in a secular occupation, since your intent in this is to serve G-d, as we mentioned previously (in ch.4 of the "Gate of the Service of G-d" - *TL*).

But when you will be in a position to give up the secular occupation (if you have enough to live on for the time being - *PL*) - leave it and spend all of your time in the service of G-d.

But during the times you are unable to serve G-d due to the need to earn a livelihood, do not be satisfied with what we said (rather let all your thoughts and desires be to hope and pray and make efforts that G-d will free you from toiling for worldly matters - *MH*) . Because He who watches your thoughts will help you to fulfill your desire in regard to His service, as our Sages said: *"He who fulfills the torah from poverty will eventually fulfill it from wealth, and he who neglects the torah from wealth will eventually neglect it from poverty"* (Avot 4:9). (i.e. if he puts off [serving G-d] until he amasses wealth, in the end he will neglect it from poverty, namely, that even his daily need he will not have - *TL*)

It is proper for you, to train yourself to curb your senses and movements as I will explain to you:

## GUARDING THE TONGUE

Begin at first by restraining your tongue and clamping down your lips. Refrain from idle words, until you will regard moving your heaviest limb to be easier than moving your tongue. For the tongue sins more quickly than all of the other limbs, and its sins are more numerous than the sins committed by all of them. Because it moves easily and swiftly, it easily completes its deed, and has the power to do good or evil without any intermediary.

> *Pas Lechem*: One does not need any intermediary for his work, i.e. any tool, or other thing for doing the sin. For example, in eating prohibited food, the food is the intermediary, or for prohibited relations, that woman is the intermediary, and perhaps he will not have the opportunity so quickly for that food or that woman, unlike the tongue which does not need anything to sin.

Therefore, my brother, it is incumbent on you, to train yourself to restrain and rule over your tongue. Do not unleash it to speak words except for what is indispensable for your torah needs and your worldly needs. Diminish extra words of your tongue as much as you can, perhaps you will be saved from its damage, as the wise man said: *"Life and death are in the power of the tongue"* (Mishlei 18:21).

They (the Sages) began exhorting on the tongue before the other senses and limbs, because it is more difficult to control than all of them as David said: *"Who is the man who desires life... guard your tongue from evil, and your lips from speaking deceit [depart from evil and do good; seek peace and pursue it]"* (Tehilim 34:13). In our holy books, the exhortations to minimize speech are so numerous and well known that it is not unfamiliar to anyone.

*Tov Halevanon*: Scripture correlated the eternal afterlife and the good in this world with the tongue, and also exhorted on it before the other limbs - to teach you that the success of a person in this world and in the next world depends on the tongue.

If you wish to attain a clear understanding of what I mentioned of the many sins of the tongue, take on yourself to remember what comes out of your tongue during the course of one day in your association with other people and consorting with them. If you can write it all, do so. Afterwards, at night, when you are free from your matters, go over it and reflect on it. See which of them were necessary and which of them were superfluous and without benefit; and which of them were harmful to you, such as falsehood, tale bearing, swearing, lashon hara (negative speech about others). Then you will recognize your faults and you will see your iniquity.

Remember them always just like you remember the faults and iniquities of your enemies. Do not be diligent in this for a short time, so that your tongue will be rectified and your words will be few.

*Marpe Lenefesh*: This last statement has a double meaning:
Either 1: You will not need to be diligent in this. For even after a short time your tongue will be quickly rectified when you do as before to remember or write down [your words].
Or 2: One can also explain this as: Do not be diligent in this only for a short time, to remember or to write [your words]. Rather do it many times until your tongue is rectified.
[Both meanings are intended and] everything according to the nature of each person.

And in exchange for much talking, substitute prolonged thinking, continuous reflecting, and spiritual accounting (see previous gate), because reflection is a candle which enters your heart, and the spiritual accounting is like the sun which illuminates the darkness of your interior being, to reveal to you what is hidden inside whether of good or of evil.

The tongue is the gate of this inner being. If the tongue is unbridled and does not keep careful guard over what is in the inner being, then the gate to the treasury will be open, and things will go out which you do not wish them to go out, and things will become visible which you do not wish them to be visible. But if you guard the gate, you guard the treasury and what is in it, as the wise man said: *"even a fool who keeps silent is considered wise"* (Mishlei 17:28). He also said: *"do not be quick with your mouth, do not be hasty in your heart to utter anything before G-d"* (Koheles 5:1), and: *"permit not your mouth to cause your flesh to sin"* (Koheles 5:5).

## GUARDING THE EYES
Afterwards, endeavor to shut your eyes and shut your sense of sight from seeing that which you do not need, or that which will distract your mind from thinking of what will be of use to you. Separate yourself as much as you can from superfluous sights, just like you separate from looking at things which are forbidden to look at. The Creator has already exhorted on this in saying *"you shall not wander after your hearts and after your eyes"* (Bamidbar 15:39), and our Sages said: "the heart and the eyes are the two agents of sin (the eye sees, then the heart desires...) " (Talmud Yerushalmi Berachos 81). Rather use your eyes to gaze at the works of the Creator, to examine them, to contemplate them, and to understand the omnipotence of the Creator, and His wisdom and benevolence from them, as David said: *"When I consider your heavens, the work of Your fingers, the moon and the stars, which You have ordained"* (Tehilim 8:4), and *"The heavens declare the glory of G-d; and the firmament proclaims His handiwork"* (Tehilim 19:2).

*Marpe Lenefesh*: (advanced) The author did not mention regarding guarding the Brit Kodesh, and this is a stumbling block before many. It is proper to bring here a bit of the severity of the punishment for a man who wastes seed, r"l. Here is an excerpt from Seder Yom (hanhaga halayla): The Sages said in tractate Nidah: "says Ula: 'if a thorn was lodged in his belly (near his organ) (Rashi: and he must rub there in order to extract it), let his belly split rather than he be considered wicked one moment before G-d'" See just how far the holiness of Yisrael goes before their Father in heaven! One who sees and hears this, how could he not be disdained all of his life before G-d because he has already transgressed this many times! Who out there is clean from this, and more than this... And all the more so, if he willingly brought himself to an erect ion that he is chayiv nidui (excommunicated by the heavenly court), and all the more so still if he wasted seed to fulfill his lust, that he is hated and banished before G-d, and will not merit to behold the Shechina (Divine presence in the future), as written: *"the evil will not dwell with You"* (Tehilim 5:5), and evil here refers to those who do these kinds of deeds. He is considered evil towards heaven and evil towards the public (the living). He destroys above and destroys below, damages above and damages below, woe to him and woe to his soul, etc. The gates of atonement and repentance are almost locked to him were it not that G-d does not desire the death of the wicked... these things bring destruction to the world, plagues, death, tragedies ... see there for more)

## GUARDING THE EARS

Afterwards endeavor to block your ears from listening to that which you have no need for. Separate as much as you can from listening to anything superfluous. Do not lend ear to listen to what will not be beneficial to hear such as superfluous words, lies, tale bearing, slander. Separate from hearing what will lead you to rebel against G-d or neglect His commandments such as the various types of songs and melodies (which draw a man after the superfluous pleasures which in turn lead to the forbidden pleasures - *TL*), comedy and merrymaking, which distract you from fulfilling the commandments and performing good deeds. Rather, lend your ears to the words of the Sages who know G-d and His torah, as the wise man said: *"Incline your ear, and hear the words of the wise"* (Mishlei 22:17), and *"The ear that hearkens to the reproof of life, abides among the wise"* (Mishlei 15:31).

## GUARDING THE TONGUE (from superfluous food)

Afterwards, endeavor to bridle the sense of taste, that you take of food and drink only as much as you need for your sustenance, and abstain from what is beyond this.

The strategy to adopt in this matter is to reduce the various types of accompaniments (to bread) and limit them to only one course (such as meat, fish..or the like - *ML*) if you can. And also to minimize this accompaniment as much as you can, and to also have intent that this (dish) is to facilitate the transfer of bread to your stomach - not for enjoyment.

Habituate yourself to sometimes eat your bread without accompaniment in order to lead your nature in this, so that it will be easy for you to do this when the accompaniment is not available (and you have only bread). If you can relinquish accompaniments which require effort and labor to prepare (cooking, etc.), and you rely instead on what needs no labor to prepare such as olives, cheese, dates, grapes, or the like - do so.

If you are used to eating two meals a day, let your meal by day be lighter than your meal by night, so that the movements of your body will be lighter during the day, and your religious and secular occupations will be easier on you.

*Manoach Halevavos*: Excessive or heavy eating, weighs on the body, making him lazy in all of his occupations.
*Tov Halevanon*: Eating brings sleepiness and heaviness of the limbs.

Afterwards, practice fasting if your body is strong enough, even if this is only one day per week. Whatever you can do to train yourself to be indifferent to matters of eating and drinking, do so. Regard what you eat as a medicine (to heal your hunger) rather than as food. Your drinking should be only water, unless your intent in drinking wine is to benefit your body, or to remove distress from your heart, as written: *"Give strong drink to he who is ready to perish and wine to the bitter soul"* (Mishlei 31:6).

Be careful not to drink (wine) too frequently or too much, or to join drinking parties, because it is a great sickness to religious and secular matters, and the wise man already spoke sufficiently on this in saying: *"Wine is a mocker, strong drink is raging"* (Mishlei 20:1) (a man who loves wine is a mocker who is hot after drunkenness - *LT*), and regarding eating and drinking, he said: *"be not among winebibbers; among gluttonous eaters of flesh. For the drunkard and glutton shall come to poverty"* (Mishlei 23:20).

> *Tov Halevanon*: it is the way of those who drink (wine) together to speak slander, and lashon hara (evil speech) due to their drunkenness and joy of heart, as scripture says (Tehilim 69:13): "They that sit in the gate speak against me; and I was the song of the drunkards".

## GUARDING THE HANDS
Afterwards, endeavor to restrain your hands from touching worldly possessions that are not yours. Separate from the various types of theft, fraud, robbery, and from doing any evil to any human being. Restrain the movements of your hands and think of its consequences (do not do any action with your hands quickly without being in a calm and collected state of mind - *ML*). Guard your ethics and modesty by being elevated from doing evil with them, as written: *"keeps his hand from doing any evil"* (Yeshaya 56:2). It also says: *"that shakes his hands from holding bribes"* (Yeshaya 33:15). Rather, use your hands for fulfilling the commandments of G-d, open them to give to the poor and needy, as written: *"you shall surely open your hand unto your brother, to your poor, and to your needy, in your land"* (Devarim 15:11), and it says: *"she stretches out her hand to the poor; she reaches forth her hands to the needy"* (Mishlei 31:20).

And likewise, you need to use them for what will provide your livelihood, so that you will be saved from borrowing and stealing, and from needing the kindness of people to support you and to benefit you, thereby giving away to them your merits, and giving your piety to he who was pious towards you (one who gives to you and does you kindness, will take for himself a part of your reward - *ML*). Likewise, so that you won't be a burden on people, as one of the Sages said: "G-d will have [great] mercy on His servants who separate from this world. But only if his separation has not become a burden on his friends. Namely, he engaged in a trade thereby freeing them from troubling themselves for him", as written: *'For you shall eat the labor of your hands: happy shall you be, and it shall be well with you'* (Tehilim 128:2)".

It has already been said: "the beginning of abstinence is the securing of a livelihood". And it was further stated: "the beginning of abstinence is to think properly on arranging the obtaining of one's needs", which means to work to secure one's needs. (so as not to be distracted by one's need for food, and thereby neglect one's torah study and good deeds - *TL*).

## GUARDING THE FEET
Afterwards, habituate your feet in this way, and refrain from going with the wicked, who seek the superfluous things, as written: *"Blessed is the man that walks not in the counsel of the wicked, nor stands in the way of sinners, nor sits in the seat of the scornful"* (Tehilim 1:1). Rather, hasten to do all good deeds, and to the gatherings of the wise, as written: *"He who goes with the wise will become wise [but he who befriends the fools will be broken]"* (Mishlei 13:20), and it says: *"in order that you go in the way of the good..."* (Mishlei 2:20).

Scripture has already gathered together everything we introduced on curbing the senses in saying: *"Who among us shall dwell with the consuming fire? ... He that walks righteously, and speaks uprightly; [he that despises the gain of oppression, that keeps his hands from the holding of bribes, that stops his ears from hearing of blood, and shuts his eyes from seeing evil]"* (Yeshaya 33:14).

And afterwards, the wise man gathered them and added to them the heart in saying: *"There are six things that the L-ord hates, and the seventh is an abomination of His soul; Haughty eyes, a lying tongue, and hands that shed innocent blood; A heart that thinks wicked thoughts; feet that hasten to run to evil; A false witness who incites quarrels among brothers"* (Mishlei 6:16), and likewise they are found in the Psalm 15: *"O G-d, who will dwell in Your tent?..."*

## ALL OR NOTHING
It is proper for you to know, my brother, that it will not be possible for you

to fulfill any of these things, unless you do all of them and you don't omit even one of them. For they are like a string of pearls. If you release one of them, (the string will break and - *TL*) all of the others will be scattered and their unity will be destroyed.

> *Pas Lechem*: if you abandon one of them, behold, all of them will become annulled.

Therefore, strive to be careful in all of these rules, and then each one of them will help the others, as our Sages said: "a mitzvah brings another mitzvah, and a sin brings another sin" (Avot 4:2), and the wise man said regarding the close connection of all good deeds: *"Fortunate is the man that listens to me, watching daily at my gates, guarding at the posts of my doors"* (Mishlei 8:34). At first he said: *"listens"*, and after *"watching"*, and after *"guarding"*.

INWARD ABSTINENCE
The abstinence which applies to the third type, namely, what applies exclusively to ourselves - our thoughts, inner life, and our inclinations, good and evil.

The beginning of this type of abstinence is to separate in heart and mind from material possessions, except for your food and living needs. Not to engage them (heart and mind) for securing any physical pleasures, or to attain through them leisures, or a position of power, or to feel proud over owning possessions of this fleeting world.

Let your abstinence in them be for G-d, may He be exalted, not to acquire a name, not to feel proud for abstaining from pleasures, and not to save your money due to your abstinence. Do not go out of the bounds of the torah in it, such as fasting on the Sabbath, Holidays, or Rosh Chodesh (new month), or to refrain from what the Creator obligated you in the commandment of having children. Rather, your matters of abstinence should be inwardly and outwardly in line with the torah and the religion.

Afterwards, to diminish your desires for this world, as if you were journeying from it in the evening of this day. Afterwards, make a spiritual accounting with yourself as we mentioned earlier in the gate of spiritual accounting. You should abandon all thought of what belongs to other people while trusting in G-d, and being contented with His decrees and judgments. Realize that you are under obligation [to fulfill] all the duties of the heart, which were previously clarified - and that they are the pillar of abstinence from the world. Investigate them closely and bind them to your heart. You will attain through them to all good.

### *** CHAPTER 6 ***

*- what scriptures says on abstinence*

The explanation of what is written in the holy books and the words of our Sages regarding abstinence from the world.
Among them, what Yaakov said: *"[and Yaakov vowed saying:] If G-d will be with me, and will keep me in this way that I go, and will give me bread to eat, and a garment to wear"* (Bereishis 28:20).

Among them, the fasting of Moshe for 40 days and nights three times. Likewise, Eliyahu for 40 days, as written: *"And he arose and ate and drank, and he went on with only this meal for forty days and forty nights up to the mountain of G-d"* (Melachim 19:8).

> *Lev Tov*: Hence whoever wants to ascend the mountain of G-d and to receive the torah must first purify himself and to separate completely from all matters of this world.

Among them what was said of the Nazir, which G-d calls him "holy", as written: *"All the days of his abstinence he is holy to G-d"* (Bamidbar 6:8). Because he abstained from the fruits of the vine and allowed his hair to grow [long]. All the more so for one who abstains from all physical pleasures that he has greater reward and recompense.

Among them, what was said to Aharon (Vayikra 10:9): *"do not drink wine or beer"*, and then *"to separate between holy and mundane"*, and to teach the Jewish people. That through this, G-d exhorted everyone who is engaged in religious service, to not occupy himself with anything that would distract him from completely doing the service (with devotion) to G-d, as our Sages said: "one who drank a reviis (about half cup) of wine is forbidden to teach, if he drank a chamishis (almost same as half cup) should not pray" (Eruvin 64a).

Among them: The matter of the sons of Yonadav ben Rechav whose father commanded them to never drink wine, nor sow, nor plant a vineyard, nor build a house, that they dwell in tents, outside settled places. This is the custom of those who separate themselves from the world. The Creator praised them for this as written: *"Therefore Yonadav the son of Rechab shall not lack a man [descendant] to stand before Me forever"* (Yirmiya

35:19).

Among them, the story of Elisha when Eliyahu passed by him, as written: *"And he went from there and he found Elisha, the son of Shafat, as he was plowing; twelve yoke were before him and he was with the twelfth. And Eliyahu passed over unto him, and cast his mantle upon him"* (Melachim 19:19), and Elisha dropped everything and followed Eliyahu as written: *"And he left the oxen and ran after Eliyahu and said: 'Let me, please, kiss my father and my mother, and then I will follow you'..."* (Melachim 19:20). Likewise, this was the practice of the disciples of the prophets in that generation and in previous ones, that they renounced occupying themselves with affairs of this world and neglected their physical well-being by going out to deserts in order to devote their souls and minds to G-d.

Among them, what the torah has commanded us to fast during the season of repentance and seeking forgiveness, in order to curb our lusts for all the pleasures, which are the greatest causes of sin as written: *"According to their pasture, so were they filled; they were filled, and their heart was exalted; therefore have they forgotten Me"* (Hoshea 13:6), and it says regarding the opposite: *"in their trouble they will seek Me"* (Hoshea 5:15).

Among them: what is written *"neither shall they wear a robe of coarse hair to deceive"* (Zechariah 13:4), and this teaches that it was the attire of the early pious ones, and some of the other [non-pious] men of that generation would wear it to appear pious.

And what David said: *"Before I was afflicted, I did err"* (Tehilim 119:67) (i.e. before I learned the ways of abstinence, afflictions fasts, and not seeking the superfluous - but then I discovered how to serve G-d - *TL*), and also: *"It is good for me that I have been afflicted, in order that I might learn Your statutes"* (Tehilim 119:71), and also: *"The torah of Your mouth is better unto me than thousands of gold and silver pieces"* (Tehilim 119:72) (hence he renounced wealth - *PL*).

Among them the practice of Iyov (Job) who described of himself how he scorned this world and its material wealth, curbed his senses, bound his hands and his tongue from all that may lead to rebelling against G-d, chose the truth, saved the oppressed, provided for the poor and lost - like the practices of those who separate themselves from the world.

Among them, what Daniel did in praying to G-d on the lengthiness of the first exile, and his mourning on it, that he said: *"I ate no decent bread, neither came meat nor wine in my mouth"* (Daniel 10:3), and the angel said to him: *"from the first day that you did set your heart to understand, and to chasten yourself before G-d, your words were heard"* (Daniel 10:12), and the rest of the matter. This is the best of all the practices of separation.

Among them, that which the people of Nineveh did, when they heard what the Creator decreed on them, as written: *"So the people of Nineveh believed in G-d, and proclaimed a fast, and put on sackcloth, from the greatest of them even to the least of them"* (Yona 3:5), and similarly what our fathers did in the days of Haman, as written: *"And in every province, where the king's commandment and his decree came, there was great mourning among the Jews, and fasting, and weeping, and wailing; and many lay in sackcloth and ashes"* (Esther 4:3), and many like this in our books, when you investigate it, you will find it scattered frequently in the words of our ancestors.

Among them what Shlomo said: *"Be not among wine-bibbers; among gluttonous eaters of flesh"* (Mishlei 23:20), and *"A little sleep, a little slumber, a little folding of the hands to lie"* (Mishlei 6:10), and what the mother of Lemuel said: *"Do not give your strength to women, nor your ways to the pleasures of kings; It is not for kings, Lemuel, it is not for kings to drink wine, neither is strong drink for rulers; Lest he drink and forget what was decreed"* (Mishlei 31:3-5).

Among them what is written: *"For to the man that is good in His sight He gives wisdom, knowledge, and joy (in his portion - TL) [but to the sinner He has given an occupation to gather and to accumulate]"* (Koheles 2:26), and it says: *"The heart of the wise is in the house of mourning; but the heart of fools is in the house of merrymaking"* (Koheles 7:4).

*"It is better to go to the house of mourning, than to go to the house of feasting: [for that is the end of all men; and the living will lay it to heart]"* (Koheles 7:2), and it says: *"The sleep of a laboring man is sweet, [whether he eats little or much: but the abundance of the rich will not allow him to sleep]"* (Koheles 5:11), and *"for childhood and youth are vanity"* (Koheles 11:10), and *"The end of the matter, all having been heard: fear G-d, and keep His commandments; for this is all of man"* (Koheles 12:13).

Regarding what our Sages said in the mishna and talmud. These are too numerous for this book, and most of it is found in the tractate Avot. Our Sages said: "this is the way of the torah - eat bread with salt, drink water in measure, sleep on the ground..." (Beraitha in Avot 6:4), and that which is near their words: "the torah is acquired in 48 ways (ibid 6:6): (minimal business, minimal pleasures, minimal sleep, minimal speech, minimal laughter...)". And in the chapter of the pious in tractate Taanit, many things teach on their great separation from this world. He who investigates this matter, will find it in scripture, reason, and in the oral tradition.

Put your heart to it, reflect on it in your inner being, you will reach it with G-d's help, as written: *"If you seek it as silver, and search for it as for hidden treasures; Then shall you understand the fear of the L-ord, and find the knowledge of G-d"* (Mishlei 2:4).

## *** CHAPTER 7 ***

*- The difference between the early ones and us*

The difference between us and our predecessors regarding separation is as follows. For the early ones such as Chanoch, Noach, Avraham, Yitzchak, Yaakov, Iyov and his company, their intellect was pure and their evil inclination was weak. So their souls were drawn after their intellect. The few mitzvot they had combined with their heartfelt faith in G-d were sufficient for them to complete their service of G-d, as written by Avraham *"You found his heart faithful before You"* (Nehemiah 9:8). They did not need the abstinence which goes out of the middle way which the torah prescribes.

But when their descendants descended to Egypt, and dwelled there 70 years in peace during Yosef's lifetime, their lust became strong, their desires grew, and their evil inclination overpowered their reason. They then needed, an abstinence, which would be counter to their lusts, and which would allow them to resist their evil inclination. The Creator added on them additional commandments, which reason does not obligate. This would serve as a substitute for the abstinence which was proper for them, according to their ability, and even less than that (so as not to be too much for them - *PL*).

When they conquered the land of Israel and settled it, and enjoyed its good, they started to seek superfluities in food and drink, indulgence with women, and in erecting buildings. The more the land was developed, the more their intellect deteriorated, as written: *"Lest when you have eaten and are full, and have built goodly houses, and dwelled therein...[then your heart be lifted up, and you forget G-d..]"* (Devarim 8:12). And the more the lusts increased and strengthened, the more the intellect weakened, and delayed grasping the correct way.

Therefore, they were in need for severe abstinence, through which they would be able to resist their lusts, as in the way of the Nazir, and the disciples of the prophets, which we mentioned previously in this book.

In later generations, the intellect has become weaker still while the lusts have strengthened more. Whenever people are occupied in secular matters, they are distracted from being concerned with matters of the next world. Therefore they need separation from this world, to free themselves from it, whenever they are doing anything of the next world.

The early ones, with their strong intellect and pure souls were capable of working for this world and also for the final one. Neither one would be detrimental to the other, as written: *"did not your father eat and drink, and do justice and righteousness, and then it was well with him?"* (Yirmiya 22:15), and it says: *"it is good that you should take hold of this, and also from this you shall not withdraw your hand"* (Koheles 7:18).

I saw, my brother, a powerful parable on the matter of separation from one of the pious, who commanded his son in it as his last testament. It pleased my eye, and I placed it as the final words for this gate as I found it, instead of ending with my own rebuke and teaching. Understand it and examine it, you will reach the good and the just with G-d's help.

Here it is (see hebrew commentaries for detailed explanation):
"Now my son, may G-d place you among those that will hear and listen, and that listen and think, and that think and know and do, and not among the people who drown in error, who are drunk with the wine of foolishness, which the evil inclination has enslaved them, and ruled this world over them, and which the lusts have overpowered them, and swayed them towards the pleasures, and enticed them to the desires, and drawn them to coveting.

And they, in their darkness are smitten, and swiftly move dazzled in their error, they hear but don't lend ear, they say but don't do (they verbally say that it is good to serve G-d but they don't do - *PL*). They sought the leasures but fell in the frustrations, endeavored to reach the pleasing, but reached instead the hard suffering, their soul is tired, and their body is weary.

Their minds are empty, and their understanding is shattered. They hoard gold to be lost and fleeting silver, which becomes an inheritance to their enemies or to their traitorous wives. They erect mansions and lie down in graves. They build and don't dwell, they amass and don't spend, each man among them buries his father and his son (i.e. someone older and someone younger than himself but does not put to heart the day of his own death - *MH*), yet still does not do religious deeds which endure forever. He forgets his end, but remembers his desires, what will you say of a middle piece, which lost both end pieces, and of a child whose parents abandoned him?

Look my son, at whose heart the Creator has broadened, and who G-d has helped him to rule over his thoughts, opened his eyes for what is good for him, showed him the straight path, and drew him close to it. People are assured of him, and he is assured of them, he is at peace with them, and saved from them. People serve their evil inclination, but he serves the G-d of heaven and earth, who grants life, who brings death, the Creator, who is gracious, and there is no god besides Him.

Look at the difference between them (the men who serve their evil inclination - *TL*) and the men with pure interiors (who serve G-d) - their eyes are at rest (unlike the desirous whose eyes are always scanning to spot desirous things they enjoy and to afterwards strive to attain them - *PL*), their hearts are secure (they are not worried or pained by anything - *PL*), and in their solitude, they delight in remembering G-d, thank Him for His goodness in all their situations. They quickly grasp all forms of deep wisdom. They ripped off the veil from their eyes (the [inner] eyes of the intellect - *PL*) which prevents seeing the interior ways. They reached the true tranquility through their toil (to conquer their lusts - *PL*). Their tranquility led them to delight, their desire does not distract them, nor does their long life make them procrastinate. They are zealous to prepare for the day of death, and from what is after it. They prepare, call to G-d, seek Him, hope to Him, and serve Him, They speak truth, converse righteousness, without fear of the Sultan, and without being ruled by the Satan. They are more precious (to G-d) than any man, and more guarded than any nation. Their splendor and grandeur is greater than all of them, honored in the houses of G-d, and great in the eyes of men. Nothing distracts them away from remembering G-d, and nothing prevents them from thanking Him. Their tongue is habituated in praises and thanksgivings, and their hearts are full of purity and unity.

This world disguised itself but they recognized it, and they tread it and told of it. Its deception was not hidden from their eyes, neither was its fraud concealed. This world adorned itself to them with beautiful garments (enticed them to pursue the enchantments of this world), but they considered it naked and empty. It deprived them (of livelihood), but it was forced (to provide for them their basic need in its proper time since they trusted in G-d - *TL*). It tried to befriend them (with wealth), but they scolded it. It tried to sway them, but they distanced from it. They gazed at its evil deeds, and understood its disgraceful acts, and it has no dominion over them, and nothing with which to approach them. They are the choicest of G-d. The pure ones, and the treasured of the pious, possessors of discerning eyes, noble desires, favored deeds, who dug after G-d and became rich, did business with Him and profited G-d was gratified with them, purified their hearts and became pure. They equipped themselves with fear of G-d in the path of evil and were saved. They rode the wagon of piety and arrived, met with the eternal joy, and the delight which never erodes, were spared from the assembly of judgment, and were saved from the punishments (of gehinom).

And you, my son, choose the good for your soul, before the regret which will not avail, and the worry which will never end." (end of the letter of the pious man)

> *Pas Lechem*: *"regret...worry"* when the wicked person sees there (in the afterlife) how much good he lost, he regrets a tremendous regret, and on his worry and pain in paying the price for his sins, he wrote: *"and the worry which will never end"*, because this is a crookedness which he can no longer straighten out there, and a loss which he can no longer recover.

May G-d teach us the just path, and incline us to the road of salvation, in His mercy and great kindness, Amen.(see the next gate for more on abstinence)

# ****** SHAAR AHAVAS HA-SHEM - THE GATE OF LOVE OF G-D ******

## *** INTRODUCTION ***

Since our previous discussion in the ninth gate dealt with clarifying the subject of separating from this world, and our intent in it was to unify the heart (away from the lusts of this world - *LT*) and free it for love of the Creator, and for yearning to do His will, I saw proper to follow with a clarification of the ways of love of G-d, because it is the purpose of all the steps, and the final stage in the levels of the men who serve G-d. I will begin, and I seek from G-d to help me.

It is proper for you, my brother, that you understand and that you know, that everything we previously mentioned of the duties of the heart and limbs, and the volunteering of the soul (that the soul must volunteer on its own, and devote itself to Him, as already mentioned many times in this book - *PL*), they are all rungs and steps leading to this sublime matter, which is our intent to clarify in this gate. It is also proper for you to know that every duty and every good quality, whether it comes through reason, scripture, or tradition, are all steps and stages by which one ascends to this matter, and it is their ultimate purpose and destination. There is no level above it or after it.

Therefore, because of this, the prophet (Moshe), peace be upon him, placed it immediately after the unity of G-d, in saying: *"Hear, O Israel: The L-ord is our G-d; the L-ord is one; And you shall love the L-ord, your G-d..."* (Devarim 6:4), and he exhorted on it, and returned to it many times, as written: *"To love the L-ord your G-d, to hearken to His voice, and to cleave to Him"* (Devarim 30:20). The meaning of cleaving is: faithful love, and wholehearted devotion, as written: *"there is a friend who cleaves closer than a brother"* (Mishlei 18:24).

Frequently the torah places fear of G-d before love of Him, as written *"And now, Israel, what does the L-ord your G-d require of you, but to fear the L-ord your G-d, to walk in all His ways, and to love Him"* (Devarim 10:12), and it says: *"You shall fear the L-ord your G-d; and to Him shall you cling"* (Devarim 10:20). It is correct to place fear of G-d before love of G-d because [fear of G-d] is the final purpose and furthest end of abstinence, which in turn is the nearest level approaching the lowest level of love of G-d, and the first gate of its gates, and it is impossible for a man to reach it without preceding fear and fright of G-d. (fear is from far, while fright (pachad) is from close - *PL*)

And therefore, we have preceded the gate of abstinence, because it is impossible to establish love of G-d in our hearts if the love of this world is established there. But when the heart of the believer is empty from the love of this world and free of its lusts, out of recognition and understanding - the love of the Creator will establish in his heart, and it will be set in his soul according to his yearning to Him, and his recognition of Him, as written: *"In the way of Your judgments, O L-ord, have we waited for You [the desire of our soul is to Your Name, and to the remembrance of You]"* (Yeshaya 26:8) (hence, the souls of the perfect yearn to Him - *PL*).

It is fitting that we clarify of the subject of love of G-d seven matters:
1. What is the matter of love G-d?
2. How many kinds of love of G-d are there?
3. What is the path to it?
4. If it is possible or not for a human being to love G-d
5. matters detrimental to it
6. Its marks, through which it is identified in a believer
7. The practices of those who love G-d.

# *** CHAPTER 1 ***

What is love of G-d? It is the longing of the soul - and its turning, on its own, to the Creator, so that it can cleave to His supernal light. For the soul is of an essence which is pure and spiritual, it tends towards spiritual things similar to itself. By nature, it removes itself from what is opposite to its nature, namely the coarse physical bodies.

When the Creator, blessed be He, bound the soul to this coarse physical body in order to test it, how it would guide the body (i.e. the test being whether the soul would be mindful and strengthen itself to guide the body or whether it would be lazy and be drawn after the body - PL). G-d aroused the soul to care for the body, and further its welfare, through the partnership and companionship which was naturally ingrained between them from the beginning of the development (of the body).

When the soul senses something which will benefit the body or further its welfare, she will turn in her thoughts to that thing and desire it, in order to secure for herself peace from the pains of the body and the external things (worries, drives) which pain the body. This is similar to the desiring of a sick man for an expert doctor who appoints a helper to (the doctor) so that the doctor can focus on him.

| (so too the soul thinks on things which are for the benefit of the body, so the body can be free to heal the soul which is love sick for G-d - ML, PL)

But when the soul (becomes complete and the intellect strengthens, then the soul - TL) senses, that there are matters which will increase light in her own essence and power in herself. (and that the body is only secondary to the soul - TL) The soul will then tend instead towards G-d, and will cling to Him in its thoughts, and in its imagination will ponder instead how to come closer to Him, and will desire to Him and long to Him. This is the highest level of pure love (of G-d).

| (namely, that you wish to become a chariot to the Divine presence, like the patriarchs - ML)

But since the matter is so (that the soul also worries for the needs of the body), and the callings of the body are numerous, and its callings for that which will fill its lackings are constant, at all times, and all periods, (and potential problems of the body can happen at all times, one is not assured from them for even one second - *PL*) and the soul is not able to pause from thinking on all of this, because she has no tranquility and no rest without having peace from the ailings of her body (which always has a demand, lust, or worry) - therefore the soul became constantly distracted with the matters of the body from the things she loves which are fitting for her, and resemble her essence, through which are found her success in the abode of her tranquility (in the afterlife).

But when the light of the understanding penetrates to the soul, and it will reveal to her the disgrace of having turned to the body in love, and having been drawn after it in her thoughts, along with ignoring what will bring her salvation in both worlds - she will desist from this, and leave all of its worldly interests to the gracious Creator, and will turn in her thoughts to seek ways of her salvation from the great trap she is ensnared in, and by which she had been so greatly tempted. Then she will separate from the secular world and all of its pleasures, and will despise the body and its lusts.

> (*Pas Lechem*: "*despise the body and its lusts*" - either due to the baseness of the physical lusts or due to the pettiness of the body, that it is not worthwhile to expend effort for it and fulfill its lusts.)

Not so long after this, the soul's eyes will open, and her vision will clarify from the cloud of ignorance of G-d and His torah, and she will discern the truth from the false, and the truth of its Creator and Guide will be revealed to her.

When the soul understands His omnipotence, and His infinite greatness, it will kneel down and prostate before Him, in fear, fright, and awe of His power and greatness, and she will not leave this state until the Creator will reassure her, and quiet her fright and awe - then it will drink from the cup of love of G-d, and will enjoy the bliss of being alone with G-d, devoting herself wholeheartedly to Him, loving Him, putting her trust in Him, and yearning for Him. She will have no other occupation than the occupation of His service, and no musings other than of Him and no thought other than of Him. She will not move any of her limbs except to do something which will gain His favor. She will not unbind her tongue except to recall Him, praise Him, thank Him, and laud Him out of love for Him and out of longing to do His will. If He bestows a benefit on her, she will thank Him. If He brings suffering on her, she will patiently bear it, and will only increase her love for Him and trust in Him (since He punished her for her sins in this world to spare her from the [harsher] punishments in the next world - *PL*), as said about one of the pious who would rise in the middle of the night and say:

"My G-d, You have starved me, left me without clothing, and set me in the darkness of night (he had no money for a candle - *PL*), and I swear by Your might and greatness that if You burn me in fire, I will only increase in love of You and joy in You. This is similar to what Iyov said: *"Though He slay me, yet will I hope in Him"* (Iyov 13:15).

On this matter the wise man alluded to in saying: *"a bundle of myrrh is my beloved unto me, between my breasts he shall rest"* (Shir Hashirim 1:13), which our sages expounded this verse saying: "even though my beloved is causing me pain and bitterness like myrrh, 'He rests between my breasts' " (Shabbat 88b) (love of Him is stuck in my heart, since the heart is between the breasts - *PL*). Similarly the prophet (Moshe) said: *"And you shall love the L-ord your G-d with all your heart, and with all your soul, and with all your might"* (Devarim 6:5).

## *** CHAPTER 2 ***

In how many ways is the love of G-d? I will answer this question as follows. The love of a slave for his master is in one of 3 ways:
1. The slave loves him because the master benefits him and shows kindness to him.
2. The slave loves him because the master frequently overlooks his transgressions, abundantly forgives him, and atones for his sins.
3. The slave loves him due to his great and exalted character, and reveres him for his inherent nobility - not out of hope [for benefit] nor out of fear [of punishment].

Analogously is the love of G-d by us.
1. Either we love Him due to his abundant kindness on us, and continuous goodness to us. Thus we will love Him out of hope for more future benefit.
2. Or we love Him due to His ignoring of our sins (to give us time to repent), forgiving our transgressions, in spite of our abundantly rebelling against Him and transgressing His commandments.
3. For some, their love of G-d is due to reverence of G-d Himself - His glory, His greatness and His exaltedness - this is the pure love of G-d, blessed be He.

The prophet (Moshe), peace be unto him, has already exhorted us in this [latter way] in saying: *"And you shall love the L-ord your G-d with all your heart, and with all your soul, and with all your might"* (Devarim 6:5).

His intent in saying *"And you shall love the L-ord, your G-d, with all your heart and with all your soul, and with all your might"*, is to correspond to the different types of people, with their different mindsets with respect to their giving of themselves versus not giving of themselves of their bodies, money, and honor. For some of them are prepared to give of themselves their body and money, but not of their honor, which they withhold. Others, are prepared to give of themselves their money and honor, but not their body. Others, still are prepared to give their body and honor, but not their money, as our sages said: "If it says 'with all your soul', why should it also say, 'with all your might (means)' and if it says 'with all your might', why should it also say 'with all your soul'? (Answer) Should there be a man whose life is dearer than his money, for him it says; 'with all your soul'; and should there be a man whose money is dearer than his life, for him it says, 'with all your might (means)'" (Talmud Berachot 61b).

> (*Marpe Lenefesh*: Hence, it is our duty to offer to Him even the good He bestowed to us in the past (money), and to accept on ourselves even the harshest sufferings (of our body) for Him. If so, certainly, we should not love Him out of hope for future additional benefits or to be spared from suffering.)

One can also render the intent of *"And you shall love the L-ord your G-d with all your heart, and with all your soul, and with all your might"* (Devarim 6:5) to be referring to the three ways in which people love each other. This can be seen in the three types of friends.
1. One who volunteers towards doing the will of the one he loves with his money only.
2. One who volunteers towards doing the will of the one he loves with his body (by physically helping) or with his money.
3. One who volunteers towards doing the will of the one he loves with his money, body, and life, as the wise man said: *"Many waters cannot quench love, neither can the floods drown it"* (Shir HaShirim 8:7), and it is written about Yehonatan and David: *"for he loved him as he loved his own soul"* (Shmuel 20:17), and *"wonderful was your love to me, passing the love of women"* (Shmuel II 1:26).

Therefore, the prophet exhorted us in the love of the Creator, that it should include one's life, body, and money, that a man should volunteer all of these out of love of the Creator, and not be sparing in any of them in the fulfillment of the Creator's will. So our Sages said: *"'with all your hearts' means with your two inclinations, the good inclination and [resisting] the evil inclination. 'With all your soul' means even if one has to give up his life. 'With all your means', means with all your money"* (Talmud Berachot 54a). They also said: "Do His will as if it were your will, that He may do your will as if it was His will. Nullify your will before His will, that He may nullify the will of others before your will" (Avos 2:4).

One can also explain the intent of *"And you shall love the L-ord your G-d with all your heart, and with all your soul, and with all your might"* (Devarim 6:5) to be referring to cleaving to the love of G-d inwardly, and to exhibit it outwardly, until the genuineness of the believer's love will be recognizable inwardly and outwardly, privately and publicly, in a way that it will be manifested uniformly and in the proper way, in the same amount and in the same level, as David said: *"my heart and my flesh cry out for the living G-d"* (Tehilim 84:3).

One can also explain the intent of *"And you shall love the L-ord your G-d with all your heart, and with all your soul, and with all your might"* (Devarim 6:5) to mean that all of your love for anything besides Him and all of your efforts on behalf of someone besides Him be for His sake - to not associate love of someone else with the love of G-d, and if you love someone else, that it be in a way that He would be pleased with, so that this love is a branch of your love for Him. Therefore, he said *"with all"*, with each of them (love G-d), as I explained in Gate 3 chapter 5 of this book regarding the intellectual urge.

## *** CHAPTER 3 ***

What is the way to attaining love of G-d? I answer this question as follows: This request is not possible for the seeker without many prerequisites. When the prerequisites are fulfilled, there will emerge from them the love of G-d. But one who has intent to it directly will not reach it.

The prerequisites which it is proper for the believer to first acquire in his soul are: two types of unity of heart, two types of humility, two types of spiritual accountings, and two types of examinations.

The two types of unity [of heart]:
1) Wholehearted acknowledgment of the Creator's unity.
2) Wholehearted devotion of all of one's acts to G-d, and to serve Him for His honor's sake alone.

> (*Lev Tov*: That in every act that one does, there should be in his heart only one sole intent - to do this act for G-d, and to serve Him only for His honor's sake.)

The two types of humility:
1) Humility before G-d
2) Humility before the G-d fearing (who turn from bad), and those who choose in Him (who do good and choose His service - *PL*).

The two types of spiritual accountings:
1) To make a spiritual accounting with oneself on what one owes to G-d in return for His continuous benefits.
2) To make a spiritual accounting with oneself for (what he owes G-d for - *LT*) G-d's hiding of his sins (from other people so that he will not be a disgrace in their eyes - *PL*), and withholding (punishment) from him for a long time, and His forgiving (those he repented on - *TL*).

The two types of examinations:
1) Reflecting on what happened to the early ones (of the miracles, wonders, and salvations of G-d - *TL*), by studying the books of the prophets, and the books of the early ones, as written: *"I remember the days of yore; I meditate over all Your works"* (Tehilim 143:5).

2) Reflecting on the world (nature), wherein one sees some of the wonders

of the Creator exhibited in His creations. I have already clarified in this book, some general principles in this subject, according to my ability, what is sufficient for one who understands and intends for what leads to his deliverance and salvation in this world and in the next.

When one will fulfill all of these and combine them with abstinence from the pleasures and lusts of this world, and he understands the greatness of the Creator, His might and exaltedness, reflects how small is his own worth, how puny and lowly he is, and he comes to realize the great benevolence of the Creator on him, and His great kindness with him - then the love of G-d from the believer will come. It will come with a perfect heart and with genuine purity of soul, and with a longing for G-d that will be with exertion, zeal, and passion, similar to what was said: *"With my soul have I yearned for You in the night"* (Yeshaya 26:9), and *"the desire of our soul is to Your Name, and to the remembrance of You"* (Yeshaya 26:8), and *"My soul thirsts for You"* (Tehilim 63:2), and *"My soul thirsts for G-d"* (Tehilim 42:3).

And the most powerful things which aid in reaching this exalted level are:
* Great awe of G-d (of His greatness - *PL*)
* Dread of Him (dread of punishment for doing evil - *PL*)
* Fear of His commandments (fear of neglecting to do good - *PL*)
* A constant awareness that He contemplates your hidden and revealed, your inner and outer life, and that He is guiding you, and has compassion on you, and that He knows all of your thoughts and deeds which you did in your past and will do in the future, and that He has promised to you (reward for doing His service - *LT*), and has drawn you close to Him.

With all of this, you will not be able to refrain from turning to Him in your heart and in your inner being, with a pure heart and a perfect faith, and you will cling to love of Him, and trust on His compassion (in saving you from damages - *PL*), His great grace (in providing your needs - *PL*) and His mercy (for not exacting justice on a man for his sins - *PL*). You will not associate love of Him with love of anyone else. And He will not observe you and see in you fear of something else besides Him. You will never find Him absent in your thoughts, and He will never depart from being opposite your eyes. Your companionship will be in solitude, and He will dwell with you in the deserts. A place full of people will seem in your eyes as if it is not full (that their matters will not frighten you - shinui nusach), and a place empty of them will seem as if it's not empty. You will not feel lonely when they are gone nor worry in their absence (since you have no desire for them and don't need them - *PL*) You will always be rejoicing with your G-d, delighting to be with your Creator, seeking His favor, and longing for His visitation, as written: *"The righteous will rejoice with G-d and take refuge in Him"* (Tehilim 64:11), and the prophet said: *"Yet, I will rejoice in the L-ord; I will jubilate in the G-d of my salvation"* (Chavakuk 3:18), and David said: *"G-d is my light and salvation, from who shall I fear?"* (Tehilim 27:1), and the rest of the Psalm.

## *** CHAPTER 4 ***

Is love of G-d within a human being's ability or not? I will answer this as follows.

There are three kinds of love:

1. That it is easy in the eyes of the lover to lose money due to his love, but not his body and life.

2. That it is easy in the eyes of the lover to lose money due to his love and also [to lose] part of his body, provided he will remain alive.

3. Love for which it is easy for the lover to give up his money, his body, and his life due to his love.

We find that Avraham our patriarch, peace be unto him, demonstrated his love of G-d in all these ways, in his willingness to give up his money, his body, and his life.

With his money: He would spend it in hospitality to the wayfarers, in order to give them knowledge of the Creator; what he told the king of Sodom: *"Neither from a thread to a shoe strap, nor will I take from whatever is yours"* (Bereishis 14:23), all this is proof of his generosity of soul and that money was light in his eyes (for his love of G-d).

With his body: In the brit mila (circumcision), he did not hesitate to fulfill it joyously on himself and on others.

His generosity in willingness to give up his life out of love of G-d, he demonstrated by his energy and zeal in the matter of [offering up] Yitzchak (who he loved like himself - *TL*) which showed his pure love of G-d, and the faithfulness of his heart in the service of G-d.

This is the highest of the levels of love of G-d. It cannot be reached by every human being because it is beyond the capacity of ordinary flesh since it runs against the nature of a man and is opposite to it.

> (*Pas Lechem*: Since human nature is to guard one's life, which is the opposite of losing it. Hence, when one's soul offers to give up her life for the Creator, the human nature stands opposite it since this runs contrary to it.)

When it is found among exceptional individuals, it exists only due to the

Creator's strengthening them and His helping them so that the evil inclination will not overpower them. This comes as a reward for their [great] exertion in His service and their fulfillment of the commandments of His torah with a faithful soul, perfect heart, and pure mind. Such were G-d's prophets and His elect and treasured ones. It is not possible for every human being to bear what we mentioned due to love of G-d, because nature and the evil inclination are against it. But the former two kinds are within the ability of most people provided they exert themselves to fulfill the prerequisites we mentioned in this gate.

(*Tov Halevanon*: "*it exists only due to the Creator's strengthening them and His helping them*" - except for Avraham, who reached this level without G-d's help because since the Creator tested him in this, certainly He did not help him to attain it)

(Even though love of G-d by willingness to give up one's life is a lofty level, nevertheless, the first two levels are also evidence of genuine love of G-d - *LT*) That which teaches that the first two kinds are evidence of genuine love of G-d in a person, we can see from what Satan said: "*Does Iyov (Job) fear G-d for nothing? Have not You made a hedge about him, and about his house, and about all that he has on every side? You have blessed the work of his hands, and his possessions are increased in the land. But put forth Your hand now, [and touch all that he has, surely he will blaspheme You to Your face]*" (Iyov 1:9), which he meant: "he is like a merchant doing business with You, since with his love and fear of You, his price from you in return is honor and wealth of the world. But if You take away from him what You have bestowed on him and he remains in his piety with You - then he is faithful in genuine love of You". The Creator answered the Satan: "*behold, everything of his is in your hands...*" (Iyov 1:12). And then Satan did what you know from the text with his money and his children, and Iyov did not change, neither inwardly or outwardly towards G-d. He maintained his faithful love to G-d, as he said: "*Naked came I out of my mother's womb, and naked shall I return [to the grave]: the L-ord gave, and the L-ord has taken away; blessed be the name of the L-ord*" (Iyov 1:21).

Then the Creator said to Satan: "*Have you considered My servant Iyov, that there is none like him on earth, a wholehearted and upright man, that fears G-d, and shuns evil? And he still holds fast his integrity, though you moved Me against him, to destroy him without cause*"" (Iyov 2:3). And Satan answered: "*Skin for skin, yes, all that a man has will he give for his life; But put forth Your hand, and strike his flesh and bones, and he will curse*

*You to Your face"* (Iyov 2:4). What Satan meant was: "many people will give up their money, their wives and their children, in order to keep their own bodies unharmed. But the genuineness of Iyov's love for You can only be demonstrated when he is tried and tested in his own body and flesh, through pains inflicted on him, and which he will resent".

(*Marpe Lenefesh*: even though a son is dear to his father, as before with Avraham, here it is not the same, since to slaughter him with his own hands like Avraham, that is equivalent to sacrificing oneself, but for Iyov, the Satan killed his children without his knowledge, and he merely accepted the decree - this is not like giving up one's own body, therefore he needed to be tested further to demonstrate his genuine love)

Then the Creator answered Satan: *"Behold, he is in your hand; but spare his life"* (Iyov 2:6). Satan then did as he said of afflicting Iyov's body, and Iyov beared it patiently and did not change in his faithfulness and good heart to G-d, in saying to his wife: *"You speak as one of the foolish women speaks. What? shall we receive good at the hand of G-d, and shall we not receive the bad?"* (Iyov 2:10).

Thus the genuineness of his love and his purity of heart to G-d was demonstrated to he who doubted it, in his bearing the loss of his money and the suffering of his body, and he did not condemn the judgment of G-d, and even said in answer to his friends: *"Though He slay me, yet will I hope in Him"* (Iyov 13:15).

Hence the Creator praised him for this, and did not praise his friends for rebuking him, as written: *"the L-ord said to Eliphaz the Teimanite, My wrath is kindled against you, and against your two friends: for you have not spoken of Me the thing that is right, as My servant Iyov has"* (Iyov 42:7).

You can observe that the Creator associated two righteous men with Iyov and brought them up as examples in saying: *"though these three men be in its midst - Noah, Daniel, and Iyov - they would save themselves with their righteousness, says the L-ord, G-d"* (Yechezkel 14:14). And afterwards G-d restored to Iyov his prosperity as written: *"the L-ord restored the prosperity of Iyov"* (Iyov 42:10).

Such too were the sentiments and conducts of the early pious ones who were subjected to trials, such as Daniel in the lion's den and his three companions in the fiery furnace, the ten martyrs, and those who conducted themselves as them.

> (*Tov Halevanon*: those tests are not comparable to the test of Avraham, because the tests of other pious ones came from other human beings' wickedness and free will on them, and G-d helped those pious ones to stand up to the test, and sanctify His Name. Sometimes G-d even performed miracles for them. But in the test of Avraham, however, G-d Himself tested him, and Avraham himself stood up to the test on his own, without help, out of his great piety.)

The prophet (Moses) exhorts on us to attain this degree of love in saying: *"And you shall love the L-ord your G-d with all your heart, and with all your soul, and with all your might"* (Devarim 6:4).

Nevertheless, if one strives always to reach the degree of love of G-d motivated by hope for benefit or fear of punishment in this world and in the next world, which is in the ability of most human beings to attain, the Creator will strengthen and help him, on the genuine love, which springs from reverence of the greatness and exaltedness of the Creator, which is beyond the ability of flesh, as the verse says: *"I will cause love to those that love Me (i.e. help them to love Me beyond their natural ability - LT); And those that seek Me diligently shall find Me"* (Mishlei 8:17), and *"But he who sins against Me harms his soul; [all who hate me, love death]"* (Mishlei 8:36).

> (*Pas Lechem*: since it is difficult on the nature of a man to reach this level without divine help, and through coming to purify oneself on his own by reaching the first level, G-d will help him to reach this second level...and when exerting to reach the first level, one should have intent to not remain there and be satisfied with it, but rather he should have intent that through it, G-d will help him to reach the second level, which is that G-d's will is more primary to you [than your own will], and that you are more joyful in fulfilling it, than you are joyful in fulfilling your own will.)

## *** CHAPTER 5 ***

The things detrimental to the love of G-d are exceedingly numerous. Among them, that a man falls short in fulfilling the prerequisites from which the love of G-d emerges.

Among them, the things detrimental in the previous gates, which we have explained earlier in this book, and it is not necessary to repeat them, so that the matter does not become lengthy.

Among them, hatred of those who love G-d, and love of those who hate Him, as written: *"Should you help the wicked, and love them that hate the L-ord?"* (Divrei Hayamim II 19:2), and it says: *"...justify the wicked"* (Yeshaya 5:23), and *"He that justifies the wicked, and he that condemns the just, [even they both are an abomination to the L-ord]"* (Mishlei 17:15), and *"Those who forsake the Torah praise the wicked"* (Mishlei 28:4), and *"He that says unto the wicked, you are righteous; [him shall the people curse, nations shall abhor him]"* (Mishlei 24:24).

## *** CHAPTER 6 ***

The signs of genuine love recognizable in one who loves Him:
* Abandoning every unnecessary thing that distracts him from the service of the Creator. (since unnecessary things distracts one away from the service of G-d, therefore he abandons them - *PL*)
* That signs of fear and awe of G-d is visible on his face, as written: *"that His fear may be before your faces, that you sin not"* (Shemot 20:20).
There are two kinds of fear of G-d:
1. Fear of G-d's punishment and trial. This person fears G-d only out of fear of what will bring him suffering and ruin, because if he were assured against the suffering, he would not fear G-d. Of such a person, our sages said: *"let us be concerned lest he come to serve out of fear"* (Megila 25b). This type of person is falling short in the levels of the fear of G-d, and this is what our sages warned us against in saying: *"Be not like servants who minister unto their master for the sake of receiving a reward"* (Avot 1:3).

One of the pious would say: "I would be ashamed before G-d to serve Him for receiving reward or to avoid punishment, whereby I would be like a bad servant, that if he fears or hopes for reward - he will do his duty, but if not - he will not do it. Rather, I serve Him because it is befitting to do so."

The second type of fear is awe inspired by His glory, exaltedness, and almighty power. This awe never parts from a man for all the days of his life. It is the highest of the levels of the G-d fearing, which are mentioned in the books which deal with this topic. It is the introductory path to pure love, and the painful (burning - *TL*) yearning. Whoever reaches this level of fear of G-d, will not be frightened by anything nor fear anything besides the Creator, as one of the pious would tell over on a G-d fearing man which he found sleeping in the wilderness. He asked the man: "are you not afraid of lions, that you sleep in a place like this?". The man answered: "I would be ashamed before G-d, if He saw me afraid of other than Him".

(it must be the man got lost or the like and wound up in a dangerous wilderness, because one who deliberately goes to a dangerous place is a reckless fool, and the sages forbid one to put himself in danger and rely on a miracle - R.Yaakov Emden zt'l, *Translator*: Perhaps he was given special permission from G-d.)

# MORE SIGNS OF ONE WHO GENUINELY LOVES G-d

* Another sign (of love of G-d) is that in fulfilling G-d's will, it is equal in his eyes, if people praise him or scorn him when, to please the Creator, he bids them on doing good or refraining from evil.

* Another sign, that he is willing to give up his life, body, money, and children to do the will of the Creator, as written *"For Your sake are we slain all the day long;"* (Tehilim 44:23).

* Another sign, that he always has the name of G-d on his tongue, in praise, thanksgiving, and psalms, as written: *"And my tongue shall utter Your righteousness, Your praise all day long"* (Tehilim 35:28), and *"my mouth shall be filled with Your praise"* (Tehilim 71:8), and he will not utter the name of G-d in vain, in falsehood, or in a curse.

A vain oath means to utter an oath idly, without need and without necessity such as when not being forced by a Beit Din (court). A false oath is an oath that the court obligates a person in the course of business rulings and he swears falsely.

Out of honor for G-d, one is obligated to guard from everything that might lead to making an oath in the name of the blessed Creator, whether to confirm truth or refute false, and all the more so to confirm false or refute truth, as written: *"He who has clean hands and a pure heart, who has not taken My name in vain and has not sworn deceitfully"* (Tehilim 24:4), and *"to fear this glorious and awesome Name, the L-ord, your G-d"* (Devarim 28:58), and *"But unto you that fear My Name shall the sun of righteousness arise with healing in its wings"* (Malachi 3:20), and our sages said: "this refers to men who are afraid of uttering G-d's Name unnecessarily." (Nedarim 8b).

In a curse: They are the curses, insults, blasphemies, in which the Name of G-d is uttered. This is a great disgrace for a believer. Common people already permitted themselves on this until they have reached the ultimate in disgrace, and their intent in this is to emphasize their provocations and increase and aggrandize their insults, and they are similar in this to what the wise man said: *"It is as sport to a fool to do wickedness"* (Mishlei 10:23), and *"on his orphans and his widows He shall not have mercy, for all of them are hypocrites and evil doers, and every mouth speaks obscene language"* (Yeshaya 9:16), and *"The tongue of the righteous is choice silver"* (Mishlei 10:20).

> (*Marpe Lenefesh*: it is obvious from many sources that the prohibition of uttering G-d's name in vain does not differentiate whether it is in Hebrew or any other language in the world. Likewise it is obvious that it doesn't matter whether it is the Tetragramaton or any other (Kinuyim) substitute name.)

* Another sign: That he makes a condition before promising to do something and says: "G-d willing", even when the matter is to be done very shortly, This is due to two things: One, out of fear of the swift coming of his death and he will not be able to fulfill what he promised. Two, because he does not know if it was decreed by G-d that he should carry out the promise.

* Another sign: That he straightens people and teaches them the path to the service of G-d, whether with soft words or with harsh words, according to what is needed for the time and place, and according to the class and level of the people, and that he does so to everyone, from the great men down to the men of the shuk (market), as the wise man said: *"a wise man will hear, and will increase in learning;"* (Mishlei 1:5), and *"To give prudence to the simple, to the young man knowledge and discretion"* (Mishlei 1:4).

It is proper for you to know, my brother, regarding the merit of the believer, that even if he reaches the furthest extreme in the rectification of his soul in its devotion to G-d and came near to the prophets, in their good traits, praiseworthy conduct, zeal in the service of G-d and pure love of Him, it is not like the merit of one who leads people to the good path, and straightens the wicked to the service of G-d, because his merits multiply according to their merits, every day and at all times. (their merits will be attributed also to him - *PL*)

The analogy of this is to two merchants who came to a country. One of them profited from the merchandise in his hand ten times the original value (of 10 gold coins), bringing to a total of one hundred gold coins.

The second merchant profited only two times his original value, but he brought many types of merchandise (worth 5,000 gold coins), bringing a total of ten thousand gold coins.

Therefore, the profit of the first merchant, even with his profiting 10-fold amounted only to 90 gold coins, while the second merchant profited 5000 gold coins even though he profited only two-fold.

Likewise, my brother, if one rectifies only himself, he will have a small merit. But if one rectifies himself and many other people, he will have his merit multiplied according to the merits of all the people who he rectified to G-d, as our sages said: *"Whoever brings merit to the masses will not come to any sin"* (Avot 5:18), and our sages said: *"Moshe was righteous and caused the multitude to become righteous, the merit of the multitudes is attributed to him, as written 'he performed the righteousness of G-d and His judgments with Israel'"*, and the wise man said: *"But to them that rebuke shall be delight, and a good blessing shall come upon them"* (Mishlei 24:25), and *"The law of truth was in his mouth - and turned many away from iniquity"* (Malachi 2:6), and *"those who bring merit to the multitudes will be like the stars forever and ever"* (Daniel 12:3).

> (*Translator*: *"he will have his merit multiplied"* - but if a person focuses only on rectifying others, and does not rectify himself, then his merit multiplied is like zero x 100 = zero. See also Michtav M'Eliyahu vol.3 pg.32)

Therefore, the Creator commanded us to rebuke those that fall short in the fulfillment of their duties, as written: *"you shall surely rebuke your fellow"* (Vayikra 19:17), and our sages taught: "until when is it one's duty to rebuke? Rav said: 'until he curses you', Shmuel said: 'until he assaults you' " (Erechin 16b), and it is said: *"He that rebukes a man shall find more favor afterwards than he that flatters with the tongue"* (Mishlei 28:23).

* Another sign (of love of G-d) is joy and delight in one's merits, not out of pride or arrogance but out of rejoicing in them (because he drew close to G-d - *ML*), while mourning and grieving over his sins, repenting and regretting them as David said: *"Rivers of waters run down my eyes, because they did not keep Your Torah"* (Tehilim 119:136).

* Another sign: That he prostrates himself at night and fasts by day, if he is able to do this, because prayer at night is purer than prayer by day for several reasons:
1. A man is more free (from his affairs) during the night than he is during the day.
2. the cravings of the body for food and drink are quieter at night than they are by day.
3. Pause from social interaction with other people, such as being visited by a friend, or a neighbor who wants to converse with him, or a lender claiming payment from what is due to him.

4. At night, the senses have tranquility from the numerous sensations, because he does not see things that distract him, nor hear things that interrupt (his thoughts).

5. Being saved and distanced from flattery, due to the few number of people who are awake at night with him, while during the day, it is possible that he will not be able to spend any time in solitude.

6. He is better able to commune with G-d in thinking of Him, and being in solitude with Him, at a time when every lover communes with the one who loves him and every desirer is alone with the one who desires him, as written: *"My soul yearns for You in the night"* (Yeshaya 26:9), and *"By night on my bed I sought him whom my soul loves"* (Shir Hashirim 3:1).

Prayer at night is praised in the holy scriptures, such as: *"At night I remembered Your name, O L-ord..."* (Tehilim 119:55), and *"At midnight, I rise to give thanks to You.."* (Tehilim 119:62), and *"I rose before the dawning of the morning, and cried out"* (Tehilim 119:147), and *"My eyes preceded the watches to speak of Your word"* (Tehilim 119:148), and *"at night I was opposite You"* (Tehilim 88:2), and *"Arise, cry out in the night, Pour out your heart like water before G-d"* (Eicha 2:19), and many more like this.

I have already prepared some strong words, which rebuke and shame the soul, so that it be stirred in the service and aroused to pray at night. These are in the Hebrew language, and I called it: "Rebuke" (Tochecha). Afterwards, I have appended to these some poetic words in Hebrew of praise and thanksgiving to G-d and request of forgiveness and supplications, soft words, which arouse the heart of the reader, and stir his nature, and I called it: "Request" (Bakasha). I appended them at the end of this book, for one who wishes to recite them as prayers at night or by day.

One who would like to take on himself this matter should do as follows: He should recite the "Rebuke" sitting down after having read some known religious songs or others (if one composes his own praises according to his will - TL), and then to stand up and in a bowed posture, to read the "Request" until the end, and then to kneel and say whatever supplications he wishes, and after that Psalm 119 and the Shir Hamaalot Psalms (120-134), until the end. If one would like to say different prayers or use any other order, he may do so. I merely suggested the ideal conduct in it.

The main thing, my brother, is the purity of soul and intent of heart while you are offering up the prayer, and that you recite it slowly, and likewise for the things near it (the things before and after it - *LT*). Let not your tongue hurry before your heart, for a little of it with your heart in it is better than a lot of it with the swift movements of your tongue and a heart devoid of it.

One of the pious would say: "do not praise empty praises, meaning, empty of having your heart in it. Rather, it should be with your heart in it, as David said: "With my whole heart have I sought You" (Tehilim 119:10), and *"I entreated You with all my heart"* (Tehilim 119:58), and *"my heart and my flesh cry out for the living G-d"* (Tehilim 84:3).

* Another sign: Joy and gladness in G-d and in knowing Him, and longing to find favor with Him, delighting in love of Him, clinging to His torah, compassion on those who fear Him, as written: *"I am a friend to all who fear You and to those who keep your precepts"* (Tehilim 119:63), and *"All who seek You shall exult and rejoice"* (Tehilim 40:17), and *"I have rejoiced in the way of your testimonies, as much as in all riches"* (Tehilim 119:14), and *"Your testimonies have I taken as a heritage forever: for they are the rejoicing of my heart"* (Tehilim 119:111), and *"Yet, I will rejoice in the L-ord; I will jubilate in the G-d of my salvation"* (Chavakuk 3:18).

## *** CHAPTER 7 ***

The good practices of those who love G-d (i.e. that result from love of G-d - *TL*) are too numerous to enumerate. Nevertheless, I will mention of them a few that occur to me.

These men know their G-d (which is the head of all knowledge, as in Divre Hayamim 28:9 'know the G-d of your father and serve Him' - *ML*) (see Gate 1), and they recognize what He wants from them (and why He brought them to this world - ML, alternative: that He desires in human beings, i.e. He chose them (humans) to serve Him - *PL*), and that He guides them, maintains them and provides for them, and that everything religious or secular which He gave them permission and free will to do is still under His control and bound by His rule.

> (*Marpe Lenefesh*: even though man has free will, nevertheless, every matter, secular or religious, is in His hand and under His authority regarding whether the matter will be successfully carried out or not. Therefore, they placed their trust in G-d in all of their matters.)

It has become clear to them and they believe that all of their affairs and movements proceed according to the decree and desire of the Creator. Therefore they no longer prefer to be in a different situation than the one they are in, and they trust in the Creator, that He will choose the best and most proper situation for them.

When it became clear to them from the torah, that G-d exhorts them on fulfilling the mitzvot (precepts), commands them to choose the service of the Creator (such as *"I have set before you life and death, blessing and curse, and you will choose life"* (Devarim 30:19) - *ML*), and warns them to avoid choosing after bodily pleasures, but rather abstain from them - they chose to follow what He wants, namely, to long for Him, to yearn to do His will in their hearts and inner being. In their hearts and souls, they ceased yearning for this world and its enchantments, but they hope to receive help and strength from Him in order to achieve their ambition in His service, and to complete the work they have chosen in fulfilling His commandments.

For what they have accomplished, they will praise and thank G-d for it, and G-d will praise them for their efforts and choice. And for what they were not able to accomplish of their ambitions, due to their weakness in reaching it, they excuse themselves before G-d (in prayer and explain their impediments in this - *PL*), and will resolve to do it when they will be more capable. They hope to the time when the Creator will help them to do it, and they will beseech Him on this with a pure soul and a faithful heart. This is their greatest desire, and final wish from G-d, as David said: *"My hope is that my ways be established, to keep Your statutes"* (Tehilim 119:5). And the Creator will praise their choice of His service, even if they are prevented from fulfilling the acts, as He said to David *"Since it was in your heart to build a house unto My name, you did well that it was in your heart"* (Melachim 8:18).

In their hearts and minds, they abandoned matters of this world, and care of their body's welfare, except for what is necessary and urgent, due to its pettiness by them, and insignificance in their eyes. They concentrate their hearts and souls to their religious matters and to the service of G-d, due to His glory and exaltedness. Their bodies are on earth but their hearts are in the heavens. Due to the knowledge of the greatness of G-d in their hearts, they serve Him as if they were with the holy angels in the highest heavens.

The [physical] lusts have melted away from their hearts, and the desire for pleasures has been uprooted from them, due to being replaced with the yearning for the Creator's service and their love of Him.

The fire of the evil inclination has extinguished from their hearts, and its heat is gone from their thoughts due to the magnitude of the light of divine service which has engulfed them, similar to a candle in the presence of the light of the sun. They are humbled by awe of their G-d. They confess their shortcomings before Him. They bore their shoulders to His service, not caring about any losses (incurred in matters of this world - *TL*)

When coming in contact with them, they seem shy, but when one speaks with them, their wisdom will appear. When one asks them something, they seem knowledgeable. When they are sinned against, their humility will appear.

When you look at them, their faces appear radiant, and if you could peer in their hearts, you will see a broken heart to G-d. In His word they are resident, but in worldly matters they are desolate.

(*Marpe Lenefesh*: in conversations of the everlasting G-d they are full of all wisdom and knowledge, because that is their primary occupation and residence, but in worldly matters, it is the opposite. They know nothing, as if the world is desolate without inhabitants. They don't even know the picture on a coin.

*Translator*: perhaps this explains the author's statement in Gate 4: "the deer to trap snakes")

Love of G-d has filled their hearts. They have no desire for joining the conversations of men, nor do they derive any pleasure therein. They are disgusted by corrupt ways, and chose the choicest paths,

In their merits, sufferings go away, and the rains fall. In their merits man kisses the ground (the earth produces food and men are happy), since they refrained themselves from lewdness, retracted their hands from all treats, and their souls have fled from forbidden things, and because they went in the good and righteous path. They reached exalted levels for bearing a short time (the few dozen years allotted to man in this world), profited in both worlds, combined both goods, and achieved two distinctions, as written in the psalm: *"Praiseworthy is the man who fears G-d..."* (Tehilim 112), until the end.

What is wondrous in their matters, is that (since their clinging to the Creator is so strong that - *TL*) the commandments which the Creator has commanded them in seem few in their eyes compared to their duties to repay Him for the good He bestows on them, and compared to the exertion, devotion, bearing, and patience which they took on themselves in order to cling to the Creator, as I will now explain.

According to how the sages counted the commandments of the Creator, the total number was found to be 613. Of these, 365 are negative commandments, to not do, 65 of them are commandments for the congregation but not for the individual. Further, some of them are positive commandments whose fulfillment depends on time, namely, they apply at certain times but not at others, such as the Sabbaths, festivals, fast days. There are also commandments which apply only in the land (of Israel) such as the offerings which an individual is obligated in, the teruma, maaser (tithes), and the offerings of the festivals, or the like. Some commandments depend on other things, and are only obligatory when the things are found, but if they are absent one is exempt from them, such as the mitzva of Brit Mila (circumcision) for one who does not have a son, or pidyon haben (redeeming first born male) for one who has no first born male, and the mitzva of making a roof-fence for one who does not own a house, or honoring father and mother for an orphan, and others like this.

When they counted the commandments, they said: "we will not count in the negative commandments because merely refraining from them is their performance and the fulfillment of their obligation". Such service of G-d seemed too insignificant in their eyes, and their service seemed little to them due to their desire and longing for reaching the favor of G-d. Therefore they sought positive commandments of the limbs for individuals which apply at all times, places, and circumstances. They did not find any precepts that fits this except reading the torah and studying the commandments, as the verse says: *"These words, which I command you this day, shall be in your heart; And you shall teach them diligently unto your children, and speak of them.."* (Devarim 6:6). And the prophet (Moshe) exhorted on this a second time in saying: *"You shall teach them to your sons, speaking of them, when you sit in your house and when you walk on the way and when you lie down and when you rise up"* (Devarim 11:19).

And all of this seemed too small in their eyes due to what they perceived of their duties of service and deeds to the Creator. So, they served the Creator with rational precepts (not prescribed in scripture - RMH), special disciplines, and good spiritual customs. In their pure hearts to G-d, they appended to the known commandments and they learned from the ways of the prophets and the regiments of the pious ones, how to seek the favor of G-d by them, and obtain His acceptance of them - these belong to the duties of the heart, which was our intent to clarify their fundamental principles and to speak of their divisions in this book. This is the wisdom hidden in the hearts of the wise and concealed in their interior. If they speak of them, everyone will see that they are correct in them, because all intelligent men can testify that these things are true and just.

By it they reached the lofty heights and the precious levels in the wholehearted service of G-d, in love of Him with a faithful love, with their heart and soul, body and means, as the prophet, peace be unto him, exhorted in saying: *"And you shall love the L-ord your G-d with all your heart, and with all your soul, and with all your might"* (Devarim 6:5). Men of these levels are nearer than all other men to the level of the prophets, the pure ones, and the pious one, which scripture has termed them: *"those who love G-d"*, and *"those who love His Name"*, and on them it is said: *"That I may cause those that love Me to inherit substance"* (Mishlei 8:21).

And if, my brother, you desire to be one of them, and to be included in their class - abandon the superfluous things of this world and avoid them. Be contented with taking only your [necessary] food from them. Train yourself to do without the superfluities. Lighten the burden of the affairs of this world from yourself, and free your mind from thinking deeply in them. Hasten to do the things necessary for you with your body only, but not with your heart and will, just like one who drinks a bitter medicine, who drinks it with his mouth, not with his desire, and he abhors the drinking itself, but he allows himself to bear its bitterness in order to cure himself from the illness. Likewise, should be the worldly needs in your eyes. (i.e. his intent in drinking is not for enjoyment but rather to remain alive, so too one's intent in all eating and drinking should be to remain alive - *TL*)

You know, my brother, that your mental exertions about your secular matters will not add anything to your livelihood in the least [because this is pre-determined by G-d]. So too, minimal exertion and zeal in them will not decrease your allotted portion in the least. Your mental distraction in them will prevent you from thinking in what will benefit you in your torah matters and in the Creator's commandments, which are in your hands, and that you undertook to toil in them all the days of your life. Thus you will wind up losing in this (religious) without gaining from the other (secular).

Therefore desire for yourself that which furthers your salvation and peace in your religious and secular life. Apply your mind to stand with all your strength to [perpetuate] the wellspring of your way of life.

> (several interpretations:
> *Manoach Halevavos*: "wellspring" - habit and custom that a person habituates in is like a wellspring, that once it is opened, it flows constantly, without interruption. i.e. put your mind, heart, and attention on this - that it "stands", and does not cease - this wellspring of your good conduct, that you have forced yourself to habituate in.
> Or, apply your mind on this, will all your strength, that the wellspring of your evil conduct stands, as written (Bereishis 8:21) *"the inclination of a man is evil from his youth"*..
> *Marpe Lenefesh*: put your mind like an iron pillar against the wellspring, i.e. evil habit, which is like a flowing wellspring, and that this be with all of your strength.)

Precede zeal before yourself for matters of your end (the hereafter). Appoint understanding as your king, humility as your deputy, wisdom as your guide, and abstinence as your close friend. Proceed slowly and thoughtfully in acquiring the good traits, according to how your matters allow you to bear. Beware of taking on too much, or too quickly, without moving gradually, lest you become lost, because too much oil in a candle is a cause to extinguish its light.

Beware of becoming neglectful, lazy or lax. Let one level of zeal follow with another level of zeal, and one level of endurance with another level of endurance. Strive to follow each level of good traits, with the next higher level which is near it. Do not neglect checking your heart and making a spiritual accounting always. Engage in the in-depth study of this book, read it, review its matters, and memorize its roots. Investigate its deductions always. You will reach through it to the pinnacle of exalted and treasured qualities, and the utmost of the noble traits that are pleasing to G-d. Straighten yourself with it and then straighten others with it.

Do not hope that you will reach this without having freed your mind of the worries and distractions of this world, even if you abhor them (it won't help as long as you worry for them and distract your heart on them - *TL*), just like it is not possible for a drunkard to heal himself from his craving for wine until he is completely free from it. One of the pious would say: "if we were truly ashamed of the Creator['s presence], we would not be speaking of love of the Creator, so long as we are drunk from the wine of love of this world" (i.e. the troubles of this world and its lusts which our hearts tend to love - *TL*).

Therefore, endeavor, my brother, let your mind be free of this world when your body is free of its affairs. Because when your body is in solitude, your soul should also be in solitude. For it is still possible for the mind to be absorbed in worldly affairs even when the body is free from them and is at rest from engaging in them.

> (*Marpe Lenefesh*: i.e. even if you are in solitude in a special chamber, it won't help in the least if your mind is tied to the affairs of this world, etc. Rather you need along with this also "spiritual solitude", i.e. that you reflect on matters of the next world, G-d's torah, closeness to G-d, or the like of spiritual things... until you habituate yourself that your body is free of its affairs, and even the opposite - that you free your body from itself, i.e. your heart contemplates on G-d all day long - [as long as you didn't reach this,] you have still not arrived.)

Check yourself in this always, my brother, and strive to keep the lusts of this world far from your heart. Replace them with matters of your end and duties of your heart. Ponder them in your thoughts always, you will attain through them that the Creator will be pleased with you. His face will shine upon you, and He will accept your good deeds, forgive your sins, and you will find favor in His eyes, as written: *"I love them that love Me; And those that seek Me diligently shall find Me"* (Mishlei 8:17), and *"those who honor Me shall I honor, and those who despise Me will be disgraced"* (Shmuel 2:30).

I saw proper for the completion of your benefit and instruction, my brother, that I summarize the main topics of the matters of this book into ten Hebrew stanzas, where each one contains a summary of each of the gates, and according to the order of the book. I conclude my book with them in order that they serve you as a reminder, so that you can memorize them and set them in your heart and mind, day and night, when you rest or are active, so that you will not cease to investigate the matters of this book and remember its fundamental principles.

When you are involved in an act of service, these phrases will remind you to devote your heart wholly to G-d in it. If you are involved in a secular work, they will remind you of your spiritual accounting. If you are in some trouble in a worldly matter, they will remind you of trusting in G-d. If it will be in a situation which brings to arrogance and haughtiness, they will remind you of submission. If your heart is free, they will remind you to reflect on the favors of G-d on you. If you are in a situation of physical joy or pleasure, they will remind you to abstain from the pleasures of this world. If you are involved in some matter where you are rebelling against G-d, they will remind you on repentance. If you are neglecting your torah and faith, they will remind you to cling to the service of G-d. If you are engaged in declaring G-d's Unity, they will remind you that your declaration should be wholehearted.

And likewise they will remind you during your recital of prayers, musings of your heart, bridling your tongue, binding of your senses, ruling over your lusts, restraining your limbs, checking your thoughts, weighing your deeds against your knowledge, and the rest of what I have discussed in this book of good conduct, and higher ethics.

May G-d teach us and you the way to His service in His mercy and greatness, Amen.

These are the ten stanzas:
Which include the topics of the gates of this book. One stanza per gate. (Meter: Yated, two Tenuot, Yated, two Tenuot, Yated and Tenuah in the

first half of the stanza, and likewise repeated in the second half.)

(Unity of G-d) - My son, devote your unique soul wholly to its Rock, when you declare the Unity of the One G-d who formed you.

(Reflection) - Examine, investigate, and contemplate His wonders, and let understanding and the law of righteousness be your girdle.

(Service) - Fear G-d, and guard His testimonies and laws always, so that your steps shall not stray.

(Trust) - Let your heart be confident and assured, trusting in G-d, the Rock, that He will be your help.

(Devotion) - With a pure heart do His laws for His sake, and exalt no human being in your generation.

(Submission) - See, that the end of a creature is to the dust, be lowly for sand, and dirt will be your dwelling place.

(Repentance) - Let the speech of your understanding contend against your folly, and repent from the brazen of your heart and [evil] inclination.

(Accounting) - The ways of G-d, in just and proper judgment, search with wisdom in your thoughts and inner being.

(Abstinence) - Remove from your heart the childish and adolescent, and do not desire the desires of your youth

(love of G-d) - In your yearning, you will see the face of the everlasting G-d, and your unique soul will commune with your Rock (you will merit Ruach Hakodesh - *ML*)

> (*Marpe Lenefesh*: ...therefore he did not mention anything of love of G-d since one who has attained all the levels, undoubtedly has also love of G-d, but if he lacks even one of them, it is not possible for the love to exist, as was explained in Gate 3 chapter 3.)

(*Translator's Note:* I did not translate the Rebuke (Tochecha) and the Request (Bakasha) appended to the hebrew version, due to the highly poetic nature and the allusions to verses in the Tanach. I recommend learning it in hebrew if possible.)

(here's an excerpt by Rabbi Yaakov Emden on the conclusion of this book zt'l written some 200 years ago, from the Masoret Yisrael edition of this book: "In this gate, the author was brief, relying on what he already mentioned in the gate of reflection. There are three primary causes on love of G-d:

1. when a man reflects on the great kindness that the Creator has brought him to existence, after he did not exist, and guarded him from all the many harmful things, until G-d also graced him with an intellect which shines on him more than the light of the stars if he uses it as He commanded and instructed him.

2. Not only did G-d create him from nothing, but He also endowed him with a holy soul, of Divine origin, and through this also established man's eternal existence.

3. G-d granted us increased qualities, exalted greatness, and immense favor in exclusively giving to us the holy, perfect torah, that through it we are called "sons to G-d" (Devarim 14:1), and He made us the treasured people of all the nations, and through it we are hoping for the redemption, etc.....

The sign of the truth of these things are from two faithful, visible, witnesses:
One, our situation and survival in this long exile, which the Creator fulfilled His promise: *"But despite all this, while they are in the land of their enemies, I will not despise them nor will I reject them to annihilate them, thereby breaking My covenant that is with them, for I am the L-ord their G-d"* (Vayikra 26:44)...

Two, the matter of our land, because from the day we went out of it, no nation was able to dwell in it, it was like a woman whose husband went on a faraway trip, and she waits for him, and the verse *"I will make the Land desolate, so that it will become desolate [also] of your enemies who live in it"* (Vayikra 26:32), tells us it is guarded for us...all these are clear signs that our hope is not lost and G-d's love has not left us, and on this eternal love is based Shir Hashirim, and just like G-d loves us a strong love, *"Torrents of water are not able to extinguish the love"* (Shir Hashirim 8:7), so too it is our duty to show our powerful and complete love, like *"As water reflects a face back to a face, so one's heart is reflected back to him by another"* Mishlei 27:19...)

These are the ten stanzas:
Which include the topics of the gates of this book. One stanza per gate.
(Meter: Yated, two Tenuot, Yated, two Tenuot, Yated and Tenuah in the
first half of the stanza, and likewise repeated in the second half.)

(Unity of G-d) - My son, devote your unique soul wholly to its Rock, when
you declare the Unity of the One G-d who formed you.

(Reflection) - Examine, investigate, and contemplate His wonders, and let
understanding and the law of righteousness be your girdle.

(Service) - Fear G-d, and guard His testimonies and laws always, so that
your steps shall not stray.

(Trust) - Let your heart be confident and assured, trusting in G-d, the Rock,
that He will be your help.

(Devotion) - With a pure heart do His laws for His sake, and exalt no
human being in your generation.

(Submission) - See, that the end of a creature is to the dust, be lowly for
sand, and dirt will be your dwelling place.

(Repentance) - Let the speech of your understanding contend against your
folly, and repent from the brazen of your heart and [evil] inclination.

(Accounting) - The ways of G-d, in just and proper judgment, search with
wisdom in your thoughts and inner being.

(Abstinence) - Remove from your heart the childish and adolescent, and do
not desire the desires of your youth

(love of G-d) - In your yearning, you will see the face of the everlasting
G-d, and your unique soul will commune with your Rock (you will merit
Ruach Hakodesh - *ML*)

> (*Marpe Lenefesh*: ...therefore he did not mention anything of love of G-d
> since one who has attained all the levels, undoubtedly has also love of G-d,
> but if he lacks even one of them, it is not possible for the love to exist, as
> was explained in Gate 3 chapter 3.)

(*Translator's Note:* I did not translate the Rebuke (Tochecha) and the

Request (Bakasha) appended to the hebrew version, due to the highly poetic nature and the allusions to verses in the Tanach. I recommend learning it in hebrew if possible.)

Made in the USA
Las Vegas, NV
26 December 2023

83516282R00184